The Braxton County
Updated & Revised Edition
The Cover-up of the "Flatwoods Monster" Revealed
Expanded

Frank C. Feschino, Jr.

The Braxton County Monster
Updated & Revised Edition
The Cover-up of the "Flatwoods Monster" Revealed
Expanded

Cover Illustration by Frank C. Feschino, Jr.
Interior Illustrations by Frank C. Feschino, Jr.

For more information go to:
http://www.flatwoodsmonster.com

Books may be ordered by contacting:
http://www.flatwoodsmonster.com

Printed in the United States of America
By Lulu Enterprises

DEDICATION

Dedicated to Kathleen May, Colonel Dale Leavitt, A. Lee Stewart, Jr., Jack Davis, Margaret Clise, Harvey Wolf, Dr. Christopher Unger, Robin Gokey, Major Donald Keyhoe, Ivan T. Sanderson and Gray Barker.

An honorable dedication to 2nd Lt. John A. Jones, Jr., 2nd Lt. John S. DelCurto and the numerous airmen who gave their lives to protect America.

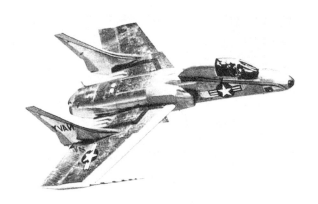

Most laymen live in an obsolete world -
in the sense that the concepts which form their view of it
were formulated without the benefit of the multitude of facts,
which are being born each day.

Author and Writer,

Peter Kol, 1963

CONTENTS

ACKNOWLEDGEMENTS

I would like to thank everyone who assisted me throughout the many years of my research. I would especially like to thank my biggest supporter, my Mom Shona, and the rest of my family for their help and encouragement.

I wish to thank Rob Tabasky and his devoted family for believing in me. Their continuous support of my "Braxton County Monster" project made this book a reality. I thank Stanton T. Friedman, Hal Povenmire and the many other scientists who assisted me with their knowledge, which was used in this book. Also, I would like to thank Michael Maroney for his computer expertise and assistance in formatting this book, "No, is a word never accepted under this roof."

I am grateful for the assistance of all my fellow UFO researchers including, Barry Greenwood, Dave Rudiak and Daniel Wilson. I am especially grateful to Fred May and the May family for their continued support and dedication to this book. I extend a sincere thank you and appreciation to John Clise and my friends in Flatwoods for their help over the past several years. I wish to thank my cousins, Cindy and Douglas, who have been there for me since the beginning, I appreciate all of your support.

A special thank you to Mr. Larry Bailey of "Brothers Bailey Promotions" for his support, I am obliged. I sincerely thank my attorneys at the law firm of Bowles, Rice, McDavid, Graff & Love-LLP, for making this book possible. I am grateful to them. I would especially like to thank all the American military veterans who assisted me throughout the years of my research. Their knowledge and help has been invaluable to me. I also wish to thank my entire team of people for their help, guidance and ongoing support, which has been invaluable.

FOREWORD BY STANTON T. FRIEDMAN
Nuclear Physicist, Author and Researcher

Several years ago in 1996, I met Frank Feschino, Jr. at a UFO Conference in Gulf Breeze, Florida. We talked briefly about his investigation of the Flatwoods, West Virginia "monster" story. I wished him well having read just enough about the case to think it was probably worth pursuing. It was only after Frank telephoned in 2002 to invite me to participate in a 50th Anniversary Celebration of the event in Flatwoods on September 12, 2002, that I decided I had better review the case more carefully. I did and agreed to attend at the expense of Frank and an associate. It was a fascinating experience.

Most importantly, I had a chance to meet with Mrs. May and her two sons, who were among the most important first hand witnesses. I also met the mayor of Flatwoods, Mayor Clise, and to my surprise, she had been a witness to a UFO that flew over Flatwoods that night. Frank led a group of people attending the anniversary celebration in a trek to the actual locations on the farm where the incident occurred. I had the opportunity to see the flat mountaintop pasture where the craft had landed, the gully down below to which it had moved and the remains of the tree from behind which "the monster" emerged. We were all there on the farm exactly 50 years to the minute after the event took place.

As soon as I was on the site, I realized I could add some new information. For example, once I saw the mountaintop location on the farm where the object landed, it was clear that it was the highest flat empty pasture in the area and a natural place for any pilot in trouble to try to land. One pilot I spoke with explained, "Look for a flat place and avoid mountains and trees."

I was particularly intrigued to find that Frank's persistence and hard work had involved important and unique resources including first-time videotaped interviews with key witnesses. He interviewed Colonel Dale Leavitt, the West Virginia National Guard commander who led his troops out onto the farm in Flatwoods, in secret, on September 12, 1952, gathering evidence, which was shipped off. He received no feedback.

Also interviewed was A. Lee Stewart Jr., a local newspaper publisher and reporter, who was "Johnny-on-the-spot" with interviews with the main witnesses' right after the event. From my experience and my investigations of the Roswell Incident since the mid 1970s, I know how much work it takes to find people and then convince them to talk. Frank did it. Both Leavitt and Stewart are now dead, but Frank, fortunately won those races with the undertaker. Their testimony (backed by video) is included in this book.

Since the 2004 edition of this book was printed, Frank continued his relentless Flatwoods research and has added much more information to this new updated book. Over the past eight years, we continued to collaborate, met at several UFO conferences and discussed his recently found information. This information includes Air Force documents that supply evidence connected to the UFO events of September 12, 1952. This new information contained here, fits into the timeline of events that Frank has established and shows us that a massive cover-up was indeed in place. Additionally, I was also able to obtain President Harry Truman's telephone call memorandum for September 12, 1952, which I gave to Frank. That information also appears in this revised edition book and adds greatly to the timeline of events that occurred on that day.

It is well known that 1952 was a very big year for UFO sightings. Project Blue Book noted more sightings in 1952 than in any other year. During a radio show a few years ago, the host and

I were talking about the famous July 1952 Washington area sightings. Pilots and radar operators made observations of UFOs over Washington, D.C., including certain areas that had forbidden flying zones above them such as the White House.

As part of that radio show, a man called in saying he had been stationed at Andrews Air Force Base just outside Washington in 1952. He said there were frequent scrambles of Air Force jets after UFOs over the next year. He was particularly impressed with a case where two fighters went up and only one came back. The caller, with whom I spoke later, said that the pilot who did come back kept repeating, "It went straight up." Weeks later there was a newspaper article indicating that that particular plane had been "lost at sea." Frank had also noted and investigated a documented incident involving an Air Force jet interceptor that simply vanished at sea on September 12, 1952, shortly before the "Flatwoods Monster" incident occurred.

With the very welcome assistance of researchers Dr. David Rudiak, Barry Greenwood, and Daniel Wilson we discovered, to our surprise that the situation was much more complex than we had known. Barry Greenwood, who possesses a huge collection of scrapbooks of newspaper clippings about sightings, also, found at my request a number of UFO related articles from that era. There was unambiguous evidence revealed in July of 1952 that military pilots had been ordered to "shoot down" UFOs who failed to land when instructed to do so including an Air Force Major General who said, "interceptor planes" were scrambled "several hundred times" after them.

We also found an abundance of information in old out of print books and periodicals about such related events as told by past researchers. It was also clear that there were very many crashes of military fighter aircraft during that time, most over the United States. In three instances pilots, each with over hundred missions in Korea, fighting off MIGs, had come back to the USA and then crashed. Accident records were quite incomplete or missing at the National Archives. Words such as "disappeared" and "disintegrated" appeared in brief news accounts of such events. *It is clear that there was a real battle going on, unheralded in the press, between UFOs and our aircraft.* Why such orders and activities, if UFOs were not considered a threat to the security of the United States?

Obviously, there were now two countries testing more and more powerful nuclear weapons. Great Britain tested its first Atomic Bomb near Australia on October 3, 1952. If aliens were concerned about new aircraft and new radar, imagine the splash as seen from above when the first H-bomb with its three-mile wide fireball was tested at Eniwetok on November 1, 1952. The rating was 10.4 megatons (10.4 Million tons of TNT equivalent) compared to Hiroshima's "mere" 15 kilotons (15 thousand tons of TNT equivalent). Thinking of UFOs as alien spy satellites, one should note that the preparations took months. The test actually involved 242 Navy ships and 156 aircraft out in the middle of nowhere.

Equally impressive to alien visitors and closer in time would have been Operation Mainbrace, the NATO Naval exercise, which began on Sept. 13, 1952, near Norway and Denmark with headquarters in Scotland. It was the largest NATO military maneuver up to that time, involved 80,000 men, 1000 aircraft and 200 ships, and lasted 12 days. Contingents were present from nine countries and obviously would have been heading that way for the week preceding the Flatwoods event on Sept. 12. Furthermore, several UFOs were sighted during the Operation Mainbrace maneuvers, which are all well documented.

An important aspect of the Flatwoods case besides the United States government's endeavor to cover-up this incident, is the attempt by UFO debunkers to try to explain away this astounding and important event. Particularly persistent in his negative attack has been Dr. Joe Nickell, a full time employee of the Committee for the Scientific Investigation of Claims of the Paranormal. Dr. Nickell, whose three degrees are in English, not in science, has worked as *a stage magician*. One can see some situations where this expertise might come in handy, but with a case like Flatwoods?

During a one-day investigation, Nickell did visit Flatwoods, West Virginia. During his investigation, he did not talk to or interview witnesses Mrs. May or Fred May. Furthermore, Nickell did not even visit the actual site where the encounter occurred near the tree. His explanation of a 6-foot tall barn owl and a meteor crash is absurd. There were a number of witnesses who saw a large object fly slowly across the sky at a low altitude, which then made a controlled landing shortly after on the farm. Most noteworthy, there was no shock wave, no crater or impact pit upon landing, no meteorite fragments in the ground and most importantly, there was no meteor shower on that day. Astronomy experts have provided Frank with the fact that there are only three instances on record in West Virginia of recovered meteorites and none were on September 12, 1952.

A six-foot owl that puts out a noxious vapor, has never been reported before or since, and certainly sounds like trying to fit a square peg into a round hole...especially when there were no reports of moving wings. All the eyewitness testimonies of the so-called "monster," actually indicate it was a mechanical device about 12 feet tall. The myth of the so-called "monster" has finally been revealed in this book. Pilots, witnesses or persons who have any information about the Flatwoods case can call me toll free at **1-877-457-0232**. My email is **fsphys@rogers.com**

My website address is: www.stantonfriedman.com

My mailing address is PO. Box 958, Houlton, ME 04730-0958.
Names won't be used without permission.

Stanton T. Friedman

INTRODUCTION BY FRANK C. FESCHINO, JR.

Illustrator, Author and Researcher

This book, *"The Braxton County Monster Revised Edition-The Cover-up of the Flatwoods Monster Revealed,"* has taken several years to be published correctly. Behind the scenes of my original 2004 book, a major problem had developed with the West Virginia publisher that controlled and printed the book. The editing of my manuscript was handled erroneously and was drastically changed without my knowledge or consent. It was poorly edited, and contained major errors, which led to a botched and confusing storyline. Furthermore, maps were incorrectly labeled, lists were incorrectly edited and numbered wrong, typos were abundant and scientific and military terms were misused.

From the start, I had many conflicts with the publisher because I disagreed with the editing process, which included the storyline, the choice of photos and use of my illustrations. Sadly, I didn't know that the final manuscript was changed, rewritten and incorrect until the book was out in circulation. Once I realized that the book was a published disgrace, I stopped endorsing it.

Yet, there was another problem; I was bound to a contract with this book publisher because of a single clause and couldn't get out of it. The publisher had a "first right of refusal" to publish a subsequent book, which included a revised edition of "The Braxton County Monster," which needed to be corrected. Needless to say, I didn't want to work with this publisher any more but he absolutely refused to let me out of the contract to go elsewhere. At this point, I was in a stalemate. Ultimately, I couldn't publish my book in a corrected version for my dedicated readers unless I worked with the same publisher, which was not going to happen!

Meanwhile, I painstakingly documented the publisher's mistakes and editing errors. Once finished, I presented my case to a Florida attorney to break the contract, and he accepted it. After years of conflict with the publisher, my attorney was unable to terminate the contract. Then, I contacted the law firm of Bowles, Rice, McDavid, Graff & Love-LLP in Charleston, West Virginia. This reputable firm accepted my case, filed a "Civil Action" suit against the publisher and fought the company to end my publishing contract.

A few months later, my attorneys contacted me and I was informed that a "SETTLEMENT AGREEMENT AND RELEASE" had been reached. Finally, the publishing contract was "terminated." The official document stated that the "intellectual property rights" of the publisher, "in plaintiff's story that is subject to the December 15, 2003 Publishing contract are revoked and/or surrendered." Finally, I got the publishing rights of my book back and I was able to publish it once again so the public could finally read the corrected version of the 2004 book.

Furthermore, since 2004, I continued my investigation into the "Braxton County Monster" incident and had many new findings to add to the case. As a result, the 2012 "Revised Edition" contained more information, new photos, maps, graphics and illustrations that were not in the original 2004 book. However, since my investigation into this is case is still ongoing, my research has continued since the release of the 2012 "Revised Edition" book. Subsequently, I found an overwhelming amount of new information, which has warranted an updated edition. I have now added all this new information and greatly expanded the book to strengthen my case.

Now, I will give a synopsis of my ongoing investigation and the events of September 12, 1952. My research into the "Braxton County Monster" or "Flatwoods Monster," began in 1991, while visiting family in Braxton County, West Virginia. I soon discovered a long lost UFO story that occurred on the night of September 12, 1952, which was one of the biggest news stories of that year. The incident involved a fiery UFO that flew over the small town of Flatwoods, and then passed over a group of boys playing football on the school playground. Flying at tree top level, the object crash-landed on the mountaintop of a nearby local farm moments later. The group of curious Flatwoods boys went to the house of Mrs. Kathleen May, mother of two of the boys in the group. Excited, some boys yelled it was a flying saucer, while others said it was a meteor. Mrs. May and Gene Lemon then escorted the younger boys to the nearby landing site to see what had landed.

Moments later, the group left the house on their trek and arrived on the farm about dusk. As they walked across a large field, some of the group noticed a pulsing red light, while others heard strange noises coming from another field. The group continued across the field, and then reached a metal gate. On the other side of the gate was an inclining dirt path that led to the back mountain where the object was seen going down. With darkness coming down, they quickly opened the gate and closed it. Lemon led the excited group up the path with his flashlight and toward the mountain. Along the path, a wooded area was to the left, a second field to their right.

Shortly after, the air along the path became filled with a strange low-rolling fog, which engulfed the area ahead of them. Lemon and May walked ahead of the boys who were strung along the dirt path behind them. The two adults and nearby boys walked into the fog and stated the odor was similar to burning sulfur, which irritated their eyes and nostrils. Regardless of the circumstances, Gene Lemon, Mrs. May and the boys continued up the path toward the back mountain. About half way up the dirt path, Mrs. May and Lemon heard a strange noise emanating from the woods to their left. The two adults pushed on, continued to lead the boys up the path, and then noticed something to their left and just ahead of them.

May and Lemon saw two glowing lights about twelve feet in the air in the vicinity of a large tree. These they thought were the eyes of an animal perched on a tree limb. Curious, May then walked ahead of Lemon in the beam of his flashlight to investigate the lights off to her left and stepped toward the tree. Lemon then redirected his flashlight beam at the two glowing lights as Mrs. May simultaneously turned on her flashlight and beamed the light at them as well. As the flashlight beams hit the area of the glowing lights, they revealed a towering 12-foot tall figure, which lit up and floated toward them in a bounding motion. The horrified group fled back down the hill and back to the house. This was the story of the "Braxton County Monster."

Intrigued by the story, I started to research this incident and have not stopped since the day I began. During my ongoing 21-year investigation into this incident, I researched government documents, collected and read articles from around the country and read the works of past investigators. Most importantly, I interviewed several first-hand eyewitnesses that were directly involved in this terrifying incident. During those interviews, I was informed about something that proved to be a major inconsistency in the event. The huge 12-foot tall figure that the witnesses saw on the farm that night, in reality was not a "monster."

A week after the incident, Mrs. May and Gene Lemon appeared on a national television show and told their frightening story. Before the live broadcast, a TV sketch artist sat down with the two witnesses and talked with them about the incident. From their descriptions, the artist drew the figure of the "monster" on a large poster board, which was later shown on the show. There was a major problem though. The artist's depiction of the figure was incorrect. He portrayed its likeness, as a huge claw-waving figure, which wore a hooded garment and dress.

I learned that this so-called "monster," was not a flesh and blood being with claws in a garment. Witnesses told me that the figure actually resembled a 12-foot tall metal-like structure, similar to a rocket. It was compared to a small craft or metal suit with a helmet and lower torso exhaust pipes, which performed as a hovering probe. Furthermore, my investigation reveals that this close encounter incident in Flatwoods was not an isolated event. The "Braxton County Monster" incident was only a segment of a much larger picture of what occurred that night. I discovered, yet another incident that occurred in Wheeling, West Virginia, which involved a dead alien occupant that was found by local residents. This incident led to a cover-up that was implemented by local authorities and has been kept a well-kept secret for years...until now. The more I dug into the case over the years, the more information I found.

I also discovered there were several other nationwide UFO episodes that occurred that day, which were reported by the press, radio and television. Moreover, these events were very well documented by the United States Government but here was a major draw back to all of these UFO events. They were extensively covered-up by Air Force Intelligence, military authorities and other government agencies. My updated research now reveals 116-documented locations, throughout ten eastern states, where witnesses reported Unidentified Flying Objects on September 12, 1952 plus a sighting over California. Moreover, I have discovered another major event that involved another crash of a damaged object that occurred on a farm in South Carolina.

My research also discloses hundreds of witnesses across the United States that reported UFOs, which were flying, crashing and landing over 21-hours of sustained activity that day. What I now call the "September 12, 1952 UFO flap," includes civilian and military personnel who reported these UFO sightings to; The Pentagon, Air Force bases, Air Defense Command headquarters, Government offices, Civil Aeronautics Administration officials at airports, State and local police stations, radio stations and newspaper offices.

Even though these UFO sightings spanned over 21-hours and different objects were on several different flight paths over ten eastern states, government records tell us differently. Intelligence officials concluded the September 12, 1952 UFO sightings were actually caused by a single "Fireball" meteor that passed over Washington, D.C. at 8:00 PM. EDT that night! Furthermore, the "Duration" of this so-called "Fireball" was only said to be "5-6 seconds," before it supposedly burned up! This story was bigger than I thought, but the cover-up was even bigger. I often compare and liken all of these UFO events, to a large jigsaw puzzle with thousands of pieces scattered about the country. After spending several years to gather all the information about these events, I then had to put all the pieces together.

I used the eyewitness accounts of the 116 east coast locations where the UFO sightings occurred and plotted them on regional geographic and topographic maps. Subsequently, all of this information was then transferred onto a huge "master map." I then placed the UFO events of that day into a chronological order and put together a precise time line. I worked with retired military persons, pilots, tower operators, police officers and several others then tracked the flight paths of the UFOs over those particular areas.

Once everything was in order, we were able to recreate an entire scenario of events that occurred on that day, which now includes new locations and landings. Those events actually involved search and rescue missions by extraterrestrials, which attempted to retrieve two of their comrades that were downed and stranded in West Virginia. This updated book is a recreation of the military strategies, tactical maneuvers and operations, which they used that night.

In this book, you will also read about my ongoing investigation into the missing USAF F-94 jet fighter that vanished into thin air shortly before the "Braxton County Monster" crash-landed in Flatwoods. In 1993, when I discovered the story in a Daytona Beach newspaper, I hunted down information about this missing jet incident and discovered several other Florida newspaper articles about it. I then contacted the United States Air Force for more information but only received a run-around. Again and again, I contacted the Air Force but their files had no official records of the missing jet incident or its 2-man crew.

I continued my research and then discovered the government had actually wiped every public record clean of the two missing airmen. Determined to find some answers, I tracked down and actually spoke to the older brothers of the two lost airmen. Shortly after, the missing pilot's brother gave me the official Air Force notification and death documents that were sent to him by the Air Force. Yes, I had finally found official records of this heavily guarded incident, which was covered-up by the US Government. I then released this cover-up story to the public in the first edition of this book. Then, more than fifty-years after the incident, the Air Force released the official records of the missing jet in an Aircraft Accident Report.

After obtaining this 65-page report, I spent hundreds of hours reviewing it and was appalled with its contents. The contents of this Aircraft Accident Report are an absolute disgrace and a slap in the face to the two men that had vanished that day! I discovered the report was incomplete, contained countless discrepancies, was filled with lies and contained false documentation. Moreover, the accident report was so convoluted, that the Air Force had actually recorded three different times that the jet vanished! I dissected the report, combined it with my previous data then clarified and recreated this extraordinary event. Without a doubt, my investigation exposes a massive cover-up that was implemented by the United States Air Force on September 12, 1952.

Additionally, I also discovered that the Air Force had actually removed two September 12, 1952 Aircraft Accident Reports from their case files and sent them to a higher classification! These two missing cases were actually the case before the missing jet report and the case following it! Yes, the events and aircraft accidents that occurred on that day were being covered-up and hidden by the United States Air Force.

Here, you will read how I exposed the Air Force's attempt to cover-up this missing jet episode, the "Flatwoods Monster" incident and all of the UFO events that occurred on September 12, 1952. Moreover, I have researched and written about another UFO case connected to the Flatwoods case, which occurred on August 19, 1952, the Desvergers Scoutmaster incident. You will see that there is much more to the "Braxton County Monster," and Desvergers close encounter incidents than meets the eye. These two UFO incidents were extensively covered-up and debunked by the Air Force, with the intentions to mislead the American public...almost!

In closing, I am very saddened to say that since the publication of the first book, my friend Mrs. Kathleen May passed away on June 13, 2009. I consider it a privilege to have known her for so many years; she was a strong and sincere woman who only wanted the truth to be known. I will never forget something that Kathleen said to me the last time I saw her and we talked. She looked at me and said, "Now Frank, I really believe you were born and put here to tell the truth about this 'monster' story. It is your destiny." Mrs. May, I believe that you were right. I now present to my readers, new additional information, photos, maps and illustrations about the "Braxton County Monster" incident and the startling UFO events of September 12, 1952.

Frank C. Feschino, Jr.

The Braxton County Monster
Updated & Revised Edition
The Cover-up of the "Flatwoods Monster" Revealed
Expanded

September 12, 1952 Project Blue Book UFO Reports

 Unidentified Flying Object: The stimulus for a report made by one or more individuals of something seen in the sky, which the observer could not identify as having an ordinary natural origin, and which seemed to him sufficiently puzzling that he undertook to make a report of it.

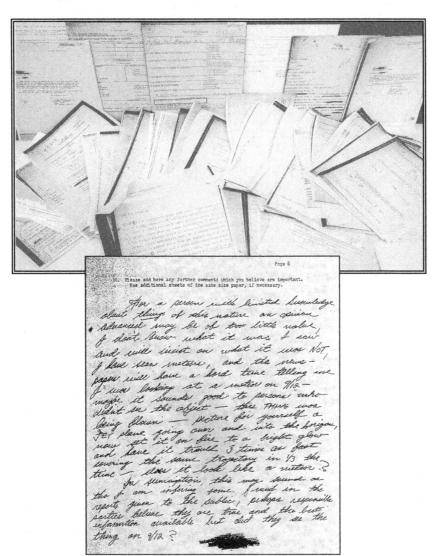

The Master Map that Reconstructs the Sept. 12, 1952 UFO Events

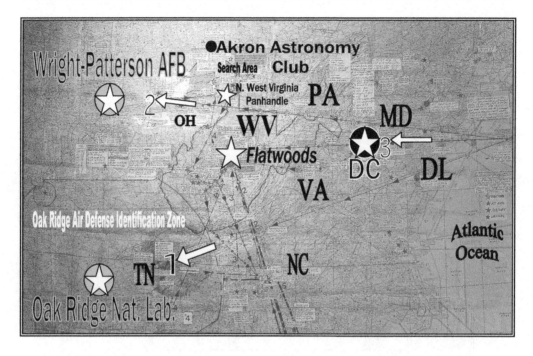

Detail of Sept. 12, 1952 UFOs on Master Map

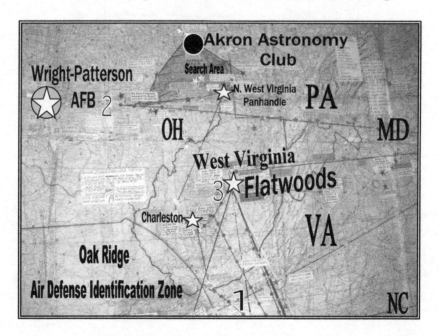

Frank C. Feschino, Jr.

He who is a slave to the truth is a free man.

Arabian Proverb

CHAPTER ONE

DESTINATION FLATWOODS

The year was 1952. The United States was involved in the Korean War. The Cold War raged throughout the world as President Truman anticipated the threat of a smashing Soviet nuclear aerial assault against the United States. Radar networks around the country were insufficient and defense gaps existed under their 5,000-foot level. Nearly 200,000 civilian volunteer sky watchers of the "Ground Observers Corps" worked with the Air Force to monitor the skies over the United States and fill the low-level gaps. Yet, the Air Force was in need of 300,000 more volunteers to help in the air defense effort.

As the eyes of America were focused on the skies and ready to report Soviet bombers at a moments notice, another problem had arisen. The United States was being plagued by another aerial intruder that flew throughout its airspace at will. The Air Force called them UFOs, but Americans commonly called them, "flying saucers," and they had become a real problem during 1952. Moreover, government officials became concerned that if Russia launched an aerial attack on the United States, UFO reports might clog communication channels and block other reports from being received.

In 1952, Project Blue Book at Wright-Patterson Air Force Base in Dayton, Ohio was the Air Force's investigative body for the acquisition and analysis of UFO data. Located at the Air Technical Intelligence Center, a small staff of officers and civilians were in charge of investigating and evaluating these UFO reports in the United States, its foreign bases, stations, and properties in other countries. The first Air Force UFO project, Project Sign began in 1947, was renamed Project Grudge in 1949 and was in operation until 1951. In late 1951, Project Grudge was renamed Project Blue Book and was headed by Captain Edward J. Ruppelt. Project Blue Book was in operation for 17 years until December of 1969, before it was disbanded.

The year 1952 had the highest amount of UFO reports and unidentified reports in Blue Book's 17-year history. Furthermore, in the twenty-two years that the Air Force was in charge of the UFO projects, the UFO reports sent to the staff at Project Blue Book in 1952 were the highest. That year, Captain Ruppelt and his intelligence officers received 1,501 official reports and evaluated 303 of those reports as unidentified or "Unknown" cases. During the summer of 1952, Blue Book officials received 1,134 reports, and evaluated 111 of those reports as "Unknown" cases. June had 148 reports, July had 536 reports, August had 326 reports and September had 124 reports. Moreover, the summer of 1952 set a record high of UFO reports received by ATIC.

Even though the UFO reports slowed down in September, one particular day of that month stands out more than any other day that year, September 12, 1952. I was able to document 102 locations over the United States where witnesses saw and reported strange aerial objects over nine east coast states during a 21-hour span. Furthermore, several of these UFOs landed and crashed around the country. Furthermore, on several occasions, the alien occupants of these UFOs were seen outside of their crafts.

A "Washington, Sept. 12," News story carried by *The Greensboro Daily News* dated Saturday, September 13, 1952 reported, "AIR FORCE PROBES FLYING SAUCERS-Four State 'Disc' Reports Unexplained." This September 12 story references the recent "unexplained phenomena cited in North Carolina" and states, "So you wanna believe in flying saucers. Gather around, tuck in your credulity, and listen to what the Air Force has to say. To date, the airmen haven't been able explain about 400 of 2,000 reports that have come in on 'unusual aerial phenomenon.' Four of the reports are from the old north state…25 percent are reported by military personnel" This article also states, "Nonetheless, since these unexplained sightings persist, the Air Force will continue its investigations, giving the problem adequate but not frantic attention, spokesmen said." This quote made by the United States Air Force was an absolute understatement, to say the least.

On Friday, September 12, 1952, all hell broke lose over the skies of the United States; hundreds of Americans reported seeing UFOs up and down the east coast as well as a UFO sighting over California. The UFO flap of September 12, 1952, "Defense Day," began at approximately 1:30 a.m. over Knox County, Ohio, near the small town of Bladensburg. This UFO incident appeared in the February 1953 issue of FATE magazine in an article titled, "Circling Object." It explains that two oil well drillers, William Darling and Donald Davis of Bladensburg, had an early morning sighting on September 12 while working the midnight shift. The next day, the two witnesses told their friend Jack Montgomery about the sighting. Montgomery said, "The incident was related to me by the two men the following morning." In turn, he then reported the incident to FATE magazine.

Mr. Montgomery explained, "They sighted an object about 2,000 feet from where they were working and about 150 feet from the ground. It was lit up very bright in the side [inside] and seemed to have windows only on one side. It circled near the ground for nearly half an hour making very little noise. Then all once it made a loud noise like steam blowing, and with a bright flash flew out of sight with the speed of a falling star." Shortly after this incident, another close range and low altitude UFO sighting occurred in Pennsylvania.

At 2:35 a.m. EST, the quiet star-filled sky over Middletown, Pennsylvania was shattered with a shocking noise that echoed through the night air. The noise that shook the area was the sound of heavy artillery being fired into the sky. A lone figure, a patrol guard on duty at Olmstead Air Force Base, gazed at a maneuvering craft as it flew across the sky near him. This aerial craft was neither a plane nor a helicopter. It was an unconventional aircraft, which had no wings and was elliptical in shape. It was a large UFO.

In 1952, Olmstead AFB housed an air materiel area set up by the Air Materiel Command of the United States Air Force. The patrol guard's sighting was then reported to Project Blue Book officials at Wright-Patterson Air Force Base. Subsequently, the guard received a Tentative Observers Questionnaire from the Air Technical Intelligence Center (ATIC) at Wright-Patterson. He documented the incident and returned it to ATIC.

The witness stated that he first noticed the object because he heard a noise that "sounded like heavy projectile artillery and saw a blue light in the sky." The object was oval-shaped and "solid." The guard made three sketches of the elliptical object and illustrated it as making unconventional maneuvers by drawing trail lines behind it. He added that the object "changed speed and direction as well as brightness." The "bright blue" light it emitted was brilliant. The guard said, "When the object disappeared the noise ceased."

A question on the form asked, "In your opinion what do you think the object was and what might have caused it?" The witness answered, "Do not know." What had the patrol guard heard? Was the Air Force test firing their heavy projectile artillery guns at 2:35 a.m. or was our military actually firing upon a nearby UFO? Was it a coincidence that a UFO was seen over the area of Olmsted AFB at the same time heavy artillery fire was heard? On September 12, 1952, an unusual heat wave blanketed the eastern United States with temperatures reaching around 90 degrees.

2

Other than the intense heat, which scorched the country that day, nothing else seemed out of the ordinary.

On the west coast, a low-flying UFO blatantly flew south over Santa Monica, California at "about 4:00 p.m." Pacific Time/7:00 p.m. Eastern Time. Subsequently, this UFO sighting prompted the Air Force to scramble jet fighters from March AFB, which is located at Riverside, about 75 miles west of Santa Monica. This incident was documented in the May 1961 issue of *Flying Saucers-The Magazine of Space Conquest*. Additionally, Project Blue Book also documented this UFO incident, but only in part. The case report was not very accurate.

Mr. L. Taylor Hansen wrote the magazine article that explained this UFO incident. The editorial introduction to this article states that Mr. Hansen was "a trained scientist and researcher." Mr. Hansen then gives his first-hand testimony of the incident and tells what happened on that hot afternoon over California. The story begins at Hansen's home in Indio, California, located about 135 miles southeast of Santa Monica. The following is Mr. Hansen's narrative of the incident as he heard it live on a radio broadcast from Brawley, California:

This sighting was broadcast on the Brawley radio by the disc jockey on the afternoon of September 12, 1952. It was Friday, and I was watering my lawn in Indio in the idle fashion in which desert dwellers water lawns on September afternoons-from an easy chair in the shade with a tall glass of lemonade close at hand. Suddenly my neighbor exploded from the door with entirely too much enthusiasm for the weather, and in fact made me turn in surprise. "Quick! Turn that portable radio to Brawley!" I had forgotten the radio playing something uninteresting from the porch. "Why" I asked, moving toward the machine. "They have spotted a flying saucer." "A what?" stopping dead in my tracks. "You heard me. We are missing it!"

I broke into a run and turned the dial to Brawley, "as I said before, it is metallic apparently," the disc jockey was saying. "I will repeat the directions, as calls are swamping our switchboard. Please do not call right now. It is just below and to the left of the declining sun." (As the hour was about four the sun was approaching the San Jacinto range of mountains.) My neighbor had been scanning the skies with a pair of binoculars but shrugged his disappointment and returned to the radio, offering them silently to me. I was about to take them when the announcers voice arrested my movement toward more open space between the trees. "I will put the mike where you will hear my answers to this call to the air-base, but not the officer's voice. Yes sir. I was calling you about a large silvery object...oh you have it under observation? It looks like metal...you would say it seems so? What is the...I mean what are you...oh, the jets are on their way? Thank you. Goodbye sir." Then the disc jockey's laugh, "I will lay money on the line that our visitor will soon leave...this I must see..."

We hurried to a more open spot. Neither of us could find a saucer, but a moment later the sound of a line of jets. We both hurried back to the radio. "Yes, here they [jets] come in the distance, and OH...OH...there he [UFO] goes! And apparently straight up. Did I have any takers on that bet?" As I clicked off the radio, we both moved out again into the open but saw nothing... "Funny we couldn't see the thing. Brawley is only about eighty-five miles southeast." "Yes, it must have been too low." Thus, we talked it over, and I returned to watering the lawn.

This incident was also documented in the September 12, 1952 Project Blue Book archives. An Intelligence document states this UFO report had originated from, "FM COADIV 12 MARCH AFB CALIF." It was then sent to, "INT HQ USAF WASH DC...AIR TECH INT CEN WRIGHT

PATTERSON AFB OH...CG ENT AFB COLO...CG SAC OFFUT AFB NEBR." The document then explains the following information:

FLYOBRPT. REPT UNIDENTIFIED OBJECT SEEN BY MR [**Blacked out**] RADIO COMPANY, SANTA MONICA, CALIF. OBJECT SEEN AT 1917 PDST 12 SEPT IN NORTH-WESTERLY DIRECTION FM SANTA MONICA CALIF. SHAPE AND SIZE NOT DISCERNED. OBJECT DISAPPEARED IN SOUTH-WESTERLY DIRECTION EXHIBITING BRIGHT INTENSE WHITE LIGHT AND TRAVELING AT HIGH RATE OF SPEED. ALTITUDE APPROX 1500 FEET.

The Project Blue Book "PROJECT 10073 RECORD CARD" states the "LOCATION-Santa Monica, Calif." It also states the "TYPE OF OBSERVATION - Ground Visual" and then reports the source as, "SOURCE - Civilian." The document then states, "NUMBER OF OBJECTS - 1" and the "COURSE - SW." The record card also states, "BRIEF SUMMARY OF SIGHTING - White color. Light shape."

The final evaluation of this UFO report states, "CONCLUSIONS - Possibly Aircraft." This record card also states the incident occurred at "1917 PST," or 7:17 p.m. Pacific *Standard* Time, yet according to Mr. Hansen, it occurred at "about 4:00 p.m." Pacific Time. The original Blue Book document about this incident recorded the time as, "1917 PDST" or 7:17 p.m. Pacific *Daylight* Saving Time! The Blue Book officials actually had contradicting times of the actual sighting! Mr. Hansen reported this UFO incident actually occurred "on the afternoon of September 12, 1952. It was Friday, and I was watering my lawn in Indio in the idle fashion in which desert dwellers water lawns on September afternoons."

Why was there a contradiction in the time of the UFO incident as documented by the Project Blue Book officials? Moreover, the UFO report originated from the Commanding Officer of the Air Division at March AFB, "FM COADIV 12 MARCH AFB CALIF." Why was there a failure to mention the Air Force jets that attempted to intercept the UFO that afternoon? Moreover, why did this object receive a "Possibly Aircraft" evaluation instead of a UFO? Additionally, why is this case incomplete and why are documents missing? A blatant and massive cover-up was in the making. This California UFO incident as told by Mr. Hansen actually occurred on the afternoon of September 12, 1952, at "about 4:00 PM." Pacific Time.

Meanwhile, another series of events simultaneously unfolded at 7:00 p.m. Eastern Standard Time on the east coast of the United States. Around 7:00 p.m. EST/8:00 p.m. EDT, the Air Defense Identification Zone (ADIZ), the United States airspace in which the control and recognition of aircraft was required, had been violated by an unidentified craft. This UFO, which was ablaze, soared west over the Atlantic Ocean through the coastal Air Defense Identification Zone and headed toward the mid-Atlantic coast.

Because this aircraft had not given warning or properly identified itself according to protocol, it was considered a threat to the United States. Under the Air Force rules of engagement, the unknown aircraft had shown just cause to be intercepted by jet interceptors. In Washington, D.C., military radars tracked the object, which was on a direct course for the Capitol.

As the object headed further west, President Truman and Pentagon officials declined to intercept the incoming UFO and waited patiently. Shortly after, it approached and passed over Washington, D.C. then continued west. Who was this enemy, and where did this unidentified aircraft originate? Moreover, why was it flying over the Capitol and further more, why was it engulfed in flames?

4

Approximately two hundred and six miles west of Washington, D.C., located in the rolling mountains of West Virginia, is the small town of Flatwoods. Set east of the Allegheny Mountain plateau, Flatwoods is the geographic center of the state.

Located in Braxton County, Flatwoods was a thriving little town of farms and mills surrounded by forests of towering pine and oak trees. Friday night was just beginning, and the residents of Flatwoods settled in for another quiet evening.

About twenty-five minutes later, as dusk settled over Flatwoods, the shouts of boys were heard in the local schoolyard. The center yelled, "Hut-one, hut-two, hut-three, hut, hut, hike!" The boys dashed across the football field, scrambling into another play. An incomplete pass brought the boys back to the line of scrimmage, yelling at each other in opposition. Seconds later, someone shouted and pointed skyward.

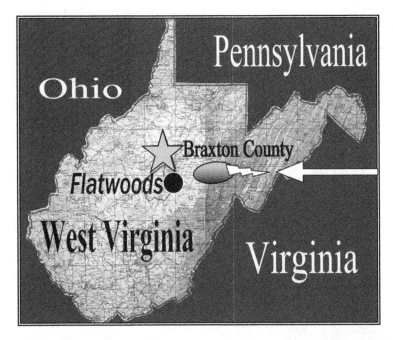

The Flatwoods Schoolyard Today

The Elementary School Circa 1952

For a few moments, an eerie silence fell over the schoolyard. The game stopped as the bewildered boys focused their attention on a nearby mountaintop. Gazing toward the sky, they saw a low-flying flaming aerial object soar over the mountain and toward them.

Seconds later, this large object flew directly above their heads as it passed over the Flatwoods Elementary School playground. This low-flying object then turned and proceeded over the nearby road and headed in the direction of a farm, barely clearing the treetops.

Investigator Frank C. Feschino, Jr. and Eyewitness Freddie G. May

During my investigation, I contacted witness Freddie May, who still lived in the area. On my initial telephone call with Freddie, he refused to speak with me. After several follow-up calls, he remained reluctant to talk with me. I had fallen into the category of a pestering, fly-by-night reporter. Mr. May had been hounded by the press for years about the incident. He had seen reporters distort the truth of the incident, and he quit talking to them. He was tired of seeing misquotes and distortions released to the public.

What this case needed was a thorough investigation, instead of reporters and writers who just wanted a quick, flashy story. As the years passed, these writers did more harm than good to the story. The incident had become just another fast, quirky story for the press. After countless telephone calls, I finally convinced Freddie of my sincere interest in the case. Finally, he agreed to be interviewed at his home and we met shortly after.

Upon meeting Fred, the interview that I had been patiently waiting for was quickly reversed. Freddie began to interview me. He wanted to know about the seriousness and depth of my investigation. After I finished explaining what I had uncovered in my research, he was amazed, even overwhelmed. After all those years, he had found the person he was waiting to talk with and I began to interview him.

Since our initial conversation, Freddie and I have spent years and countless hours discussing the incident in detail. Much of the newspaper information that I discovered and had shown Freddie was verified by him. I also showed him the Project Blue Book documents about the Flatwoods case, which he never saw until we met. Now, I will share the information from my first-hand interviews with eyewitness Freddie May. The primary interview was videotaped in Flatwoods. There, he agreed to be interviewed on the various locations where the incidents occurred. For the first time ever, a witness to all the events of that evening was willing to tell the true story of the "Flatwoods Monster."

Freddie's testimony began on site at the school playground, "The new school here sits on what used to be the old playground, where we were playing ball, and we were down about fifty yards or so from where the actual site used to be." Freddie then pointed to a mountain ridge in the northwest and said, "Somebody yelled, 'Look there,' and we all looked up and saw a fireball coming from over the mountain here. It came right over the top of our heads."

He said it looked like a "round ball of fire," and looked "oval-shaped." The colors of the object were "red, yellow, and orange." Freddie said the fireball emitted a "small trail of fire," and "flames were trailing behind it." From his position on the playground, he "saw the object for three seconds" as it passed over the group. Less than one week after the incident, journalist and science writer Mr. Evert Clark visited Flatwoods to investigate the incident and interview some of the key witnesses for a newspaper article. During an interview with Eugene Lemon, he explained the object to journalist Evert Clark, "It just looked like sheets of flame, like the top of a washtub – kind of silver-like. We all saw it."

One week after the incident, scientist/author Ivan T. Sanderson, a former British Naval Intelligence officer, visited Flatwoods with his assistant Eddie Shoenenberger. They spent several days in Braxton County investigating. Sanderson was on assignment to cover the story for the North American Newspaper Alliance and for *True Magazine*. Sanderson stated, "One of the kids looked up and he said in so many words, 'What on earth is that?' And they all looked around the edge of a hill behind the village, the north of the village but lower than the peak of that hill—or the one [hill] opposite it, came a pear-shaped glowing red object, which was pulsing from cherry red to bright orange.

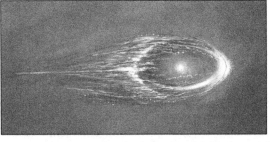

It was traveling blunt-end first. It traveled quite slowly across the valley over their heads and managed to top the mountain on the other side." The boys who witnessed this event were, Eugene Lemon (18 years old), Neil Nunley (14 years old), Olin Shaver (14 years old), Ronald Jordan (14 years old), Edison May (13 years old), Teddie Neal (13 years old), Freddie May (11 years old), and Ronald Shaver (10 years old). Unknown ages of other boys are Don Eubank, John David Jordan and Lawrence Squires.

The Charleston Gazette newspaper reported the following information in an article "Did It Ride Meteor" dated September 14, 1952, "One boy told this story. ' We saw this fiery object go overhead and seem to come down in the hills. We started to look for it. It was just about dusk.'"

In their excitement, the boys began shouting as the fireball went flying over the playground. There were some mixed opinions. One boy shouted, "It's a flying saucer!" Another yelled as the object landed, "Watch out. It may be a flying saucer and a man from Mars will jump out and get you!" One of the other boys remarked, "I bet it didn't land up there at all." Another boy in the group, who saw the object as it descended upon the mountaintop, said about its trajectory, "[It] looked like a door falling flat wise."

Eyewitness Eddie May stated the following to journalist Evert Clark, "It tilted up as it started to land." Freddie May clarified the description of the object's landing. He gestured toward the southeast and said, "It came down and lit on the other side of the mountain right up there." He pointed to a mountaintop, "Just over the edge we could tell it came down up there."

The object came down across the street from the playground on a mountaintop. The mountaintop is on the property of a farm, then owned by a Mr. Bailey Fisher. Some people also refer to this as a hill or a hilltop. For consistency, I will refer to it as a mountain or mountaintop. Next, Freddie and I went across the street and walked up to the farm. We hiked up a series of long paths and proceeded to the rear of the property.

Upon reaching the foot of the mountain, I set my equipment down and took a break. The terrain of the mountain was not rough and rugged; rather it was a steep, grassy slope, which ascended to a level plateau on top.

When we made it to the top, I was amazed to find a wide, open field. The area was nearly level, completely covered in grass and surrounded by trees. On the top, Freddie May said, "It's almost perfectly flat up here, a nice place for it to touch down." He added, "As you can see, we're right on top of the mountain. It would have been a quick spot for an emergency landing." Freddie described the plateau area where he saw the object land, "There used to be an old cistern that was torn down." (A cistern is defined as, a receptacle for holding water, especially rainwater.)

The Author Stands at the Landing Site on the Fisher Farm Mountaintop

Freddie pointed to some trees along the outlying perimeter of the field. He said, "It lit right over the top of the trees in this area." The object flew over the playground, about a mile away, passed over the trees, and then landed in the field on the mountaintop. Freddie continued by gesturing into the field where he was standing. He stated, "We could tell that it lit right here, and in this area is where we figured the thing [object] would be." He then reiterated the geography of the mountaintop, "A nice, flat spot, it makes a perfect landing place."

This portion of my interview with witness Freddie May concluded when I asked him his current opinion on what the object was. He stated, "I don't have any way, actually, of knowing what it was. My opinion is that it was a UFO from someplace else. We didn't have the technology in 1996, [to build] something that could come in as fast as I saw it come in, and slow down at the same time, and make a soft landing on earth, on the ground, and not explode or leave any evidence. I know what I saw and it's nothing that we built here on earth."

8

Lemon told Mr. Clark, "It looked like it landed right thar [there] on the hill on Bailey Fisher' farm. I said lets' go up.' Some of 'em [boys] wasn't going." Ivan T. Sanderson stated, "This object, this large, glowing object, which appeared to be about the size of a house, seemed to pause when it topped the hill and then [began] to sink, instead of going down in a sort of trajectory. It stopped and sank slowly down the hill and they could see this light pulsing behind the crest of the hill." He added, "It had stopped and landed. I know that it landed because where it landed it had pushed a large circular depression into the ground. It was an overgrown field, knee and waist high and filled with lots of twigs and bushes."

Sanderson explained, "All of that was completely flattened." He also stated, "The ground itself was flattened and there were considerable [sized] stones, not boulders, but stones the size of a man's head that had been pushed down. Also, at three points equidistant around [the area], there were three holes jammed into the ground at the edge of the circle which looked as if the object stood on a tripod, is what it looked like."

Freddie May conveyed what most of the boys thought the object was, "Well, we thought it was a meteorite, and we wanted to run up and see the meteorite burning and see if there were any rocks or anything we could save off of it, and stuff like that. That's what we were thinking when we went up." Another witness to the fiery object was fourteen-year-old Neil Nunley. He suggested the object was probably a meteorite and that they should go find it. His teachers at school said that any meteorite fragments should be gathered up for the West Virginia State Geological Department.

During the course of my investigation, I met a Flatwoods resident named Jack Davis, a prominent businessman in the area. Davis explained that he witnessed the passing of the object as it flew over the area and landed. Mr. Davis agreed to be interviewed at his home. The following testimony is from that interview. He stated, "I went over and visited my mother-in-law and father-in-law. I stayed there a little while that evening. Then I decided to leave as it was getting near dark. So, I was coming out and on the other side of the hill from the main road. When I topped the hill at the Stout Cemetery, why, [pauses] I saw a lighted object coming through the sky. It crossed where the railroad cut is today and it was an oblong-shaped object, lit up. Well, my first thought when I caught the first glimpse of it, was there was an aircraft coming down and it was in trouble."

Davis continued, "Then I recognized it wasn't - and it was bigger than an ordinary aircraft you'd see in this area at that time. It wasn't traveling at a great rate of speed in terms of that day and age. It came a little bit above the height of the trees at that time." Jack Davis then explained the color of this oblong object as it passed by. He stated, "It had a clearer, brighter illuminated light from the top and kind of an orange-red. Then as it came on down a little farther, the object was a little duller orange-red. The top of it had the reflection of a light that I would describe today as a mercury vapor light."

Drawing of the Low-flying UFO that Jack Davis Sighted over Flatwoods

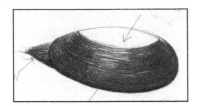 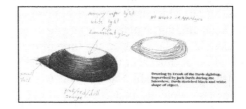

I asked Jack Davis if the object he saw pass over Flatwoods resembled a meteor. He replied, "It didn't resemble a meteor to me. To me, the object that I saw was a craft." Jack went on to describe the shape as "oblong" in nature. I then asked him, "Did it look like it was being controlled or did it look more like the flight of a meteor?" He said, "No, it looked like it was something controlled.

Like I said, it wasn't traveling at a high rate of speed, and it basically seemed like it was slowing down when it was coming in, from where I was looking at it." I then commented, "It was decelerating then." Jack replied, "Yeah, decelerating." My next question was, "Did you hear any noise, Jack?" He answered, "I didn't hear any noise." I questioned, "And there was no sonic boom noted, no noise, no rumbling?" Jack answered, "I heard none."

I then asked, "The object that you saw over the trees, Jack, did it just clear the trees, or was it a thousand feet above the trees?" He replied, "No, it was just clearing the trees, just a little bit above the height of the trees there. I had the general feeling that whatever it was, had landed. Naturally, it was coming down, not very far over the treetops until it came in behind the trees that follow the ridge out- that ran parallel to the railroad at the time. The school building [was] down below that. I knew it was up there and I knew with the reflection, the light stopped there, and I could see the reflection of it through the trees. It was very obvious to see."

Jack lived in a house that actually bordered the farm where this incident happened. After the interview, Jack walked me to my car. I looked up toward the farm and walked up the road a few feet in that direction. I asked Jack, "Why didn't you go up there that night when you saw the thing land?" Pointing up to the farm he said, "I wanted nothing to do with it. Frank, if you had seen it, you wouldn't have gone up there either." Then he joked, "Well, maybe you would have."

During a visit to Flatwoods, I spoke to the Mayor of Flatwoods, Margaret Clise, who lived in Flatwoods in 1952. A youngster at the time, she was outside in her yard and had seen the object pass nearby enroute to the Fisher Farm. Mrs. Clise told me, "The thing was oval-shaped and red. It was bright and glowing." She said, "It was big and it was flying at a very low altitude. It startled me when I saw it."

She continued, "It was so low, it was barely clearing the treetops." Mrs. Clise offered to take me to the yard where she sighted the object as it passed over the town. This section of Flatwoods is just west of the school playground at a higher elevation and overlooks the school area. While standing in the front yard near the house, Mrs. Clise pointed out a row of trees. She said, "The object passed over that area."

According to my research, the flight path trajectory she pointed out to me was correct. The witness emphatically stated, "The treetops had all turned brown and were discolored," She informed me that, "You could only see this from certain elevations in town." Furthermore, Mrs. Clise said that the tops of the trees had remained "brown" for about a year or more.

About two weeks after the incident, Mr. William Smith and his wife Donna of the "Civilian Saucer Investigation" research group of Los Angeles, California visited Flatwoods. During their stay, they visited the Fisher Farm and interviewed the witnesses. They reported their findings to the organization, which later appeared in their quarterly news bulletins, "CSI NEWS."

One such finding explained a jarring concussion that was said to have shaken the house of Eugene Lemon in Flatwoods at the time of the craft's landing on the Fisher Farm. This is the only documentation of this event that I was able to find. It was reported, "Inquiries at the Lemon house revealed that Mrs. Lemon and a friend were having coffee at the time of the landing, and their house shook so violently that coffee spilled over the table and they thought the house had fallen off its foundation. The radio went off for 45 minutes and came back on by itself."

The Boys Ran Down Main St. to State Route 4 then Depot St.

After the object landed, the boys raced down Main Street in hot pursuit of the flying object. They ran along Main Street and then ran onto State Route 4 for about a half-mile. They continued south toward the Flatwoods Train Depot, turned left on Depot Street and crossed over the railroad tracks. Depot Street was the main access road that led up to the Fisher Farm.

A Train Parked Near Depot Street in Flatwoods

The road had a steep uphill, then immediately bent to the right behind the train depot. Located on this street were three homes. At the crest of the street was the home of the Mays. Joe Lemon, Freddie May's grandfather, owned the house. Mr. and Mrs. Lemon lived in the house with their two grandsons and the boys' mother, Kathleen May, age thirty-five. As the boys approached the Lemon home, they raised quite a commotion, which drew the attention of the neighbors.

Sanderson stated, "As they ran between the houses, several people had come out on their verandas and wanted to know what was going on. One of the younger kids said, "A flying saucer has landed." As the chaotic group of boys scurried to the house, fatigued and out of breath, they started yelling in excitement. They piled through the front door of the house. Moments later the boys were met by Mrs. Kathleen May.

During this commotion of mixed anxiety and excitement, some of the boys claimed the object was a meteorite, while others insisted it was a flying saucer. Ten-year-old Ronald Shaver blurted out to Kathleen May, "A flying saucer landed up on the back hill [Fisher Farm mountaintop], and we wanna go look at it!" By then, dusk was turning into night and the boys were anxious to get to the mountaintop.

Frank C. Feschino, Jr. and Eyewitness Mrs. Kathleen May

Throughout my years of contact with Mrs. May, I compiled large amounts of notes and taped her testimony with regard to the case. Mrs. May's account of the incident begins here, she stated, "I was sitting. I had just got home from work. I was working in Sutton at the beauty shop and still had my uniform on. I hadn't even taken it off or taken a shower. I bet I hadn't been home for ten minutes when the boys came running in the house.

They had been in the lower end of town playing ball and said there was a flying saucer landing up there on the hill behind the house, and they were going up. My father had a flashlight on the coffee table in front of the couch. I reached down and got it. I said, 'You're not going by yourself. And I just took off with them.'"

This next segment of Freddie May's interview took place on the mountaintop of the farm. Freddie explained to me where he told his mother the object had landed, "It lit right in here some place." Freddie continues, "So that's where we told our mother that it lit, up on the old Fisher Farm, up close to the old cistern. This is where we were coming, to this area right here." At the house, Eugene Lemon heard the boys and decided to join the group going up to the farm. Lemon also had his dog at the house and decided to take it along with him. The May boys also had a dog. His name was Ricky. This dog was Freddie's faithful companion, and accompanied the boys. As a side note, both of these dogs were actually from the same litter.

I tried to clarify who was carrying the flashlight. (Over the years, there had been many conflicting reports about who carried the flashlight up to the farm that night.) Freddie May explained, "Gene had walked over to the house that night. When it got dark, you would need a flashlight to get around."

He added, "You wouldn't walk around these parts of the woods without a flashlight at night. Gene and mother both had flashlights that night." Mrs. May continued, "So, I grabbed the flashlight and took off with them, because it was getting pretty well dusk, and we started out and as soon as I stepped down into the road and was startin' up to the hill, I noticed this great big red flare, a purplish-looking flare." Gene Lemon stated, "When we got outside the house we could see it lit up the trees a little bit. It was orange looking – the light."

One of Mrs. May's neighbors, Mrs. Neal (Teddie Neal's mother), heard the commotion as they headed toward the farm. She came outside to see what was going on and observed the light being emitted from the farm. The boys told her that something had landed on the mountaintop on the farm, and they were going to look at it. Mrs. May said, "Little Teddies mother, well, she seen the light when we were going up there, but she didn't want to go on up. She just stayed on home."

Mrs. May adds, "I said; 'Now boys, we'll just go. We won't go clear up to it. We'll just go get the direction and the location of where it landed and then we'll just come back and call the law, and let them go up and investigate.'"

At this point, some of the original boys from the playground decided to go home instead. Five boys from the original group of witnesses proceeded up to the farm. They were Gene Lemon, Neil Nunley, Teddie Neal, Edison May, Freddie May, and Ronald Shaver. One more boy joined the group and tagged along with them. He was six-year-old Tommy Hyer. At about 7:40 p.m., the group departed in search of the mysterious object. They proceeded east of the May residence.

The main access road dead-ended only a short distance away, at the boundary of the farm. The group followed a grass path uphill a short distance that leveled off into an open field, the first field.

The Entrance to the Bailey Fisher Farm

A few hundred yards away, toward the back of the property, was the small mountain where the boys saw the object land. Along the way a neighborhood dog, a Collie, joined the group and walked along with Mrs. May, the boys and the two other dogs. As they headed in that direction, darkness began to blanket them. Their apprehension steadily increased and their pace quickened.

Their breathing became labored as the level path began to ascend. To the right of the path, out in the distance, was a fence line made of wire and wooden posts. It ran nearly parallel to the grass path. Inside the fence line is a wide-open, sloping pasture, which is set down in a valley. This area is the second field. Beyond the second field is a small mountain at the back of the farm. This is the area where the boys saw the object go down. Lemon, May, and Nunley led the group and came upon their first obstacle about ten minutes into their quest. The obstacle was a five-foot high metal gate, which was wired shut to a large wooden post. The gate was the entrance to the main section of the farm area, where livestock periodically grazed. The dirt path beyond the metal gate was an old dirt "wagon path," which had not been used by the farm owner for some time.

The older boys unwired the gate and allowed the group and the three dogs to pass through onto the dirt wagon path. Then the gate was closed and rewired. They entered a thinly wooded area, leaving the grass path behind them. The wagon path continued, but the ground became hard-packed, rough, and rocky. The path cut sharply to the right. A wooded line of trees lay to their left, the fence line continued on their right, and beyond that was the sloping valley pasture.

Feschino Stands at the Metal Gate on the Fisher Farm

The group all moved together, following a winding path that made four bends. Far off to their right, down the slope of the pasture, a large oval-shaped object rested in the valley. Some of the group became aware of the object's presence. It seemed to pulsate, dim, and brighten. Some of the people in the group did not see the oval-shaped object as it sat in the valley near a pear tree orchard. The people in the group who did see the object said it looked as big as a house off in the distance. One of the boys said it looked like a big ball of fire.

Investigator Ivan T. Sanderson

During Sanderson's investigation, he interviewed the boys who did see the object sitting in the valley. He said; "They pointed out to me, an outhouse, a sort of little barn and I said, 'How big was it?' And they said 'about that size.' We [Sanderson and assistants] measured that little two-story barn and it was about twenty-two feet high. They said this thing landed with the nose, the blunt end down."

On one occasion, during an interview with Freddie, I escorted him as he retraced the path made by the group that night. We kept our eyes focused on the beam of the lead person's light. As we continued retracing the footsteps of the witnesses toward the first gate, we noticed there was brush surrounding the valley and along the path to our right.

I asked Freddie how high the brush had been and whether it would have prevented some witnesses from observing the object. Freddie replied, "Back then, there was a lot of brush in the

14

area, a lot of tall brush, more than there is now, which made it difficult to see [down into the valley]." Taking into consideration the location of the object as it sat down below eye level on an inner slope to the right, I knew it would not have been readily visible, through tall brush.

In 1952, Ivan T. Sanderson spoke to witness, 6-year old, Tommy Hyer. Ivan said, Hyer "was at one of the houses and he tagged along behind, and to me, he is one of the most important witnesses in the whole case because of his extraordinary honesty."

Looking Up the Dirt Path that was bordered by Tall Grass and Brush to the Right

In reference to the tall grass and the object that sat in the field of the valley, Sanderson said, "When we asked him certain things he said, 'But, mister, I couldn't see. I am too low down. There was grass in between me.'" Another point that Freddie brought up as he walked up the path that night was the direction some of the boys had focused their attention.

On site he stated, "We were looking up the path to where we saw the object land on the back of the farm on the mountaintop. I was looking ahead up the path to where I saw the object land. I was not looking to the right down into the valley. We [the boys in the schoolyard] thought it was a meteorite that landed back there. We were unaware that it had moved."

Another factor prohibited some of the witnesses from seeing the object. In 1952, there were several large trees in a pear orchard and the object had landed on the opposite side of those trees. Today, very few of those pear trees remain. Freddie stated, "The boys who saw the object, the older, taller boys, told me later that the thing they saw sitting down in the valley was pulsing. A couple of them said it would get a little brighter, then dim. They saw it to the right of the path in the grass on the inner slope."

About then, a warm fog-like mist began to linger through the area and drifted down the path. The group detected a pungent, nauseating sulfur-like odor that permeated their noses and throats. They tried to ignore the odor and continued up the path. *The Charleston Gazette* newspaper article, "Did It Ride Meteor" reported the following statement made by one of the boys, "As we were going up the hill, we saw lights flashing on and off and got [whiff of] a horrible odor. It smelled like sulfur and really sort of made you sick."

Mrs. May described her account of the misty fog as the group continued up the path. She said, "Before we got up there, we could smell a kind of metallic odor, and it looked like it was getting foggy. I turned around, and looked toward the town to see if I could see the streetlights. And that metallic odor, oh, I can still smell it yet today. It was real misty." The fog obviously was not an ordinary early-evening fog that was settling through the mountains. That fog was emanating from an isolated source that was located up the path and ahead of them.

Freddie May recalled the odor. He stated to me, "The smell was similar to the old TV tubes burning out in the old TV sets years ago. A tube would burn out and have that, what we'd call that metallic smell." I asked Mrs. May about her reaction to the smell. She said, "I had a little irritated throat. It [The odor] was very penetrating. It affected me a good bit, in the chest area [inhalation]." Mrs. May also said that some of the boys were severely affected by the smell. She recalled that

Neil Nunley was almost overwhelmed by the smell. Lemon told Clark, "We just ran into this mist. It wasn't like any regular mist, just a funny looking mist. Burnt you up. It burnt your eyes and throat." Mrs. May said this about Eugene Lemon, "He did have some irritation in his throat and nose, as well as I remember." The day after the incident, *The Charleston Gazette* stated, "The atmosphere in the vicinity was reported as being 'close and hot, with the foul odor prevailing.'"

During Freddie May's interview with me on the path, he said, "Coming up the road, on down there at the beginning of the path, you could hear a whining noise which at the time [his 1952 interview], I think maybe I described it as a whining noise, but I had never heard anything like it before. Since then, with my employment - I have heard electrical compressors when they've been shut down, and they're what they call, 'whining to a stop.' Same kinda noise…same kinda noise." Here, he talks about his job at Union Carbide in Charleston, WV.

Major Donald Keyhoe and the ATIC Entrance to Project Blue Book

Pioneer UFO researcher and author Major Donald Keyhoe, USMC retired, was a prominent figure during the early era of flying saucers. He had an ongoing relationship with the U.S. Air Force and corresponded with them for several years. Keyhoe also had numerous inside sources within the Pentagon, the U.S. Government and military circles.

Major Keyhoe often spoke with Albert Chop, the USAF press officer and public liaison for Project Blue Book as well as Blue Book's Chief, Captain Ruppelt. Major Keyhoe, through his sources, was often privy to Blue Book reports that were considered classified at the time and wrote about many of these cases in his books and magazine articles. During his career, he researched many UFO cases, led many an investigation into well-known incidents and was an accomplished writer. Today, Major Keyhoe is still considered by many, as one of the best researchers to have been involved in the UFO field from the late 1940s and early 1950s through the 1970s.

Furthermore, Major Keyhoe also investigated the "Flatwoods Monster" incident between 1952 and 1953 on a governmental level. Keyhoe referred to this case as the "Sutton Monster Incident," Sutton being the nearby county seat of Braxton County. In his 1953 book, *Flying Saucers from Outer Space*, Major Keyhoe reported his findings on the "Flatwoods Monster" incident.

Also in that book, he unknowingly reported a "whining noise" heard in another UFO incident, which was similar to the noise Freddie May heard on the farm that night. That incident occurred only ten days after the Flatwoods incident on September 22, 1952, at Camp Drum in Canada.

16

Major Keyhoe states, "For 30 minutes that night, the duty officer and several soldiers watched a round, red-orange object circle above the camp.

At least three times, they heard what they later described as 'the whine of a generator or rotating discs.'" It seems that an electrical generator, which was part of the craft's propulsion system, may have been the cause for the whining noises heard in both cases.

It was now about 8:00 p.m. in Flatwoods, and Eugene Lemon was leading the group up the path with his flashlight. Suddenly, the Collie froze, and then started to growl and its ears went straight up. The dog darted up the dirt path ahead of the group, ran into the mist and disappeared from sight in seconds.

Gene Lemon continued and followed the path to the inside of the tree line to his left accompanied by his dog. Beside him, to the right, was Neil Nunley. Kathleen May was following closely behind Lemon. To Kathleen's right was her oldest son, Edison. Ronald Shaver was a few feet behind Kathleen May and was following along close to the tree line. Freddie May, his dog Ricky, Teddie Neal, and Tommy Hyer were the last of the group and followed them.

Gene Lemon, his dog, Mrs. May, Eddie May and Neil Nunley approached the fourth and final bend in the path when they heard the Collie barking violently ahead of them. Moments later, the large Collie raced by them and headed back down the path toward the house. Regardless, the group pushed on and only had only about a hundred yards to go until they reached the top of the mountain.

The location of the landed object was my main concern at that point. While in the schoolyard, the boys saw the object land on the Fisher Farm's rear mountaintop. The group did not realize that the object had actually moved from the mountain, relocated and was now sitting in the valley.

While on the mountaintop, Freddie explained the relocation of the object. He said, "Where we'd seen it come down there [he pointed down and off into the distance at the schoolyard], the angle it was coming in would have knocked trees over to get where it was [in the valley], and it didn't do that."

The Object Landed on the Mountaintop then Relocated

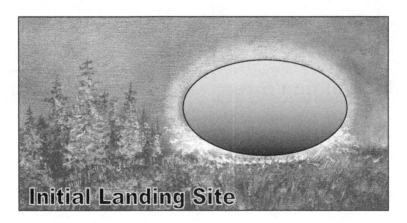

Initial Landing Site

The boys' who did not know any better and had thought the object was a meteorite were wrong. Pointing into the field of the gulley Freddie May stated, "It had to go down to there, or part of it moved down to there, whichever. This right here [mountaintop], if you're coming out of the sky, is the only place it could have lit," he said while pointing. Reiterating his stance Freddie said, "Right here."

Until my interview that day, no one had realized that the object had actually moved from the mountain and relocated down into the valley. It had actually changed its location on the farm, landing twice in two different locations.

This object actually made an emergency landing and strategically placed itself on the plateau of this mountaintop. Shortly after, it retreated into the lower valley of the farm where it would be less conspicuous to the locals in the nearby area.

<u>Looking Up at the Landing Site</u>
<u>Ring Indicates Landing Area</u>

<u>Looking Down from Landing Site</u>
<u>Object Relocated into the Valley</u>

Initial Landing Site

Initial Landing Site

CHAPTER TWO

EYES IN THE SHADOWS

The group ventured up the mountain, went around a bend in the path and encountered another gate across the dirt path. Mrs. May said, "We just kind of went around this little swag and it was kind of around this little gate there – a wooden gate." This wood gate had horizontal slats nailed from post to post and did not open.

The fence line to the right of the path also ends here at the wood gate. Beyond the fence line, to the right of the witnesses was the sloping field that was filled with tall grass, pear trees and irregular clumps of brush. This was the valley. Beyond the wood gate in front of them, the path inclines and continues up to the back mountaintop where the boys and Mr. Davis saw the object land on the plateau. Mrs. May said, "Well, me and some of the boys climbed over the gate." At this point, Mrs. May, Lemon, and Neil Nunley went over the gate, but Lemon's dog refused to go any further. Moments later, Eddie May and Ronnie Shaver climbed over the gate and followed.

Freddie, his dog, Teddie Neal and Tommy Hyer were the last of the group. They straggled along and were nearing the wood gate where Lemon's dog was standing. I interviewed Freddie May at this location. He stated, "Right down here was a wooden fence and that's where we [Freddie, Teddie, and Tommy] stopped. We came right up to that wooden fence. We didn't cross that wooden fence," he stated.

Frank Stands at the Post of the Wood Gate Remains:
An Arrow Indicates the Location of the Oak Tree along the Dirt Path of the Farm

Now past the gate, the five people headed up the incline of the path, which leads to the back of the property. Some had focused on the path ahead and followed the beam of Lemon's flashlight, while others had focused their attention on the object, as it sat down in the valley.

At this point, Gene Lemon was still walking along the inside of the path near the tree line of the woods. Kathleen May had now moved just ahead of him and was walking in the beam of his flashlight.

Neil Nunley was behind them and walking along the right of the path when Eddie May ran up behind Eugene and his mother. As they proceeded further up the dirt path, the sickening odor of burning sulfur became stronger and the misty fog started to engulf the area ahead of them. Mrs. May told me lightheartedly in the interview, "They let me lead the way. Just like an old buck, they sent the old doe out before them. We just kind of went around this little swag, [bend in the path] and it was kind of around that gate there." To their left, along the tree line, was a large white oak tree that was set back from the dirt path about four feet.

Overview of the Farm: The Dirt Wagon Path, Oak Tree and Mountaintop

Mrs. May said that she heard strange noises as they neared the large White Oak tree to her left. Getting closer, the sickening sulfur odor became stronger and the misty fog began to bellow from the area of that particular large tree. Regardless, they pushed forward. I asked Freddie about the misty fog as they walked along the path. He stated, "It was very hazy in the area along the path. It was also very misty along the tree area."

Mrs. May explained, "We got up there and it was making a hissing noise, and it just sounded like it was frying bacon and flipping a silver dollar or something against a piece of canvas, stretched canvas." Mr. and Mrs. Smith of the "CSI" research group reported, "Although some irritating odor had been noticed before, now a violent thumping began on the inside of the monster and a dense cloud of mist escaped with a hissing noise." May and Lemon, the closest of the individuals to this tree, saw something near it. Mrs. May said, "As I turned, I thought I could see it in eye view, eye level. I thought I saw something there."

Lemon also saw something. He noted a pair of eyes thought to be those of an animal set high in a nearby tree. The eyes were glowing through the fog that had engulfed the area. Lemon redirected his flashlight beam toward the direction of the eyes. At the same moment, Kathleen May turned on her flashlight. Lemon made the following statement, "I saw a pair of eyes near a tree and threw my flashlight on them. I thought it was an opossum. Then there stood this—thing."

Shocked at the ghastly sight peering over them, the boys gasped and Lemon let out a blood-curdling scream that was heard throughout the town. They were not the eyes of an animal perched on top of a 12-foot high tree branch; they were the eyes of a tremendous towering figure, which stood to the right of the tree. That colossal figure is still commonly referred to as the "Braxton County Monster," also known as the "Flatwoods Monster." Mrs. May added, "I turned the flashlight on, and the thing [the figure] lit up from the inside." She then emphasized, "I turned on my flashlight and it lit up like a Christmas tree."

20

Lemon described it as, "A 10-foot monster with a blood-red face and a green body that seemed to glow." Just after the beams of the witnesses' flashlights struck the monster, its dully-glowing eyes lit up brilliantly. The light from those eyes suddenly projected outward and cut through the fog, illuminating the area.

The stunned witnesses watched as the light beams shot forward and shone over their heads. The entire area glowed from the huge so-called gigantic "monster." During Sanderson's interviews with the witnesses, he was told about these beams of light.

He stated that, "Coming out of what appeared to be glass on the front of the head of this creature were fixed beams. The thing was turning slowly around, wavering from left to right and right to left as if it was searching the horizon with those beams. Somebody [a witness] suggested that the thing was looking for its colleagues or looking to find out where it was."

Mrs. May told me that the "monster" lit up when she aimed the flashlight on it. I asked her, "So, it reacted to you." She replied unequivocally, "Yes." Sanderson also said, "Apparently, when the flashlight came on, the object [figure] turned so that those two little beams came over and concentrated on them."

Once the area lit up, the "monster" was seen in its entirety for the first time. Some of the witnesses claimed the "monster" was green; others said it was dark. One of the boys said, "The monster was obviously black really, but as it was hot. It was getting red hot like a poker." Sanderson reported, "[It] was a sort of aluminum-gray color but reflecting the color of the bushes and such, which gave the idea of green." Hence, the "Green Monster" nick name.

Meanwhile, Freddie, his dog Ricky, Teddie, and young Tommy had reached the wood gate where Lemon's dog was standing. The boys were about to climb over it when they saw the encounter unfold in front of them near the large Oak tree.

On site, Freddie said this about the encounter, "She [Kathleen] aimed the light on it, and it was standing in this neighborhood right here under this big tree, which was a big living tree at the time." Lemon stated this about the figure that lit up, "Just flared up in front of us." Over the years, I visited the tree dozens of times. That towering Oak now stands only about nine feet tall, and is a decaying hollow shell. The remnants of the tree are steadily deteriorating, leaving little evidence of its former shape. It leans against a barbed wire fence and continues to decay.

On site during an interview, Freddie said, "From where you're filming right now, is where it was, the 'Braxton County Monster,' it was the main thing that we saw. It was standing right there." I wanted to know if Mrs. May initially approached the "monster" or if it approached her. She explained, "We came up on it. We got close enough to it so I could see exactly what it was, and we all saw the same thing. I was as close to it as the length of a car, a small car."

The ironclad figure had risen up, hovered above the ground near the vicinity of the tree, and barely cleared the tree limb just above its head. It moved away from the tree while propelling itself then glided down toward the dirt path. It then hovered over the path and passed directly in front of a horrified Kathleen May and Eugene Lemon. The immense figure hovered past a terrified Lemon, who fell to the ground and dropped his flashlight. Eddie May who was behind them, had looked, turned and then ran. The giant figure continued moving across the path in front of a shocked Neil Nunley.

Kathleen May told me what happened immediately after the "monster" moved toward her and Lemon. She said, "Gene fell over first, but he wasn't long in getting up. I don't know if he passed out, or his legs got rubbery, or what. Now anyways, he just fell to the ground." Lemon stated, "I screamed and fell over backwards."

Neil Nunley said that as the "monster" was coming toward them, it was actually moving in a downward direction as it crossed the path. Nunley reported the figure was also "circling at the same time toward the globular object." Nunley described the movement of the "monster" as it passed in front of him. He said, "I couldn't move as it did. It just moved. It didn't walk. It moved evenly. It didn't jump." Kathleen May clarified its movement, "It was just kind of floating. It was about a foot to a foot and a half off the ground, but it didn't have any kind of feet or anything that we could see."

As the "monster" glided over the dirt path in front of the three closest witnesses, it moved from their left to right, and passed in front of them. Initially, Kathleen May was the closest to the "monster." She said, "I was as close to it as the length of a small car." As the towering figure passed in front of her from behind the tree, it was hissing, making frying noises, and spewed an oily substance all over her clothing. Mrs. May explained to me, "I was close enough that it [the "monster"] squirted oil out all over my uniform." I then inquired and asked if this oil had burned her skin or work uniform. She answered, "No! I didn't even notice it on my uniform until after I got home."

Next, I wanted to ascertain the actual height of the "monster." Various publications over the years had said the height of the figure ranged from seven to fifteen feet tall. On location, Freddie May described the height of the "monster" to me, "This was the tree, what's left of the tree, right here. It had a limb that came over the road, like this limb right here. [He gestured toward another tree]. It was a little better than twelve feet up to that limb, and it was standing out and under that limb, so we figured it was about twelve feet tall, or in that neighborhood.

We estimated from where we saw him that it was approximately twelve feet tall, and I would have been oh, about five feet [tall] at the time. Now, I was not half the size of the height of it. It was [gestured with arms spread wide apart] big, you know, wide at the bottom, and the top was [indicated with his arms the width of the top of the "monster" as approximately three feet], it was, [he sighed] it was scary." Eugene Lemon said, "It was in the neighborhood from 8 to 10 feet tall." Kathleen May said, "They [investigators and townspeople] measured, and it was right under this limb of the tree, ten to twelve feet." One of the investigators who measured the height of the tree was Ivan Sanderson, "The first branch growing out of the oak tree, when measured from the [bottom] of the branch to the path on which they were standing, was 12 feet 6 inches."

The gigantic figure towered over the terrified witnesses just beneath the tree limb. It cast an eerie orange light over the area as it overlooked them. The beams of light cut through the mist, and the entire area glowed, making the so-called "monster" and everything around it visible. The group stared at the surreal image in utter disbelief.

Their first instinct was to take flight, but their feet seemed welded to the ground. They were in a dream-like state for what seemed like an eternity. The boys gazed wide-eyed and terrified as if trapped in a nightmare. Their legs finally started pumping madly as they careened back down the path into the darkness. I asked Kathleen May to describe the events directly following the encounter, "We just took off running!"

<u>Left: Frank Stands in the Area where the "Monster" was Located by the Tree</u>
<u>Right: Original Investigator Gray Barker at the White Oak Tree in 1952</u>

A shocked Gene Lemon gathered himself up off the ground and quickly caught up to the fleeing group. He said, "A boy standing near me jumped over me and took off down the hill with the rest of them behind him. I got up and took off too." Lemon also added, "Nobody said anything- everybody ran." Witness Neal Nunley, who was the boy who jumped over Lemon, said he saw the monster for a very short time. He said, "We just got a good look at it and left."

Front View Photograph of the Steadily Deteriorating White Oak Tree in 2009

At the wood gate, the three terrified boys and the two dogs turned and ran back down the path. On location near the tree, I asked Freddie May what his reaction was when he first spotted the "monster." He said, "To get out of here, we could have done the Olympics proud."

Freddie and I then walked back down the path. He turned, pointed up the path and said to me, "We had come up this direction and we took off in that direction [gesturing back down the path], the same direction which we came in."

Mrs. May expanded on her trip back down the path. She explained her encounter with the wood fence across the path. Kathleen told me, "There was a wooden [pause] ya' know how they lay the wooden pieces up across to make a little fence-gateway. That's what I jumped over and I don't even remember touching it. They [reporters] asked me if I ran, and I said I passed several of them [the boys] while I was running, and no one said a word all the way back to the house."

In what was supposed, to be only a search for a meteorite, Kathleen May said this about the younger boys, "They were just small tykes, you know, and naturally it would scare 'em, but they were of interest and they wanted to see what it was." The terror-struck witnesses raced back down the path through the mist and darkness as adrenaline surged through their bodies. Eddie May, Mrs. May, Nunley and Lemon reached the wood gate, cleared it and fled down the path. Meanwhile, Freddie, Teddie, Tommy and the two dogs reached the metal gate at the beginning of the path, the five-foot-tall metal gate that they had wired shut. Freddie told me, "I climbed over that metal gate in no time! Teddie too."

Uncertain whether the monster was following, Freddie and Teddie climbed over the top of it. Little Tommy Hyer and the two dogs went through the bars, being coaxed by Freddie. Finally, they were out of the woods; they then ran onto the first grass field where they gained momentum. Moments later, Mrs. May and the four other boys reached the metal gate, climbed over it and ran across the wide-open first field behind Freddie, Teddie, Tommy and the dogs.

The ground of the first field was much easier to traverse as it flattened out. The only sounds were the witnesses pounding footsteps and their hearts thumping in their ears. Each individual ran out of the field and down the stretch of road leading to the May home. One of the boys actually passed by the May house and continued running to his own house. Kathleen May said, "Teddie

MONSTER

Mrs. May's Point of view

Neal got so scared he ran home. He lived in Shaversville, I'd say about half a mile away. He ran all the way home, opened the door, and ran in, and his mother knew that something was wrong."

Mrs. May told me that Mrs. Neal said, "It looked like he was scared to death. And he ran into his bedroom and turned his radio on, and he just would not talk to her for ever so long." One by one, the other boys piled through the front door of Kathleen's home. Mrs. May explained, "After we all ran off the hill, the boys and I went in the house and we were all scared silly!"

Once in the house, the atmosphere had an air of chaos as they tried to regain their senses. Kathleen May instinctively tended to the traumatized boys and was assisted by her mother. All of them had difficulty breathing. Some of the boys needed more attention because they were bruised and bleeding, while others were coughing and gagging. Their eyes were glassy and tearing. Their noses and throats were inflamed. Eugene Lemon, overcome by the gas, rushed straight to the bathroom and vomited profusely. During this time, Mrs. May's parents were trying to comprehend the situation and find out what had happened. Soon, they discovered what occurred on the farm.

Freddie May recalled the scene, "When we got back to the house, we were all very scared. We were all pacing around the house, our adrenaline was pumping, and we couldn't stand still. As a matter of fact, it scared me so badly for weeks after the incident I didn't go out of the house after dark...that big thing on the hill scared us real bad." On September 19, 1952, *The Braxton Democrat* newspaper article "Flatwoods Folks See Monster" reported, "The Lemon boy was so overcome that ammonia and camphor were administered to him before he was fully restored."

Kathleen May told me, "Gene vomited all night and I had to take my boys to the doctor the next morning. Their mouths and throats were as raw as a piece of meat. I got so scared it's a wonder I hadn't vomited my head off, but I hadn't eaten and that made the difference." Mr. and Mrs. William Smith of the "CSI" research group reported, "Gene Lemon was so severely ill during the night that he was in convulsions and had attacks of vomiting." They also stated, "Soon the throats of the boys were so swollen that they could not even drink water. Examination by the doctor showed symptoms similar to those of Mustard Gas."

Meanwhile, Kathleen May called the local sheriff's department. She placed the call at 8:15 p.m. or shortly thereafter. Mr. and Mrs. Smith of the "CSI" research group reported, "The May boys were cared for by their grandmother who wiped the oily substance from their faces, while their mother phoned for the sheriff." Mrs. May told me about the call, "Cecil Rose [the jail keeper] answered the phone and he told me all the law enforcement had gone down to the river, investigating what they thought was a plane crash. But it was one of these things [the spacecraft] that landed - I'm sure. It was across the river though."

The Sutton Court House in Downtown Sutton

The area of the plane crash investigation was in Frametown, approximately twenty miles away, near the Elk River. Sheriff Carr could not respond to her call until he searched for survivors of an alleged small airplane crash.

The West Virginia State Police had their Braxton County substation located in the Sutton Courthouse. It was located down the hall from the sheriff's office. Jack Davis said this about the state trooper offices, "They had one or two troopers, at the most, assigned to Sutton. A lot of times, it was just one trooper at a time. Two troopers would handle the whole county.

CHAPTER THREE

THE BRAXTON DEMOCRAT

Jail keeper Cecil Rose walked down to the State Troopers' office to request assistance after he received Mrs. May's phone call. No one was available. State Troopers Gumm and Tribett were out on calls. Soon, trooper Corporal Ted Tribett called headquarters and spoke to Mr. Rose. Rose told him of Mrs. May's call and asked if he could respond. Corporal Tribett was detained but promised to send a representative in his place. Tribett then contacted photojournalist, A. Lee Stewart, Jr., who was working late in his office at *The Braxton Democrat* in nearby Sutton, the county seat.

Mr. Stewart was an outstanding photojournalist for the newspaper and worked closely with the Sheriff's Department and State Troopers' office. During that era in a small community, photojournalists often worked side by side with law enforcement officials. They would frequently work with the authorities and assist them on accident and crime scene investigations.

In Mr. Stewart's case, he would travel with the police to various scenes. He would help analyze the scene, report on it, and then photograph the scene for the police department. On the night in question, September 12, 1952, Mr. Stewart was empowered by the West Virginia State Police to represent the Braxton County Sheriff's Department, in the absence of Sheriff Robert Carr.

In the meantime, the news of the encounter with the "monster" had spread like wildfire throughout the small community of Flatwoods. Within ten minutes, the town had been alerted. After witness Jack Davis saw the object land, he walked back into town to retrieve his car parked in front of the mill building. As he was driving on his way out of town, he saw a gathering of people at the local country store. He explained, "This building was operated as a pretty good sized country store. It was owned at that time by a gentleman by the name of Steorts. I pulled in there to kinda' see what the gathering of people was and I learned what they were describing." Davis said the locals were talking about a "green monster."

One resident who lived nearby was eighteen-year-old Junior Edwards. Edwards was one of the first to hear about the story. About half an hour after the incident, he went up to the farm with his friend, nineteen-year-old Joey Martin. Uncertain as to where the actual encounter took place, they searched the area anyway. The boys did not see, hear, or smell anything unusual, and left the farm not knowing where the actual event took place.

Another neighbor, accompanied by some friends, drove his pickup truck to the May home and walked in on the hysterical group. He questioned them, trying to determine what had happened. Most of his queries were answered except for the exact location of the sighting. Since all the witnesses were still terrified, none of them would go with him.

The neighbor drove up to the Fisher Farm, through the first field to the metal gate. He opened the gate, and drove up the path. He continued up the path looking for the tree along the woods where the "monster" was seen. He never saw the correct tree and never reached the second field where the object had relocated. Since he was unescorted on this trip, his search was fruitless and unsuccessful. In comparison, it was similar to looking for a needle in a haystack.

During the time of my early investigation, I kept trying to locate a man who played a key role in the "Flatwoods Monster" incident, A. Lee Stewart, Jr. He was the first person of authority to arrive at the May residence after the encounter. There were many missing pieces to the incident, that only he knew the answers. After many frustrating attempts and countless inquiries to locals, I was still unable to find him. After six years of traveling to Braxton County, the only thing I had learned about him was that he had left the area in 1958 and might be living in Ohio or Indiana.

My Ohio and Indiana leads turned out to be dead ends. Luckily, I learned that the old Sutton High School had opened a new alumni archive. The collection consisted of past yearbooks, documents, and local memorabilia, overall a very impressive account of the school's history. Then I found a photograph of A. Lee Stewart, appearing among his graduating class. While I was photographing the picture of Stewart, the curator mentioned that Stewart had recently visited the town. As it turned out, Mr. Stewart's wife had passed away and been laid to rest in her native Braxton County. Subsequently, I went to the funeral home in Sutton and obtained Mr. Stewart's current address in North Carolina.

After an appropriate amount of time had elapsed, I telephoned Mr. Stewart. When Stewart left Braxton County in 1958, six years after the incident, he also left the story of the "Flatwoods Monster" behind. As we spoke, Stewart had not realized that the "Flatwoods Monster" incident was still popular. When I explained to him the amount of research I had compiled over the years, he was impressed. When I mentioned the horrendous inconsistencies of the case that had been recorded throughout the years, he was shocked.

Stewart said the story should be told once again, but this time to an investigative field reporter who would quote the facts correctly. I asked him if I could interview him and record him. He suggested we meet in person. With only a few days' notice, I set out on the thousand-mile trek to Mr. Stewart's home with my research.

My excitement grew as I made the trip to North Carolina, as years of questions raced through my mind. I arrived at his home at two o'clock in the morning. Mr. Stewart, especially considering the time, greeted me courteously. We immediately sat down and talked about the incident. I showed Lee my compilation research book, which to that time, had contained forty-four years of publications on the "Flatwoods Monster."

We talked until four o'clock and then I went to bed in the guest room. Later that morning when I awoke, I walked into the living room and found Stewart intently reading my research book. Unknowingly, I thought he had just begun reading the book, but to my surprise, he was just finishing. What had taken me seven years to accumulate, Stewart had read overnight. As I looked at Lee, he raised his head, shaking it in disgust at how the incident had been portrayed. Moreover, he did not like the fact that he had been grossly misquoted and portrayed by reporters, writers and some of the Flatwoods locals. After reading all the articles and stories about the incident, Lee spent the next four days in an in-depth discussion with me, hoping to get the real story told.

Then I set up my video camera and taped A. Lee Stewart, Jr. The following is the account of the incident as told by A. Lee Stewart, Jr. He began, "In 1952, I was co-owner and publisher of *The Braxton Democrat*. I broke the story on what is known as the 'Braxton County Monster,' or the 'Flatwoods Monster,' as it is referred to in modern day." For the record, Stewart explained to me that the nickname, the "Braxton County Monster," was coined back in 1952 because most people outside of the area hadn't heard of the small town of Flatwoods. However, many people knew Braxton County. Subsequently, after the incident became popular and Flatwoods was put on the map, the public started to refer to the "Monster" as the "Flatwoods Monster."

Stewart continued, "I have not discussed this subject since I left West Virginia in 1958. I would like to bring to light some of the things that have been said, and clarify some of the problems that have been written on this subject over the past forty years."

Stewart stated, "An artist from Florida by the name of Frank Feschino contacted me some time ago concerning this. He has done extensive research concerning this particular thing, and has spent a lot of time in West Virginia. A lot of the material that he has picked up, which he has given to me, and we have gone over, is not true. A lot of tongue-in-cheek, a lot of disclaimer material that has no bearing whatsoever on what actually happened at that particular time [1952]." He stated, "The reason I am doing this [interview] is that I'd like to bring into focus some of the things that happened and what actually transpired on the night of the particular incident. It was not easy for the people who went through this incident, and it wasn't easy for the people who tried to report it."

Photojournalist A. Lee Stewart, Jr.

Stewart's involvement with the story began about 9:00 p.m. Stewart stated, "On September 12, 1952, I was contacted at my office at *The Braxton Democrat* by Corporal Ted Tribett of the West Virginia State Police. Tribett told me about the incident. He also said the sheriff was out on a call [the supposed Frametown airplane crash] and could not answer Mrs. May's call immediately. I proceeded out to the home of Kathleen May. As far as I know, and I'm saying as far as I know, it is the only involvement that the West Virginia State Police had with this particular reporting."

He told me, "On the road out to Flatwoods, I passed Steorts' store, and Bill Steorts was working at the store with his father, and I picked him up. He directed me to the house and, in fact, was there when I talked to the people. He also went up on top of the mountain with me that night. I was the first person [of authority] to get to the Mays. It was sheer turmoil. Three boys were very sick, sick to their stomachs, and all of them were wheezing and coughing. Mrs. May's eyes were as red as they could be and sort of weepy, and everybody talked at once, so I just sat and listened for a while. As soon as I realized that the whole thing took place on the mountain [on the Fisher Farm] right behind the house, I started asking if I could get somebody there to direct me to the spot. Of course the answer was a very emphatic, NO.

After learning some of the details of the story, Stewart tried to find a willing volunteer to guide him to the exact area. Finally, he talked two of the witnesses into guiding him to the farm. Stewart explained further, "After a little coaxing, I convinced the two older boys [Lemon and Nunley] to go up to the mountain with us. So we left, the boys, Bill Steorts, and I. We were armed. We had a twelve-gauge automatic shotgun and a couple handguns. Two or three other people who lived right around there came up and went with us; they were also armed." Mrs. May had informed me that her father, Joe Lemon was part of this group. Stewart stated, "On the way up, the boys were hesitating and wanting to go back [home], and we coaxed them on."

28

In 1952, Evert Clark reported, "In no time at all the word had spread to A. Lee Stewart, Jr., editor of the weekly Braxton Democrat in Sutton, six miles away. Within an hour he had talked Gene into going back up the hill with him to have another look." Stewart explained to me, "As a matter of fact, I had my hand up around one of the boys' necks, and under his breath, he was actually crying like a whipped pup. We went on up to the tree where this thing was supposed to have happened." With shotgun in hand and his backup revolver readily available, Stewart went into the area where the "monster" had been seen. He said, "Upon arriving at the scene, we were always reminded by the boys about the odor that made them all sick. We got down close to the ground, and we could still pick up an odor. They [Lemon and Nunley] identified it as the same odor that made them sick." Mr. and Mrs. Smith of the "CSI" group reported, "Mr. Stewart, the owner of the paper immediately went to the hill and could still smell the odor on the ground."

The Charleston Gazette 1952 article, "Did It Ride Meteor," reported, "According to Stewart, there was a strong, sickening burnt metallic odor prevailing, but there was no sign of the monster." They made a thorough sweep of the area near the tree where the monster had been seen. Stewart said, "We had two large flashlights-electric lanterns, so we quickly picked up the skid marks."

The skid marks that Stewart found were actually two paths running parallel to each other, each one about thirty feet long. The marks were located to the right of the tree and the wagon path. The markings were on the grass, leading from the valley up to the area where the "monster" had been seen. Evert Clark also reported, "Mr. Stewart found no monster, but found the evil smell all right. He said he could not recall smelling anything like it before." Stewart also told Clark, "There were two sort of skid marks, about 8 or 10 feet apart...down a steep slope from the wagon path...The grass up there is about waist high, and in these tracks it was pushed down to the ground. At the end of them there was an area about 10-feet wide that was trampled down." Mr. and Mrs. Smith of the "CSI" research group talked about the pasture near the dirt path, "No wagon had been in this part for many years and the weeds were several feet high. The grass was freshly depressed."

Stewart explained the following to me, "We just spotlighted around because not one of us was inclined to hunt for something we didn't know what it was in the dark. We decided we would go back to the Mays. We were on the mountain probably thirty to forty minutes." Sheriff Carr then went to the farm with a pair of dogs. Major Keyhoe had learned about the Sheriff's participation and explained the results of his investigation into the incident. Keyhoe said, "When the sheriff arrived, a fog was settling over the hillside. Twice he tried to get his dogs to lead him to the spot where the monster was seen. Each time they ran away, howling, and he gave up until morning."

Freddie May said, "When the sheriff got to the house someone told him where we saw the "monster." He went to the farm with two dogs, but they didn't get very far before heading back. He never even got up near the tree where we saw it. When Carr got back with his dogs, Joe Lemon [Kathleen's father] even offered to take him up there to show him where it happened." Mr. and Mrs. Smith of the "CSI" research group reported their finding, "When the sheriff arrived, he listened to Mrs. May but did not investigate further during the night, when [his] dogs howled and ran away frightened."

Stewart said, "I went in and talked to the Mays, saying that maybe I could come up with a tape recorder the next day and interview the boys." Meanwhile, Sheriff Carr, who was very skeptical of the whole incident, went back to headquarters in Sutton. Stewart stayed and continued talking to the witnesses. Gene Lemon, who had arrived back at the house with Stewart, was still feeling nauseous from the fumes he had inhaled and consequently stayed the night. Mrs. May explained, "Gene is the only one who vomited and my aunt sat up with him and put cold cloths on his head and took care of him until about 12:30 that night."

Stewart explained what happened when he left the home, "I left the May residence between 10:30 and 11:00 and returned to Sutton. I took Bill Steorts home at that time. I came back to my office, and I called Buck Thayer in Gassaway to see if I could borrow his tape recorder, a big reel-to-reel he used in the theaters. So I called him and picked that tape recorder up about midnight for use the next day with the kids."

Stewart picked up the tape recorder about 12:30 a.m. and drove back to Sutton. Mr. Stewart told me he needed legal advice on breaking the story to the media because he wanted to receive the credit for it. He said, "Then I called my attorney, Olin Berry, who I got out of bed, and asked him if I should contact the *Associated Press* or *The Charleston Gazette* or both. I went over to his house (About 1:00 a.m.) we ran over this thing, and he actually made the initial call to *The Charleston Gazette* himself. This was probably about two o'clock in the morning." Attorney Berry explained the legality of the situation to Lee and said he should be credited with the story. They concluded their conversation and Stewart left Berry's house about 2:45 a.m. Stewart's involvement in the incident ended shortly after. He stated, "I got home about 3:00 a.m. and slept the night."

I also found out that the United States Army National Guard had played a significant role in the "Flatwoods Monster" incident that night. The West Virginia National Guard was actually mobilized into Braxton County on the evening of September 12, 1952 under the direction of the United States Air Force. National Guard Army troops were also mobilized to the Frametown area to look for an alleged crashed airplane. Frametown was the area that Sheriff Carr was investigating when Corporal Tribett of the West Virginia State Police called State Police headquarters in Sutton.

The time that this call was made, was at approximately 8:45 p.m. Earlier that evening, Sheriff Carr had responded to another call involving another alleged airplane crash. That call was received shortly after 7:30 p.m. from the small community of Sugar Creek. Sugar Creek is located between Frametown and Gassaway. Frametown, Sugar Creek, and Gassaway all lay along the Elk River. After the Frametown and Sugar Creek investigations had discovered nothing, a small contingent of those troops was led to Flatwoods to investigate the Fisher Farm.

Back Angle Views Comparing the White Oak Tree

  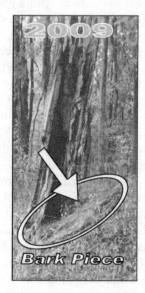

Front and Side Angle Views Comparing the White Oak Tree

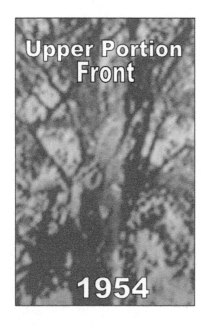

CHAPTER FOUR

WASHINGTON TAKES COMMAND

On April 19, 1953, *The New York Times* reported an article titled, "SAUCERS - Air Training, published by the Air Training Command." It reported, "more than one thousand reports of flying saucers were received at Wright Patterson Field, Ohio, in 1952. Twenty percent of these apparitions are of unknown origin. A team of four- two officers and two civilians – is evaluating all reports." This team was the understaffed intelligence group at Project Blue Book located at the Air Technical Intelligence Center.

They made up only a small percentage of those in the United States Air Force who were trying to solve the UFO dilemma; there were much higher Air Force powers in the hierarchy of the U.S. Government at Washington, D.C. that wanted UFO answers. They were quick to become involved in the Flatwoods case.

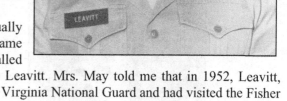

I discovered that the long arm of the United States Air Force actually reached into Braxton County on the night of the "Braxton County Monster" encounter and had actually contacted the West Virginia National Guard. Witness Mrs. Kathleen May spoke to me about the military commander of the WVNG, who was involved in the case.

This Braxton County resident was actually contacted by the United States Air Force. His name was Dale Leavitt of Sutton, but the locals called him by his retired military rank, Colonel Dale Leavitt. Mrs. May told me that in 1952, Leavitt, then a captain, was the commander of the West Virginia National Guard and had visited the Fisher Farm with some troops the day after the incident.

Colonel Dale Leavitt was the commander of the Special Forces Augmentation Section of the state headquarters of the West Virginia National Guard. Leavitt entered military service as an enlisted man in 1941. In 1943, he commanded a recruit training detachment at Fort Richardson in Alaska with the 4th Infantry Regiment. Leavitt then went to jump school in 1944 at Camp Kilmer, New Jersey. After qualifying, he was assigned to the 541st Parachute Regiment at Camp McCall, NC. He then saw service in New Guinea and Luzon, where he joined the 11th Airborne Division.

Colonel Leavitt then went to Japan and was among the first troops to land in Japan on August 28, 1945 a few days before the peace treaty was signed. Leavitt separated from active service in November 1945 and became a reservist. He transferred to the WVNG in 1948, as the commander of Company G, 150th Infantry, at Gassaway until 1955. He served as chief of staff for the West Virginia Guard from 1967 until 1968 and retired from active duty in 1973.

I asked Mrs. May if she thought that Colonel Leavitt would talk to me if I contacted him. She paused for a few moments and then replied, "Maybe you should let me call him first and tell him about you." Mrs. May did not have to say anything else. I knew what she meant. Outsiders who came into these parts were not always readily welcomed, especially outsiders who were snooping around, talking about the "monster." Fortunately, I had some relatives in Braxton County, which made me more acceptable to the locals. Mrs. May called Colonel Leavitt on my behalf, and Leavitt told her that he would talk to me.

The following day, I called Colonel Leavitt. I told him that I was surprised by the fact that there was very little known about the National Guard's involvement. Leavitt became very quiet and then asked me what I knew about the case. At that point, I gulped and had to decide quickly whether to divulge the amount of information I had. Knowing not to tip my entire hand, I was vague in my response.

I did not know this retired United States Army colonel and I was leery of negative repercussions. As the conversation progressed, it was a touch-and-go situation, and I was uncertain whether I would get any information. Leavitt set the boundaries of the topic, and his demeanor was clear. However, toward the end of the conversation, Leavitt stated that he admired my persistence and agreed to talk again soon. Over the next few months, Leavitt told me a little bit more of the story via telephone.

I brought my mother with me on my next visit to Braxton County. I wasted no time in calling Leavitt. He said to meet him at his home in Sutton. When I called him the next morning for directions, he surprised me by saying, "Make sure you and your mom wear your sneakers or boots, because I want to take you both up to the Fisher Farm to talk to you." We drove to Leavitt's house, picked him up and went to the Fisher Farm.

Leavitt explained to us that he went to the farm with several West Virginia National Guardsmen to investigate the site on the night of the incident. He said that his presence on the farm that night was strictly covert. The locals and the public were unaware that the National Guard was on the farm only hours after the incident occurred. Leavitt also explained that he had had troops down on the Elk River, looking for a crashed airplane in the nearby Sugar Creek and Frametown areas.

Leavitt told me that National Guard members throughout West Virginia were alerted and ordered to report to Braxton County for duty. He explained that he believed something highly unusual had occurred there. Shortly after our meeting, Colonel Leavitt mailed me a brief unsigned note. The note is as follows:

Dear Frank, and your mother, I was glad to go back to the hill at Flatwoods, and to know that those people and I did what Washington wanted us to do. However, there are many sightings in various states in our world. Some people laugh and think people are crazy. It appears that there are beings on other planets that want to come and land on our planet. And they may have more knowledge of outer space from their planet than we do. I do think that sometime they will continue to come to our world and try to live on our world.

Upon receiving this short unexpected note, I was shocked. Even though Leavitt stated his opinion about extraterrestrial life, he left his note unsigned. This seemed unusual, but considering his rank in the military and his involvement with this case, I could understand his desire to remain cautious.

After several repeated telephone calls with Leavitt, I pleaded with him to tell his story in front of a video camera. I knew the truth about the government's involvement that night, and his testimony would lend more credibility to the incident. In a last-ditch effort to obtain this interview, I brought up the point that the people of Flatwoods deserved better treatment than all the ridicule they had received.

Without Leavitt's testimony, the truth of the Flatwoods incident would be forever lost. Leavitt finally agreed to the interview and shortly after our conversation, I was headed to West Virginia once again. The videotaped interview was conducted on the Fisher Farm. When we began the interview, Colonel Leavitt caught me completely off guard by discussing facts that he had never disclosed before.

<u>Frank Interviews Colonel Leavitt on Site at the Fisher Farm</u>

Due to the complexity of the case and the wealth of new information that Leavitt gave me throughout the interview, I have arranged the most important information in sequential order.

For the purpose of accuracy, the following interview consists of quotes and a straight question-and-answer format as the interview progressed during the videotaping.

I began the interview with Colonel Leavitt as we stood on the dirt path near Mrs. Kathleen May's home, which leads up to the farm. The following interview with Colonel Leavitt is the only one in existence!

Frank: "Is this basically the same path you came up with your troops?"
Leavitt: "On the other side, down over the side a little bit. It was near the tree. It was close, not too far away from where we went."

When Colonel Leavitt and his troops arrived in Flatwoods to investigate, they didn't travel the main access road to the farm. The troops came through on a logging road on the back part of the property. They arrived at approximately 1:30 a.m. Leavitt was called by the United States Air Force and was ordered to deploy National Guardsmen from around the state into Braxton County. The first target zone of investigation was the Sugar Creek and Frametown area along the Elk River where a downed aircraft had been reported. The second target zone of investigation was Flatwoods.

On the scene at the Flatwoods farm, Leavitt said, "When I got the word on it, I had to detour some of our people to come up here and look at it. What happened, is they [USAF] wanted us to go, so I got the people together and brought it [the contingent of troops] up here, and then the airplane, that's the other part of it, and the car [UFO encounter with car]." Realizing that Leavitt had arrived on the farm with a contingent of troops, I asked him how many troops he had with him:

Leavitt: "There were about thirty, when these guys came out [gesturing toward the Elk River direction], because they had to fan out and try to find that airplane. But there wasn't anything there." An additional twenty to thirty troops joined the thirty initial troops that came with Leavitt to Flatwoods.

Leavitt: "I had a total of 180 something people but a whole bunch of them went down the river."

Frank: "Now how many stayed up in this area?"

Leavitt: "Oh, I'd say about 50 or 60."

Frank: "How long were you on this actual spot right here?"

Leavitt: "I'd say about 45 minutes."

Frank: "Now how long was everybody up here…a total time?"

Leavitt: "Well, we had about 50 people here, and I don't know how long. Well, they stayed the night."

Frank: [shocked reaction] "They did?"

Leavitt: "Yeah, to see if something else was going to happen."

Frank: "Now all this time your troops were out looking for a crashed airplane?"

Leavitt: "Well, yeah. Most of my people had to because it was a big area. We didn't find anything!"

During the 45 minutes that Leavitt investigated the scene of the "Flatwoods Monster" incident, he had two specific missions to carry out. His first task was to form a cordon to prevent unauthorized entry into the area. Second, he had to gather specimen samples from the area in question. Leavitt then explained the involvement of the USAF. "They called me on the phone and asked me to get them what they wanted, and I told them I would send it back to them. I did. And I came up here and got it. I dug some dirt, and all that sort of thing, leaves off the trees, and sent them in. That's all I did." I continued:

Frank: "Where did you have to send all this? Did you have to send it to Washington?"

Leavitt: [sternly] "The Air Force, that's what they wanted me to do."

Frank: "And they never told you any of the results?"

Leavitt: "No results. Never. They never do."

Frank: "Why do you think that? Do you think? . . ."

Leavitt: [interrupting] "You think something's wrong"!

Frank: "Do you think they were trying to cover something up?"

Leavitt: [Caught off guard by the question, he answered] "Maybe."

My next question involved the tree area where the witnesses saw the so-called "monster" hovering:

Frank: "What about the tree limbs or leaves? What did they look like? Were they wilted or burnt or singed at all?"

Leavitt: "No! It wasn't burned at all, the ones I got. I got them off the tree. But I got some of this oil, the little bits of this and that to see what it was, and I never did know what it was."

Frank: "Now this oily substance that was on the ground, did you have to take samples of that also?"

Leavitt: "I did, I did, and I took dirt, and leaves and some of the wood."

Frank: "Now, when these samples were sent out, they were sent to Washington directly. How did that process work?"

Leavitt: "Air Force People, that's who wanted... [Frank interrupts]"

Frank: "Now, they contacted you?"

Leavitt: "Yeah."

Frank: "Through Washington?"

Leavitt: "Yeah and they wanted to know what it was."

Frank: "Were there any other reports from Washington?

Leavitt: "No! They never, they never gave me anything back."

Frank: "It was just this one time that they called you and you sent the samples?"

Leavitt: "Yeah."

Frank: "Yeah and that was the end of it?"

Leavitt: "That was the end of it for them."

The following conversation concerned the mysterious object that was seen sitting in the valley of the Fisher Farm and was reported to have been the alleged vehicle of the monster.

Leavitt was standing along the path pointing to the grass in the valley pasture when he said, "I saw all this stuff pushed over and everything [high grass] and it landed right here. Well, it landed gently and undoubtedly. It didn't go down in the dirt or anything like that [Gestures his hand toward the ground]. "The conversation continued:

Frank: "So, it was a soft landing?"

Leavitt: "I don't know what they had underneath that place where they landed."

Frank: "What was it, just set down and pressed?"

Leavitt: "It just set down and got back up."

Frank: "How big was the section of grass that was pressed down?"

Leavitt: "Oh, it was probably about twenty feet."

Frank: "Was there much of a burnt area? Could you actually - [Leavitt interrupts]"

Leavitt: "No! Nothing burned."

Frank: "So this object was definitely maneuvering. It didn't just crash down out of the sky? It was definitely able to maneuver?"

Leavitt: "No, they could go right or left I imagine."

In 1952, journalist Evert Clark spoke to Colonel Leavitt a few days after the incident. During one conversation, Leavitt told him the following information about the grass, the odor and the oil he had found on the farm, which he referred to as grease "I saw some of the grass, and I got the odor like burning celluloid. The grease is like graphite grease, and they say there is an oil grass in West Virginia, but I never saw anything like this before."

An important point arises concerning the object that sat in the valley. Because this object was seen in flames just prior to its landing, I assumed it would still be very hot when it relocated in the valley. To my dismay, the Colonel told me there was nothing burned. This seemed odd to me. It did not seem feasible that the object's shell was able to cool down in such a short time after being on fire. Ivan Sanderson also had a discussion with some of the boys about the object as it sat in the valley. Sanderson had asked the boys if it was hot. The boys said that it had not been so.

Sanderson expounded on this. He stated, "One of the younger kids, and I don't remember which one now said, 'But mister, it wasn't hot!'" Sanderson said, "Everyone supposed [it would be hot], because of the tremendous light [and] that the thing [downed craft] was hot and pulsing, but the boy said, 'No! No! No! It's not hot. It wasn't hot.'"

The Second Landing Site in the Valley of the Farm

In 1995, I found an original 1969 newspaper clipping of an article, which is shown above, in the archives of the Charleston Public Library. I made a copy of the article and photo then later digitized it. This September 16, 1969 newspaper article is from the *Charleston Daily Mail*. The caption states, "LANDING SPOT – Marked by a different type of growth is a circular area where the vehicle of the Braxton County Monster was reported to have landed the evening of Sept. 12, 1952. Back to the spot last month to investigate were three South Charleston boys: Jim Ware and George Webb, pictured, and photographer Rick Ware." Note the elliptical pattern between figures.

Mr. Sanderson added, "The boys also kept saying that it was black. I said that if it was pulsing cherry red to orange, how do [sic] you say it was black? And they said it was obviously a black object, which was giving out this light."

It seems that the shell of the object that was just in flames only a short time before was able to cool down quickly after it landed. Another important piece of evidence that was found in the field was the mysterious tracks, which were called skid marks. Colonel Dale Leavitt also investigated those tracks. He explained the correlation between the tracks and how they were made, "The tracks just stopped here and that's all there was to it, and it [the 'monster'] got out just the same way." After the craft relocated into the gulley and landed, the "monster" exited and hovered away from it. It then proceeded across the field and headed toward the nearby woods.

Then, the "monster" went across the path and toward a large oak tree for cover. It barely passed under a 12-foot high limb that extended from it. Leavitt explained that this limb extended out over the path and then arched downward across it.

Leavitt said this about the so-called "monster" once it went under the branch, "It could move even though it went under this limb…it couldn't raise up very much or anything, but it must of backed off or turned around." At this point, the figure was now facing the path and the direction it had just come from and then settled down.

Leavitt explained the area of the tree where the monster was seen, "It just sat down. It just sat down under a limb. There was a limb here, and it scooted in underneath it. He went underneath something here [gestures upward] but it wasn't very high, maybe ten or twelve feet." Leavitt said that the proximity between the monster's head and the tree limb was close. He stated, "It was pretty close and that THING ["monster"] couldn't have got out very far. Cause it was a low limb that was down [gestures downward] through here."

Mrs. Feschino took this Photograph of Frank and Colonel Leavitt

When the three closest witnesses saw the so-called "monster," it was next to the tree and looking down the path toward them. When the two closest witnesses, Mrs. May and Lemon, shone their flashlights on the figure, it moved out directly away from the tree and under the highest point of the limb. It then hovered over the path and crossed in front of them.

Earlier in this interview, Leavitt stated how he brought his troops to Flatwoods then spoke about the alleged "airplane crash" and "the car." On a break during the videotaping session, I asked Leavitt what he was referring to when he spoke about "the car."

He told me how witnesses in a car had encountered a craft on the night of this incident. This actually happened near the Elk River, at Duck Creek, which is about six miles west of Frametown. To my knowledge, this incident had never been documented.

The following conversation transpired:

Frank: "Now, could you explain about the craft that flew over the automobile and what happened with that? That's never been documented!"

Leavitt: "No, it hasn't been documented, but other people have said what happened. They [the witnesses] said it [a UFO craft] shut their car motor off and they couldn't get it started. Then when it [the UFO] left,
they [the witnesses] went on up the road."

Frank: "And the engine just started up again?"

Leavitt: "Yeah, well they started it up."

Frank: "But while the craft was over the top of it, the engine went completely dead?"

Leavitt: "Yeah, that's what they said."

Frank: "Was that the same night this crash-landing happened here?"

Leavitt: "Yes, it was on the same night."

Frank: "Do you remember what part of town that was in?"

Leavitt: "Well, it was—do you know where Duck Creek is? It was back this way, it was."

The Duck Creek incident, the "Flatwoods Monster" incident, and the massive search for a downed aircraft in the Sugar Creek area, were the major events discussed by Colonel Leavitt. It is apparent that the craft that crashed in the Sugar Creek and Frametown areas was not an airplane.

The aircraft in question had actually crashed in Sugar Creek, took off and crashed again in nearby Frametown. Unlike a crashed airplane, this craft was capable of taking off after it crashed. This is the reason no aircraft wreckage was found during the search.

Colonel Leavitt and the West Virginia National Guard

Moreover, the Air Force was aware about what had actually occurred that night and knew an airplane hadn't crashed at Sugar Creek. They were aware that the "Flatwoods Monster" incident had occurred only a short distance away and made an obvious connection between these crashes. This is the reason the West Virginia National Guard was called out in large numbers in Braxton County that night. Colonel Leavitt expressed his opinion about the events of that night, stating to me, "Something was a cover-up! There was something down below too, but I don't really know what it was." I then asked Colonel Leavitt if he had been involved in any other UFO cases:

Frank: "When you were here in 1952, is this the only involvement you've had with this type of case?"

Leavitt: "Yes."

Frank: "That's the only one?"

Leavitt: "That's the only one. I've heard of some [others], but I've never gone to the place where it happened. This is the only one I know [had firsthand knowledge of] about."

In Donald Keyhoe's 1955 book, *The Flying Saucer Conspiracy*, he stated, "As I thought about these sightings, I wondered—and not for the first time—if I could be wrong in probing this mystery. And yet in 1952 Air Force intelligence had fully cooperated with me. Since then more than one Air Force officer had urged me to tell the whole story. In spite of this, I felt a growing uneasiness. Could the silent group be right after all? Had they found something too frightening to tell the public?" Yes, Mr. Keyhoe, I believe that they had!

Up to this point in the story, the National Guardsmen who were involved in the search party area along the Elk River departed after a fruitless search. The contingent of troops remaining in Flatwoods "stayed the night," then departed before sunrise. These troops returned to central National Guard headquarters in Gassaway, where Leavitt released them to go home. The United States Air Force had covertly entered the picture and had Leavitt and his troops take control of the situation.

However, Leavitt and his troops were not totally aware of all the other activity UFO activity over West Virginia and the Washington, D.C. area that night. The news of the visitor, which had terrorized Flatwoods, was received too late by *The Charleston Gazette* to make it to press on the following morning. However, the Gazette did publish an article on Saturday September 13, 1952, about an alleged meteor seen over West Virginia and Front Royal, Virginia. The headline read, "Meteorite Spotted in Kanawha Area." The article stated in part:

A large meteorite presumably landed or exploded within a 50-mile radius of Charleston last night. . . . The object was sighted not only in the Charleston area, but in Wheeling and Parkersburg as well. . . . A pilot en route to Wheeling from the east reported sighting the object from the vicinity of Front Royal, VA over this general area.

According to the article, it was believed that the object seen over Wheeling, Parkersburg, and Charleston was the same object seen over Front Royal, Virginia…it was not. Although the Gazette reported the object seen over the Charleston area as a meteorite, it printed this contradictory statement, "The object was also variously reported to have made hissing sounds and to have **'backed up and started over.'"**

The Charleston Gazette also printed the following article on September 13, 1952, under the subtitle heading, "Who Heard [the] Crash?" that stated:

Geologists said that the appearance of the meteorite was not uncommon, although a crash in this area would mark the first time it had happened. Meteorite fragments should have been found somewhere in the area if the object came down near here. No one reported any sort of explosion accompanying the disintegration or disappearance of the object. Presumably, a meteorite of this size would leave a depression in the earth near its disintegration point.

Meteorites are composed chiefly of nickel and iron and are fragments of other planets or meteors, which have been loosened by an explosion or by a collision. When they fall into the earth's atmosphere, they are traveling at a high rate of speed and are set afire by the extreme atmospheric friction. Normally, they disintegrate before striking the earth. Those that do hit, however, leave their mark. Large meteorites have fallen in the southwestern part of the U. S., and one which fell some years ago in Siberia wiped out an entire forest. When one caller was told these facts, he replied, "That may be, but whatever it was it sure scared the hell out of me."

The Charleston Daily Mail also reported on this story on September 13, 1952. Their headline read, "Fiery Objects Flash Across Sky in W. Va.—Many From Wheeling to Bluefield Puzzled Over Weird Spectacle." Unlike the Gazette article, which reported a single meteorite, *The Charleston Daily Mail* reported many objects. It begins, "Hundreds of West Virginians from Wheeling to Bluefield reported last night seeing strange meteor-like objects flashing through the sky."

The Charleston Daily Mail article also named locations where sightings occurred throughout West Virginia. It states, "Residents from Wheeling, McMechen, Fairmont, Parkersburg, Elkins, Morgantown, and Bluefield all reported seeing fiery objects in the sky about 7 p.m. About 40 persons in the Fairmont area said the object looked like a spotlight with a greenish tail and was traveling from 100 to 500 miles per hour."

The article also informed us of the following revelations, "Pilots of two or three commercial planes reported to the CAA in Wheeling they saw meteoric objects flash past their planes while aloft. One pilot said an object had nearly clipped the wing of his craft. This article also reported a sighting over McMechen, WV, about thirty miles south of Wheeling. It stated, "Mrs. Mary Curitti of McMechen said she saw an object which appeared without noise, and was spitting blue and white fire from one end." In reporting these sightings as multiple objects rather than one meteor, I find *The Charleston Daily Mail* was more accurate in its rendition of the story than the Gazette.

Next, I researched all the locations where sightings were reported throughout West Virginia. When I plotted these points on a map and analyzed them, they formed irregular patterns, which could not have been the flight path trajectory of any one object. In reality, there were actually two separate objects on separate flight paths, which flew over West Virginia around 7:00 p.m. EST that night.

I plotted a definite flight path of the object that flew on a southwest trajectory into the Charleston area. I was also able to pinpoint its path within the city and then follow its departure route once it left Charleston and continued south over the state.

This object flew over the following West Virginia cities, towns and vicinities:
1. Preston County
2. Morgantown
3. Fairmont
4. Wheeling-Ohio County Airport
5. Wheeling, Oglebay Park,
6. Wheeling
7. McMechen
8. Parkersburg
9. Nitro
10. St. Albans
11. Charleston/Spring Hill Cemetery area
12. West of Charleston
13. Charleston/South Hills area
14. Charleston/MacCorkle Ave
15. Ward
16. Chelyan/Cabin Creek
17. Bluefield

West Virginians actually saw a single aerial object pass over the above listed areas. The object that passed over Front Royal, Virginia was a completely different object on a western heading. A September 13, 1952, *Associated Press* news article from *The Daytona Beach Evening News* titled, "Saucer Talk In 4 States…Baltimore (AP)" states, "a pilot en route to Wheeling from the east reported sighting it in the vicinity of Front Royal, Va."

There were actually two separate aerial objects on two separate trajectories, *not* a single meteor as many newspaper articles had stated. The information from which I formed these two object's flightpath trajectories are very well documented in the media. No one took the time to figure it out; they assumed it was one object!

2-In-One Meteor
Seen Over Ward

Saucer Talk
In 4 States

Meteorite Spotted
In Kanawha Area

Fiery Objects
Flash Across
Sky In W. Va.
Many From Wheeling
To Bluefield Puzzled
Over Weird Spectacle

CHAPTER FIVE

"MONSTER" OR MACHINE?

During their trip to Flatwoods, Mr. and Mrs. Smith of the "CSI" group reported they were told about a "flying saucer" sighting that occurred in Flatwoods during the early morning of September 13, 1952. The Smiths stated the sighting was quickly reported to "Mr. Stewart" at "the Sutton newspaper." Here is their documentation, "At 6:30 the next morning, the director of the Board of Education saw a flying saucer take off, not far from his house, and immediately reported it to the Sutton newspaper. Only then was he informed of the happening the night before. Mr. Stewart, the owner of the paper immediately went to the hill and could still smell the odor on the ground. He discovered two tracks where the reported object had landed."

At about 7:00 a.m. on Saturday morning, A. Lee Stewart, Jr. walked onto the Fisher Farm and was the first person to set eyes on the scene in daylight. As he looked across the scarred landscape of the property, he scribbled notes on a pad, absorbing all the information he could, before curious onlookers besieged the area. Stewart stated, "I was back on the mountain at seven o'clock the next morning. I scanned the area of the tree as best I could, then stepped out into the tracks—the skid marks. There were several rocks that were turned over."

The two skid marks in the tall grass of the valley were each about thirty feet long. The grass was pushed down as if something had passed through it. Even though there was no ground contact made in these tracks, some outside force had turned over some rocks. Stewart then explained his investigation. He stated the following:

I walked up both of the skid marks and examined the area around [them]. That is when I realized I was getting the oil on my clothes. Upon examination, and of course I had gotten the same thing [on me] the night before—I actually thought of it the day [the previous night] that I ran into it, that it could be from the grasses. There is a grass in West Virginia called tar grass that leaves marks on your clothes, but the marks wash off. But these marks didn't come off. The oil that came from the scene adhered to your clothes, and was darker than anything you would normally get [from anything] such as tar grass.

Stewart analyzed one theory of how these track marks were made. He then said, "Somebody made the statement that the skid marks were probably made by a tractor. Well, these skid marks were probably ten or eleven feet apart and two feet to thirty inches wide." He sarcastically stated, "That takes a damn big tractor."

Journalist Evert Clark stated the following information about the skid marks and oil, which was also called grease, "Editor Bob Earl and Advertising Manager Creel Cornwell of the weekly *Democrat* in Weston, 40 miles to the north, did some investigating too...Mr. Cornwell found what is left of the skid marks, and the strange gray grease-like substance, which Mrs. May got on her beautician's uniform." Mr. Cornwell reported the oil or gray greasy substance to Mr. Clark, "There is a small plant sort of like plantain that is native to West Virginia and most of the gray seemed to be on these. We found some of this – chemical, or whatever – almost like a crank case grease."

I also spoke to Lee about the landing area that was near the two track marks. He told me, "Just a few feet away from the skid marks was a large pressed down area of grass. It was round and I'd say, about ten to twenty feet across. It looked like something had set down there in a way that the tall grass was pushed down." This was the area where the craft landed after it relocated into the gulley of the Fisher Farm.

I will now explain the true story of the so-called "Flatwoods Monster" and dispose of the folklore aspect of the story. This will also explain how the tracks were made in the gulley of the field and why the oil was found in them. The "Flatwoods Monster" was not an entity wearing a cloth garment. The original drawing of the "Flatwoods Monster" was drawn back in 1952.

One famous photograph shows Mrs. May holding this poster-sized drawing; the other shows Eugene Lemon and Mrs. May. One week after the incident, on September 19, Mrs. May, Eugene Lemon and Mr. Stewart appeared on a nation wide television show in New York called, *We the People*. Mrs. May and Gene Lemon sat down with an artist in the studio before the show aired and spoke of their encounter with the so-called, "Monster." The artist then drew a pencil illustration of the so-called "monster" from their descriptions.

It was then shown to the national television at the opening of the show with scary orchestra music setting the scene, as the host narrated the beginning of the show. In talking with Mrs. May and Fred May, I discovered that the artist's depiction of the 12-foot tall figure was actually incorrect. The artist turned the entity into a claw –waving "monster" that was outfitted with a garment similar to a hood and flowing cloth robe worn by a monk. It was depicted as wearing a tunic top, a pointed hood that covered its large red head, and wore a long pleated dress.

After this picture was shown, the media then ran with the story and further distorted figure. The overall description of the figure was misinterpreted. The press then had a field day, turning this entity into its own fictional creation. The incorrect physical portrayal of the monster is still seen today, and the entity is still represented as a Hollywood monster to the public.

After several discussions and in-depth interviews with the May family, I was able to make a composite image of the "monster's" true appearance. During one particular interview with Freddie May, I brought along some pencils and a sketchpad. He assisted me in drawing an actual likeness of the "Flatwoods Monster." I did thumbnail drawings based on his description and sketched my way into a rough draft.

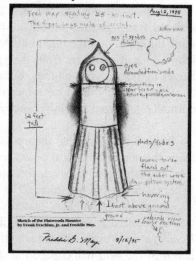

Here in the eyewitnesses' own words, are their descriptions of the entity seen on September 12, 1952, in Flatwoods. Freddie May said, "For publicity, the 'monster' got attention, and I think that's why the papers played it up with claws and things like that, as something alive. It was mechanical; it was not alive. Maybe inside the thing-there could have been something that was alive. What I saw was either a small spaceship or suit of some kind. Something it was wearing. It was mechanical."

Freddie told me while we were drawing the "monster," that, "There was something in the upper torso area that I could see. From what I saw, they could have been antennae. I'm not sure what they were, but they were coming out from the body." In Mrs. May's interview, she said, "Now! It didn't have arms. The drawing showed arms [the drawing shown on the New York TV show], but it didn't." Mrs. May adds, "It looked like, something like antennae sticking out from it, between the body and the head." The antennae-like devices protruded out from the upper torso area, on the same horizontal plane as the shoulders. Mrs. May's description of the antennae that were protruding from the shoulder area of the upper torso was interpreted incorrectly. They were changed by the TV show artist to arms with claw-like hands. The ace of spades shape that was shown in the original 1952 drawing illustrated the shape of a cloth hood that surrounded the monster's head.

As I sketched the "monster," Freddie clarified the head apparatus, "Over the head was a big ace of spades covering, it was something that looked like a helmet, and I think it was. I would describe it as a helmet." May also explained the head apparatus to me, "It looked like—over the top of its head, was a great big black thing that looked like the ace of spades.

8 Charleston Daily Mail Sunday, Sept. 14, 1952 **Braxton Co. Residents Faint, Become Ill**
Blaze Levels **After Run-In With Weird 10-Foot Monster**

The Charleston Daily Mail was one of the first newspapers to report the "monster" incident. On September 14, they printed an article titled "Braxton Co. Residents Faint Become Ill After Run-In With 10-Foot Monster." This article contained information about the head apparatus. It stated, "Both Mrs. May and Lemon described the thing. They said it had a black shield affair in the shape of an ace of spades behind it." What the TV show artist interpreted as a monk's cloth hood surrounding the head was actually some kind of a helmet. Set inside this large black helmet was a red sphere-shaped head. Mrs. May explained, "The head and face were round."

She added, "The head was a red color. Now right around the neck it looked like the neck would rotate." This red head actually sat upon a neckpiece or cylindrical collar that would pivot and rotate. The eyes of the "monster" were another area of discrepancy. The press portrayed them as bulging eyeballs that emitted light and having a wide variety of colors, mainly red. Freddie said, "The 'monster', as the TV show and papers led us to believe, came out with the claws and the big red eyes and things like that."

The "Monster"

Freddie explained what the large eyes actually were. He stated, "The eyes were portholes. It's the way I described them, and the way most of us [the other witnesses] described them, as portholes. Say like a window in a house at night, with the light on, and you're looking in. That's what it looked like." Mrs. May told me, "It had great big eyes, portholes or whatever you want to call them, and basically lit up. It was a funny-looking orange in the portholes. It looked like there'd be lights behind them." The portholes described here by the witnesses were actually eye openings.

Next, the original drawing showed a tunic-type flap of material hanging down over the chest of the monk-like garment. I thought the original portrayal of the chest area in the drawing was some type of armor plate covering. Mrs. May described the actual shape. She said, "It just came up, just like a human body."

The depiction of the monk-like robe and tunic were a complete fabrication. Freddie said that the upper torso was nearly cylindrical in shape. He explained to me, "The overall body was metallic not cloth."

Freddie emphasized, "The figure was made of metal." I also asked Kathleen, "Did it look cloth-like or metallic?" She said, "No! It looked more metallic."

Moreover, the 1952 sketch of the lower torso depicted a figure or "monster" wearing a pleated dress. This was illustrated as the lower robe section of the monk-like garment. Kathleen told me this about the lower torso. She stated, "It was shaped like drapes but it came out. It wasn't straight down like they had in that picture. It came out on the sides. It flared out." In Mrs. Mays' description of the lower torso, the original TV show artist and media writers interpreted her description literally.

The misconception of the figure showed a "monster" wearing a robe-like dress, which extended downward from the waist toward the ground. The contour of this dress was shown to have great folds running vertically from the waist to the bottom, like a pleated fabric. Based on Mrs. May's life experiences, drapes were the best example she had to describe the lower portion of the "monster's body." The description of the "monster" in *The Charleston Daily Mail* September 14 article mentioned the pleated lower torso, but made one small mistake.

The article stated that the "monster" or figure, "wore what looked like a pleated metallic shirt." The word "shirt" was mistakenly substituted for "skirt" thereby changing the description of the metallic figure and its likeness. Freddie May clarified the pleated lower torso section of the "monster" and told me, "What really stood out was [sic] the big pipes on the bottom of the 'monster.' They were metallic and silver in color and very bright." He explained, "What mother described as the pleats of hanging drapes, were actually tubes running vertically." We continued working on the pencil drawing and as I sketched his descriptions onto paper, I drew tubes running from the waist area of the body toward the bottom. Freddie said, "The lower torso flared out." As I continued to draw, Freddie told me the tubes were equally spaced apart around the circumference of the body.

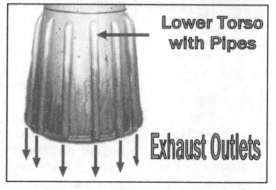

Lower Torso with Pipes

Exhaust Outlets

He said that the thickness of the tubes could be compared to that of a "fireman's hose," but explained, "they were metal, they were actually metal pipes." Freddie then extended his arm out and said, "Frank, they were big as, [Pauses] they were thicker than my arm." As the drawing began to develop, it appeared to resemble a booster rocket. The lower torso was actually said to be metallic-like and conical shaped, according to the witnesses. The so-called vertical folds or pleats were actually pipes that ran from the waist to the bottom of the figure and equally spaced. I asked Freddie what he believed those tubular pipes to be.

He said, "I think those tubes were some sort of propulsion system. It was hovering about one foot off the ground." He then took my pencil and drew his own sketch of the tube pattern, circling the torso. He drew the end of the tubes as exhaust pipes.

After I saw his drawings, I believed that those tubes were part of an exhaust system where the sulfurous mist/gas smell originated. Freddie May agreed with me. During an interview with Mrs. May, I wanted to know if the "Flatwoods Monster" was throwing off any heat. Being so close to it, she may have noticed this detail. I asked her," Did you feel any heat from it?" Mrs. May answered, "Yeah, you could feel-it was just like a warm mist."

Hearing this, Mrs. May reinforced my theory that the mist she described as a "warm mist," was actually exhaust that was spewed out of the metal pipes. Moreover, the original drawing shows a drop cast shadow under the "monster." This actually illustrates the point that the figure had actually hovered and was mobile. I now had a working visual image to aid me in illustrating a rendition of the "monster."

I combined the descriptions from Freddie and Kathleen May and made an illustration of the "Flatwoods Monster." My illustration shows the "monster" as described by the actual witnesses. In making comparisons between the old and new renditions of the "monster," I was able to establish several conclusions. The media portrayed a "monster" wearing a monk-like garment, but it was actually a machine, spacesuit, or a large transport vehicle. Now, it made sense as to why the "monster" was said to have hovered a foot above ground!

Surrounding the head area was a large ace-of-spades shaped covering. The early depiction of this covering was portrayed as a cloth hood with an opening in the front facial area. In reality, the hood was actually a black metallic-like helmet with a circular opening that was covered by a transparent barrier. It resembled a pane of glass, similar to a window. An inner helmet was contained within the ace-of-spades shaped helmet. This inner helmet was sphere-shaped and red. It was thought to be the actual head and face of the "monster."

The inner helmet and outer helmet described here, actually reminds me of a jet fighter pilot in a cockpit wearing a helmet, the outer helmet a canopy. The eyes were described as large and about one foot apart. The early depiction of the eyes portrayed them as large and protruding. Descriptions of eye color varied from red to green to orange.

The eyes were actually thought to be eyeballs. In reality, they were porthole-type openings one foot apart. Behind the eye openings was a light source. (Note: When the "monster" reacted to a beam of flashlight cast upon it, the light source behind the eye openings increased. This forced the light through the openings into a beam like pattern.) The light source color changed from orange to green.

The original depiction of the neck indicated it was wrapped in a dark cloth. This was thought to be an extension of the cloth-like shirt, similar to a scarf. According to witnesses, the neck was short, stout and cylindrical in form. The sphere-shaped inner helmet sat upon the neck that rested upon the top area of the upper torso. The upper torso from the shoulder area to the waist was depicted as wearing a monk-like robe. This was a total fabrication.

The "monster" then, was illustrated as wearing a dark cloth like undergarment with a tunic type material across the chest. Actually, the figure had a metallic, cylindrical body, wide at the shoulders, which widened slightly down to the waist.

After reviewing all the eyewitness descriptions of the color of the metallic-looking outer shell, I concluded that the space suit was aluminum-gray and that the shell was hot and was becoming a darker color. As the metal turned "dark," it became "black," as "it was getting red hot like a poker." The dark oily-like substance that the structure was emitting covered portions of the metallic shell as well, adding to the dark appearance. When the flashlight beams hit the so-called "monster", it reacted and lit up from the inside and projected beams of light from the eye area. Mr. and Mrs. Smith reported this, "It was as though a light had been turned on inside the figure."

At that point, the area became illuminated, "reflecting the color of the bushes and such, which gave the idea of green" against the metallic-looking body shell of the figure. The visitor in question was definitely not a "monster" shrouded in a monk-like garment but rather a mechanical apparatus or probe; the occupant that was contained inside the probe is another matter.

THE SPACE SUIT

Inner Helmet

Shell of Outer Helmet

Upper Torso Shell of Suit

Suit Separates at Mid-Section

Lower Torso with Pipes

Exhaust Outlets

Shortly after Mrs. May returned from New York after appearing on *We The People*, she claimed she was notified in a letter by the United States government that the "monster" was actually an experimental craft. This explains her government craft story.

The Charleston Gazette printed the following story, "What Happened to the Monster?" The sub-headline read, "Braxton County Woman Feels Glowing Object Was Jet Ship Discovery in 1952 Stirred up Nation-Wide Martian Debate." The article stated, "Flatwoods, Oct. 6 - The woman who set off a four-year debate when she saw a mysterious object near her home here said today she was convinced she didn't stumble on a craft from Mars. Mrs. Kathleen May said the 'Braxton County Monster' was nothing more than some new type governmental-owned jet or rocket plane."

Shortly after, Mrs. May returned from New York after appearing on *We The People*. She claimed she was notified in a letter by the United States government that the "monster" was actually an experimental craft. This explains her government craft story. When I interviewed Leavitt, he also knew the "monster" was some kind of a machine. He stated the following to me in our interview, "Well, there was something here that could fly backwards or anywhere it wanted to go, just anywhere, as long as it didn't tear up its equipment. But it was right here."

Colonel Leavitt's comment about equipment being damaged was in reference to oil that he found that night. This oil was emitted by the figure, the same oil that spewed on Mrs. May's clothing during the encounter. Leavitt actually found an oil puddle near the tree where the "monster" was seen. This puddle was obvious to see at night with flashlights.

Leavitt explained, "It just sat down. It just sat down under a limb. There was a limb here, and it scooted in underneath it." I also asked Colonel Leavitt if the oil that he found near the tree was splattered about the area. The following conversation transpired:

Leavitt: "No, not all over the place. Where it sat, it had some oil coming out. Whatever-it was."
Frank: [lightheartedly] "I guess spaceships have oil leaks too."
Leavitt: "Maybe so."

I then asked Colonel Dale Leavitt his opinion about the craft, called the "Flatwoods Monster."

Frank: "Do you seem to think it was an experimental craft, or do you think it came from someplace else?"
Leavitt: "No. I think it came from someplace else, personally."
Frank: "What was the general thought of the local people around here?"
Leavitt: "They thought it was silly, crazy."
Frank: "Did they ridicule, make a big joke of it?"
Leavitt: "Yeah, they made a joke out of it. They made all kinds of different pictures [he laughs]. I saw some of 'em."

By analyzing A. Lee Stewart's findings of the strange oil-like substance in the grass and Colonel Leavitt's findings near the tree, I had reached a conclusion. Based on witness testimonies and news reports, I theorize the marks were actually two separate paths made by the "monster" as it hovered and glided across the field. The force of the propulsion system parted the grass and over turned small rocks as it hovered over the area. The oil-like substance was emitted from the "monster" after it had departed its craft, through, and over the grass. This created the path en route to the tree. Once near the tree, the "monster" continued to emit or leak the oil.

Upon reaching the tree, it sat down and leaked more oil. This was the oil puddle that Leavitt and his troops found and collected. Shortly thereafter, the witnesses encountered the "monster". In my interview with Kathleen May, she said, "I was as close to it as the length of a car. I was close enough that it squirted oil out all over my uniform.

After the witnesses saw the "monster," it hovered back toward the landing area, leaving a second track that ran parallel to the first one. The "monster" continued to

Sketch by A. Lee Stewart Jr. of piece of metal found on Sept. 13, 1952, in field of Fisher farm near tree where Flatwoods monster was sighted.

Dec. 1996

drawing by Frank Feschino Jr. assisted by A. Lee Stewart Jr.

METAL PIECE DRAWINGS

leak oil on its return trip back to the craft. Stewart found something else while walking through the large tracks. He said, "It was at that time that I found a piece of metal."

Stewart explained, "It looked like somebody had taken a soldering iron and just dripped solder. The piece of metal was shiny and silver, very easy to see in the daylight." He further stated, "I don't think we would have ever found it at night, even if we looked. It was about this big [making a circular shape with thumb and forefinger], rugged on the edges like any dripped metal would be."

After examining the scene for about an hour and a half, Stewart went back to his car and got the large reel-to-reel tape recorder to record the witnesses. He went to the May residence and spoke to Mrs. May, the Lemons and Kathleen's two boys.

The other boys and their families congregated at the house throughout the day and the Mays were swarmed by curious visitors from the town. Stewart eventually interviewed four of the witnesses that morning, and the remaining three in the afternoon.

Drawings by Five of the Boys who saw the "Flatwoods Monster"

Stewart said, "One point that you've got to remember on this, is that you're dealing with an age range of from six to eighteen years of age. These kids were not modern street punks; they were country kids. They had not been exposed to TV or monster movies [or the sophistication] that kids [have been] in this day and time. You've got to remember, this was 1952 in central West Virginia." Mr. Stewart also explained his procedure in interviewing the young witnesses, "I interviewed each one of these people separately and privately and asked each the same questions."

He further explains, "Approximately thirty questions on anything and everything I had heard the night before, and ones [questions] I had been able to come up with since that time. After I finished with each one of these kids, I'd change the questions. I would take a couple or three of the questions and change them around so I could expect another answer. They'd always come back to the same things they had said before.

Then I would jumble the thing up in such a way that, I said, 'Well, you said so and so,' but they always, [he paused] always went back to the same answers." Stewart also said, "They were sincere, truthful, [and] to be quite honest with you, I believe they believed everything they said. It is surprising to be able to sit down, go through that many questions to kids of that age, and still get the same answers, regardless of what you did to the question.

Ivan Sanderson also talked about the witnesses that he and his colleagues interviewed throughout Braxton County and stated, "None of those people were telling lies. They never deviated from their story, one single iota. They never deviated in their overall story and I think that's a very powerful factor."

As the day progressed, hundreds of people over ran Flatwoods. Droves of local residents and outsiders congregated near Kathleen May's home. Flatwoods had now become a target of investigation by both amateur and professional information seekers. Before long, local West Virginia newspaper reporters arrived on the scene. Some of the people who visited the area were from the local sheriff's department and the West Virginia State Police.

In addition, there were local political figures Glen Cochran, the mayor of Flatwoods, and J. Holt Byrne, the mayor of Sutton. Byrne was also the owner, publisher and editor of the Braxton

Central, the rival of *The Braxton Democrat*. Olin Berry, the prominent attorney who broke the story to the Gazette, was also present. Arriving that afternoon was the small group of National Guardsmen led by Colonel Dale Leavitt.

I also talked to several people who actually visited the Fisher Farm after the incident. They told me that the farm was over run with people in the days following September 12. Several of them saw the "pressed down" area in the lower field and the "two path marks" near it. At least twenty people that I spoke to, told me about an odor that was described as a "sulphur smell" scattered all across the farmland of the Fisher Farm. According to one man's account, he visited the farm over a week later and the "sulphur smell" remained in the area.

Photo of Witnesses Tommy Hyer, Fred May, Gene Lemon (back) and Ed May

A *Charleston Gazette* article written by James Haught on October 31, 1954, titled "Martian or Mirage" stated, "The day after the sighting [September 13, 1952] visitors reported finding 'large marks', oil spots, scraps of metal and pieces of black plastic-like substance on the ground." A photograph of Leavitt appears in the story showing him in his civilian work uniform holding a pencil with his thumb pointing to the tip of the pencil. The caption stated, "Metallic fragment the size of the tip of a pencil was found at the spot where the 'monster' was seen by National Guard Capt. Dale Leavitt. Also, found were 'skid-marks, oil spots and pieces of black, plastic-like material."

I found this article 10 years after my videotaped interview with Colonel Leavitt. It seems as though Leavitt actually found at least one scrap metal fragment on the site where the "monster" had been. At the time of my interview with Leavitt, I was unaware that Leavitt and some visitors had actually found "scraps of metal" fragments and "pieces of black, plastic-like material" on the farm.

I retrieved my videotape of Leavitt from storage and reviewed it again. Leavitt did mention something to me that I did not understand at the time of the interview when I asked him about the samples he collected.

When we were standing in the field on the farm, Leavitt was explaining and gesturing his hands across the field and talking about the grass and dirt samples that he had collected. He then stated, "I got some of this, - all of this, little bits of that [pauses] to see what it was, and I never did know what it was." I was not aware that there was a black-plastic like substance and metal pieces found on the farm at the time of Leavitt's interview.

It was not until I spoke to Stewart in 1996, about three years after Leavitt's interview, that I realized fragments were found on the farm. James Haught's 1954 article was very useful when he informed that, "The day after the sighting visitors reported finding 'large marks', oil spots "scraps of metal and pieces of black plastic-like substance on the ground."

Colonel Leavitt also went to the farm with some of his troops on that following day to control the overwhelming number of visitors. He told me, "There were so many people that came up here and ran all over the place, they might have gotten killed or something." Freddie May said, "When

Leavitt and his troops arrived, there was a lot of people at our house and on the farm. It was chaotic. The access road to the farm was cordoned by the Guard so no one else could get in."

Mrs. May stated, "The amount of people that came up here later the next day was unbelievable. The National guard roped of the area at the access road." I ask; how many visitors found and picked up pieces of the metal and black plastic-like material on the farm that day?

When Sheriff Carr arrived on that Saturday, he spoke with some of the witnesses and local newspaper reporters. Carr spoke with J. Holt Byrne. He told Byrne that he and Deputy Long had previously investigated another crash-landing of what was thought to be a small cub airplane at Sugar Creek. Woodrow Eagle, a resident of Duck Creek, made a call, saying he had witnessed a flaming object crash into a hillside while traveling in his car.

Mr. Byrne reported the following statement to *The Charleston Daily Mail* dated September 15, 1952, "Woodrow Eagle of Duck Creek, along the Braxton County line, was traveling toward Flatwoods as the aerial phenomenon made its appearance. He reported to Braxton County Sheriff Robert Carr that a small airplane had crashed against the mountainside. A later search [by the sheriff] failed to disclose any remnants of the wreckage."

During one of my interviews with Mrs. May, she said that about one month after the incident she read a government letter explaining the events that took place on September 12. She told me that the government had an explanation for the objects seen in Braxton County. She was informed that they were actually experimental crafts being tested in the area. The one craft that had trouble was the one that landed in Flatwoods.

She said, "They notified us that there were four crafts in Braxton County that night. One of them lit here [Flatwoods], one down the river [Sugar Creek crash- Frametown crash, same craft], and one up in Holly [a town just south of Flatwoods]. And I don't know what happened to the other one [James Knoll crash in nearby Frametown]."

Interestingly, I discovered that the federal government denied being involved with this case. Officially, they made no public investigation. I have combined my research findings with Keyhoe's early governmental findings. Together, they show a correlation between the United States government and the "Flatwoods Monster" incident. When Keyhoe first heard about the case, he said, "I found myself faced with another puzzle, the case of the Sutton Monster. Of all the eerie saucer stories, this was the weirdest. When the story first appeared, I put it down to hysteria. As a joke, I phoned Chop."

Keyhoe asked Chop, "How many intelligence officers are you rushing down to Sutton?" Chop answered sourly, "You too? We're not even bothering to investigate. Several astronomers said a meteor went over there. Those people must have dreamed up the rest." Keyhoe, during the course of his investigation, said, "Later from a source outside the Pentagon, I heard that intelligence had followed this up by sending two men in civilian clothes who posed as magazine writers while interviewing witnesses. Even if this was not true, and the Air Force denied it, their check through the state police showed more interest than they had admitted."

I found out from Kathleen May that intelligence actually did send men to Flatwoods the day after the incident. She said, "Two men came and knocked on my door and they told me they were editors from Clarksburg. Well, they said they were reporters from Clarksburg at first and they would like to go up and see the place where it landed. Freddie went up with me, Eddie was too sick to go, and we went up there."

Mrs. May, Freddie, and the two supposed reporters left the house and went to the Fisher Farm. This was the first visit to the farm for both Mrs. May and Freddie since the incident had occurred. Upon reaching the farm, they went to the field in the valley. Mrs. May said, "And one said he was going to cross over the fence and go down toward Shaversville. That's the way the thing came in that night and landed."

While Kathleen, Freddie and the two supposed reporters were standing in the valley near the track marks and second landing area, they conversed about the events that had taken place. Kathleen said, "We were just talking about the thing and they saw the skid marks. These skid marks went right down a little slant. One stayed there with Freddie and me, and one went across [the fence] and went down. Well, he was gone about thirty minutes and came back."

Mrs. May explained what happened when the supposed reporter came back from the tree area covered in oil. She said, "He came back and said to the other guy, *'Now what do you think Ed's gonna think of this when we send these in for analysis?'* That's just the way he said it [Gesturing with her arms down at her sides and held out away from her body]. And he was covered. They had beautiful, nice suits on with hats to match, and he was striped. He looked like a zebra, with oil. Everything he touched left oil marks on his suit and hat." Questioning her further, I asked, "So when this guy came back he held his arms out and he was covered with oil?" She replied, "Yeah, he was just covered, on his arms, his legs, his hat and everything. He had oil all over him." Shortly after these events, the two supposed reporters left the scene.

One of the legitimate reporters on location that day was a representative from *The Charleston Gazette*. He worked with A. Lee Stewart, Jr., and the following article appeared in the Sunday morning September 14, 1952 edition. (Special to the Gazette). "**Did It Ride Meteor?** Boys Spot Appalling Creature Near Flatwoods, Link It to Passage of Fiery Object in Skies." The article began, "The 'meteorite' which flashed through eastern skies Friday night may have had a passenger, according to reports from nearby Flatwoods."

The newspaper had made a correlation between the alleged meteorite Friday night and the "Flatwoods Monster." The alleged meteor was seen over numerous parts of the state between Morgantown, Fairmont, and Wheeling. It was also seen over the city of Bluefield along the southern border of West Virginia. It was also, "Considered to be one of the most brilliant meteors to streak across the sky in recent years."

The Charleston Daily Mail reported on September 14, "Braxton Co. Residents Faint, Become Ill After Run-In With Weird 10-Foot Monster." This article gave the "monster" an inaccurate description, "Seven Braxton County residents Saturday reported seeing a 10-foot Frankenstein-like monster in the hills above Flatwoods." Not only was the "monster's" description reported inaccurately in the article, but also the following remark was included. It discredited the story even more, "However, state police laughed the reports off as hysteria. They said the so-called monster had grown from seven to seventeen feet in 24 hours."

Donald Keyhoe said this about the West Virginia State Police involvement, "I discovered that the Air Force had not ignored the Sutton report. To avoid public attention, intelligence had worked through the West Virginia State Police, securing all the details."

I spoke to Jack Davis about the involvement of the state police in the Flatwoods case. He stated, "I was in Sutton and a patrolman, by the name of Gumm talked to me a little bit. He expressed to me that any remarks or anything that people might ask about it [the "monster"], not to give them any information and not to discuss it." Davis then told me about other state troopers that spoke with him in Flatwoods, concerning the "monster". "They told me just not to discuss it with anyone. They said, 'that [it] was to be discussed with no one and not to tell a bunch of tales about something I'd seen that I didn't know anything about,' That if you couldn't tell them what it was, then you didn't tell them some phenomenon [sic] tale."

Davis also told me about seeing the state police in Flatwoods. He told me, "I would notice that very, very often they'd just come along and stop at the local stores in the areas of Flatwoods—basically, just in my opinion, to disperse the loafers or whatever you would want to call them." The debunking phase of the government's plan had actually begun at this point through the West Virginia State Police.

On Sunday, September 14, the two supposed reporters who spoke with Mrs. May returned and took her back up to the farm. She said, "And then the next day they came back and they begged apologies. They said they were from Washington, D.C. They said they were from Washington and they had flown in and rented a car and came up here." I asked, "Why do you think they didn't tell you the truth the first time?" She replied, "They were afraid that if they wanted information and we knew they were investigators we wouldn't tell them anything." Mrs. May and the two men conversed about the incident. Pressed further, Mrs. May mentioned that during her encounter she was squirted with oil. One of the investigators was adamant about getting a sample of it.

She said, "They did go down to the house and scrape some oil out of my uniform." Mrs. May added, " So I guess he just wanted it for analysis or something, to see what kind of oil it was." I asked, "Do you remember the oil in particular? Did you get it all over yourself when the "monster" sprayed it on you?" She replied, "No. It just hit the front of my uniform." I asked, "What did you do with your uniform? Did you keep it or did you throw it out?" She answered, "I kept it for a while and then I think I threw it away. I'd never have gotten that (oil) out of it anyway." These statements by Kathleen May demonstrated the government's involvement and interest in the case. It also corroborated Keyhoe's source who had heard that intelligence had sent two men in civilian clothes posing as magazine reporters while interviewing witnesses.

Project Blue Book Chief Captain Edward J. Ruppelt

A striking part of this interview was the name that Mrs. May clearly remembered after her first encounter with the intelligence officers on the Fisher Farm. She remembered the officer who was covered in oil specifically using the name Ed. He stated, **"Now what do you think Ed's gonna think of this when we send these in for analysis?"** The Chief of Project Blue Book at that time was none other than Captain Edward J. Ruppelt. He was a World War II veteran who later earned a degree in aeronautical engineering from Iowa State College.

When the Korean War began in 1950, Ruppelt, a reserve navigator, was recalled to active status on November 4, 1950. He worked at the Air Technical Intelligence Center doing aeronautical analysis of the Russian jet fighter, the MIG-15. Here at ATIC, they were in charge of the Air Forces' UFO project as well. In November of 1951, Captain Ruppelt was appointed the Chief of Project Grudge later named Project Blue Book and held that position until September 1953. After Captain Ruppelt retired from the Air Force, he wrote a groundbreaking book titled, *The Report On Unidentified Flying Objects*, published in 1956.

In Flatwoods, the two men who visited Mrs. May were undoubtedly officers from Blue Book. At the time, Ruppelt had three officers who were available for field investigations, Lieutenant Kerry Rothstein, Lieutenant Robert M. Olsson and Lieutenant Andrew Flues. During their visit to Flatwoods in September of 1952, Mr. and Mrs. Smith of the "CSI" research group had learned, "Samples of ground and vegetation were also collected by airforce [sic] officers."

I now ask; which two men met with Mrs. May and who needed a new hat and suit? The level of participation by the Federal Government in this case far exceeded the interest they were willing to admit. The two intelligence officers returned on Sunday and revealed their identities in a desperate attempt to get further information and obtain the oil sample from Mrs. May's uniform.

Colonel Leavitt was also on the Fisher Farm on Sunday, September 14. Leavitt had talked to journalist Evert Clark about the witnesses and the farm and stated, "I talked to every one of them, looked over the hill Sunday, checked to see if there had been any horses or cows in the pasture that night [Friday], and so on. There weren't. Their stories are all identical."

Project Blue Book Investigators Captain Ruppelt, Lt. Rothstein and Lt. Olsson

AT ONE OF the four desks in the small, 30-by-15-foot rooms, partitioned off from the rest of the Air Technical Intelligence center, Rothstein and Ruppelt check off one of the 1,000 sightings reported to their office in the past two years.

CHAPTER SIX

DOUBLE JEOPARDY

At this point, I knew there were actually two objects that flew over West Virginia about 7:00 p.m. EST that night. It had become clear to me, that not all the reported sightings across the state could be blamed on one single meteor. My next step was to trace the flight paths of these two objects back to their origins.

I searched through newspaper archives for information. My first goal was to locate articles related to alleged meteor reports for that evening. Once I located those articles, I was overwhelmed by the fact that there had been multiple sightings of supposed meteors throughout the east coast. The newspapers had inadvertently combined all the sightings of this supposed single meteor, not realizing there had been more than one.

Donald Keyhoe said the following about the "Flatwoods Monster" incident, "I found myself faced with another puzzle, the case of the Sutton Monster." Investigator Gray Barker also referred to the "Flatwoods Monster" case as a puzzle, He stated, "I can only begin to cope with the mass of data and the correspondence, the pieces of the jigsaw puzzle containing the answer to the entire mystery—if it could only be put together!"

The overwhelming number of UFO sightings that occurred that night throughout the east coast was indeed similar to pieces of a jigsaw scattered about in a shotgun pattern. It took me several years to search out and collect a list of locations where these so-called meteor sightings occurred. I used newspapers from around the country, including daily and small weekly regional publications. I also used actual Project Blue Book documentation to obtain information about these UFO sightings and spoke with actual eyewitnesses who saw the objects.

To put this gigantic jigsaw puzzle together I used several maps and plotted all the areas where the UFOs were sighted that night. My master map consisted of several aeronautical maps that I pieced together that made one huge map of the eastern United States. I used this master map throughout the course of my investigation and as I discovered new sightings, I would plot the points on the map. I also used several regional maps to plot UFO sightings that occurred over local areas and then made several maps of my own. I then combined all of the information that I had accumulated, including times and started connecting the plotted points on my maps. In other words, I connected the dots and started forming flight path trajectories across the country. This is how I was able to reconstruct the events as they unfolded on the night of September 12, 1952.

I discovered an article that provided the first half of the flight path for the object that was seen from the Wheeling area. It appeared in *The New Haven Evening Register,* September 13 AP news article, "Fiery Object Streaks across Skies of 4 States—A Meteor? Could Be." The article in part reported, "The streak of fire first was reported over Baltimore shortly after dusk about 8:00 p.m. EDT. In quick succession came reports to the west from Frederick, Hagerstown, and Cumberland, MD, and Charleston, Wheeling and Parkersburg, W. Va." The first object seen that night over this vicinity was the object passing over Baltimore that proceeded into northern West Virginia. I will now refer to this as the Baltimore/WV Object.

This object passed over Baltimore, Maryland on a northwest trajectory as it flew over the United States. However, witnesses from nearby Pennsylvania sighted it before it reached Baltimore. *The Mercury* newspaper of Pottstown, Pennsylvania reported the sighting of this object as it flew enroute to Baltimore, Maryland. Their article stated, "Reported Plane Crash is Just

Another Meteor. It wasn't a flying saucer and it wasn't a burning plane that flashed across the sky to the southwest of Birdsboro about 8 o'clock last night – it was nothing more than a particle of dust speeding through the atmosphere. Dr. I.M. Levitt, director of Fels Planetarium in Philadelphia said a meteor passed over the area at the time, lasting three seconds...Mrs. Eva Hilbert, Monocacy, reported to *The Mercury* soon after she had seen the 'flaming object' in the sky that she and her sister saw a burning airplane fall to earth...Edward Rea, 783 Haycreek Road, Birdsboro, saw the meteor."

This UFO was traveling at a very high altitude as it rapidly descended towards Baltimore, Maryland. The Philadelphia sighting of the object that was said to be a meteor was the **first** sighting of the object and the Monocacy sighting was the **second** sighting, which also involved a "burning airplane" falling to earth. The object was sighted "to the southwest of Birdsboro" for the **third** time. This object was then reported flying over Baltimore, MD shortly before 8:00 p.m. EDT/7:00 p.m. EST. This was the **fourth** reported sighting of the object. The object was described as, "a fiery object that streaked through the night sky with a great greenish-white light."

On September 13, *The Baltimore Sun* featured an in-depth article about the object, "Scores of Baltimoreans See Meteor-Like Objects In Skies." The article reported:

What was it? It definitely was not an airplane streaking across North Baltimore, its engine on fire. And it was not a comet. It could have been a meteor. In fact, it probably was. But you cannot convince scores of Baltimoreans who witnessed its spectacular dash over the city that it was not a flying saucer. Not since Baltimore, with the rest of the world, first began to read about flying saucers several years ago has anything approaching so close to what local residents considered the 'real thing' made its appearance here. The first excited call came in a few minutes after 8 p.m. And they kept up for more than an hour. Mrs. Felix Blair, for example, said she and her husband were sitting on their back porch in the 1300 block of West North Avenue, when: "Suddenly this thing came swooping down from the eastern skies. It looked like it was right above the housetops. It was a ball of bright greenish fire with a long tail." Then there was the army veteran who was driving along Cold Spring Lane, near Loch Raven Boulevard. He would not give his name ("people might kid me"), but to him, it was a flying saucer. "I thought it was a flare at first," he recounted. "That is, I thought it was a flare until the darn thing swooped down, and then up again. It seemed to follow the contours of the road.

The **fifth** sighting occurred shortly after. The object passed over Catonsville, located on the outskirts of Baltimore. *The Baltimore Sun* reported this sighting in a September 13 article titled, "Scores of Baltimoreans See Meteor-Like Object In Skies." A subtitle states, "Seen In Catonsville" and gives the following information, "Numerous Catonsville residents saw it too. Most of them thought it would hit the ground in that area. It didn't though." After passing over the Catonsville region, the blazing object continued on its westerly flight path. It veered slightly to the north and passed near Frederick, MD., where it was reported for a **sixth** time. This same article stated, "A few minutes later, four farmers near Frederick described a ball shooting across the horizon."

This object, engulfed in flames and searing through the sky, continued on its northwest trajectory before passing over Hagerstown, MD., where it was reported for the **seventh** time. *The Baltimore Sun* also reported this sighting by stating, "And it was next heard of in Hagerstown, where at least a dozen persons called police or the local newspaper." The **eighth** sighting was made over Cumberland, MD, where it was still heading in a northwesterly direction. Police and newspaper switchboards were flooded with reports in Cumberland. As the object continued on its path, it was seen for the **ninth** time over Garrett County, Maryland.

A Baltimore Sun September 12 (AP) headline read, "A Meteor Seen Whizzing across Maryland Skies." This article stated, "It first was sighted over Baltimore and traced westward across the state over Frederic [sic], Hagerstown and Cumberland, 140 miles away. It was last seen by a state trooper atop Negro Mountain in westernmost Garrett County, headed into northern West Virginia."

After passing over Garrett County, along the Maryland-Pennsylvania border, the object continued on its northwest flight path and was sighted a **tenth** time by several residents in Preston County, West Virginia. The time of this sighting was about 7:00 p.m. EST. (Preston County observed Eastern Standard Time.) Soon thereafter, the object was spotted for the **eleventh** time over Morgantown, WV. *The Dominion News* printed an article on Saturday, September 13, 1952. The headline states, "Large Meteorite Reported Sighted in This Section." The article reported:

Several Morgantown and Preston County families called *The Dominion News* last night to report the appearance of a "large glowing ball" streaking through the heavens. One resident who phoned was certain it was a "flying saucer." Another was more cautious, reporting only that what he saw appeared to be "a large ball of fire." It appears, however, that the object traveling through space was not one of those mysterious and elusive "saucers." Instead, it apparently was a large meteorite, and it appeared possible that it landed and exploded in the Charleston area.

The **twelfth** sighting of this supposed meteor was by residents of Fairmont, WV. Fairmont is located about 15 miles southwest of Morgantown. The time of this sighting was about 7:00 p.m. EST/8:00 p.m. EDT. *The Charleston Daily Mail* reported this sighting in its Saturday evening, September 13, 1952 edition, "About 40 persons in the Fairmont area said the object looked like a spotlight with a greenish tail and was traveling from 100 to 500 miles per hour." *The Wheeling Intelligencer* reported the object on the front page on September 13, 1952. It reported this article:

Mystery Lights Zip Through Skies Here Stirring Mild Furor—Flashing Light Believed Caused By 'Low' Meteors—Night Sky Watchers Swamp Phone Circuits In Reporting Event.

A series of brilliant flames flashed across the sky over the Ohio River last night and jittery valleyites feared they were in for another siege of "flying saucers." Hundreds of calls flooded area law enforcement offices, local airports, and The Wheeling *Intelligencer* last night describing a brilliant flaming object blazing across the sky at a low altitude.

The CAA office at Stifel Field, Wheeling Ohio County airport, received a call late last night from a Martins Ferry man who claimed to have seen what looked like a light plane on fire crash to the ground between the transmitters of radio stations WHLL and WKWK atop Glenwood Heights. State Police from the Triadelphia barracks were searching the countryside late last night but the unofficial report was that the flying objects were thought to be meteors flashing through space.

W. A. Garrison of West Liberty called the *Intelligencer* to report seeing an object resembling a Roman candle flash over his home at 8:06 p.m. [EDT] toward the southeast, approximately the same direction as the object seen by the Martins Ferry man (later sighting). The CAA office at Stifel Field said that offices in Pittsburgh, Morgantown, Zanesville, OH, and several other points were swamped with calls from persons who thought they saw burning planes crashing to the ground.

Pilots of two or three commercial airliners, however, reported seeing meteoric objects flash past their planes while aloft. The mysterious brilliant flames were even sighted over the nation's capital last night and jittery Washingtonians flooded newspaper offices with calls giving all sorts of stories to describe the phenomenon. Descriptions of the "flames" varied widely, but all the witnesses agreed the blazing objects moved horizontally across the heavens and came "awfully low."

At the U.S. Naval Observatory, a spokesman said the reports "sound like a typical meteor." The National Airport Observatory said flatly the objects were not "flying saucers." There was no trace of any unidentified object on radar screens, observers said. Mrs. Mary Curitti and her parents, Mr. And Mrs. James Butler, of McMechen were on their lawn last evening when they witnessed the strange fire-spitting display in the sky. Mrs. Curitti said it appeared without any noise and was spitting blue and white fire from one end. It disappeared over the Riley hill at McMechen. The Brookside station of the Ohio highway patrol received a number of calls from eastern Ohio concerning the strange visitor in the sky, spotting it in the vicinity of Piedmont and Tappan Lakes. Mr. and Mrs. H.F. Penney of Shawnee Hills witnessed the light.

Mr. Penney described it as a luminous ball that was moving downward diagonally and apparently parallel to Route 88. Mrs. Penney stated that there was no noise and she was confident it was not a plane. Apparently, it should have come down in the vicinity of Oglebay Park. The Cambridge station of the Ohio highway patrol reported calls from Columbus and Akron, where persons reported seeing the meteor. Many thought it was a plane that was about to crash.

When I reviewed this article, I realized there were several other objects sighted in the northern West Virginia panhandle as well as eastern Ohio later that night. Some of the sightings occurred later that night and were not the damaged UFO that I was tracking here along its northwest trajectory. I also found additional information about other aerial activity that occurred that night throughout this area. The Columbus Citizen reported the following incident on September 13, 1952. It also tells of two additional UFO sightings, which occurred after 8:00 p.m. EDT as well. These occurred at 8:06 p.m. and 8:30 p.m. EDT. The article headline read, "Fireballs Shower City Area: Meteor Fall Blamed as Cause of Scare." The article stated:

Reports were made at Columbus, Mt. Vernon, Zanesville and Chillicothe, in addition to a number from eastern Ohio points, Pennsylvania, Virginia, West Virginia and Washington, D.C.
Mt. Vernon state patrolmen said they received a report at 7:05 p.m. [EST] from G. S. Gallopy of Danville, reporting a "plane on fire going down." He said the crash seemed to be near Millwood, 12 miles east of Mt. Vernon. Patrolmen said no crash could be found, however.

In Zanesville, CAA officials at the Municipal Airport said an Army pilot at 10,000 feet reported what looked like a burning plane. Other calls to newspapers there described "flying saucers" and "flaming planes." Other people said they saw a streak of light in the southeast. In Chillicothe, patrolmen said a Frankfort man reported a "burning plane falling" north of town about 8:30 p.m. No plane could be found they said.

Columbus patrolmen said they received no local calls on the reports but did receive a number from other posts. CAA officials at Port Columbus concurred with Zanesville CAA officials in describing the phenomenon as probably a meteor shower. In Washington, residents of the nation's capital feared they were in for another siege of "flying saucers." Residents in Harrisonburg, VA reported a "cigar-shaped object trailing blue-green flames" streaking across the sky.

Police in the "bombarded" states reported they were searching the countryside for some clue to the strange phenomenon. However, police officials said they believed the objects sighted were meteors. A spokesman at the U.S. Naval Observatory said the reports "sound like a typical meteor display." Descriptions of the weird spectacle varied widely but all witnesses agreed the blazing objects moved horizontally and zoomed "awfully low." Reports of "balls of fire" and "flaming planes" deluged newspaper offices and police stations in four states Friday night. Civil Aeronautics Administration officials said today [that] witnesses probably saw a meteor shower.

15. St. Clairsville, Ohio
16. Wheeling-Ohio County Airport, West Virginia
17. Oglebay Park, West Virginia
18. Wheeling, West Virginia
19. McMechon, West Virginia
20. Proceeded Southwest to Parkersburg

Next, the Baltimore/WV object made an astonishing maneuver for a meteor. After proceeding from Baltimore on its northwest path, it changed directions. This object made a 45-degree turn near Selma, OH turning northeast, passing over Columbus. The object continued on a northeast trajectory passing over Zanesville, OH, fifty-five miles from Columbus towards WV.

These two episodes are plotted as the **thirteenth** and **fourteenth** sightings respectively, and occurred shortly after 8:00 p.m. EDT. This alleged meteor then went approximately 60 miles northeast of Zanesville and passed over St. Clairsville, OH at approximately 8:02 p.m. EDT.

The St. Clairsville location was the **fifteenth** sighting of this object as it headed towards the northern WV. Panhandle. *The Wheeling News Register* reported the St. Clairsville sighting on September 13, 1952. The headline states, "Residents of Ohio Valley Excited as Heavenly Meteor Hurls Off Bright Fragments." In part, it reads:

A gleaming meteor sped silently over the Ohio Valley at 8:02 last night throwing saucer-conscience residents of four states into excited speculation…Many Ohio Valley football fans saw the object as they trooped into stadiums up and down the river. The massed bands of St. Clairsville and Powhatan had just finished playing the national anthem, when the meteor flashed over the west horizon, sped toward the east, broke into several pieces and vanished in a sparkling shower at the south end of the field.

The **sixteenth** sighting occurred approximately 20 miles northeast of St. Clairsville, over the vicinity of the Wheeling-Ohio County Airport, in West Virginia. *The Wheeling Intelligencer* article above reported, "Pilots of two or three commercial airliners reported seeing meteoric objects flash past their planes while aloft . . . one pilot said the object nearly clipped the wing of his aircraft. Tower control men at the Wheeling CAA reported a bright ball of fire flashing through the sky and disappearing to the south or southeast. According to the spotters, the thing appeared simply to disintegrate in their general area." At this time, I will raise the point, that this UFO actually followed the directional radio beacons of nearby airports and traveled their flightpath corridors.

The next sighting occurred four miles away. This object reappeared and was now in the area of Oglebay Park. This marks the **seventeenth** sighting of the object along its path. The sighting was described as a "luminous ball," which made "no noise," was not traveling at a high rate of speed, and was about to land. The object at this point was descending but not engulfed in flames it had cooled.

This UFO was looking for an isolated area to land after several pilots sighted it. The following report came from Triadelphia, located about five miles east of the Oglebay Park area. *The Intelligencer* stated, "State police from the Triadelphia barracks were searching the countryside late last night, but the unofficial report was that flying objects were thought to be meteors flashing through space." Were the police interested in looking for meteorites or really searching for downed aircraft? Again, an article refers to, "flying objects," not a single object. Moreover, one of the objects that were being searched for was this damaged UFO, which went down in nearby Oglebay Park. It was not found because it departed the area shortly after it landed.

After the craft took off again, it headed in a southerly direction along the Ohio River toward Wheeling. Many residents in Wheeling sighted this UFO. *The Wheeling News Register* reported, "Hundreds of calls flooded area law enforcement offices, describing a brilliant flaming object blazing across the sky at a low altitude." The sightings over Wheeling account for the **eighteenth** location where the UFO was seen.

The object was still blazing southbound after passing Wheeling, trying to ascend to a higher altitude. Shortly thereafter, the UFO was sighted for the **nineteenth** time over McMechen, approximately five miles south of Wheeling, also along the Ohio River. When the craft followed the river to McMechen, it was sighted and reported by local residents to *The Wheeling Intelligencer*. This damaged object was having problems, as it was seen spitting fire over McMechen. The object "appeared without any noise," which meant it was not a conventional airplane, jet, or helicopter.

The Charleston Gazette September 13, 1952, edition reported this information:

The object was sighted not only in the Charleston area, but in Wheeling and Parkersburg as well. Tower control men at Civil Aeronautics Commission stations in the latter cities reported a bright ball of fire flashing through the sky around dusk and disappearing to the south or southeast. According to the spotters, the thing appeared simply to disintegrate in their general area...Appearing at the same time in those cities, the meteor was at a very high altitude.

Parkersburg observed Eastern Standard Time. Wheeling observed Eastern Daylight Saving Time. After the object passed over Wheeling, it passed in to the Eastern Standard Time zone. The UFO followed the radio directional signal of the Wood County Airport in Parkersburg, flew southwest through the flight corridor and passed over that area. The Parkersburg report made by the towermen made this the **twentieth** sighting of the craft. Even though "the thing" appeared to simply disintegrate in their general area, as the sky watchers gazed on, it reappeared once again.

The object continued south, followed the flight corridor and headed toward the Kanawha County Municipal Airport in Charleston. The **twenty-first** sighting of the object was made southwest of Parkersburg over the town of Nitro, which is located on the east side of the Kanawha River. Witnesses there stated the object was seen about 7:00 p.m. EST.

The Damaged Object Flew near the Kanawha County Municipal Airport

The flight path showed that this object was actually seen after 7:00 p. m. The object also showed major signs of damage upon reaching the Nitro area. *The Charleston Gazette* received this Nitro report, "Sergeant Major L.C. McDougal of the Salvation Army, his wife and sister-in-law, Mrs. Homer Murray, also reported sighting the object."

He said the following, "It was about 7 p.m., and we were driving through Nitro. I saw the thing and told the rest of the passengers in the car to look. My sister-in-law said she saw something dropping from the thing. It [the flying object] was a greenish color, shaped like a top. Two Nitro high school boys were also with us. It seemed to disappear about the edge of the entrance to the rubber plant."

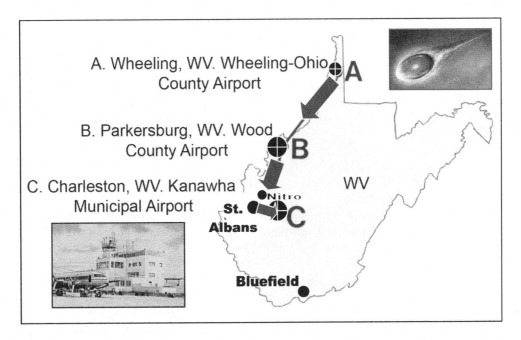

Like the two previous sightings, the object again seemed to disappear or disintegrate and was also having trouble staying airborne. After passing over Nitro, the damaged object flew south along the Kanawha River, crossed over it and landed on the outskirts of the city of St. Albans. This unscheduled landing was the **twenty-second** sighting of the UFO. On September 23, 1952, The *Charleston Gazette* reported, "two residents of rural St. Albans," had reported, "they saw a lighted object float lazily to the ground and disappear." It was also reported by the newspaper that, "A search of that area by two Gazette reporters failed to turn up anything." The Object was not found because it had already taken off by the time that the reporters arrived.

After leaving St. Albans, the object flew southeast toward the beacon of the Kanawha Municipal Airport, flew above the Kanawha River, and headed toward the airport. *The Charleston Gazette* reported in a September 13 article "Meteorite Spotted In Kanawha Area" that, "The Gazette switchboard was deluged with calls from anxious Charlestonians who saw the object."

The next series of sightings took place over the Charleston area. Charleston observed Eastern Standard Time like the rest of the state, except Wheeling and the northern panhandle. The sightings of the object in Charleston and the following areas that occurred after 7:00 p.m. Eastern Standard Time, translate to 8:00 p.m. in the Eastern Daylight Saving Time zone areas.

I plotted the **twenty-third** sighting of the object over the city of Charleston. *The Charleston Gazette* reported in the same September 13 article, "One woman was standing in the Spring Hill Cemetery at the time the meteorite appeared. The witness said, 'One of the small planes had just landed, and my daughter and I were still looking at the sky.'"

The witness then explained what she saw while still looking at the sky, "Suddenly this enormous thing appeared and veered in the general direction of Shadowlawn or Meadowbrook." The Kanawha County Airport is located just southwest of Meadowbrook. This is the area where the witness saw the "enormous light" appear and veer. She also said, "It looked like a big star and was brighter than anything I have ever seen before. It made a sort of a putt-putt noise. One corner seemed to fall off, and I saw sparks for a moment. Then it just seemed to disappear." This craft was definitely damaged as indicated by this witness's description.

Over this area of Charleston, the object appeared as an enormous light, which veered. Meteors do not veer during flight. Moreover, the object was noted to have "made a putt-putt noise," also uncharacteristic of a meteor. This kind of noise indicates an engine noise, possibly stalling or having problems. The only sound a meteor would make is a sonic boom. If this witness were close enough to the object to hear a putt-putt noise, she clearly would have been close enough to hear a sonic boom. *The Charleston Gazette* also received the following information from local eyewitness accounts:

1). "The object was variously reported to have made hissing sounds and to have 'backed-up and started over.'" This startling eyewitness account, defies the laws of physics and logic by describing a meteor going in reverse.
2). Another eyewitness, Andrew Burkhardt, gave the following description of the "thing." He stated it, "had sparkles all around it. It was white. I was standing out in our front yard and it went to the right, behind a neighbor's house and just went away."

It is evident that this aerial object was not a meteor but in reality, was an unidentified flying object. It was damaged, giving off sparks with pieces falling off it. Even after the object disappeared, it actually reappeared once again. This time it was seen west of Charleston. This was the **twenty-fourth** location where a sighting occurred. A Mrs. Alice Williams witnessed a glowing object, which was seen to be flying low and moving slowly. Williams was a member of the Speleological Society and a very credible witness. She said it, "disintegrated in a rain of ashes" at a height of "no more than a few hundred feet," above her. The strange disappearances the object made seemed to form a pattern. These locations are listed in sequential order from the St. Clairsville, OH area sighting to the West Virginia sightings:

   1). St. Clairsville, Ohio: "broke into several different pieces and vanished in a sparkling
        shower."
   2). Wheeling and Parkersburg: "The thing appeared to simply disintegrate."
   3). Nitro - "It seemed to disappear."
   4). St. Albans: "float lazily to the ground and disappear."
   5). Charleston/Spring Hill Cemetery area: "It just seemed to disappear."
   6). West of Charleston: "Disintegrated."

It seems that the object was actually dematerializing and then reappearing at different locations. It was sighted for the **twenty-fifth** time by Mrs. F. W. Emory of Forest Hills, who made the following report to *The Charleston Gazette*, "[She] reported seeing the object appear to land in or near South Hills." This location indicates that the object had once again crossed over the Kanawha River. Mrs. Emory also told the Gazette, "It was very close, and at first I thought it was an airplane in trouble. Then it appeared to be a very bright light, and it looked as though some little pieces fell from it. It seemed to fall right in South Hills." This is the third time a witness reported seeing something falling from the object and the second time the craft appeared to land in the area.

After the damaged UFO took off from South Hills., it was sighted again for the **twenty-sixth** time. On this occasion, it was seen east of South Hills, Charleston over Watt Powell Park. According to *The Charleston Gazette* in the September 13 article, "Another woman reported seeing the same thing near Morris Harvey College." The witness stated:

I was driving east on MacCorkle Avenue when I saw it. It appeared to be falling in a very slight arc to the south, in the hills back of Watt Powell Park. It looked like a giant skyrocket and there was a very bright light. The light seemed to go out just before the thing hit, and it looked like a very, very faint puff of smoke rose where it landed.

The object seemed to be in drastic trouble, which would explain the reason it landed a third time in the area. I analyzed the flight path of the craft after it flew away from the Kanawha County Airport in the Charleston area. The damaged object appeared to have flown purposefully over the outskirts of the city, disappearing and reappearing as it proceeded southward. In doing this, the craft was able to locate one isolated area after another, desperately hoping to land because it was damaged. Examples of the damaged craft sightings are listed in order below:

1). Nitro: "saw something dropping from the thing."
2). Charleston/Spring Hill Cemetery: "one corner seemed to fall off and I saw sparks for a moment. It made a sort of a putt-putt noise."
3). West of Charleston: "a rain of ashes."
4). Charleston/South Hills: "At first I thought it was an airplane in trouble. It looked as though some little pieces fell from it."
5). Charleston/MacCorkle Avenue: "It looked like a very, very faint puff of smoke rose where it landed."

The Charleston Gazette reported in the September 13 article, "Meteorite Spotted In Kanawha Area" that "A large meteorite presumably landed or exploded within a numerical 50 mile radius of Charleston last night, according to reliable reports received by the Gazette." The NASA FIRST EDITION book, *Dictionary of Technical for Aerospace Use* defines a meteorite as, "Any meteoroid, which has reached the surface of the earth without being completely vaporized."

The same Gazette article also stated, "Geologists said the appearance of the meteorite was not uncommon, although a crash in this area [Kanawha Co.] would mark the first time it happened. Meteorite fragments should be found somewhere in the area if the object came down here."

These same geologists also made the following statement to *The Charleston Gazette*, "Presumably a meteorite of this size would leave a depression in the earth near its disintegration point." Contrary to normal documentation procedures applied to astronomical discoveries, this object that landed in Kanawha County was neither documented nor recorded in any official scientific reports. This so-called "large meteorite" was actually the damaged Baltimore/West Virginia object.

After landing in Watt Powell Park in Charleston, the object took off, headed southeast and followed the Kanawha River. The next sighting was over the town of Ward, WV, approximately 7 miles southeast of Charleston. This was the **twenty-seventh** sighting of the damaged craft. On September 14, *The Charleston Daily Mail* reported, "2-In-One Meteor Seen Over Ward." The article stated the following information:

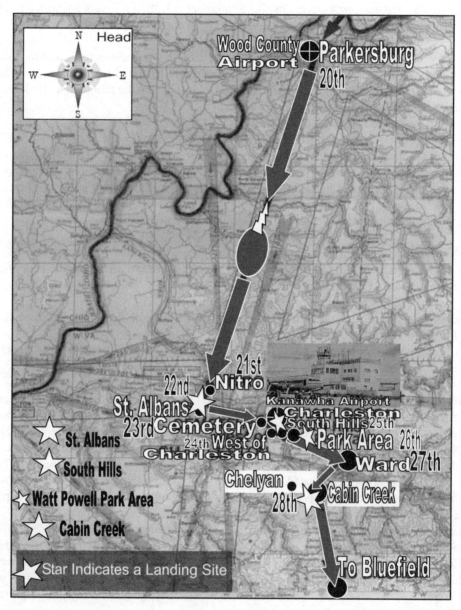

James Blount of Ward, an employee of the state Liquor Control Commission, said he viewed the object and that it appeared to be two balls of fire, one over the other, with a connecting tail. He said the bottom ball was about 14 inches in diameter, the connecting tail about 3 feet long, and the top ball about 4 inches in diameter (Relative size of objects seen at a distance). Blount said the color of the object was orange.

Here, the witness to this sighting referred to the object as two balls of fire, never referring to it as a meteor, as the headline stated. When the craft passed over Ward, it was on a southeast trajectory. It then changed direction, headed southwest and passed across the Kanawha River again. A witness from the nearby town of Chelyan then sighted the object. This man reported that he saw the object land in Cabin Creek.

This was the **twenty-eighth** sighting of the craft. The *Charleston Gazette* reported in the September 13 article, "A man in Chelyan said it seemed to land at the point of a hill near Cabin Creek." The witness described the object as, "about twenty or thirty feet across . . . It looked like it dropped either in Mill Hollow or the hollow to the right." However, the key statement that the witness made was, "I don't think it was a meteor because it looked like it stopped right in mid-air just before it came down." This amazing maneuver actually marks the fourth landing of the craft in the area after it departed the Wheeling, West Virginia area.

After the object landed in Cabin Creek, it took off and headed south. Shortly after, it was reported over the area over Bluefield. This was the last location where the object was reported along its flight path in West Virginia.

This final sighting was made approximately 65 miles southeast of Cabin Creek near the state's southern border. This was the **twenty-ninth** location where it was sighted along its flightpath. The in-depth flight path I have re-created shows that this object was not a meteor. Rather, the evidence that I have shown here indicates this object, was an intelligently controlled craft, which was being maneuvered across the United States and making repeated landings.

In 2004, I met and spoke to radio and television engineer, Mr. Johnny Barker from West Virginia. Between 1945 and 1954, Barker ran the control room at the WCHS-Radio station in Charleston, before going to WCHS-TV, until the time he retired in 1994. During the late 1940s and early 1950s, Johnny also investigated and reported on West Virginia UFO sightings.

Mr. Barker worked with nighttime disc jockey, Hugh McPherson, who reported on the local West Virginia UFO activity during that era. After several conversations and meetings with Mr. Johnny Barker, he explained the following to me, "Our news machines, AP and UP, were constantly reporting sightings from all over the world."

Mr. Barker then talked about the September 12, 1952 UFO sightings, "Concerning the Flatwoods epic, we started getting calls that night (Friday), and all the next day. Most of the calls were about witnesses that said they saw lights traveling in the sky. All the lights were reported to be moving, with no sound." Besides the calls received about the local Charleston area sightings, Mr. Barker stated, "We had calls from as far away, as 50 -60 miles from Charleston."

Recapping this UFOs flight path, the first of 28-plotted locations where it was sighted, indicates it was first seen from Philadelphia, just before it passed over Baltimore before 7:00 p.m. EST /8:00 p.m. EDT. It continued on a northwest flight path along the northern border of West Virginia and then passed over eastern Ohio. Then, it turned and redirected northeast over the northern West Virginia panhandle. Again, it turned, then redirected and headed on a southwesterly flight path over the Wheeling area.

The object continued to fly southeast over West Virginia and headed toward the city of Charleston. In that area, the UFO landed four times; it went down in St. Albans, South Hills, Watt Powell Park in Charleston and Cabin Creek. After the fourth landing, the damaged object took off and flew south once again. Shortly after, the UFO flew south over Bluefield and exited the state.

Most importantly, this object was not the craft that landed in Flatwoods, WV, which was previously seen in flight over Front Royal, VA. by the pilot of a small plane. The pilot of that aircraft said it was "tremendously large" and "seemed to disappear in a bunch of sparks."

On September 13, *The New Haven Evening Register* headline read, "Fiery Object Streaks Across Skies Of Four States—A Meteor? Could Be." It stated, "Washington viewers flooded the weather bureau, Naval Observatory, and even the Pentagon there (sic) with calls...No blips showed on Washington area radar screens to record the object's passing." The article continued and reported, "Operations personnel at Andrews Air Force Base near Washington put a similar label on it. And Naval Observatory officials said reports they received made it sound to them 'like a typical meteor.'"

The alleged meteor seen over the Washington area and the alleged meteor seen over Baltimore were actually reported by the press as the same object. The confusion of what was thought to be a single meteor over Washington, D. C. and Maryland by the press appeared in an article in *The Massachusetts Springfield News* on September 13. The headline read, "Flaming Object Seen at Capital." The dateline was, "Washington, Sept. 12" by the International News Service or "(INS)."

The newspaper reported, "A flaming object believed to have been a falling meteor tonight flashed across the skies startling hundreds of Washington area residents. The object was seen over the capital and near Maryland and Virginia. The Weather Bureau, Naval Observatory and newspaper offices were jammed with a flood of calls from persons wanting to know what the mysterious looking object was. National Airport observation tower crewmen said there was no trace of an unidentified object on their radar screens. A U.S. Naval Observatory spokesman said, 'It sounds like a typical meteor' which probably burned itself up before it hit the ground."

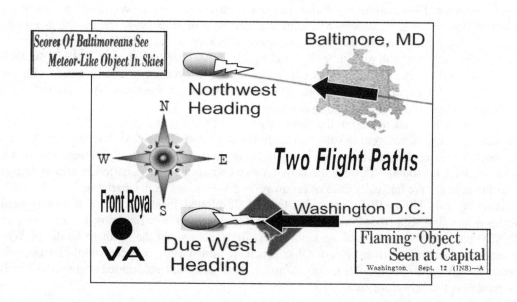

To establish a second flight path I needed more information about this supposed meteor sighting over Washington, D.C. The Saturday, September 13, 1952, edition of *The New York Times* reported the following article, "Flame Over Washington—Brilliant Streak Across the Sky—Probably a Meteor." It reported:

A brilliant flame, apparently a meteor, flashed across the sky near the nation's capital tonight prompting jittery Washingtonians to believe they were in for another flying saucer scare. Newspaper offices were flooded by calls from witnesses of this phenomenon who sought an explanation. Descriptions of the flame varied widely, but they agreed the blazing object moved horizontally across the heavens and came "awfully low." The National Airport's observation tower said the object was not a "flying saucer. There was no trace of any unidentified object on radar screens. At the United States Naval Observatory, a spokesman said the reports "sound like a typical meteor." The Air Force said it knew absolutely nothing about the object.

First, I would like to stress two points from this article, 1. The "Flame over Washington" was said to be "apparently a meteor," which was 2. "Prompting jittery Washingtonians to believe they were in for another flying saucer scare." This comment refers to the numerous UFO sightings that had taken place over the skies of Washington, D.C. during July and August at the height of the UFO flap during the summer of 1952.

FLAME OVER WASHINGTON

Flaming Object Seen at Capital

Washington, Sept. 12 (INS)—A flaming object believed to have been a falling meteor tonight flashed across the skies startling hundreds of Washington area residents.

The object was seen over the capital and nearby Maryland and Virginia.

Most importantly, the object was reported to have, "flashed across the sky near the nation's capital." It was also said to have "moved horizontally across the heavens" and "came awfully low." How could this object, which flew "awfully low" to the ground "near the nation's capital," have flown over Baltimore, thirty miles away, at the same time? The sightings, which occurred over those two cities, were not of the same object!

The following three segments of this article show official statements made by prominent organizations in the D.C. area. The truth of these statements is questionable. Based on my research they show a discrepancy:

1). "The National Airport's observation tower said the object was not a 'flying saucer.' There was no trace of any unidentified object on radar screens." The observation tower declared the flame as an "object," which would make it a solid target. If this object was not a UFO, it was an IFO (Identified Flying Object). If this object was identified, why was it not reported as such? Furthermore, the reason that there was no radar trace of this "object" over Washington is because it had actually flown under the radar when it passed over the city.

2). At the United States Naval Observatory, a spokesman said the reports "sound like a typical meteor." This statement has little relevance, being made by a non-witness, and only based on other reports.

3). The Air Force said that it knew absolutely nothing about the object. They did not want to admit that, again, Washington had UFOs over its skies in great numbers, as it had in July, and August. Furthermore, they were not going to tell the public that they had called Colonel Leavitt in West Virginia, and activated the National Guard in Braxton County. In addition, they would not report, as they did to Leavitt, that they wanted to know what the object was.

The UFO Flew over DC - Front Royal, VA – Elkins, WV then toward Burnsville

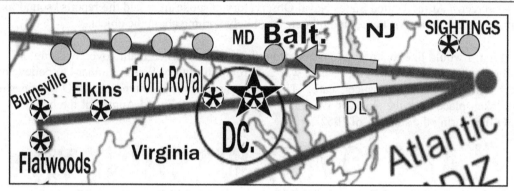

The UFO cover-up had continued. Again, a curtain of silence was dropped in front of the American public, which was deceived once more. A disinformation directive, developed by the U.S. Government, was quickly being implemented. I plotted the easternmost area where an alleged meteor had been seen over Washington, D.C. Then I plotted the town of Flatwoods, which lies approximately two hundred miles due west of Washington, D.C.

I connected these points with a solid line, representing a flight path. This line ran almost parallel to the 39-degree latitude meridian line. I examined this flight path line and found the answer I was seeking. Sixty miles west of Washington, D.C., along the flight path line I had drawn is Front Royal, VA. This is the area where a pilot reported an object thought to be a meteor. Continuing along this straight line to the west, 85 miles away, is the town of Elkins, WV.

The Charleston Daily Mail article on September 13 referred to "Fiery Objects Flash across Sky in W.Va." and reported, "Residents of Wheeling, McMechen, Fairmont, Parkersburg, Elkins, Morgantown, and Bluefield all reported seeing fiery objects in the sky about 7 p.m." The town of Elkins did not fit into the flight path of the Baltimore/WV Object, which I plotted from Baltimore to Bluefield. Elkins did fall in line with the Washington, D.C. - Front Royal object's flight path. Fifty miles west of Elkins is the Braxton County borderline.

Based on the geographic locations of all of these UFO sightings, I had discovered there were actually two different objects that flew on two separate flight paths. One object passed "over the city" of Baltimore, Maryland; *The Baltimore Sun.* article stated, "Scores of Baltimoreans See Meteor-Like Object in Skies." Witnesses reported it as a "mass of flaming, incandescent material" which flashed across the sky about 8 p.m." The newspaper also said it "probably" was a "meteor" and added, "But you can not convince scores of Baltimoreans who witnessed its spectacular dash over the city that it was not a flying saucer."

The other flight path indicates that this craft passed over Washington, D. C. and proceeded west. It then traveled 60 miles, veered slightly to the southwest, passed over the vicinity of Front Royal, Virginia and was seen by an airborne pilot. Continuing westward, the object was next sighted 85 miles away over Elkins, West Virginia.

It continued to fly another 50 miles farther west and then reached Braxton County. This westward flight path went directly over the town of Burnsville, located about ten miles northwest of Flatwoods. Several Flatwoods residents told me that there was a man who had witnessed the flight of this craft before it reached Flatwoods. The witness lived in the town of Burnsville at the time of the sighting. Eventually, I found out the witness' name was Wally Hefner and located his current residence in Flatwoods. I asked him if he witnessed the passing of the object over Burnsville, West Virginia before it reached Flatwoods.

He told me, yes that he did see it. Mr. Hefner agreed to do an interview, which I videotaped. Mr. Hefner stated, "I was sitting in front of the taxi stand. It came from my right heading left toward Flatwoods. It was so much lower. That is what caught my attention, and it wasn't an airplane or a weather balloon, but it was traveling fast, and I'd say it looked like a ball. It wasn't on fire, but it was reddish-orange and went very fast but I knew as low as it was, just clearing the treetops, that it was going to land someplace close, someplace very close in our county. And of course, I'd heard the next day about it landing in Flatwoods, and I knew that I had seen it."

When I analyzed the westward flight path of this craft after it had passed over Elkins, I was astonished. This alleged meteor, which was traveling from east to west, had made an amazing aerial maneuver.

It had made a 90-degree turn toward the south and proceeded over Burnsville en route to Flatwoods. While en route to Flatwoods, the object had traveled due south.

It passed to the west of the small community of Heaters and then proceeded about five miles farther to Flatwoods. This object I will now refer to as the Washington/Flatwoods Object.

The Damaged UFO Redirected South over the Town of Burnsville

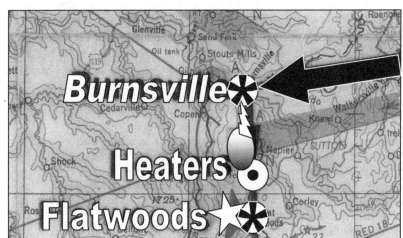

CHAPTER SEVEN

TENNESSEE TRAMPLED

My plotted flight paths indicate that there were two objects seen flying on westward paths over the mid-Atlantic United States. These two objects were both seen at approximately 7:00 p.m. EST/ 8:00 p.m. EDT. They were the Baltimore/WV and the Washington/Flatwoods objects.

After establishing the flight paths of what was supposedly one meteor, I referred back to the Baltimore, September 13, AP article. "Fiery Object Streaks Across Skies Of Four States—A Meteor? Could Be." It stated the following:

A ball of fire seen in the sky over Kingsport, TN, about the same time, set off a fruitless search for a wrecked plane. There were no reports of missing aircraft, but Tennessee highway patrolmen, the Kingsport lifesaving crew and several ambulances combed an area of almost 15 square miles after an aerial object was reported to have struck the ground after streaking across the sky. A spokesman at Tri-Cities Airport near Kingsport said the object had been identified as a meteor.

When the newspaper reported the Baltimore sighting at "about 8 p.m. EDT" and that the Kingsport, TN ball of fire was seen "about the same time" they were correct. Because Kingsport observed Eastern Standard Time instead of Eastern Daylight Saving Time, the Kingsport area sighting that occurred at 7:00 p.m. EST, was actually occurring "about the same time," as the object sighted over Baltimore at 8:00 p.m. EDT.

The Kingsport Times-News sent me a detailed article about an object seen in their area. After I read this article, I discovered that the object was actually seen at 6:50 p.m. EST. The actual time the Baltimore, Washington, and Tennessee objects were sighted was about 8:00 p.m. EDT. *The Kingsport Times-News* published the following article, dated Saturday, September 13: "Sky Object Seen Here—Search Ends for Wrecked Aircraft." The opening paragraph is about an object that landed about two miles to the northeast of Kingsport, "A flying object described variously as 'like a full moon with a tail on it', 'a streak of silver' and as 'big as a car with a flaming exhaust,' reportedly fell to the ground somewhere in the Bloomingdale area about 7:00 p.m. Friday."

The path revealed that this was a completely different object from the two seen over the mid-Atlantic about 8:00 p.m. EDT and was an isolated incident. The landing of the Tennessee object brought the total number of objects that flew into the United States at about 7:00 p.m. EST to three. The following documentation is the plotted flight path of the Virginia/TN object arranged in sequential order:

1). It was first reported by "airport communication sections from Roanoke to Pulaski, VA."
2). "Tri-Cities Airport tower operators in Johnson City sighted it," as it crossed into Tennessee.
3). "A communications office operator said the tower sighted the object at 6:50 p.m. [EST] in the sky northeast of the airport in the direction of Kingsport. The source said operators described it as a 'bluish-green brilliant light with an orange tail.'"
4). "Tri-Cities Airport tower identified [it] as a meteor, a brilliant ball of fire that flashed across the sky in the vicinity of Kingsport Friday night. Several had reported it was a plane in distress."

As the object passed over the Tennessee border on its southwest trajectory, it suddenly went down in the small town of Arcadia, about four miles northeast of Kingsport:

5). "First to call the newspaper was Mrs. Nettie R. Taylor of Kingsport. Mrs. Taylor said she and her husband, W. G. Taylor, saw the object from their front porch. She described it as a 'flaming streak of silver.'"

6). Another witness to the passing of the object gave this report, "Guy Lewis who lives in McCrary Manor on Bloomingdale Road, apparently saw the same object, which he said looked to him like a meteor."

7). Another witness to this object was H. L. Williams, a fifteen-year-old boy, who said he was driving some cows in from a field when the object went over. He said, "It was shining bright and big as a car, and when it went down over the hill back of Joe Newland's tobacco patch, it sprouted a tail."

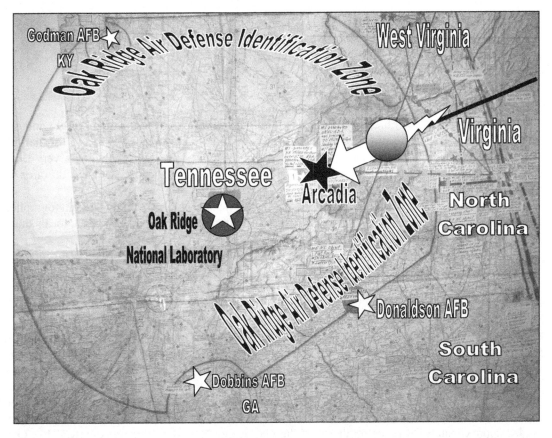

The *Kingsport Times-News* article of September 13 stated what happened shortly after the object was seen going down in Arcadia, "Since most of the early reports came from Arcadia, about five miles out the Bloomingdale Road, Tennessee Highway Patrolmen and county officers, led by persons who saw the object, formed search parties to comb the area. An ambulance and the Kingsport Life Saving and First Aid Crew sped to the area and stood by after patrolmen reported sighting what they believed to be distress flares from the ground near where the object was supposed to have fallen."

The Kingsport Times-News follow-up article of September 14, "City Dust Haze Replaces Interest in Sky Objects" stated, "Many who called in felt certain it was a plane in distress." Even though the object was classified by a communications office operator as a meteor, the Tennessee Highway Patrolmen and county officers thought otherwise. They carried out a "three-hour search" on the possibility that a private craft might have gone down, yet no wreckage was found.

The description of the object as it was seen going down stated, "it was shining bright and big as a car." This weakens the supposition it was a meteor. If it were a meteor as big as a car that fell to earth, there would have been substantial material evidence to that effect including a very large conspicuous crater. I visited the small town of Arcadia on one occasion, searched the area in question and talked to some of the local citizens.

I went to the different locations mentioned in the newspaper, looked around and photographed the area as well. However, I never saw a large meteorite impact pit, nor had any of the locals that I spoke to.

Over the many years that had passed, no one in this area had ever reported such a crater's existence.

Another point to consider here is when the object went down over the hill it was said to have suddenly, "sprouted a tail." Why was there no sign of a tail during this alleged meteor's flight?

When I examined the descriptions of the object's appearance and behavior described in the sightings, along with the complete lack of physical evidence of a meteorite or downed aircraft, it became evident that the object was *not* an airplane or a meteor. Whatever landed in Arcadia shortly before 7:00 p.m. EST on that night was capable of taking off after it landed.

The object must have taken off almost immediately after it landed, because the search parties who arrived on the scene shortly afterward found no evidence of it. I also made an observation on my Master Map about the location where this UFO landed in Arcadia, Tennessee. This object landed approximately 90 miles northeast of the Oak Ridge National Laboratory [ORNL] in Oak Ridge; a national laboratory for nuclear research. Moreover, it was on a direct course toward it.

During the Second World War, ORNL was involved in the development of the atomic bomb. An atomic-energy plant at Hanford, Washington, was designed for producing plutonium by neutron bombardment of U238, while the plant at Oak Ridge was built for large-scale separation of U235 from U238. Furthermore, in 1952, simulated hydrogen bomb tests were being tested at Oak Ridge National Laboratory. In the hydrogen bomb, at least three main nuclear reactions take place, which releases more energy than does an atomic bomb alone.

Yes, the United States Government considered this national laboratory a security sensitive area. Most importantly, before this object landed in Arcadia, it had actually penetrated and flown seventy-miles into the ORNL Air Defense Identification Zone, which surrounds the laboratory. Moreover, 3 nearby USAF bases, the closest being Donaldson AFB, didn't scramble jets after it!

The Object Landed in Arcadia, Tennessee

In Arcadia, another issue regarding this UFO sighting remains. An ambulance and the Kingsport Life Saving and First Aid Crew were called to the area by patrolmen. They reported a sighting of what they believed to be "distress flares from the ground, where the object was said to have fallen."

The Damaged UFO Sprouted a Tail

Now, consider the following questions:

1). Officials at Tri-Cities Airport said all their aircraft were safely accounted for. What craft had launched the flares seen by the patrolmen? The USAF definition of a flare is, "flare, *n.* 1. A pyrotechnic device that emits a bright light, used for illumination, signaling or identification." In this particular incident, they were referred to as, "distress flares."
2). Why was there not any wreckage or impact evidence found on the ground in the vicinity where the downed craft launched the distress flares?
3). The Tri-Cities Airport tower identified the object as a meteor. Since a meteor does not launch flares and normally leaves an impact pit, what actually landed in Arcadia?

An Ambulance and the Kingsport Life Saving and First Aid Crew Responded

The next sighting was made about 7:00 p.m. EST over the town of Rogersville, about forty miles southwest of Arcadia. Sam F. Miller of Rogersville reported seeing a ball of fire resembling a meteor about 7 p.m. [EST] headed east. Miller said, "It looked like a full moon with a tail on it." After the object reached Rogersville, heading southwest, it then made a 45-degree turn and headed east, where it was seen by the witness.

The *Kingsport Times-News* reported in the September 13 article that highway patrol officers in Rogersville said, "Numerous calls were coming in all evening reporting meteors and shooting stars." Unlike a meteor, this object had already landed once and then taken off. Once airborne again it was described as resembling a full moon with a tail on it, looking like a ball of fire, and resembling a meteor. This object was actually a damaged craft that was having difficulty flying.

The next report was made over the area of Sullivan Gardens, at about 7:15 p.m. EST. *The Kingsport Times-News* stated, "Later reports throughout the evening placed the fallen object 'just over the ridge' in Wadlow Gap, Moccasin Gap, and Sullivan Gardens." The object passed over

Rogersville headed east, then changed direction and headed back toward Arcadia, where it had originally landed. This was the Sullivan Gardens area. The information in the article stated:

Reports were still coming in late last night from residents of the Moccasin Gap and Wadlow Gap sections saying they had seen the object but had not reported it earlier for fear of "being laughed at." Edgar Bowlin and his wife said they were visiting at the home of Mr. and Mrs. Tom Lane. They were talking together on the front porch when they saw an object "almost big as a full moon and with a fluorescent glow" streak past. Bowlin said the "thing seemed to burst as it went down over some trees on top of a mountain and left only a short glowing trail."

This Tennessee object was referred to as a "thing" by these witnesses. Witnesses who saw the Baltimore/WV object also referred to the object as a "thing." This object in Tennessee was said to have burst and disappeared, just like the object in the Charleston area did several times. The final sighting of this object over Tennessee was twenty-five miles to the southeast, near Elizabethton. Highway patrol officers in that region reported receiving numerous telephone calls all evening from local residents "reporting meteors and shooting stars."

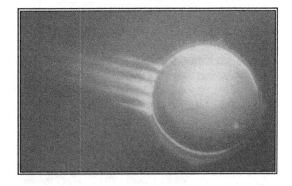

The Kingsport Times-News article of September 14, 1952, "City Dust Haze Replaces Interest In Sky Objects" reported this strange occurrence on September 13, 1952, the day after the UFO was seen in the Kingsport, Tennessee area. As the following article asks, Why was there "A strange dusty haze over the city"?

City Dust Haze Replaces Interest In Sky Objects

9-14-52

Judging from the tenor of telephone calls to the Times-News office in the last few days, there should soon be an epidemic of cricks-in-the-neck among sky-watching residents.

A strange dusty haze over the city Saturday evening put a stop to flying-saucer reports but raised the query "Why the haze?".

Officials who scan the skies from the tower at Tri-Cities Airport could offer no explanation. Visibility was good out there, they said, and winds were light. However, thundershowers had been reported in the area—at Church Hill, Gate City and Bristol—and thunderheads had been gathering here during the afternoon.

A brilliant ball of fire which flashed across the sky in the vicinity of Kingsport at about 7 p.m. Friday put the top on all previous "strange object" reports. Many who called in felt certain it was a plane in distress.

A communications office operator at the Airport tower identified the object as a meteor but not before a three-hour search had been carried out by Tennessee highway patrolmen and residents of the Arcadia section, about five miles east of Kingsport. An ambulance and the Kingsport Life Saving and First

(See HAZE, Page 5-A)

78

CHAPTER EIGHT

FLIGHTPATHS AND FIREPOWER

I have demonstrated the flight paths of three separate objects seen over the United States on the evening of September 12, 1952 that occurred over the eastern seaboard around 8:00 p.m. EDT. They are listed below:

A). The northernmost object, the *Baltimore/WV craft*, flew over Baltimore, proceeded northwest into Ohio, redirected and passed over northern West Virginia, then turned southwest over the state and exited south over the Bluefield, West Virginia area.
B). Just southwest of Baltimore, the object that flew over Washington, D.C., the *Washington/Flatwoods craft*, proceeded west over Virginia, then flew over West Virginia, turned south toward Braxton County and then landed in Flatwoods.
C). The southernmost object, the *Virginia/TN craft*, traveled southwest over Virginia, then passed over Roanoke and Pulaski, Virginia before reaching Tennessee and then landed in Arcadia, Tennessee.

At this point, I needed assistance to figure out the rest of the timeline. A man that I had met at a military show who is a historian of military strategy helped me. I took out my master map, hung it on the wall and showed it to him. He studied it intently then took a yardstick and pencil and then extended the flight path of each object back to the east coast.

Soon, I realized that the trajectories of two of these objects first passed over New Jersey, and one passed over Delaware. He continued to extend the lines of the three flight paths east and out across the Atlantic Ocean. Now the flight paths showed an amazing conclusion! Astonishingly, all three-flight paths converged and intersected ninety miles off the eastern seaboard and directly east Washington, D.C. I asked, "So what does this mean?" He told me, "You're thinking one-dimensional with this piece of paper hanging on the wall." We took the huge map off the wall, laid it down on the floor and stood over it.

He then said, "We just put this map into a three-dimensional setting." He reached in his pocket and took out three coins as I stood and watched. "This is the atmosphere above the map," he stated, and "these coins are the three objects." From waist level, he dropped the three coins one at a time over the intersection point on the map and they all landed on top of each other. He turned and looked at me and said, "This intersection point over the Atlantic Ocean indicates the area where the three objects made their descents into the atmosphere." Now it made sense to me.

He continued, "These three ships were dropped from a main craft that was hovering above the atmosphere." This three-dimensional demonstration illustrated how the three objects dropped down one at a time, hence the area where all three-flight paths converged. He then said, "Now look at the area where these three coins are sitting," and pointed to a perimeter line on the map that said ADIZ.

He picked up my USAF dictionary and flipped to a page. "Here, read this!" he said, "ADIZ. The airspace above a specified geographical area in which the control and ready recognition of aircraft is required." I read further, "The *coastal* ADIZ, an ADIZ established over an oceanic area adjacent to the international boundary lines of the U.S. or its territories or its possessions."

This intersection point ninety miles off the coast indicates that the three objects were within an Air Defense Identification Zone, the Atlantic ADIZ.

Any aircraft within this air zone must properly identify itself. If it didn't, the aircraft would be considered possibly hostile, and a threat to the United States. I looked at him and he said, "Radar picked them up. This is where the jets got them as they dropped." He then said, "Boy, they must have been surprised by our rockets!"

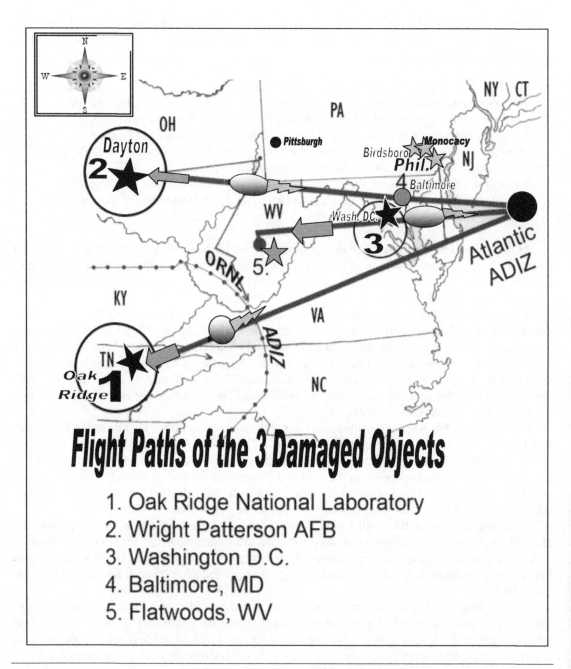

Flight Paths of the 3 Damaged Objects

1. Oak Ridge National Laboratory
2. Wright Patterson AFB
3. Washington D.C.
4. Baltimore, MD
5. Flatwoods, WV

Looking back at the map, he explained a partial scenario from the plotted points, flight paths, locations and times of the sightings. We continued to work together and I showed him more research as I found it. The timeline of events tightened up over the years and the pieces of the puzzle finally fell into place.

By following the three flight paths of the three damaged objects back to the east, they intersect at a point about 90-miles from the coastline into the Atlantic ADIZ. Retracing them back to the west indicates that they spread out in a fan-like pattern on western trajectories, over the Atlantic Ocean and across the United States.

The first UFO headed southeast toward Oak Ridge National Laboratory located in Oak Ridge, Tennessee. The second UFO flew northeast toward Wright Patterson AFB, in Dayton, Ohio and the third UFO headed toward Washington, D.C. All three of these locations are security sensitive areas within the United States.

Furthermore, each of the three damaged objects sighted on September 12, 1952, shared the same characteristics. They displayed the characteristics of being damaged as they flew over the United States. These objects were described as being on fire, exploding, emitting sparks, had pieces falling from them and seen flying at low-level altitudes across the country. Most importantly, all three of the UFOs shared another common factor; each went down within the United States. These objects were reported to have made crash landings and repeated forced landings on American soil during the course of their flights! At this point though, how had these UFOs become damaged?

In 1952, the primary jet fighters used by the USAF to protect the U.S. and its borders were the Lockheed F-94 Starfire, and the North American F-86 Sabre Jet. *The Unicorn Book of 1952 Outstanding Events of the Year* stated, "So fast and so intricate did new aircraft become that their human pilots were obsolescent [sic]. The Air Force unveiled semiautomatic interceptors such as the Lockheed F-94C Starfire, and the D model of the North American F-86 Sabre. Each fired 2.75-inch rockets rather than conventional but less lethal guns, and was laden with 1,000 odd pounds of electronic gear. This electronic brain, faster and surer than the human brain, picked up the enemy bomber, charted its course, guided the interceptor toward the target, and selected the instant to fire the rockets. Electronic gear on [the] plane picks the moment to fire rockets, each one of which could bring down (the) biggest bomber ever built."

Official Air Force Photos of the Lockheed F-94C Starfire Interceptor

On July 3, 1952, The New York Times gave details about the new "Starfire" that read, "AIR FORCE'S NEW SUPERSONIC PLANE." In part, this article reported:

The military took some of the wraps off one of its most important shoreline defenses today, a high-flying supersonic jet warplane that automatically seeks out enemy bombers in any kind of weather. The new airplane is the Starfire F-94C, built for the Air Force by Lockheed Aircraft at Burbank, California. It is the first fighting plane ever to have all-rocket armament, carrying twenty-four rockets, 2.75 inches in size, in a ring of firing tubes around the blunt nose. The plane carries a two-man crew. Radar and specialized 'brain-like' instruments enable the Starfire to spot the enemy miles away, lock onto the target, track, close, aim and open fire-all by itself, according to Hall L. Hubbard, Lockheed vice president and chief engineer...The interceptor-type plane was designed specifically to knock out invading bombers.

In July though, and the months to follow, the F-94C Starfire was primarily used by the Air Force to pursue UFOs over the United States. None of which proved to be enemy bombers, moreover, Soviet bombers. The F-94C was a two-man fighter that carried a rear seat navigator/operator. This jet was capable of attaining speeds in excess of 600 mph. The C-model F-94 Starfire was the first two-seat straight-wing combat aircraft to break mach one in a dive. Primary armament for the F-94C consisted of rockets rather than fixed machine guns.

The rockets had a greater range than conventional aircraft machine guns and were fitted with explosive warheads, which made them more deadly. There were 24 of these rockets grouped in four six-round compartments situated around the radar dome in the jet's nose. They were housed behind four retractable doors from which they could be salvoed. The F-94C Starfire also carried over 1,200 pounds of electronic equipment on board. The jet had an automatic pilot, which could be coupled with the radar for attack runs. This meant that once the autopilot was engaged and coupled with the radar, the jet would react automatically and center the steering dot on the pilot scope.

The rocket firing system was controlled automatically with a firing control system that combined radar tracking with a rocket-firing computer. This system enabled the Starfire to spot its target, lock on, approach, close, aim and fire automatically. The pilot and radar operator would principally act as monitors, although manual firing was available if needed or desired.

When these rockets were fired, they were stabilized by means of folding fins. The fins were opened by air pressure immediately after the rockets left the jet. Even though these propelled rockets were unguided, the spread they created would blanket a large area of sky in destruction. The F-94C Starfire was a prime example of a truly powerful modern-era combat jet. In the September 1952, issue of Flying Magazine, Lockheed Aircraft Corporation reported, "the 'C' was the third in the Starfire series and was now being delivered to the USAF to augment squadrons to F-94A's and F-94B's now on 24-hour duty protecting U.S. borders."

The North American F-86 Sabre Jet was the first swept wing aircraft in the United States inventory of jet fighters. The F-86D version was a single-seat all-weather interceptor that had a top speed of 650 miles per hour. This jet was also armed with twenty-four "Mighty Mouse" rockets that were carried in a retractable carriage in the fuselage. This carriage would lower on an elevator to fire the rockets and then retract back up into the body of the jet.

The D-model featured a 35 degree swept back wing and tail and was designed with an under slung engine air-intake channel at the front of the fuselage for airflow.

This jet was also equipped with aerodynamically actuated wing leading-edge slats that were used for high lift and a hydraulically power-operated irreversible controls system. These controls gave the jet an artificial feel for an all-movable tail, ailerons and its rudder.

The Rocket-bearing USAF North American F-86D Sabre Jet

The F-86D had a service ceiling of more than 45,000 feet and had a range of about 1,000 statute miles. In 1952, the F-86D Sabre Jet and the F-94C Starfire were the Air Forces top all-weather jet interceptors in their inventory and true examples of modern jet fighters.

The Vought F7U-3 Cutlass

The United States Navy also had a jet fighter that had rocket-bearing capability. The Vought F7U-3 Cutlass was a single-seat jet that was the Navy's first production aircraft to achieve supersonic flight. This jet did not have a single conventional tail surface; it actually had two unconventional tails. The Cutlass had a maximum speed of 680 MPH and had a service ceiling of 40,000 feet. This jet fighter featured afterburners for its turbojet engines, was armed with four 20-mm cannon and had an attachable belly pod that carried "Mighty Mouse" rockets.

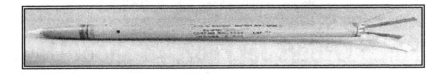

The "Might Mouse" 2.75-inch air-to-air rocket was a "Folding Fin Aerial Rocket." This projectile was four feet long, weighed 18 pounds and carried a 7-1/2 pound explosive warhead. When salvoed, it traveled at 2,500 feet per second, had a maximum range of 6,500 yards and an effective range of 3-1/2 miles.

The following July 28 news story appeared in, *The Washington Daily News*, "Jets Ready to Chase Lights - 24 - Hour Alert Ordered after Second Appearance Here." In part it states, "Jet interceptor planes of the Eastern Air Defense Command are on stand-by, round-the-clock orders today to take-off immediately if any more mysterious lights show up in the sky or on a radar screen." This article also states, "'We have no evidence they are flying saucers,' an Air Force representative said." He added, "Conversely we have no evidence they are not flying saucers. We don't know what they are."

A *United Press* news service story from Washington, D.C., dated July 28 stated the following information in an article, "Air Force Alerts Jets to Chase 'Flying Saucers' Anywhere In U.S." In part it reads, "WASHINGTON, July 28 (UP)-The Air Defense Command alerted jet interceptor pilots Monday to take off instantly in pursuit of any 'flying saucers' sighted in the country…interceptor planes are ready to go aloft at any time." Further information states, "The Air Defense Command's mission is air defense of the United States and it is virtually interested in anything unidentified that flies in the air a spokesman said."

A staff correspondent for the International News Service, Larry Auldridge, wrote the following story that appeared in the *San Francisco Examiner*. Their July 29 headline stated, "Jets on 24-Hour Alert to Shoot Down Saucers." A portion of this article states, "WASHINGTON July 28 [INS] The Air Force revealed today that jet pilots have been placed on a 24 hour nationwide alert against 'flying saucers' with orders to 'shoot them down' if they refuse to land. It was learned that pilots have gone aloft on several occasions in an effort to shoot the mysterious objects to the ground but never came close enough to use their guns. The Air Force refused to confirm this, but Lt. Col. Moncel Monte, information officer stated, 'The jet pilots are, and have been, under orders to investigate unidentified objects and shoot them down if they can't talk them down.'"

Further information states, "Disclosures of the 24-hour alert came as new reports continued to pour into the Pentagon of mysterious objects in the skies." Auldridge also stated, "Capt. Forest R. Shafer, commander of the Air Force Filter Center at South Bend, said reports of 'whirling discs' over Indiana have been increasing the past week. He stated, 'The disks seem to fall into two categories – red whirling objects like balls of fire and bluish – white disks that revolve and travel with tremendous speed.'"

On July 29, the Seattle *Post-Intelligencer* carried the International News Service story. Their headline read, "Air Force Orders Jet Pilots To Shoot Down Flying Saucers If They Refuse To Land." A portion of this article rephrased their headline, "WASHINGTON July 28 [INS]...In Air Force parlance this means that if a 'flying saucer' refuses to obey an order to land jet planes are authorized to shoot them to earth if they can get close enough to do so."

Seattle *Post-Intelligencer*, July 29, 1952, p. 1

Air Force Orders Jet Pilots To Shoot Down Flying Saucers If They Refuse To Land

The *Fall River Herald–News* of Massachusetts also covered the story. Their headline read, "Jets Told to Shoot Down Flying Discs – Air Force Puzzled But No Longer Skeptical."

Writer Darrell Garwood reported, "Jet pilots are operating under 24-hour nationwide 'alert' to chase the mysterious objects and to 'shoot them down' if they ignore orders to land. However, the Air Force confessed that none of its jets have come within shooting range of the blinking, enigmatic flying discs. Several pilots, according to the Air Force, have tried to shoot down the mysterious discs but the 'steady bright lights' in the sky have outflown the pilots."

Jets Told to Shoot Down Flying Discs

A writer from *The Washington Post*, John G. Norris also wrote about the July 28 Air Force's "shoot down" story. The Post's July 29 headline read, "Jets Poised for Pursuit; 'Saucer' Peril Discounted." In part, Mr. Norris reported the following, "Air Force interceptor planes are on alert to take off in chase of any further 'flying saucer' manifestations a spokesman said yesterday." Norris also reported, "Units of the Air Defense Command have no new or special orders to intercept 'saucers,' the spokesman said, but they will pursue any unexplained 'glowing lights' or radar 'blips' as part of their mission to protect the United States against any threat from the skies."

On Thursday July 31, *The Lawrence Tribune* ran an *Associated Press* story dated Washington, July 30 (AP) that read "Urges USAF Not to Shoot Saucers." A concerned individual wrote to the Air Force and stated the following in a telegram, "Urgently request reconsideration of your order to destroy flying saucers... people much arose and worried." An Air Force representative responded by stating, "That nobody is going around shooting at strange objects in the sky but that Air Defense planes would attempt to destroy any air craft or objects definitely identified as hostile and dangerous."

In 1952, Donald Keyhoe spoke with an Air Force jet fighter pilot who had recently returned home from the Korean War. This Captain was a veteran combat pilot who had earned the "Distinguished Flying Cross and Silver Star ribbons." Keyhoe spoke with this pilot, concerning Air Force fighter pilot intercepts against flying saucers. Reluctant to speak with Keyhoe at first, the pilot agreed to be interviewed when Keyhoe said, "I wouldn't quote you by name, Jim. But the public ought to know its serious business, chasing a saucer."

The following is part of that conversation; Captain Jim stated, "They [pilots] don't all feel the same. Some pilots never get very close." Keyhoe asked, "What about the ones that do?" Captain Jim replied, "They're on edge-what the Hell do you think." The pilot continued and stated, "All right, I'll give you the picture, but it sounds kind of silly when you're on the ground good and safe." He sets the scenario, "You're flying an F-94 jet, with a radar operator behind you. You're on a routine patrol. Ground Control Intercept calls you. They got an unknown on their radar, which is a surveillance type, with a longer range than yours [you're on board radar].

Their tracks show the unknown is making tight turns and speeds too high for any aircraft. So they give you the word - it's a UFO...right then, it stops being an ordinary intercept. Going after a MIG [Russian jet fighter], it's different. You know what you're up against. When you get him in your sights, you're ready to fire. With the saucers, you're on the spot. The orders are to intercept

85

but not to shoot-unless you're sure they're hostile." Keyhoe stated, "I knew about that. Major General Roger Ramey, chief of the Air Defense Command, had told me about the instructions."

According to Donald Keyhoe, Captain Jim "harshly" stated, "How're you going to tell if they're hostile or not." The fighter pilot also said, "All of a sudden, circling faster than any plane, your radar picks it up too, and you lock on, so you're automatically following the thing. About that time, Ground Control calls and says they got you both on their [radar] scope, and the UFO's right where your radar shows it. That does it. You know the things real-not a reflection or a set malfunction." Captain Jim then stated, "It's your job to get in close, so you open up and go in."

The fighter pilot continued, "Then it makes a quick turn toward you. You know you have been spotted, and you start getting butterflies in your stomach...sounds pretty dopey, Huh, a fighter pilot sitting behind 50-caliber guns and rockets and scared of a light in the sky. You watch the thing start a tight turn around you. Nobody on Earth could take all the gs [G-Force] in that turn. It's so fast you almost twist your neck off, trying to keep it in sight. Maybe you see a shape behind the light, maybe not. Even if you do, you can't tell its size- you don't know if the things close or a half a mile away. One thing sure, something with intelligence is in control of the thing, the way it maneuvers."

The airman then stated, "You'd give anything if it was suddenly daylight, so you could see exactly what the thing is. But all you really know is that you're a sitting duck, if whoever's watching you wants to let you have it." Shortly after, Captain Jim told Donald Keyhoe, "You're right - people should know about all those UFOs intercepts." I ask how many fighter pilots in hair-raising situations like this particular episode actually felt like sitting ducks and did fire at them?

In *The Fall River Herald–News* article, "Jets Told to Shoot Down Flying Discs – Air Force Puzzled But No Longer Skeptical," Writer Darrell Garwood reported, "Several pilots, according to the Air Force, have tried to shoot down the mysterious discs."

In fear for their lives, and the safety of their country, how many fighter pilots fired upon the discs and UFOs? On the other hand, how many UFOs have fired upon American jet fighter pilots? Now I ask, has the Air Force ever admitted that our fighter pilots have been killed or vanished because they were fired upon by saucers and UFOs during intercepts? The answer is no!

The Air Force has never admitted any loss of aircraft or pilot life during an intercept with a flying saucer or an unconventional craft. Why, you may ask! In the forward of his 1956 book, *The Report On Unidentified Flying Objects*, Captain Edward Ruppelt sums it up best when he wrote, ***"The report has been difficult to write because it involves something that doesn't officially exist."*** In other words, since flying saucers and other unconventional-type crafts do not officially exist, then fighter pilots couldn't have been killed by them or lost during intercepts...officially, that is! This double-talk is a play with words to cover-up a shady situation, which has existed for years.

The July 1952 "shoot down" articles appeared in the press only a few weeks before the September 12, 1952 UFO flap occurred along the eastern United States. Yes, the Air Force had orders to "shoot them down," and furthermore, they now had rocket-bearing jets. Based on my recreation of the events that day, the three objects were well within the airspace of the Atlantic Air Defense Identification Zone; any aircraft within this air zone must properly identify itself.

Moreover, since the chances are slim that this alien race spoke English, there was a definite language barrier between the United States military and these UFOs; "In Air Force parlance this means that if a 'flying saucer' refuses to obey an order to land jet planes are authorized to shoot them to earth if they can get close enough to do so." Therefore, since the three UFOs did not properly identify themselves on September 12, 1952, they were considered possibly hostile and therefore deemed a threat to the United States. Subsequently, jet interceptors were scrambled.

They investigated the potentially hostile unidentified aircraft, attempted to intercept them, fired upon the UFOs and hit them.

This would explain the reason the three objects were all damaged. Based on the times and locations where these damaged objects were seen, they actually flew over land one after another.

1). The *Virginia/TN craft* actually flew in first and later landed near Kingsport, TN in Arcadia, just after 6:55 p.m. EST/7:55 p.m. EDT. Its flight path indicates it passed over the U.S. over Delaware.
2). The second object was the *Baltimore/WV* craft. This craft was seen over Baltimore just before 7:00 p.m. EST/8:00 p.m. EDT. Its flight path indicates that it passed over New Jersey along the coastline of the United States.
3). The third object was the *Washington/Flatwoods craft* that was called the "Flame over Washington." The *United Press*, which carried this article, did not state the time that it was seen. Since the Washington, D.C. craft and the Baltimore craft were thought to be the same, the third object passed over Washington, D.C. about the same time, actually shortly after.

Of the three objects that passed over the Eastern Seaboard, the third object had the shortest flight path before landing and had a later landing time, about 7:25 p.m. EST. The Washington/Flatwoods object passed over the United States coastline over New Jersey, and then passed over Delaware.

The "Flame over Washington," was the severely damaged craft that landed in Flatwoods. Several coastal Air Force bases were close to the three UFOs and had superior jet fighters available to scramble. The flight path of the Baltimore/WV object as it passed over Delaware, en route to Baltimore, actually passed over the area of Dover AFB.

Dover AFB is strategically located to dispatch jets over the Atlantic into the ADIZ and would have been among the first to scramble. In 1952, Dover AFB was the home of the 336th Fighter Interceptor Squadron. This Air Defense Wing Squadron possessed superior F-86 and F-94 jet interceptors that were equipped with new electronically fired rockets. About thirty-five miles to the northwest of Dover AFB is another Delaware base known as New Castle AFB.

At New Castle, the Air Force had F-94A, F-94B and F-94C Starfires in their inventory, always ready to scramble. Another nearby base located about fifty-five miles to the northeast of New Castle AFB is McGuire AFB, in Wrightstown, NJ. McGuire is the closest AFB to the Atlantic Ocean in this region of the country. This Air Force base was home of the 52nd Fighter All-Weather Wing, and was assigned to the Eastern Air Defense Force of the Air Defense Command. They possessed both Sabre Jets and Starfires, several of which were equipped with 2.75- inch rockets. These Air Force Bases were three of the nearest installations to the objects with the best jet fighters available to scramble after them. There were also several others as well as Navy and Marine Corps Air Stations.

These damaged objects were shot down over the Atlantic ADIZ by American jet fighters, and then headed inland over America. Now, I ask, how many American fighters were lost in battle that night? It is worth noting an eyewitness statement reported in the Pottstown, Pennsylvania September 13 edition of *The Mercury*; **"Reported Plane Crash is Just Another Meteor.** The witness, "Mrs. Eva Hilbert, Monocacy, reported to *The Mercury* soon after she had seen the 'flaming object' in the sky that she and her sister saw a burning airplane fall to earth. 'It could see the outline of a plane, she said. 'It looked like it was burning in the center and the flames were shooting back.'"

Was this "airplane" a jet fighter that went down in a confrontation with the UFOs that night?

In 1953, Donald E. Keyhoe made this statement in *Flying Saucers from Outer Space,* "The public ought to know its serious business, chasing a flying saucer. Right now, they read some newspaper story where the pilot says the object made a tight turn and came near his ship. Even people who don't brush it off as a joke won't feel any need to worry—and I think it's time they did begin to worry." Notice the similarities of the eyewitness descriptions that indicate the three objects were damaged.

A. VISUAL APPEARANCES

1. *Virginia/TN Object (Round-shaped UFO)*
   Arcadia, TN - "Flaming streak of silver" and "flaming exhaust"
   Rogersville, TN - "ball of fire"
   Moccasin Gap, TN - "plane on fire"

2. *Baltimore/WV Object (Oval-shaped UFO)*
   Monocacy, PA – "flaming object"
   Baltimore, MD - "streak of fire"
   Preston County and Morgantown areas - "a large ball of fire"
   Morgantown, WV - "burning planes"
   Zanesville, OH- "burning planes"
   Ohio River, OH/WV border - "brilliant flames"
   Pittsburgh, PA - "burning planes"
   Wheeling, WV area - "brilliant flaming object"
   McMechen, WV - "spitting blue and white fire"
   Wheeling and Parkersburg, WV - "bright ball of fire"
   West of Charleston, WV - "fiery object"
   Ward, WV - "two balls of fire"

3. *Washington/Flatwoods Object (Oval-shaped UFO)*
   Washington, D.C. - "a brilliant flame" and "blazing object"
   Flatwoods, WV - "ball of fire," "small trail of fire" and "flames were trailing behind it"

B. DESCRIPTIONS OF OBJECTS

In flight low-level altitudes

1. *Virginia/TN Object*
   Moccasin-Wadlow Gap area, TN – "went down over some trees on top of a mountain"

2. *Baltimore/WV Object*
   Wheeling area, WV - "across the sky at a low altitude"
   West of Charleston, WV - "low flying"

3. *Washington/Flatwoods Object*
   Washington, D.C. - "came awfully low"
   Burnsville, WV - "low as it was, just clearing the treetops"
   Flatwoods, WV - "just about cleared hilltop" and "just clearing the trees, just a little bit above the height of the trees."

Type of light from objects (overall brilliance)

1. *Virginia/TN Object*
   Arcadia, TN area – [object passing over VA and across TN border] "brilliant light"
   Arcadia, TN - "it was shining bright"
   Moccasin Gap, TN - "a fluorescent glow"

2. *Baltimore/WV Object*
   Ohio River, OH/WV border - "brilliant flames"
   Preston County and Morgantown areas - "glowing ball"
   Oglebay Park, WV - "luminous ball"
   Wheeling area, WV - "brilliant flaming object"
   Wheeling and Parkersburg, WV - "bright ball of fire"
   Charleston, WV - "enormous light" and "brighter than anything I've seen before"
   West of Charleston, WV - "glowing object"
   Charleston area, WV - "had sparkles all around it"
   Second Charleston sighting - "there was a very bright light"
   Forest Hills, WV - "then it appeared to be a very bright light"

3. *Washington/Flatwoods Object*
   Washington, D.C. - "a brilliant flame"
   Flatwoods, WV - "luminescent glow, white similar to a mercury vapor light" and "Illuminated from the top"

C. DISAPPEARANCES WHILE IN FLIGHT

1. *Virginia/TN Object*
   Moccasin Gap, TN - "thing seemed to burst" and "left only a short glowing trail"

2. *Baltimore/WV Object*
   Wheeling and Parkersburg, WV - "the thing appeared to simply disintegrate in their general area"
   Nitro, WV - "it seemed to disappear"
   Nitro, WV – "disappear."
   Charleston, WV - "saw sparks for a moment, and then it seemed to disappear"
   West of Charleston, WV - "witnessed the disintegration"

3. *Washington/Flatwoods Object*
   Front Royal, VA - "disappeared in a bunch of sparks"

D. LANDINGS

1. *Virginia/TN Object*

   Arcadia, TN - "when it went down over the hill"

   Sullivan Gardens, Wadlow Gap, and Moccasin Gap areas, TN - "later reports throughout the evening placed the fallen object 'just over the ridge' in Wadlow Gap, Moccasin Gap, and Sullivan Gardens."

   Moccasin Gap, TN - "thing seemed to burst as it went down over some trees on top of a mountain and left only a short glowing trail.

2. *Baltimore/WV object*

   Morgantown, WV- "crashing to the ground."

   Zanesville, OH - "crashing to the ground"

   Oglebay Park, WV - "moving downward diagonally" and "apparently it should have come down in the vicinity of Oglebay Park.

   St. Albans, WV – "floated lazily to the ground"

   Charleston, WV - "the light seemed to go out just before the thing hit and it looked like a very faint puff of smoke rose where it landed."

   Cabin Creek, WV - "it looked like it stopped right in mid-air just before it came down" and seemed to land at the point of a hill near Cabin Creek."

3. *Washington/Flatwoods Object*

   Flatwoods, WV - "We don't have the technology yet today [in 1996], that something could come in as fast as I saw it come in, slow down at the same time, and make a soft landing on earth, on the ground, and not explode or leave any evidence."

   Flatwoods, WV - "Well, it landed gently and undoubtedly because it didn't go down in the dirt or anything like that. I don't know what they had under that place when it landed."

   Flatwoods, WV - "It was slowing down as it was coming in, decelerating."

Virginia/TN Object

Baltimore/WV Object

Washington/Flatwoods Object

CHAPTER NINE

DREAMED UP THE REST?

In Major Donald Keyhoe's book, *Flying Saucers From Outer Space*, Albert Chop expressed the Air Force's opinion of the incident, "Several astronomers said a meteor went over. Those people must have dreamed up the rest." This statement prompted me to find the official records.

I obtained the file segment for the Project Blue Book September 1952 cases on microfilm. I was shocked when I found the September 12 and 13, 1952 segment contained nearly 200 pages of documents. I reviewed them and found the majority of the September 12 documents all pertained to what the government called a single "meteor" over the mid-Atlantic United States. Specifically, the U.S. Air Force called it the "well known Washington area meteor."

Upon further examination of these numerous reports, I discovered additional UFOs were also reported that night up and down the eastern seaboard. By segregating the information about these UFO sightings, I found many objects were actually seen at different times, had flown over various locations and flown on different directional headings! Several had actually flown over Washington, D.C., Maryland, Virginia, West Virginia and North Carolina; all were said to be a single meteor by the U.S. government. Included in the government's single meteor explanation were the Virginia/TN object, the Baltimore/WV object, and the Washington/Flatwoods object.

It was while examining Project Blue Book for clues about the "Flame Over Washington" object that I discovered the Air Force had kept a close record of the entire incident. The following quotes are from September 12 radio broadcasts aired in Washington, D.C. that evening. These pages were transcribed from Project Blue Book T1206, tape 15, 2000-2167:

1). The flying saucer fad nearly made a comeback in the nation's capital tonight. Many residents in the area saw a brilliant flaming object flash across the sky...and thought it might be a saucer. But a spokesman at the naval observatory says the reports "sound like a typical meteor." And the National Airport Observation Towner [sic] said flatly the object was not a saucer. Newspaper offices were flooded with calls from persons who wanted to find out more about what they had seen. Descriptions of the object varied...but eyewitnesses generally agreed that the blazing matter moved horizontally across the sky and came "awfully low."

2). A brilliant flame—apparently a meteor—flashed across the sky near the nation's capital tonight. Newspaper offices were flooded with calls by persons wondering about flying saucers. Most witnesses agreed that a blazing object had moved horizontally and came "awfully low." The National Airport Observation Tower said the object definitely was not a flying saucer.

3). UPR STATION BREAK - Here is station [deleted] ---'s 10 o'clock headline. "A Flaming Object Whizzed Through the Sky Over Washington Tonight. It's Believed to Have Been a Meteor. Listen at [deleted] ---o'clock for the next complete news report.

4). Objects believed to be meteors have soared through the skies in three states and the nation's capital. The display caused many residents in Virginia, Pennsylvania, and Ohio to think they were seeing flying saucers. Several commercial pilots said they saw balls of fire flash by their airliners. The show in the skies resulted in many calls to police, civil aeronautics offices, and news offices.

This following story is also contained in the Project Blue Book "12-13 SEP" UFO files:

A fiery object that streaked through the night sky with a "great greenish-white light" stirred "flying saucer" talk among residents of four states from Maryland to Tennessee last night. Weather bureau observers here saw the object but made no official report of it. The streak of fire first was reported over Baltimore shortly after dusk. About 9 p.m. in quick succession came reports to the west from Frederick, Hagerstown, and Cumberland, MD, and Charleston, Wheeling and Parkersburg, W. VA. Washington viewers flooded the Weather Bureaus, Naval Observatory and even the Pentagon. No blips showed on Washington area radar screens to record the object passing. RH943 9/13

This story is actually an edited version of the "Baltimore September 13 (AP)" article, "Fiery Object Streaks Across Skies Of Four States—A Meteor? Could Be." It appeared in the Connecticut newspaper, the *New Haven Evening Register*. Here in the Blue Book files, it was retyped by their officials and the final ten paragraphs containing explicit details about the alleged meteor have been deleted. Whether this edit was done intentionally, I do not know. Upon closer examination of the Air Force's edited version of this article, I also discovered an inconsistency from the newspaper's account. The original article stated the time of the object's passing "over Baltimore shortly after dusk about 8 p.m. E.D.T." The retyped and edited version contained in Project Blue Book states, "shortly after dusk about 9 p.m."

I wondered why this change was made; was it a typo or was it intentional? Researcher Ivan T. Sanderson stated that he discovered "a local Baltimore account later picked up by the wire services but not extensively used. It related to the passage of a 'fireball' over that city at 7 p.m. [7:00 p.m. EST, 8:00 p.m. EDT] on Friday, September 12." Sanderson also stated that he and his assistant met two witnesses while driving into Baltimore from West Virginia "who had seen a slow-moving reddish object pass over from east to west."

He also wrote that this object "was later described and 'explained' by a Mr. P. M. Reese of the Maryland Academy of Sciences staff as a 'fireball meteor.'" According to Sanderson, Mr. Reese "further stated that it 'was burned out.'" Sanderson stated, "However, a similar, if not the same object, was seen over both Frederick and Hagerstown [Maryland]." In reality, the object had passed over Baltimore, MD at about 7:00 p.m. EST, but did not burn out over that vicinity. The object actually proceeded on a northwest course then flew over both Frederick and Hagerstown.

The sighting of this alleged "meteor" that flew over the mid-Atlantic United States had become a primary topic in many of the country's newspapers for days. Then, another news story released by the United Press started to appear across many nationwide newspaper headlines. The topic was referred to by several names, but was most commonly known as the "monster."

On Monday, September 15, 1952, three days after the Flatwoods incident, the *United Press* (UP) released their story. Picked up by *The New York Daily News*, the headline read, "The Thing, 10 Feet Tall, Terrifies Party of 7."

This article described the "monster" as, "an evil-smelling fire breathing monster, 10 feet tall, with a bright green body and a blood-red face." Clearly, the misinterpretation of the "monster" had already begun. On Monday, September 15, a story credited, *By United Press"* appeared in *The Washington Daily News*. The headline read, "The Monster of Braxton County - Around a Bend They Saw a Pair of Bulging Eyes." The lead paragraph read as follows, "Sutton, W. Va., Sept. 15- A short time after a meteorite—or something—blazed across this town last Friday and seemed to land nearby, an evil-smelling, green bodied monster 12 feet tall with bulging eyes and clawy [sic] hands sent seven young citizens running for their lives."

Another story of UP origin and dated Monday was carried by *The Binghamton Press* (New York). They ran this headline, "Flashes of Life—Green Monster with Blood-Red Face Scares Wits Out of Seven Hill Folk." In part it states, "Sutton, W. Va.-(UP)-Eyewitness accounts of a tall, glowing monster with a blood-red face skulking in the hills divided Braxton County today into two camps-believers and disbelievers."

---

4 BINGHAMTON PRESS   Mon., Sept. 15, 1952

Flashes of Life

Green Monster With Blood-Red Face Scares Wits Out of Seven Hill Folk

---

On Monday, September 15, *The Fairmont Times* of West Virginia released the following article, from *United Press* information. The headline reads, "Police Say Braxton Monster Product of 'Mass Hysteria.'" Now the story of the "monster" was being given a negative slant, "Police figured the smelly boogie man was a product of mass hysteria." This article also stated, "Police laughed. They said the monster had grown from seven to 17 feet in 24 hours."

Another negative article on the "monster" was printed by *The Charleston Daily Mail* on Monday, September 15, 1952. The headline stated, "Braxton Folks Divided Over Visitor— 'Monster' May Have Been Due To Dead Tree, Meteor, Beacon." It gives its credit source as, "Special to the Daily."

It reads in part, "SUTTON - A coincidental combination of light from a revolving airplane warning beacon and the fiery trail of a blazing meteor reflected against the trunk of a dead tree standing alone atop a steep ridge at nearby Flatwoods may have been the 'glowing monster' who made a strange visit Friday night to Braxton County."

The Witnesses

Back Row: Fred May - 11, Kathleen May - 32
Gene Lemon - 18, Neil Nunley - 14
Front Row: Eddie May - 13, Theodore Neal - 13
Ronnie Shaver - 10
Missing from photo is witness Tommy Hyer - 6
Photo taken by A. Lee Stewart, Jr, on the Fisher
Farm, September 20, 1952
Photo Courtesy of A. Lee Stewart, Jr.

The story continues, "But the combination of the 'orange to green glow' of the heavenly body that roared through space to the south—casting off fragments as it sped along—and the stark white from the beacon is the best explanation yet offered about the formation whose height ranged upward from seven to 17 feet tall." Here, information actually talks about the object, "casting off fragments." Little did they realize that the object was actually a damaged craft and not a meteor!

Even though some Charleston newspaper articles were inaccurate in their description of the so-called "monster", *The Charleston Gazette* reported it quite accurately. On Monday, September 15, 1952 the headline read, "Braxton Monster Left Skid Tracks Where He Landed." This subtitled, "Special to The Gazette," credit was written with the assistance of A. Lee Stewart, Jr.

The article gives a rather accurate account of the incident. The headline nicknamed the "monster" as the "Braxton Monster." The story referred to it as, "The Phantom of Flatwoods," and one of the few articles that came close to telling the truth. In part, it stated, the "monster":

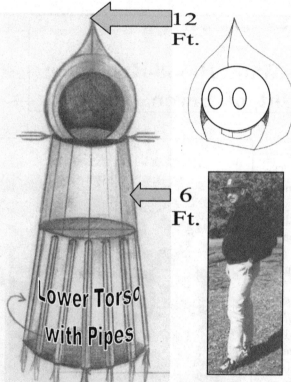

Wore a suit of green armor; looked like a mechanical man; was 10 feet tall, four feet wide; had a blood-red face; sported a black, spade-like cowl that extended a foot or more above its head. It had claw-like 'toy' hands too and orange eyes the size of half dollars, according to Mrs. Kathleen May.

This accurate description of the so-called "Braxton Monster," had actually appeared in this article five days before the inaccurate rendition of it appeared on the *We The People* TV show.

This article also marked the first time that a photograph of most (seven of eight) of the witnesses was published.

The September 15, 1952, Wheeling *Intelligencer* also reported this incident in a straightforward manner. Their source was the *United Press*. The front-page headline read, "Boogie-Man Has B.O. - Monster From Space Roaming W. Va. Hills?—Police Discount Half-Man, Half-Dragon Figure Seen in Hills as 'Saucer' Hysteria." The article states in part, "The thing... had not been reported seen since Friday night but residents of the area said a foul odor still clung to the hilltop yesterday. All of this started when Mrs. Kathleen May...found a 'fire breathing monster, 10 feet tall with a bright green body and a blood-red face,' that waddled toward them with 'a bouncing, floating' motion and sent them scurrying down the hillside. Police laughed. They said the so-called monster had grown from seven to 17 feet in 24 hours. The 'flying saucer,' officers speculated, might have been a meteor crashing to earth.

But Mrs. May stood her ground. She said she went back to the hilltop today and found 'skid marks,' one and a half car lengths long. She said Lemon was leading the party when he saw something move in a tree. Lemon said at first he thought it was a 'possum or a coon' but that when he shone a flashlight on it he saw the 10-foot monster with the flushed face and green body 'that seemed to glow.' She said the monster exuded an overpowering odor 'like metal,' that so sickened them they vomited for hours afterward. 'It looked worse than Frankenstein,' said Mrs. May. 'It couldn't have been human.' Reporter A. Lee Stewart, Jr. remarked that Mrs. May and her boys 'must have seen something.' Stewart said he and several men, armed with shotguns, returned with Lemon a half-hour to an hour later and reported a sickening odor was still present. He remarked, 'I don't know what to think, I hate to say I believe it but I hate to say I don't believe it. Those people were scared—bad scared, and I sure smelled something. The odor was still there. It was sort of warm and sickening. And there were two places about six to eight feet in diameter where the brush was trampled down.'"

After reviewing this article, I believe the information concerning the actual events to be highly accurate. The headline describing a "half-man and half-dragon" entity is not accurate in this case. I am unaware of the source of this quote, but this description was taken literally by many readers, as well as the police.

The "Flatwoods Monster" was described from the waist up as being in the general shape of a human figure. The half described as a dragon had to have been the lower torso section, where the propulsion system exhaust was emitted. Now, reread the headline, "Monster From Space Roaming W. Va. Hills?" Omit the question mark and that is exactly what happened!

On September 15, *The Wheeling News-Register* headline story read, "Metallic Odor Indicates Meteor—Officers Shake Heads Over W. Va. Ogre Tale." It reported in part, "SUTTON, W.Va. Sept. 15- (UP)...Authorities said they believed the 'flying saucer' which Mrs. May's sons saw, was a meteorite. The incident occurred during a meteor shower over a 3-state area."

Many other states reported UFO sightings that night. The entire list included Illinois, Maryland, North Carolina, Ohio, Pennsylvania, Tennessee, Virginia, Washington, D.C., California, Delaware, and West Virginia. However, if Mrs. May's sons saw a meteor go down, then where did it land? As previously stated, a "Meteorite is any meteor which has reached the surface of the earth without being completely vaporized." At the time of this incident, there were no traces of meteorites or impact pits found in Braxton County or anywhere else in the United States. These discrepancies evident in the above statements set the stage for the controversy and put in motion a cover-up that is still the official explanation of the entire series of events.

In Charleston, radio engineer Johnny Barker stated what had occurred at the WCHS radio studio, "We had calls all through the weekend. So on Monday morning [September 15], the news chief thought it would be a good idea to visit Flatwoods and interview some of the townsfolk." Mr. Barker visited Braxton County shortly after, investigated the story and then reported it.

The *Wheeling Intelligencer* also printed an article regarding the "Flatwoods Monster" on September 16. The article carried no headline, "Mayor J. Holt Byrne thinks he has the answer to the 'monster' mystery that has this little central West Virginia town all a-twitter. Byrne, who besides being mayor is also publisher of one of the town's weekly newspapers and Republican nominee for West Virginia secretary of state, said today he believed what seven persons saw on a remote hillside near here was 'vapor.'"

Additionally, "Byrne said it probably was vapor and that it was possible the vapor was left by a meteor which was reported to have flashed over the state Friday night. The 'foul odor' which witnesses said engulfed the area where they saw the 'monster' could be attributed to the vapor and some strong-smelling weeds growing on the hillside, Byrne said."

Was Mayor Byrne suggesting that seven local people could not tell the difference between "some strong-smelling weeds," which area residents would have recognized, and something alien, wholly unknown to them? According to the mayor, these "weeds" were the source of the overpowering stench—an easy, though highly unlikely explanation. Could the mayor's bid for state office have influenced his attitude? Was he seeking to please the authorities, possibly grasping at straws for explanations?

Even though most newspapers had given a negative or dubious slant to the story, the popularity of the "Flatwoods Monster" was far reaching. It had captured the public's imagination. A ballad was written about it by radio announcer Donald Lamb and sung by radio singer Cindy Coy, the title of which is The Phantom of Flatwoods. As the story spread across the country, Flatwoods became the center of attention. Even though the Air Force and others tried to stifle the story, saying the Flatwoods witnesses had dreamed it up, the story didn't die. Radio commentators repeated and continuously repeated it all over the country.

Monster Story To Be Broadcast

SUTTOJ,' W. Va. (UP) —The New York television program "We the People" has invited A. Lee Stewart, Co-publisher of the Braxton County Democrat, and two of the persons who thought they saw a 10-foot monster in the hills above Flatwood to appear on the show this Friday night, it was announced today.

Stewart said Mrs. Kathleen May and Gene Lemons will tell their story of the monster on the nationwide show which starts at 7:30 p.m e.d.t.

Sept. 17, Ohio Times leader

The *Braxton Democrat* was a weekly publication that circulated on Fridays. Since A. Lee Stewart, Jr., broke the story, his newspaper office had become the makeshift headquarters for media inquiries about the "monster". On September 16, A. Lee Stewart, Jr., Kathleen May, and Eugene Lemon received and accepted an invitation to appear on *We the People*, a popular television show aired nationwide from New York. This show was to be aired live from an NBC studio in New York on Friday evening, September 19.

Opinions throughout the country were as divergent as those expressed in Braxton County. Many people in the area doubted that the event had occurred. Long-time Flatwoods resident Jack Davis said, "You find the culture of people in this area to be very skeptical unless you can really prove something to them. People don't [believe something] if they only hear talk of it." Subsequently, May and Lemon accepted the invitation to be guests on the TV program.

UFO witness Wally Hefner stated, "People heard that they [May, Lemon and Stewart] were going to New York to be on TV and they [local residents] thought that was kind of ridiculous, that they'd be better off staying in Flatwoods than to be on TV in New York City talking about a "monster" in West Virginia." Mr. Hefner continued, "Over the years West Virginia has had [paused], you know, we haven't had the best publicity."

Kathleen May, regarding some of the local residents, said, "They razzed me. They said we were drunk and we'd seen a deer that got caught in somebody's mesh, you know. Some said we were making moonshine." Even though there were many wild and absurd explanations as to what the "monster" actually was, some people were taking this event seriously.

96

When A. Lee Stewart met with journalist Evert Clark, he explained that the West Virginia State Police visited the Fisher Farm, "The state police went up there Wednesday [Sept. 17]. They got back from a shooting match or something and went up to see." Also on Wednesday, September 17, only one day before the three Braxton County residents were to leave for New York, Mr. Stewart was paid a surprise visit. Three people came to see him inquiring about the piece of strange metal and the odd oily substance he found in the track marks. Stewart explained in his interview, "I brought that [piece of metal] back to the plant and it sat on my desk there for several days. My father suggested that I remove it, because everybody wanted it [locals], everybody that saw it."

He continued, "Well, I had taken that piece of metal and taken a torch that I had available there; a soldering torch and I couldn't melt it. I took it to a shop there in town [Sutton], and they took that particular piece of metal and put it in a prong devise and then they turned it around and put two torches, gasoline blowtorches, on it to try to melt it. We couldn't melt it. Now as everybody knows that's ever melted solder and dripped it, it comes out relatively thin."

Stewart further explained, "What happened to that metal is I had three people come to my house on Wednesday. I took them out to the site; I invited them into my house that evening. They were a man and wife and a friend of theirs who worked in Virginia. They had taken a few days off and they were driving up through the mountains to see the site, and they asked me about the piece of metal. They asked me about the stains on the clothes so we [Stewart and his wife] showed them the pair of pants that was there with the stain on them. They took a piece of paper out that they had with them, and with a hot iron transferred the stains from the pants to the piece of paper.

The following day was newspaper day. It was the day in the weekly newspaper business when you gave it your all from seven in the morning 'til the paper was out. Then it went out to the post office [for Friday afternoon delivery]. About ten o'clock in the morning they dropped by the office and wanted to know if they could get a little clipping off that [metal]. At that point they admitted to us [Lee and his father] that they worked for the Treasury Department, but were in no way connected with the federal government as far as this trip was concerned. They also wanted to take scrapings from the legs of the pants that I had worn. We quickly jumped into the car and ran to my house.

I set the little vial out with the metal in it. I went down to the basement and got out a pair of tin snips, and I cut that little piece of metal into three pieces. I gave them apiece no bigger than the end of my finger [showing his pinky finger from joint to fingertip]. My wife went into the bedroom to get the pants that the lady took and scraped. She [Mrs. Stewart] took them back. I put the little piece of metal into an envelope, and they took it with them. We jumped back in the car and they delivered me back to the shop. When I went home for lunch, I picked up the vial that had the metal in it, and the balance of the metal was gone.

I had their names, their addresses. They were to call me back with an analysis of the little piece of metal, and an analysis of the scrapings. I waited a month, six weeks. I heard nothing. I called the telephone numbers, wrote the addresses, and at that time I realized I had been taken. To this day I've never heard from them."

The metal vanished only a few hours prior to his flight to New York, where he was to appear live on a nationally televised talk show with two of the seven eyewitnesses. The strangers' appearance had to be more than coincidence. First, they transferred the evidence of oil traces from the cloth pants to a piece of paper with a hot iron. The next day, on their way back to wherever they had come from, they removed more oil by scraping it from the material of the pant legs. The only other evidence Stewart possessed was the metal fragments. They, like the oil smears, were now gone. Kathleen May had also been investigated by two intelligence officers from Washington who initially claimed to be reporters. They, too, took scrapings of the strange oily substance from her clothing. Now she, like Stewart, had no physical evidence to present on national television.

On Thursday September 18, 1952, Reporters and curious onlookers were still flocking to Flatwoods to find out what occurred on the Fisher Farm that previous Friday night. The story of the "Flatwoods Monster" was still far reaching and showed no signs of dying out. Steorts General Store in Flatwoods had become the meeting place for the locals and visitors who had come to Flatwoods. Journalist Evert Clark met and spoke to A. Lee Stewart, Jr. just before he left for New York for the Television show that Thursday. Clark explained the following, "He has had 70 or 80 out-of-town calls since that night, he said – all from what he now calls, 'monster hunters' – mostly newspaper and radio stations. Everett Clark also spoke to Mrs. may and stated, "Mrs. May has had 'more than a hundred' phone calls from 'all over the United States.' Several radio and television stations have made tape recordings." Later that Thursday afternoon A. Lee Stewart, Jr., Mrs. May, and Eugene Lemon flew to New York. The guests were given accommodations at the Belmont Plaza Hotel for their stay in the city.

On Friday, September 19, the two local Braxton County weekly papers went on the stands with their first articles concerning the "monster" incident. The first headline read, "Mysterious Monster Pays Visit to Braxton County." J. Hoyt Byrne wrote that the residents of Flatwoods did indeed see something. He gave three possibilities for the sighting, 1. That it had been a man from another planet. 2. Vapor from a falling meteorite, which took the shape of a man. 3. An omen of disaster. Mr. Byrne referred to a "meteor" that was seen on September 12 over "Pennsylvania, Maryland, and West Virginia." He also stated that the meteor passed over Flatwoods at 7:15 p.m.

The other local newspaper that carried the story was *The Braxton Democrat*. Its headline read, "Flatwoods Folks See Monster." This article gave an account of the incident without interjecting personal or editorial opinion. It stated, "The story as it appeared in the daily paper has caused much comment and many questions. Calls have come into this office from New York, Washington, Los Angeles, and many other places. Several news syndicates and magazines have shown an interest in further information, with the objective of using the story. Mrs. May has also been flooded with phone calls and letters."

Among the many people arriving in Flatwoods to investigate the incident were Ivan T. Sanderson and Gray Barker. Sanderson, a naturalist and researcher, visited Flatwoods on Friday, September 19 to research the story for an upcoming article for *True Magazine*. Later that day, Barker, local Clarksburg businessman and former English department head, came into the area. Barker investigated the incident for Fate magazine.

Both of these men were unaware that the three key figures with whom they most needed to speak were in New York for a television appearance.

Later that Friday afternoon, Mr. Stewart, Mrs. May, and Mr. Lemon were driven to NBC studios to prepare for the live airing of *We the People*. The three met with talk show host Dan Seymour and his staff, and reviewed the story with them. During the course of their initial interview, an artist stood by and drew his interpretation of the "monster". This poster-sized drawing of the creature was to be shown on air during the broadcast. I asked Mrs. May about the sketch artist and the drawing.

She told me, "They just told me they'd like to draw a sketch of it, and Gene and I together had told them what we'd seen, and he [artist] drew the sketch." I continued, "Why did he draw arms on it then, because you told me it had antennae?" She responded, "I told him that [about the antennae] too, but that's what he drew on it. To make it look more like a 'monster,' I guess." The network was probably trying to emphasize to its viewers the threatening appearance of the "monster" with arms and claws. Its inaccurate depiction of the "monster" eroded the story's credibility by showing a dress-wearing, claw-waving caricature of the creature.

Master of Ceremonies Dan Seymour began the show by setting the stage of the incident for viewers while the orchestra performed soothing background music. He said, "Imagine a scene in the autumn dusk, in a lonely secluded spot which you reach right after viewing a fiery meteor in the sky. This was easy to imagine." Suddenly the drawing of the "monster" was flashed on the screen and the music from the orchestra then turned eerie, intensifying. "This," he said, "was not so easy."

While showing me a 1952 picture of Mrs. May holding the original "monster" drawing from the TV show, Stewart said, "The picture in question that always seems to be in a lot of the articles that I've seen is the one right here. The artist at *We the People* drew that in New York on the actual day we were there. In fact, it was the focal point of the entire show. They started interviewing Mrs. May, and then went to Lemon, which was all a question-and-answer situation. They gave me the opportunity of summarizing the thing in general and then again finished with this particular picture. That was basically the entire program."

An interesting fact about the airing of this program was that the Huntington channel that telecasts into the Sutton area did not carry the show. The residents of Flatwoods saw only a garbled transmission from other, more distant markets. Messages and letters from West Virginia residents in areas who had received better reception of the show reported the story to the Braxton County residents.

Mrs. May described the scene that greeted them at the airport upon their arrival home from New York, "When we got off the plane down here in Charleston, Lord, there were photographers and everything else. They had taken pictures of me, and they were all waiting for us."

A. Lee Stewart, Jr. began handling the public relations, becoming the primary spokesperson for interviews with the media. Among numerous reporters who visited the May home after their return from New York was one from *The Charleston Gazette*. A. Lee Stewart, Jr. and a Gazette photographer took numerous photos of May in her home, while she held the "monster" drawing she had brought back from New York. These famous photographs have been published repeatedly.

Among the others in Flatwoods that day was Colonel Dale Leavitt, commander of the West Virginia National Guard. Leavitt was accompanied by local guardsmen and was soon once again on the farm. Kathleen explained an incident that happened the afternoon of her return to Flatwoods. She spoke with Dale Leavitt regarding the "monster" saying, "I hadn't been home too long until this truck came up and it had all the troops and everything on it, and Dale came in. He asked me if he could borrow the picture and he took it out and showed it to all the boys. After a while he came back in and said, 'Well, I want you to take a look at this' and he just turned it [the picture] sideways and said, 'This is a complete missile.'"

I asked Mrs. May what that meant and she responded with, "It means it was some kind of missile craft, you know!" She also told me that she had been very proud of the National Guard unit in their county, "They did all they could and they tried their best to find out—and now—but the government, I just don't know. I'm still puzzled as to what the government—[the few] answers, the government gave us. And I guess I always will be."

Investigator, Major Donald E. Keyhoe made this statement, "Then Mrs. May and the Lemon boy appeared on *We the People* and retold their frightening experience. It was obvious they believed the monster was real, and a dozen papers and magazines sent writers to Sutton for new angles on the story." Mrs. May told me how far the news of this incident had reached, "We got telegrams, even from Japan, Steve McNeil, he's over at Sutton, he was in Japan at the time and he sent us a telegram. They'd heard it over there in Japan."

USAF Public Liaison Albert Chop

Shortly thereafter, Donald Keyhoe contacted Air Force public liaison, Albert Chop. As stated in *Flying Saucers From Outer Space*, Keyhoe told Chop, "This could get out of hand." Keyhoe then asked, "Why doesn't the Air Force squelch it?" Chop retorted, "We've already said the object was a meteor." Keyhoe replied, "A lot of people don't believe it. And the way this has built up, it's bad." Chop insisted, "It'll die out."

Keyhoe responded, "But people will remember it later if something breaks. Why doesn't intelligence go down there and kill it? They sent Ed Ruppelt to Florida [Desvergers incident, August 19, 1952], and that thing didn't have half the potential danger." Chop replied, "We didn't know the answer to that one [Florida]. This time we do. All those people saw was a meteor. They imagined the rest. We can't send intelligence officers out on every crazy report. Project Blue Book hasn't the people or the funds." Not everyone thought it was a crazy report!

CHAPTER TEN

CASE #2078 - WAS ASTRONOMICAL

I have mentioned various actions taken by the U.S. Government to cover up the "Braxton County Monster" incident. These are summarized as follows:

1). False information given to the *United Press* news releases. The "Flame Over Washington" article dated 12 September 1952 UP stated, "The Air Force said it knew absolutely nothing about the object." On the contrary, Colonel Dale Leavitt stated, "They called me on the phone and asked me to get them what they wanted and I came up here and got it. The Air Force, that's what they wanted me to do."

*When Major Donald Keyhoe spoke to Albert Chop about the incident, Chop made the excuse of having insufficient funds and limited personnel. He said he could not send intelligence officers "out on every crazy report." Keyhoe apparently didn't believe this because he said, "Major Fournet [Major Dewey Fournet, Jr., Pentagon liaison for Project Blue Book] and other investigators were available in Washington; a plane from Bolling Field could get them there in one hour."

2). Through my own interviews with witnesses who had personal dealings with these individuals, I found it obvious that government intelligence agents had come to Flatwoods. Kathleen May said, "These two guys came out from, well, they said they were reporters from Clarksburg, at first, but they were investigators or some men from Washington, D.C."

*In addition, A. Lee Stewart, Jr. said, "They admitted to us that they worked for the Treasury Department, but in no way were they connected to the federal government as far as this trip was concerned. I had their names, their addresses. I called the telephone numbers, wrote to the addresses, [and never received a response]. At that time, I realized I had been taken. To this day, I've never heard from them."

3). Government officials acquired landing-site samples from witnesses involved in the case. Kathleen May said, "They scraped oil out of my uniform. They just scraped the oil out of it, that's all they did." A. Lee Stewart, Jr., spoke about the oil on his clothing, "They took a piece of paper out that they had with them, and with a hot iron, transferred the stains from the pants to the piece of paper. I put the little piece of metal into an envelope. When I went back home for lunch, I picked the vial up that had the rest of the metal in it, and the balance of the metal was gone."

*Major Donald E Keyhoe, in reference to the investigation, said, "If the Air Force had sent investigators publicly in hope of killing the story, it might have backfired. Papers and magazines would picture the intelligence officers as making a serious investigation. It might seem like proof to some people that the Air Force was soberly impressed by the report, or at least the "giants from space" were considered a strong possibility."

I was put in touch with eyewitness Neil Nunley. When Gray Barker interviewed Nunley back in 1952, Barker wrote extensively about him. I spoke to Nunley on the phone and he seemed surprised that he was mentioned in so many articles and books by Barker. Like so many of the witnesses, he had no idea that this incident had been written about so extensively. I then gave Nunley some copies of Barker's articles and writings in which Nunley was featured. Shortly after

Neil read them, he told me, "You can pretty much take that story to the bank as far as I'm concerned." Mr. Nunley concluded, "The only thing that wasn't mentioned was the fact that some people claiming to be with the federal government were shutting everybody up and telling them not to talk to any reporters. My parents both told me at the time that that would be for the best and to this day, I haven't said a lot about the whole ordeal. So you can quote any, or part, of that article, [Saucerian article] and it would be fine with me."

The "Project 10073 RECORD CARD" for Flatwoods, West Virginia

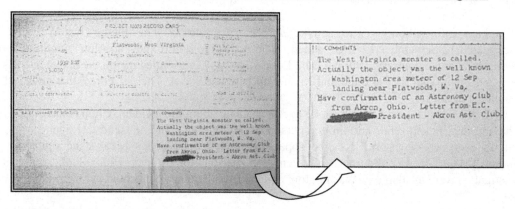

As I searched Project Blue Book for the official document stating the USAF explanation of the "Flatwoods Monster," I kept thinking about the comment Albert Chop had made to Donald Keyhoe: "Several astronomers said a meteor went over there. Those people must have dreamed up the rest." The "Flatwoods Monster" incident was given the designated case number #2078.

The definitive answer I sought I found in a "Project 10073 Record Card ATIC Form 329 (REV 26 Sep 52)." [Note: The typed-in information on the document appears in bold print.]

This document stated the following:

1. Date. **12 Sep 52**
2. Location. **Flatwoods, West Virginia**
3. Time. **1930 EST** [7:30 p.m. EST/8:30 p.m. EDT]
4. Type of observation. **Ground Visual**
5. Photos. **No**
6. Source. **Civilians**
7. Length of observation. [Blank]
8. Number of objects. **1**
9. Course. [Blank]
10. Brief summary of sighting. [Blank]
11. Comments: **The West Virginia monster so called. Actually the object was the well-known Washington area meteor of 12 Sep landing near Flatwoods, W. Va. Have confirmation of an Astronomy Club from Akron, Ohio. Letter from E. C.** [blacked out] **President-Akron Astr. Club.**
12. Conclusion: **[X]** Was astronomical.

It is interesting to note that three of the most important sections of this document were incomplete and left blank: #7, length of observation, #9, course, and #10, brief summary of sighting. Section #11 reports that the object was a "meteor" that made a "landing near Flatwoods, W. Va." Again, why was no trace of a meteorite in the Flatwoods area as the Air Force claimed?

Ultimately, Project Blue Book concluded that this object "Was astronomical." I researched the Blue Book files for September 12 and found a copy of the letter from the president of the Akron Astronomy Club sent to Project Blue Book that confirmed the sighting of this object.

The following is a verbatim copy of the letter. After this letter was received by Project Blue Book at, ATIC, handwritten notes were added. [Note: the handwritten notes appear italicized and the typed-in information on the document appears in bold print.]

EXAMPLE Typical Meteorite (Fireball)
12 Sep Fireball - September 12, 1952-Flatwoods, W.Va.

Direction: **From about 30 ° north of east to 30 ° south of west**
Angle of Flight: **About 30 ° from the horizontal**
Duration: **5-6 seconds**
Size: **about twice the diameter of the moon at zenith, but believe the object looked larger than it actually was because it was so near the horizon**
Time: **Approximately 7:00 p.m. EST**
Color: **Brilliant greenish white**
Shape: **Egg-shaped with smaller radius in front; bluish green at rear**
Distance: **Assuming that it passed over Cumberland, MD in the flight to Flatwoods, West Virginia it passed within 160 miles of Akron.**
Arc: **Was observed while passing through an arc of approximately 45 °**
Length of visible flight: **Based on a distance of 160 miles from Akron and an arc of 45 °, the flight was observed for approximately 135 miles.**
Altitude: **When first observed the object was about 65 miles above the ground.**
Velocity: **25 miles per second**
Actually (sic) Velocity: **27 miles per second**

Fireball (also see Dr. LaPaz + Dr. Olivares report) 7-3719-17
Observed by a number of people between Cumberland, MD to a point 160 miles from Akron, Ohio (All computations tally with speed description trajectory and other characteristics of a meteorite.)

The information contained in this report was used for the Air Force's final evaluation for the Project 10073 Record Card. There is no explanation for the conflicting data between this letter/report and the final Project Blue Book Project 10073 Record Card.

The Akron report stated the time the supposed meteor was seen was "approximately 7:00 p.m." The final Project 10073 Record Card stated the time of the sighting in Flatwoods was 7:30 p.m. The Astronomy Club stated, "**Assuming** that it passed over Cumberland, MD in the flight to Flatwoods, it passed within 160 miles of Akron." Since an object did pass over Cumberland, the Astronomy Club **assumed** "that it passed over Cumberland in the flight to Flatwoods." It didn't.

The distance from Cumberland to Flatwoods is approximately 110 miles. According to the Akron Astronomy Club report, they **assumed** a meteor passed over Cumberland at approximately 7:00 p.m. en route to Flatwoods. According to the Project Blue Book report card, the object landed near Flatwoods at 7:30 p.m. and 110 hundred miles away from Cumberland, Md. This shows a time lapse of about thirty minutes.

If this object's actual velocity were "27 miles per second," as the Astronomy Club stated, it would have reached Flatwoods in about four seconds, not thirty minutes. The next inaccuracy of the assumed flight path is the direction this object flew en route to Flatwoods. The direction of its flight was given as "from about 30 ° north of east to 30 ° south of west," which according to the Astronomy Club was the assumed flight path from Cumberland, MD to Flatwoods.

Project Blue Book called this object the "Washington area meteor". It is the same meteor that "flashed across the sky near the nation's capital." If this alleged meteor flew over Washington, D.C. headed due west, it would have been impossible for it to have passed over Cumberland, change direction and then head south to Flatwoods. The Akron Astronomy Club's assumption of the meteor's direction and flight path was dead wrong.

The object the Astronomy Club sighted within 160 miles of Akron was actually the Baltimore/WV object that headed toward Wheeling. What Project Blue Book called "the well-known Washington area meteor" and the newspapers called the "Flame Over Washington" actually flew over Washington, D.C. on a straight due west flight path before landing in Flatwoods. Once again, these two objects, the Washington/Flatwoods object and the Baltimore/WV object, were mistakenly thought to be the same object.

Another important item in the Akron Astronomy Club letter is their assumption about the object, "in the flight to Flatwoods, WV." They sighted the meteor 160 miles away, flying at 27 miles per second. The duration was said to be 5-6 seconds. If the Astronomy Club wrote this report based on the information from their sighting, how did they know the object was in flight to Flatwoods? This letter was perhaps written later, probably in collaboration with Project Blue Book officials!

The Akron Astronomy Club report had a handwritten message on it, written by someone from Project Blue Book. This message states, "Fireball (also see Dr.'s LaPaz and Olivares report) 7-3719-17." Dr. Lincoln LaPaz, head scientist of the University of New Mexico's Institute of Meteorites, was known worldwide as an authority on meteors. In the late 1940s, LaPaz worked closely with intelligence officers in New Mexico trying to solve the mystery of the "green fireballs." LaPaz was called upon numerous times by the U.S. government to assist in various UFO sighting cases. In the Flatwoods case, where the "monster" was explained as a meteor, the confirmation document from the Akron Astronomy Club stated in a handwritten note that LaPaz and Olivares made a supplemental report about this supposed meteor.

I was unable to find this report in the files of Project Blue Book for the September 1952 cases. Handwritten on this document are statements referring to a "fireball" meteor. Handwritten statements were obviously added after the letter was supposedly received by the Air Force. These statements seem to indicate that there was a supplemental report written by Dr. LaPaz and Dr. Olivares. This would account for the statement made by the Air Force's public liaison, Albert Chop, to Donald Keyhoe, "Several astronomers said a meteor went over there."

Now, consider the following questions about Dr. LaPaz's and Dr. Olivares' hand-written message, which appeared on the Akron Astronomy Club report:

1). Did Project Blue Book officials contact LaPaz and Olivares because they felt unsure about the report from the Akron Astronomy Club?

2). Was the USAF trying to reinforce their cover-up by using Dr. LaPaz and Dr. Olivares' opinions?

3). The letter showed a handwritten reference note that read "fireball (also see Dr. LaPaz's and Dr. Olivares' report)." This note told of the existence of an important document. If Dr. LaPaz and Dr. Olivares wrote a report, stating the object in question was a "fireball," why did officials at Project Blue Book use the confirmation of an *amateur* astronomy club report in their final Project 10073 Record Card?

4). Moreover, is it possible that the Akron Astronomy Club report was actually a complete forgery, made up by ATIC officials or other officials?

After I determined the flight paths of the three objects, I analyzed the Project Blue Book reports that explained all of the sightings as a single fireball meteor. I needed further assistance to help sort out the facts concerning the Air Force's single meteor explanation. I contacted an astronomer who is a meteor expert as well, Harold (Hal) Povenmire from Florida. Mr. Povenmire wrote a book titled *Fireballs, Meteors, and Meteorites* and was an active participant in the field of astronomy. Hal Povenmire also worked with world-renowned astronomer J. Allen Hynek, a key figure in UFO studies who served as a consultant to Project Blue Book.

I met Harold Povenmire at his Florida home and interviewed him. He began by talking about his association with Mr. J. Allen Hynek and said:

I first met Dr. Hynek when I was a high school student and he was a professor of astronomy at Ohio State University. I worked with Dr. Hynek with satellite tracking cameras out in Pasadena, CA. I also worked on board a ship with him off the coast of Africa during the solar eclipse of 1973. Later on, around 1975, I helped set up some of the lectures and demonstrations on his UFO studies. So my actual association went on with him for more than twenty years. During that time, I saw him change his attitude quite a bit toward the flying saucer-UFO phenomenon.

In the early days, Hynek did not take any of these stories seriously; [saying] that most of them could be accounted for by identified flying objects, such as aircraft, balloons, balled lightning, and things like that.

However, Povenmire also said this about Dr. Hynek, "He often said, 'I hear incredible stories from basically credible people!'" I then asked Mr. Povenmire, "What constitutes a meteoritic fireball?" He answered, "A fireball is a small Apollo asteroid, or a meteorite that is orbiting the sun along with the earth, and it happens that their paths or their orbits cross, and this small object enters the earth's atmosphere. As it does, it is retarded by the atmosphere and begins to oblate or burn, and can become incredibly bright; much brighter than the full moon. It can be bigger than the full moon. If it is heavy enough and moving slow enough, it can descend into the lower atmosphere. If it gets below eighteen to twelve miles above the surface, it can produce a sonic boom." I asked Mr. Povenmire, "Would the average person notice this boom?" He answered, "Yes, if it's close, it can be extremely intense. I felt one sonic boom from a fireball that was actually a jolting experience. On one other occasion, I could hear the reflected rumble. In both cases, the rumble sounded like distant thunder and was approximately forty seconds in length."

In reference to the Flatwoods case, there is no mention in the Akron Astronomy Club report, the Project Blue Book report or the press of a sonic boom. Even though this alleged meteor was traveling at an extremely low altitude over Braxton County, none of the witnesses who sighted this object mentioned a sonic boom. This object had traveled well under the 12-to-18 mile range and would have created a very audible sonic boom.

I then asked Mr. Povenmire, "After the object had dropped and landed, a very bright light had flared up and appeared from the area where it had landed or crashed. Is this typical for a meteor or any [celestial] body?" Povenmire answered, "Absolutely not. Whatever you're describing there, [it] is not a meteoritic fireball or a meteorite impact. I can say that with certainty."

I also asked Povenmire if oil deposits would have any relativity to a fireball. He responded, "To my knowledge, there would be absolutely no connection of any sort of an oily deposit and a meteorite impact. The two are completely incompatible with each other."

The most uncharacteristic flight path of what was called a meteor was the Baltimore/WV object. I handed Mr. Povenmire a map showing the flight path of this alleged fireball meteor. I asked him, "Is this a typical path?" He answered, "Now, I can tell you with absolute certainty that a meteoroid or a fireball could not possibly entertain such a course. Its ability to change course would only be caused by deceleration by the atmosphere, or an explosion, and at most it could only change one or two degrees in its path."

Mr. Povenmire expounded further about fireballs, "If it descends further and is slowed enough, then it may produce meteorites which are portions of the object that actually land on earth. Very few meteoritic fireballs produce meteorites." Mr. Povenmire explained two kinds of meteorite craters that would have been relative to the alleged fireball meteors seen landing that night.

He explained, "The first one is what we call an impact pit. That's where a small meteorite falls from the atmosphere and all the cosmic velocity—that's the velocity that it had in space—has been damped out by the retardation effect of the atmosphere, and so it's dropping just by Newton alone—by the force of gravity—and when it hits the ground, it's like a brick that's tossed off of a building, and it will form a small impact pit."

Povenmire continued, "A second crater would be a much larger one, called a simple crater. This is where a meteorite of some size still retains a bit of cosmic velocity and plows out a good size pit, maybe a thirty-or-forty-foot-wide crater and throws the dirt out and will always leave a raised rim." There was not one impact pit reported in West Virginia or Tennessee where these objects landed on September 12, 1952. To this day, no impact pits have ever been reported!

What the officials at Project Blue Book concluded as "the well known Washington area meteor of 12 Sept landing near Flatwoods, W.Va." was actually three separate UFOs. I have identified each of those objects by their flight locations, and have designated them numbers in the order that they appeared. They are the Virginia/Tennessee #1 object, the Baltimore/WV #2 object, and the Washington, D.C./Flatwoods #3 object. After each object passed over the eastern seaboard, they continued on western headings and fanned out across the country. These sightings occurred between 6:50 p.m. and 7:25 p.m. EST (7:50 p.m. and 8:25 p.m. EDT).

The following is a chronological list of locations where the three objects passed over and near after they flew over the mid-Atlantic coastal region of the United States:

I. VIRGINIA/TENNESSEE # 1 OBJECT (Round-shaped UFO)

1. Roanoke, VA
2. Pulaski, VA
3. Johnson City, TN - Tri-Cities Airport sighting

4. Arcadia, TN –*landed*
5. Kingsport, TN
6. Rogersville, TN
7. Moccasin Gap, TN –*went down*
8. Wadlow Gap, TN
9. Elizabethton, TN

II. BALTIMORE/WEST VIRGINIA # 2 OBJECT (Oval-shaped UFO)

10. Baltimore, MD (Sighted to the north from Philadelphia area)
11. Catonsville, MD
12. Frederick, MD
13. Hagerstown, MD
14. Cumberland, MD
15. Garret County, MD
16. Preston County, WV
17. Morgantown, WV
18. Fairmont, WV
19. Columbus, OH
20. Zanesville, OH
21. Saint Clairsville, OH
22. Wheeling- Ohio County Airport, WV-near mid-air collision between object and aircraft
23. Oglebay Park Resort, WV—*landed*
24. Wheeling, WV
25. McMechen, WV
26. Parkersburg, WV
27. Nitro, WV
28. St. Albans - *landed*
29. Charleston (Spring Hill Cemetery), WV
30. West of Charleston, WV
31. Charleston (South Hills), WV –*landed*
32. Charleston (Park Area), WV –*landed*
33. Ward, WV
34. Chelyan/Cabin Creek, WV –*landed*
35. Bluefield, WV

III. WASHINGTON, D.C./FLATWOODS # 3 OBJECT (Oval-shaped UFO)

36. Washington, D.C.
37. Front Royal, VA
38. Elkins, WV
39. Burnsville, WV
40. Heaters, WV
41. Flatwoods, WV –*landed* at approximately 7:25 p.m. EST

These sightings took place over a period of about thirty-five minutes. The Akron Astronomy Club report stated that the duration of the alleged single fireball meteor was 5–6 seconds. It would be impossible for all these sightings to have occurred within a period of 5–6 seconds over all of the areas above. Mr. Povenmire explained about the time durations of fireball meteors and meteors, "Anytime that you have a meteor that lasts for more than seven seconds, its path would be considered very long. Nine seconds is a near record for a typical fireball, and anything longer than that would be considered extraordinary."

The Akron Astronomy Club report said it was a "typical meteorite," a "fireball." On the contrary, it would not have been possible for a fireball meteor to change directions several times and be seen flying over forty locations. The characteristics, geographic locations, and flight patterns of what were sighted that night are completely inconsistent with humankind's knowledge of meteors, and instead point to unknown crafts. Could all of the different sightings been a meteor shower? I asked Mr. Povenmire, "In which months do we not see any significant meteor showers?" Povenmire answered, "The months that would be considered not to have meteor showers would be February and March. Then we go into June without any significant showers, and then September. Really every other month has some sort of known annual shower."

In 1952, Harvard University established the Harvard Meteor Project. The project was in existence from 1952-54 and photographed 2,529 meteors and their flight paths. During that time, renowned UFO debunker, Donald H. Menzel, was the director of the Harvard College Observatory. Interestingly enough, there were no photographs of meteors taken by this project on the day of September 12, 1952!

The December 1952 issue of *Sky and Telescope* magazine had an article titled "Astronomical Highlights of 1952." The article gave a list of the top ten astronomical highlights for 1952, as of October when their meeting was held. Amazingly, the overwhelming amount of alleged meteors that the military insisted occurred on the night of September 12 did not make the top ten list!

To reiterate a point, the definition of a "meteorite" is as follows, "Any meteoroid which has reached the surface of the earth without being completely vaporized." Roger Chapman, an astronomer that I know in Charleston, West Virginia, assisted me with my research concerning the alleged meteorites of West Virginia on September 12, 1952. I asked him if he could find documented information about the history of West Virginia meteorites.

He told me that he would get in touch with other astronomers in the state and ask them to look through their private astronomy book collections. Several weeks went by and Roger called me back. Several of his astronomer friends had went through their books and copied everything they could find about the history of meteorites in West Virginia. Some of the books they got information from are actually very rare and have been out of print for several years. Shortly after his phone call, I received a package in the mail with a wealth of information I was seeking.

I discovered there are only three documented cases of known meteorites in the state of West Virginia. It was no surprise that none of these meteorites fell in West Virginia on September 12, 1952. One of the valuable sources of material that I received is information from, *"THE SMITHSONIAN INSTITUTE CATALOG."* It states the following 3 meteorites of West Virginia:

1). GREENBRIER COUNTY, West Virginia. Coarse octahedrite. Found 1880. Original weight: 5 kg. Description: A mass of 5 kg. was found near the top of Alleghany Mountains, 3 miles N of White Sulpher Springs.

2). JENNY'S CREEK, Wayne County, West Virginia. Coarse octahedrite. Found 1883.

Original weight: 11,987.6 g. Description: Three masses of about 10.4 kg., 1134 g. & 453.6 g. were found in 1883-1886 but only about 907 g. have been preserved.

3). *LANDES, Grant County, West Virginia.* Iron. Silicate bearing octahedrite. Found about 1930, recognized as a meteorite in 1968. Total weight: 69.8 kg. (1) Specimen. Description: Plowed up in a hillside cornfield one mile east of the Landes Post Office about 35 to 40 years before it was brought to the attention of G. I. Huss.

Corroborating documentation about these three West Virginia "meteorites" is recorded in the "*NEWSLETTER - West Virginia Geological Survey, Morgantown*" dated, "December 1973," the "Seventeenth Issue." In an article, "WEST VIRGINIA METEORITES," writer Peter Lansing, the "Environmental Geologist and Head of the Environmental Geology Section," stated the following; "Today, about 1,600 meteorites are known throughout the world and three are known to have fallen in West Virginia. These meteorites are named, 'Greenbrier County,' 'Jenny's Creek' (Wayne County), and 'Landes' (Grant County)." Now, to reiterate my point, Project Blue Book officials recorded the following information in the Flatwoods, "Project 10073 Record Card.":

11. Comments: The West Virginia monster so called. **Actually the object was the well-known Washington area meteor of 12 Sep landing near Flatwoods, W. Va.** Have confirmation of an Astronomy Club from Akron, Ohio. Letter from E. C. [blacked out] President-Akron Astr. Club.

The following handwritten notes appeared on the Akron Astronomy Club letter that was sent to Project Blue Book:

*EXAMPLE Typical Meteorite (Fireball) 12 Sep Fireball - September 12, 1952-Flatwoods, W. Va. (All computations tally with speed description trajectory and other **characteristics of a meteorite**).*

Major Keyhoe explained the major reason that the incident was covered-up. He stated, "When the time came to admit that the saucers were real, the slightest official hint of possible menace would be quickly remembered. From that angle, the Sutton story was dangerous, with its picture of a fearsome creature intelligent enough to build and control spaceships. It was far better to brand the whole thing as a hallucination, which intelligence evidently believed was the answer."

CHAPTER ELEVEN

KEYHOE AND CHOP

It is safe to say that the Air Force's official viewpoint of the incident was one of contrived disinterest. The Air Force repeatedly claimed that the so-called "West Virginia monster" was attributed to a "meteor," which made a "landing near Flatwoods, W.Va."

In 1952, shortly after the event occurred, Major Keyhoe contacted the Air Force for its viewpoint about this case. He again spoke to Albert Chop, requesting an update in January of 1953. Chop told him, "We're simply not bothering with monster stories. We've got enough trouble with confirmed sightings." Chop's statements were misleading if not untrue.

If the Air Force was "not bothering with monster stories," why did USAF representatives contact Colonel Dale Leavitt, A. Lee Stewart, Jr., and Kathleen May, among others? If the object was a "meteor," why was the National Guard activated in Braxton County? What was the Air Force representative referring to in, "We've got enough trouble with confirmed sightings?"

Major Donald Keyhoe and Public Liaison Albert Chop

As I searched through the Blue Book files, I found documentation that the Air Force actually *was* reading and saving these "monster stories," specifically, the "West Virginia monster." I found some articles that Project Blue Book officials obtained about the Flatwoods case.

The first was a newspaper article; the headline read, "The Thing, 10 Feet Tall, Terrifies Party of 7." This article had handwritten notes across the top of it stating the source as the *New York Daily New*, "September 14, 1952." In addition, along the bottom of this page was written "in Sutton, West Virginia." Along the side of the document appeared the same code number that was also handwritten on the Akron Astronomy Club report, "7-3719-17." Another article among the Blue Book September 12 documents was from a publication, titled, *Infinity*. This article, "Sutton Monster Real?" was an interview with researcher Ivan T. Sanderson and had the same handwritten number, "7-3719-17."

Another article among these documents was information about the "Flatwoods Monster" from Gray Baker's 1956 book, *They Knew Too Much About Flying Saucers*. Here, the Air Force had actually retyped highlights of Barker's story into a brief 37- line synopsis. Also within the files was another document, this one taken from a page of the book, *The World of Flying Saucers*, by Donald H. Menzel and Lyle G. Boyd. It is a synopsis of the Flatwoods case from Gray Barker and Donald Keyhoe's 1956 books. Handwritten notes state, "12 Sept 1952" and "Sutton, West Va." Interestingly, the original copyright of Menzel and Boyd's book was 1963, which indicates the Air Force was still interested in the Flatwoods case for at least eleven years after the incident.

The monitoring of these "Braxton County Monster" stories seemed odd, considering the Air Force's supposed disinterest in the incident...but not surprising! They were actually keeping tabs on the authors and their works, much like the contents of this book! In January of 1953, a statement was made by Albert Chop to an inquiring Donald Keyhoe, who asked for additional information about the "monster." This was about four months after the "monster" incident had occurred; Mr. Chop gave the following details of the Air Force's explanation to Mr. Keyhoe:

A). "First, the glowing object seen by Mrs. May and the boys was actually a meteor; it merely appeared to be landing when it disappeared over the hill."

B). "Second, the group did see two glowing eyes, probably those of a large owl perched on a limb. Underbrush below may have given the impression of a giant figure, and in their excitement they may have imagined the rest."

C). "Third, the boys' illness was a physical effect brought on by their fright."

D). "Fourth, the flattened grass and supposed tracks were caused by the first villagers when they came to investigate."

It seems that the Air Force spent a lot of time and effort trying to explain away the details of the incident! The following points concern the Air Force's explanations, which Albert Chop explained to Major Keyhoe (in quotations) and are followed by my rebuttals:

1). "First, **the glowing object seen by Mrs. May** and the boys was actually **a meteor**." Actually, Mrs. May was not at the Flatwoods Elementary School playground playing football with the boys when the object went overhead. Mrs. May was at home when the boys on the playground saw the object pass overhead. Besides the documentation of this "meteor" in Project Blue Book, I did not find any other official record of it in any astronomical history or record books. There are no West Virginia meteorites recorded for September 12, 1952.

2). "It merely **appeared to be landing** when it disappeared over the hill." Albert Chop's quote contradicts the Project Blue Book "Project 10073 Record Card" comment; **"the meteor of 12 Sep. landing near Flatwoods, W. Va."** If it disappeared, how did they become aware of its landing near Flatwoods? The USAF actually gave two different landing versions in this incident!

3). "The group did see two glowing eyes, **probably** those of a large owl perched on a limb." The use of the word "probably" showed the Air Force was speculating. The witnesses tell a completely different story and none described an owl; some said the "eyes" were actually "portholes."

4). "Underbrush below **may have given** the impression of a giant figure." The Air Force again used speculative terminology to dismiss the sighting. Again, the witnesses tell a different story; the "giant figure" was described as a "metallic-like" structure that hovered! It was mechanical.

5). "In their excitement they **imagined the rest**." It is very unlikely that every witness along the path "imagined" the same description from different angles. In addition, the boys were separated and interviewed privately by professional writers and drew similar pictures of what they saw.

6). "The boys' illness was a physical effect brought on by their **fright**." The USAF could only guess it was caused by fear. Eighteen-year-old witness Eugene Lemon vomited for hours after the encounter due to the gaseous odor that emanated from the "monster." Additionally, several other witnesses also became ill with the same symptoms from this gas, which was compared to Mustard Gas. Some of the boys saw a doctor because of the gas. Mr. and Mrs. Smith of the "CSI" research group reported, "After two weeks, Gene Lemon still was not able to swallow carbonated drinks."

7). "The flattened grass and supposed tracks were caused by the first villagers when they came to investigate." This is another excuse given by the USAF, who was again grasping at straws. The locals did not flatten the grass fields into specific markings with well-defined patterns...nonsense!

This illustration compares the size relationship between the 12-foot tall "Flatwoods Monster" and a 6-foot tall barn owl. Note the 6-foot tall human figure for size comparison

In Donald Keyhoe's book, *Aliens From Space*, Edward J. Ruppelt told him, "We're ordered to hide sightings when possible, but if a strong report does get out we have to publish a fast explanation—make up something to kill the report in a hurry. We must also ridicule the witness, especially if we can't figure a plausible answer."

Mr. Johnny Barker went to Flatwoods on Monday, September 15, 1952, observed the Fisher Farm and spoke to the locals. He said, "Some said it was just a meteor, others said they didn't want to say, while others really believed Mrs. May and the children did see a 'monster.'"

He also explained the site, where the object relocated to in the second field, "A woman pointed to the gate involved and to where the object landed with three slight depressions. It seemed like something had been there for sure. The grass was flattened."

Johnny Barker, Freddie May and Frank C. Feschino, Jr.

Mr. Barker also stated, "I believe what was most interesting to me, was while we were interviewing people, several times they would comment about all the military people present."

The Flatwoods case was definitely a strong report that got out to the public and had received a fast explanation in an attempt to kill the incident. As far as a plausible answer, the team at Project Blue Book could not figure out an answer, their explanations were speculative and estranged.

Furthermore, Edward Ruppelt did not mention one word about the "Flatwoods Monster" in his book, *The Report On Unidentified Flying Objects*, even though the incident was one of the biggest news stories of 1952. Obviously, if Ruppelt had written about the Flatwoods case in his book, it would have brought more attention to the incident, which the Air Force was already struggling to keep silent and covered-up! Subsequently, his approach worked and Flatwoods was overlooked!

CHAPTER TWELVE

THE RESCUE MISSION

There were sightings of other odd-shaped craft that flew over Braxton County on the night of September 12. Witnesses described the objects as being oval, round and cigar-shaped. Moreover, they were seen flying on different directional headings and sighted at different times during the night. Therefore, if the alleged Washington, D.C. meteor did indeed land in Flatwoods, then how do we explain these numerous other sightings over Braxton County that night, or the lack of a meteorite impact pit? During my interview with Kathleen May, she made the following statement about the government letter she had received, "They notified us there were four of them [objects] in Braxton County that night." Colonel Dale Leavitt, in my interview with him, also told me about different objects seen that night throughout the area; the Flatwoods object, the Sugar Creek-Frametown crash (one object), and the Duck Creek UFO encounter, which involved a car.

In 1954, writer Harold T. Wilkins researched the case and made this articulate statement, "The local police, however, admit that on that day of the incident a fleet of pear-shaped objects—dull red, white and gleaming—had been seen flying in formation over the region. They hovered in mid-air, ascended almost vertically, descended, then flew level, and three strange objects had crashed in the dense woods." Investigator Gray Barker said, "Within a 20-mile radius of Flatwoods, numerous persons saw what they variously described as shooting stars, flying saucers and meteorites." The various described objects seen by witnesses within a 20-mile radius of Flatwoods that night evidently shows that Braxton County was the target of a "UFO flap." The numerous amounts of objects sighted in the county would account for the original investigator's confusion in formulating accurate flight paths of these objects.

Investigator Ivan T. Sanderson documented many of the objects seen that night. He stated, "As a result of plotting the incidents on a map," he said, "we are of the opinion that a flight of intelligently controlled objects flew over West Virginia on the evening of September 12 and further that one of them landed or crashed, a second and third crashed, and a fourth blew up in the air." Even though Sanderson's individual investigations were thorough, my research indicates his overall theory to be *incorrect*. Even though Sanderson was unable to formulate the flight paths of these individual objects, he did reach the following conclusion about them, "The one that reached Flatwoods landed rather than crashed and its "pilot" or "occupant" managed to get out before it disintegrated." This object did not disintegrate; it took off from the farm after it landed.

Gray Barker made this statement; "I can only begin to cope with the mass of data and the correspondence, the pieces of the jigsaw puzzle containing the answer to the entire mystery—if it could only be put together!" The four landing sites that Mrs. May described to me were amazingly accurate except for one point. The government told Mrs. May that there were four individual experimental crafts in the area that night. In reality, there were actually two crafts that were damaged, which repeatedly landed throughout the Braxton County area.

The first craft made two landings in Braxton County, one in Sugar Creek near the Elk River, and then in Frametown. The second craft, the "Flatwoods Monster" craft, made three landings in Braxton County. It first landed in Flatwoods on the Fisher Farm, then in Holly, and then later crash-landed on James Knoll in Frametown. Gray Barker, interviewing A. M. Jordan, described the first object seen over Flatwoods. Barker stated, "This strange event had taken place simultaneously with sightings of aerial objects over several states." Mr. A. M. Jordan's sighting in

Flatwoods occurred simultaneously to some of the earlier sightings, at approximately 6:50 p.m. EST. Barker stated in his interview with Jordan, "He saw the object, which later landed on the hill, and was able to describe it in a cold matter of fact." Barker assumed this was the object that later landed on the mountaintop of the Fisher Farm about 7:25 p.m. EST. He believed this was the "Flatwoods Monster" ship.

Mr. Jordan's description of the object did not depict the oval-shaped craft seen over the schoolyard that landed on the Fisher Farm. Gray Barker, based on his interview with Jordan, said this about the object, "Evidently it came from over the horizon from the southeast as he was sitting on the porch. He [Jordan] did not look up until it had come into his view overhead and flashed in a southwesterly direction toward the hilltop opposite him. It was an elongated object. The top of it was a light shade of red. From the rear shot balls of fire."

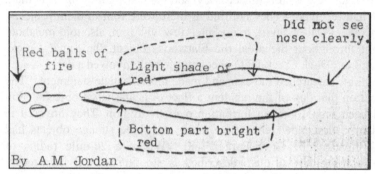

Did not see nose clearly.

Red balls of fire

Light shade of red

Bottom part bright red

By A.M. Jordan

Barker explained what Jordan believed this object to be, "He thought it was a jet plane at the time, though he saw no wings. He did not see the nose of the object clearly. It proceeded across the sky, then halted suddenly, seemed to fall rapidly toward the hilltop." This was not the same object seen passing over the schoolyard. The description given by Jordan—and his drawing—had little or no resemblance to the descriptions of the "Flatwoods Monster" ship. Moreover, it was not a jet plane because it had no wings or appendages. Gray Barker spoke to the children who witnessed the object that passed over the schoolyard. Barker said, "The children were unanimous in disagreeing with Mr. Jordan about the shape." These UFOs were two entirely different ships.

Additional witnesses saw this object pass over Braxton County on September 12, 1952. Mr. Morrison, his father, mother and a sibling saw this UFO from their backyard when they lived in "Ben's Run," near Newville.

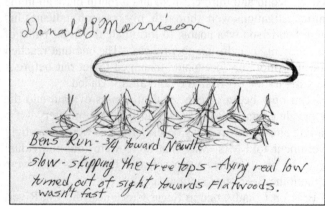

Donald J. Morrison

Bens Run - 3/4 toward Newtle
slow - skipping the tree tops - flying real low
turned out of sight towards Flatwoods.
wasn't fast

This area is approximately four miles southeast of Flatwoods. They saw this elongated object fly near them shortly before it passed over Flatwoods. I interviewed Mr. Donald Morrison and he told me what occurred on that early evening when he saw it at the age of eleven.

The witness stated, "My dad had seen it first. He was out in the yard getting stove wood and had an armload of stove wood. He hollered and said 'By God' and said 'everybody look!' When we all ran and started to look, he said, 'Look up there' and pointed right at it. It was in a low gap and it was clear at the time and we all seen it go through." Mr. Morrison told me what he saw, "I seen a big huge thing that looked like a bottle gas tank." During our interview, I also drew a picture of the object from Morrison's description.

He also stated, "It was red in color. I remember very well what I'd seen. I'd say it was probably forty-feet long - my estimation about it. The object was probably a quarter a mile away - from where I was lookin' at it. It was very low. It was skippin' the tops of the trees." He added, "It was on a mountainside" and said, "I was lookin' up at it." Mr. Morrison gave a further description of the UFO, which eliminated it as being a plane. He stated, "There was no indication that I could see anything being on the outer shell of it - at all." I emphasized the point, and asked if the low-flying craft had wings or appendages. Morrison answered, "There wasn't no wings on it - at all. When he [father] hollered, we had seen the whole thing. We even seen both ends of it and it came through that low gap. It was rounded on both ends and it was floatin' straight through."

When I asked Morrison how fast the elongated object appeared to be moving, he answered, "It was goin' very slow when we seen it. It was goin toward a little community right below where I lived at Ben's Run, Har. It [object] went ahead and vanished behind - there was another hill there, and it vanished behind it."

After speaking to a witness and resident of Har who also saw the object, Morrison stated, "They seen the same thing down there and it came toward Har then veered toward the right, came over the store. Everybody down there seen the same thing that we seen up here. They all said it was red in color and huge. They said it left and the last they seen of it, it was headed right smack dead for Flatwoods when it disappeared."

It is evident that this jet-shaped object was actually the same craft that was seen over the Fisher Farm by A. M. Jordan. Upon reaching, the farm in Flatwoods this jet-shaped object dropped a homing device onto the hilltop. This occurred when the ship appeared to halt suddenly, then fell rapidly toward the earth. The device would guide the damaged ship that was approaching the Washington area on a western heading. The damaged ship was the Washington/Flatwoods #3 object, also known as the "Flame Over Washington."

The following sequence shows the order of the objects as they appeared:

1). **The Virginia/TN #1 object** first passed over the coastline and then landed in Arcadia, TN at approximately 6:57 p.m. EST.
2). **The Baltimore/WV #2 object** passed over the mid-Atlantic coast then passed over Baltimore before 7:00 p.m. EST/8:00 p.m. EDT, heading over West Virginia and north of Braxton County.
3). **The jet-shaped UFO** was then seen by A. M. Jordan over the Bailey Fisher Farm at about 6:50 p.m. EST.
4). **The Washington/Flatwoods #3 object**. The "Flame Over Washington" was the object that contained the "Flatwoods Monster." It eventually landed on the Fisher mountaintop about 7:25 p.m. EST.

Actually more than two objects passed over Flatwoods that night besides the jet-shaped craft and the "Flatwoods Monster" ship. Gray Barker said the locals reported several other objects passing over the area of Braxton County. Harold T. Wilkins said the local police admitted, "on that day of the incident a fleet of pear-shaped objects—dull red, white and gleaming—had been seen flying in formation over the region. They hovered in mid-air, ascended almost vertically, descended, and then flew level." Ivan T. Sanderson stated, "We are of the opinion that a flight of intelligently controlled objects flew over West Virginia on the evening of September 12."

Why were there other UFOs flying over Braxton County that night? Moreover, why were objects seen over the town of Flatwoods? Furthermore, where did they come from? The answers to these questions were contained in Project Blue Book. Several other alleged "meteor" sightings had also been reported earlier that evening on September 12. These sightings did not come from the mid-Atlantic area however; they were reported south of West Virginia over "North Carolina" and were thoroughly documented in Project Blue Book.

Once again, I used my Master Map to plot the points for all of these sightings so I could decipher and make sense of these sightings. When I plotted the numerous sightings on my master map, including their origin points, locations and the times they were sighted, it indicated there was actually more than one object. I discovered there were actually five objects that descended upon North Carolina. The plotted locations of their origin points, when connected to other sighting points had all formed definitive flight paths that headed north.

The first of these alleged "meteor" sightings actually occurred shortly before 7:00 p.m. EST. At this point, we know no there is no official documentation of any meteor for September 12, 1952 other than Project Blue Book's records. It is no surprise, the USAF tried to explain the series of sightings over North Carolina as a single "meteor." The Directorate of Intelligence Agency stated in a document entitled "Air Intelligence Report," that a flying object was reported in the Lumberton, NC area September 12 at 7:00 p.m. EST/8:00 p.m. EDT.

Four witnesses at four different locations in Lumberton confirmed its appearance. This report covered sightings from Lake Waccamaw to Fayetteville, North Carolina. The object was traveling from "southeast to northwest" and described as "a ball shape with a trail three times the length of the body." The speed was so fast that most witnesses got only a hurried glimpse. According to Fayetteville and Raleigh, NC newspapers, they reported "a meteor" was observed over their regions at approximately the same time and place, with the same flight path characteristics. After examining all the official Air Force reports and eyewitness accounts contained in the Tentative Observers Questionnaires, I began to notice major discrepancies about this alleged single "meteor" sighting. I realized that here was more than one object seen over North Carolina that night.

The first discrepancy was the numerous locations that this alleged lone "meteor" was said to have passed over during the duration of its flight. The witnesses' descriptions of details were also varied. They described different objects, which were of different shapes, sizes and colors. Next, the alleged "meteor" displayed multiple flight trajectories over different locations.

These various flight trajectories are not at all characteristic of a meteor. Next, I dissected these reports, plotted the locations of the sightings on my map and analyzed the times and descriptions, reported by these witnesses. I quickly discovered that there were actually five different objects sighted, not a single "meteor." Project Bluebook received the following information from a witness to this alleged single meteor. This information was contained in a Tentative Observer Questionnaire. For clarity, I have named and numbered each of the five objects. This object is "#1 Object." The witness stated:

At about 7 o'clock on September 12, in front of [service station name blacked out] in Lumberton, NC...I saw a large seeming ball of fire, traveling from east to west . . . it seemed to be a bright glowing mass with a contrasting colored tail at least three times the diameter of the ball...I saw it for approximately two or three seconds traveling on a downward plane. When it got below apparent tree height, it seemed to level off, but never came into view again... It seemed to be traveling at least 600 mph and perhaps more...The mass or object appeared round and flat with the flat side down...I have seen many falling stars and meteors but this was larger, closer and different from any I have seen before…The object appeared to be about a mile and a half away and 12 to 15 feet in diameter...My seeing this object was not a hallucination as I saw it long enough to call [name blacked out] attention to it and he saw it also.

Another description of a North Carolina sighting stood apart from the #1 Object called a "ball of fire." This object I have designated Object #2. The following information was contained in another Tentative Observer Questionnaire. The witness stated, "On Friday afternoon, Sept. 12, 1952 at dusk, my attention was called to an unusual object in the sky. This object was round in shape and white in color, with a trailing streamer of darker color. It was traveling to the northwest at a very high rate of speed. Another witness driving on Highway 301, three miles north from Lumberton, NC, reported that he sighting the object directly in front of his windshield as it flew from right to left. In both cases [military witness and Highway 301 witness] the object was moving from the southeast to the northwest." The "trailing stream" color was described as "blue."

According to this Intelligence report, another witness "was fishing five miles east of Elizabethton, NC. He reported the object to be between 15-20 degrees [percent] of the tail of the object." The witness who sighted the object here reported he saw it "immediately after dark." It is interesting to note that the sighting of the #1 Object and the #2 Object were both made during dusk. This witness saw neither the #1 nor #2 Objects. The object he sighted was seen at dark. It is obvious that the Air Intelligence Information Report had combined all of the sightings reported in the area, and explained them as one single meteor. At that point, the object sighted, "immediately after dark" did not fall into the time frame of the two earlier reports made during daylight. This lone object passed over the area after dark, about one hour after the other two objects did.

Even though the descriptions, the flight directions, altitudes, and the times as observed by different witnesses varied, the USAF still claimed those incidents were attributed to a single meteor. The Intelligence report gave yet another account of this supposed single meteor sighted over North Carolina. It stated, "Another person in the vicinity of Lake Waccamaw, a distance of 45 miles from Lumberton, reported sighting this same object." To this point, we have learned about two different objects with two very distinct descriptions, both seen over Lumberton. They are described and listed below:

1). A large ball of fire compared to an object that was white in color.
2). A round and flat object with a flat side down compared to an object that was round in shape.

Later, an Air Force C-46 military cargo plane that was flying northwest of Lumberton had a sighting of the #1 Object when it passed over Greensboro NC, approximately 110 miles away. A Project 10073 Record Card document stated the object was a "meteor" shaped like a "ball of fire." It also stated that it was traveling at a "high speed" in a "steady dive." It said the object was the "12 Sep meteor sighting throughout east coast area."

Also contained in the Project Blue Book files was the original two-page report that told a completely different story. The original document was filed under an official "CIRVIS" [sur-vees] report. According to the *JANAP, Joint-Army-Navy-Air Force* publication 146(D), it defines and states, "Canadian - United States/Communications Instructions For Reporting Vital Intelligence Sightings."

In "Chapter I - JANAP 146 (D) - General Description and Purpose of Communications Instructions For Reporting Vital Intelligence Sightings" the scope of CIRVIS is explained as follows:

102. SCOPE - A. This publication is limited to the reporting of information of vital importance to the security of the United States of America and Canada and their forces, which in the opinion of the observer, requires very urgent defensive and/or investigative action by the U.S. and/or Canadian armed forces.

USAF personnel, who witnessed the object from a C-46 aircraft of the "514th troop carrier wing, Medium-132", filed the "CIRVIS" report. The most relevant information contained in this report is arranged in a chronological order and is as follows:

A. "Unidentified aerial object directly over Greensboro, North Carolina
   (3605 N dash 07948 W)."
B. "Observing aircraft flying over Greensboro, North Carolina at 7,000 feet."
C. "Pilot of observing craft—Colonel"
D. "Object appeared at 11 o'clock high approximately 200-500 feet above observing aircraft
   as a brilliant streak of fire"
E. "Observed one unidentified flying object traveling on heading of approximately 330
   degrees"
F. "Course of object a steady dive at extremely high speed, from altitude of approximately
   7200 or 7500 feet to a point somewhere near below altitude of and in front of observing
   aircraft"
G. "After object had passed observing aircraft it appeared as a round ball of fire which then
   erupted into sparks and disappeared."
H. "Object in view approximately five seconds."
I. "Sighting verified by 2 CR/MS [crew members]"
J. "Also observing phenomena were persons in control tower at Greensboro Highpoint
   Airport."

The Project 10073 Record Card for Flatwoods, WV stated, "Actually the object was the well known Washington area meteor of 12 Sep. landing near Flatwoods" This North Carolina Blue Book case reported the "Unidentified aerial object directly over Greensboro, North Carolina," at 2400 hours GMT. North Carolina observed Eastern Standard Time. 2400 hours Greenwich Mean Time translates to 7:00 p.m. EST, or 8:00 p.m. EDT. The Akron Astronomy Club letter sent to Project Blue Book stated the time as approximately 7:00 p.m. EST [8:00 p.m. EDT]. The alleged "Washington area meteor" flew "awfully low" over the Capitol around 7:00 p.m. EST/8:00 p.m. EDT. It was on a western heading when it passed over Washington, D.C. and was said to have an official duration time of five to six seconds. This alleged "meteor" could not have flown "directly over Greensboro, North Carolina," it was not possible.
These two objects flew directly over two different cities, located in two different states and were proceeding on completely different flight paths. An interesting point to note in this CIRVIS report is that a crew of Air Force pilots filed it. ATIC ignored the pilots' judgment and opinion and declared this object a meteor. When a Major, a Colonel, and a Captain in the Air Force filed a

report naming something as a threat to national security, it was arrogant and deceitful for the ATIC to dismiss the object as a meteor.

On September 16, 1952, *The Greensboro Daily News* featured a lengthy article about the sightings of two objects that flew over the area of Reidsville, NC. and one was in flames. The town of Reidsville is about 120 miles northwest of Greensboro. The following headline and opening paragraph detail this sighting, "Many Report Thing in Sky at Reidsville. Reidsville, Sept. 16—A strange light which streaked through the heavens Friday night in Reidsville has been described by W. E. Lambeth, postal clerk, who saw the object about 6:55 p.m. [EST] through a skylight in the post office building, as "like a traveling flashlight." According to my information and flightpath, this object sighted over Reidsville was actually the #2 Object sighted along its northwest flight path. This object was first sighted over Lumberton. It then flew toward the town of Reidsville.

This witness gave no description of the #2 North Carolina Object as being on fire. Yet, this article described another UFO that was, "A group of boys sighted two objects in Reidsville about 6:50 p.m. While watching an object in the sky they initially thought to be a star, another object passed over them trailing fire." The #1 and #2 Objects had both actually passed over Lumberton then followed parallel flight paths toward and over Reidsville.

The Greensboro Record also ran an article on September 16 about the Reidsville sightings, titled, "Aerial Whazzit Seen Here Friday." It also refers to the sightings as "strange objects" using the plural tense. A paper in the nearby town of Leaksville ran an article headlined, "'Flying Saucer' Reported Seen By Mrs. Blackwell." This low-flying object that passed over Reidsville was described as "trailing a red streak that looked just like fire." This fiery description describes the #1 Object, which flew over Reidsville after passing over Lumberton.

There was yet another sighting of a different object, which flew over North Carolina. According to the two-plotted points and its flightpath trajectory, this object was sighted over two different areas to the northwest of Lumberton near the North Carolina-Virginia border. This object was sighted 30 miles west of Greensboro after it had been sighted over Winston-Salem approximately 115 miles away. The object was then sighted over Mount Airy at the North Carolina border approximately 40 miles away from Winston-Salem. This third UFO, I have designated as the Object #3. It was described as a "shooting star" over both of these locations.

In *The Mount Airy News* dated September 19, a headline read, "Flat Rock Man Calls News to Report Flying Saucer–Local Residents See Ball Of Fire in the Sky." This article combined the reports of the various other sightings as being a single object. It reads, "A streak of fire that appeared and suddenly disappeared again was seen by a group of people last night at about 7 o'clock." The article also gave information about the sighting of the #3 Object that was seen over Winston-Salem. It stated, "At Winston-Salem many puzzled witnesses called the airport for information. Men on duty at the tower saw the spectacle and said it was a larger-than-usual shooting star that remained in sight at least two or three seconds."

The #3 Object was then sighted along its northern flight path approximately 40 miles away over the Mount Airy area. The Mount Airy witness, Bernice Harris, described the object as follows, "I thought it was either a shooting star or a falling star with a tail on it." The single meteor explanation became even more unlikely when still another description of it was given.

The next report indicated that a fourth UFO was seen over North Carolina within the same period as the first three objects. It was seen over Flat Rock, North Carolina along the South Carolina border. This is designated as the #4 Object. Information concerning this sighting was in the same article, "Flat Rock Man Calls News to Report Flying Saucer."

The article stated, "One of the observers, James Newman, of Flat Rock, called the News to report the object as a flying saucer. Mr. Newman was the only person to call the spectacle a 'flying saucer,' but plenty of other people did see it." This saucer description stood apart from the previous objects.

A fifth UFO was also seen, which I have designated as the #5 Object. The sighting of this object is the one that took place much later, "immediately after dark." It was first sighted over Lake Waccamaw, NC, near the southeast coast of North Carolina. It then headed northwest over Elizabethtown, then northwest over Fayetteville. The Air Intelligence Information Report stated, "The newspaper Fayetteville Observer, reported on 13 September [name blacked out] of Fayetteville had seen a huge ball with a tail heading northwest after 1900 Eastern Time 12 September 1952. He reported the color as a greenish blue; the newspaper reported the object as a meteor. Several newspapers in Raleigh, North Carolina, it is reported, carried articles about the sighting of this meteor." This object was actually seen well "after 1900 Eastern Time" or 7:00 p.m. It was seen immediately after dark at about 8:00 p.m. Eastern Time, about one-hour later.

According to the description in this Intelligence report, the color of the object was a "greenish blue." It was not described as a "ball of fire" or "white in color." Furthermore, this object was seen "immediately after dark," which places it into a much later time frame than the first four objects sighted over North Carolina. This fifth North Carolina UFO, the #5 Rescue Object, was described as a "huge ball with a tail and heading northwest," which was the same directional heading of the first two objects sighted earlier. The end of this Intelligence report raised a major discrepancy concerning the Fayetteville sighting of the #5 North Carolina Rescue Object and its flight path.

This information appeared in the Air Intelligence Information Report section, "Comments of the preparing officer." He stated, "I have interviewed the three witnesses in the above report. All reports, in my opinion are reliable." The final line in this report stated, "The witness at the point east of Elizabethtown reported the object to have a flat trajectory; whereas the other two said it was definitely curved." The two referenced sightings, that had "definitely curved" trajectories were the Lake Waccamaw and Fayetteville sightings. Lake Waccamaw was the first area where the #5 Object was sighted on its flight path that had a trajectory reported as, "definitely curved."

Located 20 miles northwest of Lake Waccamaw is Elizabethtown. After the #5, Object passed over Lake Waccamaw, it continued northwest over Elizabethtown where it was then noted to have a "flat trajectory." This indicates that when the object was first sighted over Lake Waccamaw while its trajectory was curved, it was arching downward as it was descending. Next, when the object neared Elizabethtown and proceeded over that area, it then leveled off, causing it to have a "flat trajectory."

The #5 Object continued on a northwest heading, proceeded another 30 miles and was sighted for a third time. I plotted this point on the map when the UFO flew over Fayetteville. It was stated in a Fayetteville newspaper that it's trajectory over the area was "curved." At that point, while the object was over Fayetteville still heading northwest, its trajectory had changed to a curved trajectory once again. This area is where the object began to descend even closer toward the earth.

During my interview with meteor expert Harold Povenmire, he made the following statement concerning a horizontal meteor's path and trajectory. He stated, "Now if it's going to have a horizontal path, that means that it's entering the earth's atmosphere almost tangent to the earth's surface and it's going to continue on until it either leaves the earth's surface, or it oblates down to essentially nothing." Povenmire then said, "Nearly horizontal meteors are not terribly rare, but they're not going to change course." If this object had been a meteor, it would not have been able to change its course three times during its flight path. When this alleged meteor was observed to

120

have a flat horizontal trajectory over Elizabethtown, it should have left the earth's atmosphere or disintegrated into nothing. This object did neither.

When the #5 Object descended over Lake Waccamaw after dark, it flew on a northwest flight course and passed over Elizabethtown then Fayetteville. Shortly after, the object passed near Pope AFB at Fort Bragg, located just northwest of Fayetteville. The object continued farther northwest and was sighted once again as it flew just to the west of Raleigh, NC, located to the northeast of Fayetteville. The plotted points of this object's northwest flightpath are indeed correct. The Air Intelligence Information Report actually confirms these sightings and states, "Four different witnesses at four different locations confirmed its location."

According to the Fayetteville and Raleigh newspapers, "a meteor was observed at approximately the same time, day, place and the direction of the flight." This alleged meteor was last observed passing west of Raleigh before it vanished. Here, it had actually ascended out of North Carolina and into the upper atmosphere. Most importantly, the sightings of this UFO over Lake Waccamaw, Elizabethtown, Fayetteville and the Raleigh area all occurred when it was dark.

The Project Bluebook Intelligence Report concerning the so-called meteor incident ends by stating, "It is the personal opinion of the reporting officer that the flying object sighted by witnesses in and around Lumberton and the meteor report made by the Fayetteville paper are the same." My research definitely shows otherwise. My Master Map plots indicate that five different UFOs were sighted as they passed over North Carolina, not a lone "meteor." The following is a list of the five North Carolina UFOs and the designated numbers that I assigned to them:

A. **# 1 North Carolina Object**. The "ball of fire" sighted over Lumberton at approximately 7:00 p.m. EST.
B. **#2 North Carolina Object**. "The white in color" object sighted at dusk over Lumberton at approximately 7:00 p.m. EST. It also "was described to be the size of an automobile."
C. **#3 North Carolina Object**. The "larger-than-usual shooting star" sighted over Winston-Salem at approximately 7:00 p.m. EST.
D. **#4 North Carolina Object**. The object reported as a "flying saucer."
E. **#5 North Carolina Object**. The "greenish blue "object seen "immediately after dark."

The following are descriptions of the five objects that were sighted over North Carolina:

A. **#1 North Carolina Object**. It did not manifest the characteristics of a meteor in flight; namely, it changed its course from a downward trajectory to a level trajectory. Its characteristics indicated it was being controlled and maneuvered. The Lumberton witness who sighted this "ball of fire" called it "the mass or object," but not a meteor.
B. **#2 North Carolina Object**. The primary Lumberton witness who saw this object, which was "white," called it "an unusual object," but did not call it a meteor. Moreover, none of the other eyewitnesses, who saw this object called it a meteor either.
C. **#3 North Carolina Object**. Winston-Salem tower men said it was "a larger-than-usual shooting star."
D. **#4 North Carolina Object**. Observer James Newman described the object as a "flying saucer."
E. **#5 North Carolina Object**. When referring to this object, the Fayetteville witness had seen "a huge ball." This object had also changed its flight trajectory three different times.

The witnesses involved in four of these sightings did not refer to the objects as meteors. The tower men though, said the object that they saw was a "shooting star" but also stated it was, "larger than usual." It is evident that these five North Carolina objects were not "meteors." Moreover, these UFOs were part of a much bigger picture and were involved in the series of events that occurred that night. They actually had a specific task when they had descended upon North Carolina. These UFOs were on a search and rescue mission, their target area – Flatwoods, West Virginia.

The first three objects descended over North Carolina at approximately 6:50 p.m. EST and proceeded on northern trajectories toward Flatwoods, West Virginia. The fourth and fifth objects had another objective in this mission. These two objects hovered high over North Carolina, guarding the area from any immediate air strikes against the three northwest bound rescue objects.

This was a military strategy in operation. Shortly after, the #4 Object described as a "flying saucer" had descended. It passed over Flat Rock, North Carolina, which is located near the South Carolina border. This area lies within the perimeter of the Oak Ridge Laboratory restricted no-fly zone. Furthermore, Donaldson AFB in Greenville, South Carolina is located just south of the Flat Rock area where this UFO descended. Even though this UFO descended into the ORNL ADIZ just north of Donaldson AFB, it was not intercepted! The #4 Object passed over Flat Rock, proceeded on a northeast flight and flanked the three rescue ships to the west to assure them of unobstructed flight to Flatwoods. It then continued north to Flatwoods and to another destination.

The #5 Object hovered out of sight and watched over the other four objects that descended earlier. It then descended about an hour later. Just after dark, the #5 Object descended over Lake Waccamaw and headed northwest toward the Raleigh area. According to the Sept. 13, 1952 Florence, SC *Morning News*, it also passed over "Fort Bragg" home of Pope AFB. Near Raleigh, it was sighted from the northeast by Rocky Mount and Arcola, NC residents according to the Sept. 13, 1952 edition of the *Evening Telegram*; "Strange Object Viewed By Many In This Area."

This flight path, which it traveled, was actually along the area of an intended escape corridor for the damaged objects to exit out of the country. The #5 North Carolina Rescue Object had positioned itself along the southeast North Carolina coastline, south of Lake Waccamaw and acted as a beacon for the damaged objects to follow toward the Atlantic Ocean. These coastal waters were the rendezvous point where the UFOs were to get picked up by the Mothership. This search and rescue operation was definitely a programmed plan, from the beginning phase to the end.

I have now designated these five southern objects as the "North Carolina Rescue Objects." The following is a list that shows the vicinities where each of the five North Carolina Rescue objects descended then passed over the state:

#1 North Carolina Rescue Object
1). Lumberton, NC – *Descended over Lumberton*
2). Greensboro, NC- (CIRVIS)
3). Reidsville, NC
4). Draper, NC
#2 North Carolina Rescue Object
1). Lumberton, NC – *Descended over Lumberton*
2). Reidsville, NC
#3 North Carolina Rescue Object
1). Winston-Salem, NC – *Descended over Winston-Salem*
2). Mt. Airy, NC

#4 North Carolina Rescue Object

1). Flat Rock, NC – *Descended over Flat Rock into ORNL ADIZ*

#5 North Carolina Rescue Object

1). Lake Waccamaw, NC – *Descended over Lake Waccamaw "immediately after dark."*

2). Elizabethtown, NC

3). Fayetteville, NC

4). Fort Bragg, NC - (Home of Pope AFB.)

5). Raleigh area, NC (Sighted by residents from Rocky Mount and Arcola, NC)

<u>Map Detail of the Vicinities where the Five Rescue Objects had
Descended over NC: The #1, #2, #3 and #4 Objects all Headed north; the #5 Object
Stayed behind acting as a Beacon for the Damaged UFOs to Follow Out</u>

Up to this point in the reconstructed storyline, the three mid-Atlantic UFOs had all met resistance from American jet fighters that were scrambled from the east coast to intercept them over the Atlantic ADIZ. As a result of this confrontation, these UFOs were intercepted, shot and suffered severe damages in an aerial battle. Subsequently, the three damaged objects were forced down, headed west and later landed within the United States.

During this time, four objects were actually observed to be damaged; they were all on fire, had flown erratically and flew at low-altitudes. They were the three mid-Atlantic objects and the #1 North Carolina Rescue Object. In contrast, the #1 North Carolina Rescue Object, did not fly across the mid-Atlantic United States on a western heading from the Atlantic ADIZ as the others did. Rather, it flew from the southern region of the United States on a northern trajectory. This object was also on fire, had flown erratically and flew at a low-altitude like the other three damaged objects. Additionally, when the three damaged mid-Atlantic UFOs were seen along their flight paths; being severely damaged, they had all made emergency landings inside of the United States.

Likewise, the damaged #1 North Carolina Rescue Object also went down. When it descended over North Carolina and headed northwest, it continued toward West Virginia and upon reaching Braxton County, it crashed twice near Flatwoods along the Elk River. This southern object displayed the same characteristics of the three-damaged mid-Atlantic ships; it was damaged, disabled and eventually went down. This profile of being "damaged" is an indication that this southern object may have also been intercepted by jet fighters, which ultimately caused it to make an emergency landing on American soil. However, where did a confrontation occur that would have caused this object to have been forced down? I continued my search for UFO and mysterious jet fighter incidents in the southern region of the United States, where some sort of altercation may have occurred. Eventually, I found what I was looking for.

Some Blue Book North Carolina Documents and Newspaper Articles

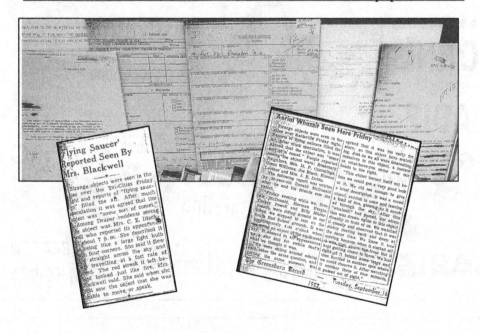

124

CHAPTER THIRTEEN

THE VANISHED AIRMEN

As I continued researching for UFO events and jet stories on September 12, 1952, I found a newspaper article that discussed a very unusual jet fighter incident that occurred that day. This story from Florida, led me on a long search to find other articles and information about this particular incident, which I eventually did. The first article I found, which tipped me off on the incident, appeared in *The Daytona Beach Morning Journal* dated Tuesday, September 16, 1952 with the heading, "Lost Pilot Was From Sanford, AF Reports." It reads:

The Air Force yesterday identified a jet pilot and radar operator missing since Friday in a flight from Tyndall Air Force Base here to MacDill Field, Tampa. The pilot was 2nd Lt. John A. Jones, Jr., 544 Palmetto Ave., Sanford, attached to the Air Defense Command. The radar operator was 2nd Lt. John S. DelCurto, of Pine, Ore., and a trainee at Tyndall.

A large-scale air-sea search has been underway for the two since their F94 all-weather night fighter and interceptor radioed it was having trouble at 5:52 p.m. Friday [5:52 p.m. EST/4:52 p.m. CST]. The search continued yesterday after shifting 200 miles west of Tampa in the Gulf of Mexico.

This incident took place only about an hour before the first mid-Atlantic UFO went down in Arcadia, Tennessee. The following points are important:

1). The lost jet was an F-94 all-weather night jet fighter and interceptor, one of the Air Force's elite jets.
2). Although the F-94 model-type was unknown, the F-94 jet fighters, models A, B and C, carried state-of- the-art radar and tracking technology.
3). The U.S. Air Force reported this jet "missing" on a routine flight from Tyndall AFB in Panama City to MacDill Field in Tampa over the Gulf of Mexico.
4). This jet fighter disappeared off the Florida coast and was never found. Yet, the pilot was in radio communication with tower controllers, and was being tracked by numerous radar systems and stations.

I found the mysterious disappearance of this F-94 jet fighter disconcerting. The article raised questions that made me want to dig more deeply for answers, in part because this incident had occurred on September 12, in the midst of 21-hours of sustained UFO sightings along the east coast. I began to research the missing airmen story in earnest. I then contacted the Air Force Historical Research Agency at Maxwell AFB in Alabama. I sent a letter to this agency requesting further details. I asked if the airmen had been found and asked for any additional data pertaining to the story.

Shortly thereafter, I received a letter from the AFHRA with this response, "Thank you for your letter requesting information about the lost pilots. Regrettably, our holdings do not contain the historical data you've requested. Sincerely, David R. Mills, Captain, USAF, Chief, Inquiries Branch." It seemed unbelievable that the Air Force had no documentation on this particular subject; they released the information to the *Associated Press* in 1952, so where had it gone? How could an incident of such magnitude, involving two missing airmen and a jet fighter, go undocumented by the Air Force, especially in light of the huge air and sea search that took place following their disappearance? I did not believe it. My next lead took me to The Air Force Safety Agency at Kirtland AFB Albuquerque, New Mexico, as suggested by Maxwell AFB officials. I called them and spoke to an Air Force representative about the two lost airmen episode.

I gave him the information I had, including the names of the pilot and radar operator, their addresses, the date of the incident and the location, including the area of search. I was even able to give him the reported time of the pilot's last transmission. He asked, "How did you find out about this incident, and where did you get your information?" I told him I had found an article in the *Daytona Beach Morning Journal*, dated September 16, 1952. I was puzzled at the officer's question about how I had found out about the incident. His response led me to believe that he was familiar with the story, and surprised by the amount of information I had. As our conversation progressed, he asked me, "Why are you fooling around with a story like this from so long ago?"

I found his questions disconcerting enough to make me uncomfortable disclosing that my research was related to a UFO incident. I told him that I had stumbled across the article. I said the fact that I lived in the area where it had occurred had made me curious as to whether the airmen had ever been found. He told me that in the early 1950s there were numerous planes for which there had been no accounting and that it would take a very long time to search through the many documents in their archives to find out about this incident.

I asked him, "Even with all the information I just gave just you about this incident? I even have the time reported that the last transmission was made by the pilot. How much more do you need?" At this point, the officer became agitated. His courteous demeanor changed, and I could tell that our conversation was ending. He said, "Doing research like this could become very expensive." Then he requested my name, address and a telephone number at which I could be reached. He said if he found any information, he would contact me.

I told him that I had not realized what a big job the search would be and that at that point I was no longer interested. He suggested that I contact the Maxwell AFB AFHRA. I realized I would have to take a different course of action to obtain the information I needed.

Since the National Archives had referred me to Maxwell, where this wild goose chase had begun, I figured I had reached a dead end. I tried contacting Maxwell AFB again in hopes that they had overlooked something in the search of their records. Again, I sent a letter of inquiry, this time directed at the missing airmen in reference to the history of Tyndall AFB. Tyndall was the base that these pilots were assigned at the time of their disappearance. I thought that perhaps by directing my angle of inquiry toward the history of Tyndall AFB, they might have a record of their missing personnel.

My response from them was not what I had expected. Their letter read, "Thank you for your letter. We checked the history of Tyndall AFB FL for the time period mentioned in your letter, but did not locate any information on the incident you mentioned. You may wish to contact the Air Force Safety Agency at Kirkland AFB. Sincerely, Archie DiFante, Archives Branch." Once again, my request was given the runaround.

I either began to think that the Air Force had lost the records concerning the incident or were reluctant to disclose the relevant information. My next step was to contact the Florida Office of Vital Statistics. As Jones had last resided in Florida, the state records should have had a death certificate for him. The letter I received stated, "Florida vital records have been carefully searched, but no record has been found that exactly matches the information on your application. The attached record which is a partial match may be the correct record."

I examined the Certificate of Death and found the partial match to be, "John Anthony Jones," not John A. Jones, Jr. This death certificate was for a man who was born in 1888 with a death date of 1953, one year after Jones and DelCurto were lost. This Mr. Jones died at age 64, far older than any jet fighter crewman. It seemed I had again reached a dead end. Because the Air Force had no records of these men or their disappearance, I thought that perhaps the names cited in the newspaper were wrong.

I had no choice but to return to the source where I had originally discovered the story, the newspapers. I searched several library collections and contacted several other libraries in Florida and Oregon. I found new articles, and after reviewing them, I began to develop new leads. I found that the missing radar operator had had his name spelled at least three different ways. The variations were John S. Del Curton, John S. Del Curto and John S. Curto. I contacted different libraries and looked through directories and Web sites to find any one of the variations of this airman's name. My big break came when I received a telephone call from a librarian in Oregon.

This librarian not only gave me the correct spelling of the name, but she had also found one of the relatives of a John S. DelCurto. She had gone far beyond what I would have expected. She had made many telephone calls on her own time to help me. Shortly after her call, I talked to John's brother via telephone. He was able to give me insight into his brother's life and death. He verified John's disappearance as the navigator of the F-94 jet. He told me of John's love for the Air Force, and the tragic impact his disappearance had on his family.

He explained to me that he had received a telegram from the Air Force informing him of John's disappearance, and that the Air Force was attempting to locate the jet and the missing airmen. The family had received several updates via telegram about the search, but there was no new information. He said, "There was never any wreckage found whatsoever, and the boys' bodies were never recovered." About six weeks after the jets, disappearance the Air Force contacted them again. John's official date of death was October 22, 1952.

One year after the incident, a military memorial was held in Pine, Oregon and a headstone was erected in memory of 2nd Lt. John S. DelCurto. I experienced a deep sadness for this family who had never had any closure on this terrible tragedy. Next, I tried to find information about the pilot of the missing jet, John Jones. The Seminole County Public Library in Florida helped in this quest. Although the Florida Bureau of Vital Statistics had no record of John A. Jones, Jr., another resourceful librarian tracked down the information. A librarian had found a microfilm copy of *The Sanford Herald*. On Monday September 15, 1952, *The Sanford Herald* ran a front-page story with the headline, "Lt. John A. Jones is Reported Missing." This article was written from information given by the brother of Lt. Jones. After reading this article, I started searching through local Sanford business facilities. Eventually I spoke with someone at a historical museum there. This small museum had records going back to the 1950s. There was no record of John A. Jones, Jr., but there was information on a surviving brother. I found a telephone listing for him and immediately called him.

I asked this man if he had a brother, John Jr., who had served in the Air Force and who had disappeared while piloting a jet fighter. I told him I was researching the entire incident involving his missing brother and the radar operator. I explained that I had found numerous inconsistencies in the available information and an odd aura of mystery surrounding the whole incident. He agreed and said that even to this day the incident was unsolved.

After nearly half a century (when we spoke), he still could not believe no wreckage of the jet had been found. He told me that the Air Force had contacted him by telegram informing him of John's disappearance. The USAF also contacted him by telephone and sent several more telegrams. To my surprise, he told me that he still had the original Air Force telegrams and a letter that had been sent to him. These did not state the type of aircraft that John was piloting when he disappeared. He told me that in one telephone conversation the Air Force had said that the jet John was flying was a "current, state-of-the-art jet interceptor." I told him that the newspaper accounts of the incident reported it as an F-94 all-weather night fighter and interceptor. He did remember, he said, being told by the Air Force that the jet was one of the most recent models in use.

In the Official GOC Magazine, *The Aircraft Flash* Vol. 1, No. 1, October 1952, Brig. General Kenneth P. Berquist made the following statement in an article titled "ADC Deputy for Operations Explains Air Defense System." He stated, "On July 14, 1952, the GOC [Ground Observer Corps] system along our eastern and western seaboards and along the Canadian Boundary went into continuous 24-hour-per-day operation. Some of the finest and fastest jet fighters in the Armed Forces have been allocated to ADC for the interception mission. They are the F-94 and the F-89, both all-weather fighter interceptors."

John's brother asked me if I wanted copies of the telegram and letter sent to him to use in my research and shortly after, he mailed them to me along with an original photo of John. The brother also put me in touch with a man who was a Civil Air Patrolman at the time of John's disappearance. This man said that he had gone to MacDill AFB to assist in the search for Jones and DelCurto, but was told by officials at MacDill that his services were not needed. They had everything under control.

The following information is the official documentation that the USAF sent to the brother of 2nd Lt. John A. Jones, Jr. These were the telegrams and letters sent to the family of John A. Jones, Jr., pilot of the lost jet.

They are presented in chronological order.

The first, a *Western Union* telegram, dated "1952 SEP 15 P.M. 348." It states:

Western Union (40)
    AB65
    A-TP A 662 Long Govt PD—MacDill AFB FLO 15 327P=
    ASHBY Glen Jones=
    Palmetto Ave Sanford FLO= DAAD-A 53042.

It is with deep regret that I officially inform you that your brother, John A. Jones, Jr. has been reported as missing. He was on a local routine training flight from Tyndall AFB on 12 Sept 1952 when the weather deteriorated. All aircraft were recalled and instructed to proceed to Moody AFB, Georgia which was the alternative landing field. Your brother was unable to contact Moody by radio and notified Tyndall AFB that he was not positive of his position. The Tyndall control tower was directing him to MacDill, AFB Flo the nearest base when he informed them that his engine had failed. Immediately thereafter Tyndall AFB lost radio contact with your brother. No further information is available at this time, however, please be assured that everything is being done to locate the aircraft. Additional information as it becomes available will immediately be forwarded to you.

General Benjamin W. Shidlaw (sic) Commanding General Air Defense Command ENT AFB Colorado Springs Colorado=

The next document is a *Western Union* telegram dated "1952 SEP 16 P.M. 851." It is an updated telegram sent out the next day. It states:

1952 SEP 16   51
    AB8I
    TPA895 Govt NL PD=MacDill AFB FLO 16
    Ashby G Jones=
    2544 Palmetto Ave Sanford FLO=

Reference is made to my message of 15 Sept 1952 informing you that your brother is missing. Being located in Florida you are probably in contact with the rescue operations now being conducted. Results of the search now in fourth day are negative. Search this far has covered area of forty-six thousand miles=

General Benjamin W. Chidlaw, Commanding General, Air Defense Comm=

The next document is a letter, which is hand typed, including the heading. It states:

Headquarters 3625TH Flying Training Wing (Advanced Interceptor)
Tyndall Air Force Base, Florida

17 September 1952

Mr. A.G. Jones
2544 Palmetto Avenue
Sanford, Florida

Dear Sir:

In addition to our telephone conversations, perhaps this letter will bring a little more light as to just what happened last Friday afternoon. John and his Radar Operator, Lt. DelCurto, were on a routine weather-training mission. When the weather started to become near our minimums, all of the aircraft were called to come back to the field. Supervisory personnel in the Control Tower advised John and three other aircraft to go to Moody Air Force Base about 15 minutes north of Tyndall; however he was unable to contact the Moody tower or the Moody Approach Control.

He indicated that he was not sure of his position at 4:20; however, the Tyndall radio directional finding gave him a steer to Tyndall Air Force Base. MacDill Air Force Base directional finding was able to pick up John's voice and gave him a directional steer also. Shortly afterward, he said he had a flame-out at 15,000 feet. Immediately, Air Sea Rescue was alerted for a search. Since last Friday, almost 125 sorties, which at one time included 52 airplanes, have been searching. Over 46,000 square miles have been searched with aircraft and surface vessels.

All available leads are being thoroughly investigated. I wish that I could give you some positive hope and information; however, at this time all I can say is that the Air Force is doing everything possible to find John and his Radar Observer.

Search is continuing. I am sure that you have received some information from newspapers that is not, in all cases, factual information; however, any leads that we get are thoroughly investigated. For example, today an area is being thoroughly searched by helicopter in an attempt to run down a lead that some fishermen possibly heard shouting. Please be assured that the Air Force will continue to search in the hopes of finding John and his Radar Observer. My deepest sympathies are with you at this time. In the event we develop any additional leads, I will call you direct [sic].

Very sincerely yours,
B. T. KLEINE
Colonel,
USAF - Commanding

Photograph of 2nd Lt. John Anderson Jones, Jr. and Tyndall Field

The next telegram update was dated "1952 SEP 20 p.m. 258." It states:

Western Union
AB56 KA251 1952 SEP 20 p.m. 258
K.CGA 139 Govt D.IPD=ENT AFB Colorado Springs Colo 20 1235P
Ashby G. Jones. Report Delivery=
2544 Palmetto Ave Sanford FLO=

Reference is made to my message of 16 September 1952.
Results of the search now in eighth day are negative=

General Benjamin Chidlaw CG HQ ADC ENT AFB Colo=

The last document is another telegram. It is dated "1952 OCT 23 p.m. 750." It is the death notification of John A. Jones, Jr. It states the following:

AB90 KB321   1952 OCT23 p.m. 750
K.CGA349 Govt PD=HQ ADC ENT AFB Colo Springs Colo 23 523P
Ashby G. Jones=
Report delivery 2544 Palmetto Ave Sanford Flo=

ADAAD-4 56 345. It is with deep regret that I officially inform you that on 22 October 1952, the Chief Of Staff, Headquarters United States Air Force notified this command that your brother John A. Jones Jr. was declared dead. The body was not recovered, however after the extensive search conducted by the Air Force it was determined that conclusive evidence existed to warrant this action. Please accept my sincere sympathy in your bereavement.

General Benjamin W Chidlaw Commanding General Air
Defense Command ENT Air Force Base Colorado Springs Col=

CHAPTER FOURTEEN

THE AIR FORCE ARTICLES

The UFO activity near Florida and along the Gulf coast was plentiful in August and September of 1952. Edward Ruppelt made this statement in his book, "September started out with a rush and for a while it looked as if UFO sightings were on the upswing again. *For some reason we began to get reports from all over the southern United States.* Every morning [for] about a week or two, we'd have a half dozen or so new reports."

The United States Air Defense Command was on a constant full alert, ready to scramble jets at any unidentified aircraft deemed a national threat. One incident involved a USAF base that had a direct encounter with a UFO occurred during the summer of 1952 at MacDill AFB. This UFO report was on file with the National Investigations Committee on Aerial Phenomena/NICAP.

According to their archives, MacDill AFB picked up a "UFO target" on its radar and tracked it. This Unidentified Flying Object was flying at an altitude of "40,000 ft" at a speed of "400 knots (460 mph)." A nearby airborne aircraft, a B-29 plane, which was manned by a USAF colonel pilot and a co-pilot, flew toward the UFO to get a closer look at it. When these airmen "investigated [the] radar target, [they] saw [a] **maneuverable egg-shaped object!**" In the report, this UFO was also described as being an **"elliptical UFO."**

Even though the exact date of the MacDill event is unknown, there were many correlations between that incident and the events of September 12, 1952. They follow:

1). Both UFO events occurred during the summer of 1952.
2). The UFO in the MacDill incident was described as an "egg-shaped object" and an "elliptical UFO." The shapes described here also fit the majority of the UFOs seen and described by witnesses on September 12, 1952.
3). The UFO visual sighting report of the object in the MacDill event stated it was maneuvering. Many of the September 12, 1952 witnesses said the objects they saw had maneuvered.
4). The UFO event in the NICAP report also involved MacDill AFB in Tampa, Florida.

I continued my research and found several other newspaper articles about the two missing airmen. They are listed here in chronological order of their publication dates. They span a period from September 13 through September 17, 1952. On Saturday, September 13, 1952, the first two articles appeared in two different newspapers talking about September 12 stories. Both were Tampa-based newspapers. The article that appeared in *The Tampa Tribune* was datelined September 12. It reported the missing flyers incident within the headline story of another incident, "Pilot Bails Out, Lands Safely After MacDill Hears Distress Call." It reads in part:

The pilot of a jet observation plane ran into technical trouble during a training flight today and bailed out after heading the plane in the direction of the Gulf of Mexico. The pilot was reported to have landed safely between Tyndall Air Force Base here and Apalachicola... Earlier MacDill Air Force Base at Tampa reported a jet has been unheard from since it radioed it was out of fuel at 5:42 p.m. [5:42 p.m. EST/4:42 p.m. CST].

MacDill and the Coast Guard base at St. Petersburg sent out planes along the course being followed by the fighter. The pilot was unable to give his exact position, and MacDill said the fighter could have been anywhere up to 70 miles northwest of Tampa at the last radio report. MacDill's Public Information Office reported late tonight that crash boats and two search planes had discontinued the search but would resume looking for the missing plane at daybreak pending conformation of the report that the pilot had parachuted to safety.

This article gave the source about Jones and DelCurto's disappearance as well as the time it was reported to the press, "MacDill's Public Information Office reported late tonight"—"late tonight," meaning late Friday night, September 12. The press received the information contained in this article late Friday night from MacDill AFB officials and also reported the "pilot of a jet observation plane," had bailed out "today." This article also stated that "earlier" on September 12, MacDill had reported a missing jet fighter—the plane piloted by Jones and navigated by DelCurto. The information given claimed that Jones and DelCurto and their jet fighter actually disappeared before the pilot of the jet observation plane bailed out and headed his plane out over the open waters of the Gulf of Mexico on September 12.

The Tampa Daily Times also ran a story about Jones and DelCurto as well as the pilot who bailed out. The headline read, "Last Heard From Late Yesterday—MacDill Searches for Pilot Down In Flight Over Gulf." This article also talks about the "jet observation plane." It states, "MacDill Air Force officials were unable to confirm an earlier report that a jet observation plane pilot headed his plane toward the Gulf and bailed out after he ran into trouble on a training flight *Thursday*." The article states:

Thirty-two planes fanned out over a wide area of the Gulf from Panama City to Bradenton in search of an Air Force jet plane last heard from at 5:42 p.m. yesterday. MacDill Air Force Base Public Information Officer Paul E. Mitchell said the plane was identified as a Lockheed F-94 all-weather night fighter and interceptor flying from Tyndall Air Force Base, Panama City to MacDill.

Lt. Col. Charles J. Rosenblatt, base operations officer, said the last coherent radio contact with the plane disclosed the pilot had engine trouble at 15,000 feet over the Gulf. The last radio sound indicated the disabled craft was down to 8,000 feet, Captain Mitchell said. The time was 5:42 p.m.

Captain Mitchell said the plane was apparently lost, and Air Force officials *speculated* that its radio compass had failed. First inkling that the craft was in trouble came when the pilot called Tyndall Air Force Base. He was directed to land at Moody Air Force Base at Valdosta, GA, but for some reason, failed to comply with the orders, Captain Mitchell said.

The next contact was made with MacDill radio tower, which gave the plane three fixes, the MacDill information officer said. It was by means of these fixes that the plane's approximate location was determined.

The assumption is that the pilot bailed out over the Gulf. The two Air Force Bases, MacDill and Tyndall, and the Coast Guard are participating in the search today. Combing the Gulf are 36 Air Force planes, six Coast Guard planes, and six crash boats from MacDill. MacDill Air Force officials were unable to confirm an earlier report that a jet observation plane pilot headed his plane toward the Gulf and bailed out after he ran into trouble on a training flight Thursday.

The information in this article was received later than the information that appeared in *The Tampa Tribune*. The Tribune had picked up the story from the Panama City, September 12- (UP) wire and used their story. *The Tampa Daily Times* printed their article from information they received later in the day, hence the headline, "Last Heard from Late Yesterday." It stated, *"MacDill Air Force officials were unable to confirm an earlier report that a jet observation plane pilot headed his plane toward the Gulf and bailed out after he ran into trouble on a training flight Thursday."* USAF officials from MacDill were unable to confirm the "Thursday" report that had come from Panama City because the "training flight" accident actually occurred on Friday September 12, not Thursday September 11. This was the reason MacDill officials were unable to confirm the report of a plane lost "on a training flight Thursday." *The Tampa Daily Times* made a mistake.

Both jets in these incidents departed Tyndall AFB in Panama City on September 12, 1952. In each case, they were reported as having radioed Tyndall and both were reported as having mechanical difficulty. The jets in both stories were lost. In one the pilot bailed out, in the other Jones and DelCurto were not reported to have exited their plane.

The following day, Sunday, *The Tampa Tribune* published a follow-up story about the two missing airmen. "Planes Hunt For Missing Jet Fighter." It reads in part:

The missing plane was identified as a Lockheed F-94 all-weather night fighter and interceptor bound from Tyndall Air Force Base, Panama City, to MacDill, according to MacDill Public Information Officer Captain Paul E. Mitchell. Thirty-two planes from Tyndall and MacDill, with six Coast Guard planes and six MacDill crash boats took part in yesterday's search for the two crewmen who were presumed to have bailed out when the plane had engine trouble 15,000 feet over the Gulf while en route from Tyndall to MacDill.

Lt. Col. Charles Rosenblatt, MacDill Base operations officer, said, "The last thing we heard was the pilot had a flameout (power failure) at 15,000 feet on course between Tyndall and MacDill. There was complete radio fadeout at 5:43 [EST/4:43 p.m. CST] at about 8,000 feet. Standard procedure is for the crew to bail out."

First notice that the craft was in trouble came when the pilot radioed Tyndall Air Force Base. He was instructed to land at Moody AFB, Valdosta, GA, but for some reason failed to comply with the orders. Captain Mitchell said the plane was apparently lost, and Air Force officials speculated that its radio compass had failed. The next contact was with MacDill radio tower, which gave the plane three radio fixes. Captain Mitchell said, "The plane took off on a routine training mission from Tyndall Field at 3:08 p.m. [EST/2:08 p.m. CST].Friday and last radio was two hours and 35 minutes later when MacDill received the last message at 5:43 p.m. [EST/4:43 p.m. CST]."

I next found an article in *The Panama City News Herald* that appeared on Sunday, September 14, 1952. The large bold print read, "Fliers Hunt Tyndall Pair." The difference between this Panama City report and the other Tampa articles was the time given when the pilot was last heard from. It reported, Public information officers said the plane, an F-94 all-weather jet fighter, was last heard from at 4:52 p.m. [Central Time]." Taking into consideration the one-hour time zone difference, the other three Tampa articles gave the time period between 5:42 p.m. EST and 5:43 p.m. EST. This is a time differential of ten to eleven minutes.

This article also mentioned a pilot reported to have bailed out. It stated, "An *Associated Press* story from MacDill said public information officers there had been unable to confirm reports that the pilot had parachuted to the ground between Tyndall and Apalachicola, but Tyndall officials said the reports 'are not correct.'"

The reason they were not correct was that they were two entirely different stories. In this article, two tragic jet incidents had been combined into one story in this article. The newspapers were having a difficult time keeping track of the two September 12, 1952 jet accident incidents. The report of the jet observation pilot who bailed out was never followed up, but the missing jet story continued to receive further press coverage.

The names of the two flyers that were presumed missing had not yet been released by the Air Force. The September 14 article titled, "Fliers Hunt Tyndall Pair," stated the following:

A vast air and sea search continued last night for two Tyndall airmen missing on a routine training flight between the Panama City base and MacDill Air Force Base, Tampa. Public information officers said the plane, an F-94 all-weather jet fighter was last heard from at 4:52 p.m. Friday when the pilot radioed MacDill that he was having engine trouble. MacDill operations told him to attempt a landing at Valdosta, Ga. and gave him a "fix." Capt. Paul Mitchell, MacDill's public information officer, said the craft had messaged earlier that it had engine trouble 15,000 feet over the Gulf.

Failure of a radio compass was believed to be the cause of the pilot's non-compliance with the order directing him to land in Valdosta. Directions to the Tampa base were also given the pilot, but the out-of-fuel message was received about six minutes later. The plane's position at the time of the last message was unknown, except that it was northwest of Tampa and probably within 70 miles of here. Names of the pilot and radar man, the only two occupants of the plane, were not immediately available.

An *Associated Press* story from MacDill AFB said, public information officers there had been unable to confirm reports that the pilot had parachuted to the ground between Tyndall and Apalachicola, but Tyndall officials said the reports "are not correct." The bulletin report article followed the main article on Monday September 15, 1952. The name of one of the missing men was released. It stated, "TAMPA (AP)" ...His name was 2nd Lt. John S. DelCurto of Pine, Oregon. DelCurto was the radar operator of the missing Tyndall jet."

The Pine, Oregon local newspaper that carried the story was *The Baker Democrat-Herald.* The headline read, "Pine Airman Lost in Flight." The article informed of DelCurto's disappearance and stated the following about Second Lt. Jones, "The pilot was attached to the Air Defense Command and his name is being withheld pending notification of next of kin. Their F-94 all-weather night fighter and interceptor has been unreported since 2:52 p.m. (PST) Friday when the pilot radioed he was having engine trouble."

At the time of publication of the Pine, Oregon article on September 15, 1952, the pilot's name was withheld "pending notification of next of kin." At the same time, a late article appeared in *The Sanford Herald,* a Florida paper, bearing the headline, "Lt. John A. Jones Is Reported Missing." The name of the missing pilot was then known, not through wire service reports but rather through Jones' brother, his next of kin. The article from *The Sanford Herald* was more personal than the other articles. It contained quotes from the "missing" notification telegram sent by ENT AFB in Colorado Springs, CO, to the missing pilot's brother on Monday.

In 1952, according to city directories, John's brother, Ashby, was listed at the address to which the "missing" notification was sent. Ashby was the next of kin and upon his receiving the telegram from the Air Force, he contacted *The Sanford Herald.* The following missing notice was reported to *The Sanford Herald,* "Lt. John Jones Is Reported Missing. Lieutenant John A. (Buddy) Jones, Jr., 22, Sanford, has been reported by the Air Defense Command as missing after he took off from Tyndall Air Force Base, Panama City, last Friday." This information actually reached the press shortly after the incident occurred on Friday night September 12. Since it was released to the press on that night when the two airmen disappeared, why was 2nd Lt. Jones' brother, who was his next of kin, not notified until Monday, September 15 about his brother's death?

Why did the Air Force wait until nearly three days had passed to notify John's brother when the MacDill Public Information Office told the press about the incident on Friday night, September 12?

I was able to put together a time line of the events that happened that night. The only discrepancy I found was the last transmission time. I used the original time of disappearance of 5:43 p.m. EST as released to the Tampa papers by the Air Force. I do not know why the time of the disappearance was changed afterwards to 5:52 p.m. EST. It remained at 5:52 p.m. in all the AP articles appearing afterward until the story was dropped.

According to the telegram received by Ashby Jones, 2544 Palmetto Avenue, Lt. Jones was on a "local, routine training flight" when the "weather deteriorated." The telegram, bearing the name of General Benjamin W. Chidlaw as the sender, further stated that all aircraft were recalled and instructed to proceed to Moody AFB Georgia, the alternate landing field. It reads, "Your brother was unable to contact Moody by radio," the telegram said, "and notified Tyndall AFB that he was not positive of his position." The Tyndall control tower was directing him to MacDill AFB, which was the nearest base, when Lt. Jones informed the tower his engine had failed. Immediately, radio contact was lost.

I raise the following points concerning Air Force statements contained in the telegram and article:

1). None of the other articles stated that the "weather deteriorated" while the jet was en route to Tyndall.
2). None of the other articles stated that all aircraft were recalled and instructed to proceed to Moody AFB.

The scenario projected by the USAF on the missing jet was that it was on a solo mission. There was never any indication given by them that Second Lt. Jones was flying with three other planes.

3). None of the other newspapers stated, "Your brother was unable to contact Moody by radio."

136

4). None of the other newspapers stated that Jones "notified Tyndall he was not positive of his position."

On Tuesday, September 16, 1952, three newspapers carried updated stories concerning the missing Tyndall airman. The names of both missing men were then finally announced but only in two of the newspapers. Oddly enough, the newspaper that did not list both of the men's names in the article was *The Panama City News Herald*, the point of origin of the event. That newspaper listed only John S. DelCurto. The two papers that named both the pilot and radar observer were *The Tampa Daily Times* and *The Daytona Beach Morning Journal*. Both of these papers carried articles that were AP press releases from Panama City. The Daytona Beach article, "Lost Pilot was from Sanford, AF Reports" stated, "The Air Force yesterday announced a jet pilot and radar operator missing since Friday…."

The Tampa Daily Times article read, "Missing Airmen's Names Announced . . . Panama City, Sept. 16 (AP)." Why didn't *The Panama City News Herald* print John A. Jones' name in its September 16 article if it was released on September 15? Both the Tampa and Daytona papers listed the time of the men's disappearance as 5:52 p.m. EST. This inconsistency from the original report made by Air Force officials of 5:43 p.m. EST was still being published incorrectly on September 16.

Were the times of the disappearance of Jones and DelCurto intentionally changed by the U.S. Air Force (by approximately ten minutes)? If so, then why? If the time change was a simple error, why was it not corrected in subsequent correspondence? If the mistake was made by news reporters, why was it not caught by the Air Force or at least by an editor who had access to Air Force information? The following article appeared in the *Panama City News Herald* on September 16, 1952:

Planes Press Search for Jet Fighter

Air Force planes today widened their Search for an F-94 jet fighter from Tyndall, missing over the Gulf of Mexico with its crew of two since Friday. Planes from Tyndall, Eglin and MacDill, plus five SB-29s of flight C, Fifth Air Rescue, Maxwell Field, shifted their hunt west of Tampa and included a land area southeast of St. Petersburg. By nightfall, the search will have covered 46,000 square miles. The SB-29s bear 33-foot rescue boats with inboard motors that can be dropped by parachute.

The final article I found regarding this incident was published in *The Tampa Tribune,* five days after the disappearance. The second paragraph of the article, "CAP To Continue Plane Search," states, "CAP planes flew six sorties yesterday [Tuesday], and one Monday in the Crystal Bay-Chassahowitzka Bay area after fishermen reported hearing calls for help in the vicinity Monday." These calls probably were not from the missing airmen because the article continued, "No trace of the missing plane or its crewmen had been found since it disappeared Friday afternoon." Was this a false alarm, or was someone calling for help in that bay area on September 15? If not the missing airmen, who was it?

I extracted Air Force information from the articles, along with the telegrams and letter sent by the Air Force to the Jones family and created a timeline. I arranged the following timeline of events according to several quotes. They appear in chronological order as follows:

1). "MacDill Air Force Base Public Information Officer Paul E. Mitchell said the missing plane was identified as a Lockheed F-94 all-weather night fighter and interceptor flying from Tyndall Air Force Base to MacDill."

2). "The Air Force reported Monday that a jet pilot and a radar operator were missing in a flight from Tyndall Air Force Base here to MacDill Field, Tampa."

3). "The plane took off on a routine training mission from Tyndall Field at [2:08 p.m. CST/3:08 p.m. EST] Friday."

4). "He was on a local routine training flight from Tyndall AFB on 12 Sept. 1952 when the weather deteriorated."

5). "Colonel B. T. Kleine, USAF commander of headquarters for the 3625th Flying Training Wing stated, 'John and his radar observer, Lt. DelCurto, were on a routine weather training mission. When the weather started to become near our minimums, all of the aircraft were called to come back to the field, John and three other aircraft . . .'"

6). "MacDill and the Coast Guard base at St. Petersburg sent out planes along the course being followed by the fighter."

7). "A vast air and sea search continued last night for two Tyndall airmen missing on a routine training flight between the Panama City base and McDill [sic] Air Force Base, Tampa."

The press was not notified by the USAF that this was a "routine weather training flight," nor was there any mention at all that they were diverted to Tyndall or Moody due to deteriorating weather. In fact, there was no mention of deteriorating weather to the press from any of the Air Force public information officers.

This key factor was left out when the Air Force briefed the news media. *The Tampa Tribune* weather report for September 12 was for "moderate variable winds with scattered evening showers." The September 12, 1952 Tampa Daily Times, published a weather map showing the symbol for rain over Tampa. It was no secret rain was coming in the direction of Tampa on that day. Air Force weather officials were quite aware of the status of the weather.

The weather map also revealed a large arrow marked rain located over the Gulf of Mexico, with a point of origin just south of Tampa. The arrow was shown as a continuous sweep from the southeastern U.S. across the Gulf heading northwest past Panama City and continuing across the entire Gulf. This indicated the rain pattern was moving from Tampa right into the flight path of the jets. The weather forecast was for rain for the entire southeast United States.

The Panama City News-Herald [the Tyndall area] reported the weather as, "partly cloudy to cloudy today, tonight and Saturday with scattered thunderstorms." This indicated that the rain pattern from South Florida was moving in the direction of the Florida Panhandle and sweeping northwest, passing over the Gulf of Mexico. Had the press found out that an F-94 all-weather jet interceptor on a "routine weather training flight" was recalled because of poor weather conditions, they would likely have raised too many controversial questions.

The F-94A and F-94B Starfires were the Air Force's first operational jet interceptors capable of operating in weather conditions described as, "adverse " and armed with .50 caliber cannons. The C-model was an upgraded jet and carried 2.75-inch rockets. Now, one must wonder if the deteriorating weather was really a factor in recalling the jets. Why was there no mention to the press that Jones was flying with three other jets? The only mention of the additional aircraft was sent to Lt. Jones' family. The USAF reported that all aircraft were ordered to return to Tyndall field. The supervisory personnel in the Tyndall Control Tower advised John and the three other airmen to proceed to Moody AFB. There was no explanation given for the change of flight orders.

The reports said, "All aircraft were recalled and instructed to proceed to Moody, AFB, Georgia, which was the alternative landing field." This was a mere puddle jump for these jet fighters. General Chidlaw said in a telegram, "Your brother [Lt. Jones] was unable to contact Moody by radio and notified Tyndall AFB that he was not positive of his position." The September 17 letter from the commanding colonel of the 3625th FTW said, "However he [Jones] was unable to contact Moody tower or the Moody Approach Control." It is puzzling that two airfields that handled the most highly sophisticated aircraft the U.S. possessed were unable to keep track of their planes. It was also interesting that no mention was made of the other three aircraft that were apparently accompanying Jones.

At this point, Jones had radioed and notified Tyndall AFB that he was not positive of his position and was unable to contact Moody AFB. Captain Paul F. Mitchell said, "He was instructed to land at Moody AFB, but for some reason failed to comply with the orders." Mitchell further said, "The plane was apparently lost, and Air Force officials speculated that its radio compass had failed." The USAF definition of a radio compass states, "A radio-receiving set mounted in an aircraft, which, together with a directional antenna, displays on instruments the heading of the aircraft with respect to a radio transmitter."

Even if Jones could not contact Moody AFB, they were still in radio contact with Tyndall AFB. Why were Tyndall officials unaware of the problems onboard? MacDill attempted to aid the two flyers. In 1952, MacDill AFB was operating a very high frequency directional finding system. This radio directional finding station was nicknamed "Homer."

Contact was established between the F-94 and Homer. Mac Dill's public information officer related the following information, "The next contact was made with MacDill radio tower, which gave the plane three fixes." It was by this means that the plane's approximate location was determined. One of the three established fixes was a landing fix. "MacDill operations told him to attempt a landing at Valdosta, Ga. and gave him a fix." Once again, Jones did not land the Starfire at Moody AFB. This was the second time that the pilot did not land when he was instructed to. Why was the crew of the F-94 jet unable to make contact with Moody AFB tower? This raises the following questions:

1). What distances were the jets from one another when the pilot, Jones, became lost? Why was Jones isolated from the other jets and why did no one realize he had become lost?

2). Why didn't Jones contact the three other jets and notify them that he was unable to contact Moody AFB? What was the radar operator, John Del Curto, doing during this time? Why is there no mention of his participation?

3). All of these aircraft should have been in communication with one another and should have been able to listen in to each other's radio transmissions. Why were they not in communication with each other? This dangerous situation could have lead to disastrous mid-air collisions!

4). Why did the other three aircraft that were flying on this "routine weather-training mission", proceed to Moody field and abandon Jones and DelCurto?

5). Why were all four jets redirected to Moody after being called back to Tyndall? Was the weather too treacherous for these "all-weather" fighter interceptor jets? This is a scary thought, especially during the time of the "Cold War," when the Soviet Union was a threat to the United States!

6). I ask, was it pilot error, mechanical failure or something undisclosed that caused Jones to become lost?

7). Why did Jones fail to attempt a landing at Moody Field?

8). Why did Jones refuse to attempt a landing at Moody the second time, after receiving further instruction from MacDill that included three radio fixes on his location? If Jones were unable to contact Moody to land, this would indicate he was near Moody AFB and planning to land. The pilot then "notified Tyndall AFB that he was not positive of his position." Moreover, "Since Jones was unable to contact Moody AFB to land," then why didn't Tyndall AFB just direct him back to their base field, 140 miles from that area?

According to General Chidlaw, "The Tyndall tower was directing him to MacDill AFB, which was the nearest base." In Colonel Kleine's Sept 17 letter he stated, "However he was unable to contact Moody tower or Moody Approach Control." He also wrote, "He indicated he was not sure of his position at 4:20. The Tyndall radio directional finding gave him a steer to Tyndall AFB...Shortly afterward; he said he had a flameout at 15,000 feet." This supposed flameout occurred at 5:42 p.m. EST. Kleine in his letter indicated that the pilot "was not sure of his position at 4:20 [4:20 p.m. CST/5:20 p.m. EST]." The letter tells us the following:

1). Jones was given a steer by Tyndall AFB tower to their base field.
2). The pilot was then given a steer by MacDill AFB, but Kleine neglected to state that the steer also given to Jones by MacDill AFB was not to Tyndall AFB. From the time, Jones indicated he was not sure of his position at 4:20 p.m. until "he said he had a flameout at 15,000 ft." at 5:42 was a span of 22 minutes. All of this leads to the following questions:

a). If all the involved bases were in radio contact with Jones, able to monitor his radio transmissions, give him positional fixes, and landing orders, then how could he have be lost?
b). What was Jones doing during the times when he repeatedly failed to land at Moody AFB?
c). Jones was supposedly lost near Moody AFB and not positive of his position, while being tracked by both Tyndall and MacDill radar systems and receiving steers. Why did he go anywhere near Tampa?
d). How could both MacDill and Tyndall be unaware of the problem with the jet's radio compass when each had had been in radio communication with Jones? Why is there no mention of the radar operator's involvement in the incident? After all, he did operate the onboard radar system of the jet!
e). Why was Jones not directed to another nearby AFB when he was supposedly lost at 4:20 p.m.?
f). At this point Kleine stated, "The Tyndall radio directional finding gave him a steer to Tyndall AFB. MacDill AFB then picked up John's voice and gave him a steer also." While Tyndall AFB was steering Jones toward their base in Panama City, MacDill AFB stepped in and redirected the pilot toward their base in Tampa. General Chidlaw stated Tyndall Control Tower was directing him to MacDill AFB. Why did Chidlaw fail to say that Tyndall AFB was steering the pilot toward their base? During this time, Lt. Jones was actually being steered by both Air Force bases.
g). Why did Tyndall and MacDill tower controllers both steer Lt. Jones away from Moody AFB toward Tyndall AFB, then attempt to direct the jet all the way across the Gulf of Mexico toward the Tampa area 245 miles away?
h). Why would Tyndall and MacDill take the risk of bringing a jet across water when it was running low on fuel? If the jet did run out of fuel, which supposedly caused the flameout, why was Jones not aware of his fuel consumption up to that point? The F-94B Starfire's fuel gauges were

140

located on the right-hand side of the main instrument panel, were unobstructed and plain to see. Moreover, the jet had "FUEL RESERVE LOW" indicators on the main instrument panel as well!

Lt. Col. Charles Rosenblatt [MacDill] said the last coherent radio contact with the plane disclosed the pilot had a flameout at 15,000 feet while on course between Tyndall and MacDill and the crewmen were presumed to have bailed out when the engine trouble occurred.

MacDill, at Tampa, reported that the plane had been unheard from since it radioed that it was out of fuel at 5:42 p.m. EST. At 15,000 feet, Jones' jet supposedly had engine failure because, "it was out of fuel." This caused a flameout, the extinguishing of the flame of the jet while in flight. 5:42 p.m. was the "last coherent radio contact with the plane," according to Rosenblatt. One minute later at 5:43 p.m., "The last radio sound indicated the disabled craft was down to 8,000 feet," according to Captain Mitchell. Lt. Colonel Rosenblatt added, "There was complete radio fadeout at 5:43 at about 8,000 feet."

i). The jet was now in a dive, dropping 7,000 feet between 5:42 and 5:43 p.m., MacDill said the plane's position was unknown at the time of the last message and the fighter could have been anywhere up to seventy miles northwest of Tampa. What did the Air Force mean when they stated the "last coherent transmission" from the jet was at 5:42 p.m.? At 5:43 p.m., "the last radio sound" from the jet indicated it was down to 8,000 feet. Was this transmission incoherent? What actually occurred at 8,000 feet when the radio transmission faded out?

j). Did the jet run out of fuel, or was this a cover story? *Since the jet was running low on fuel, why was it being directed over the Gulf waters?* Had the jet used extra fuel during the time Jones was allegedly lost? Had Jones put his plane into afterburner (which requires more fuel)? If so, why would Lt. Jones engage the jet's afterburners if he was low on fuel? The engagement of afterburners would indicate that Jones was attempting to intercept an aircraft, or was he being chased and trying to out run an aircraft?

k). During this entire time Jones' plane would have been visible on radar as well as in radio contact with three bases. Search planes would have been sent out to search along his route if his course was known. It seems unlikely that the radar systems at all three military bases as well as radar stations along the coast were unable to keep track of this jet. These radar systems were not only used to track U.S. aircraft but to detect any potential threatening aircraft entering U.S. airspace. Another puzzling question: why did Jones and DelCurto not bail out, which is standard procedure for the crew of a doomed aircraft?

The Jones and DelCurto incident was not the only unusual incident that happened in northern Florida on that night. The article, "Balloon Is Found In Tree" was published on September 16, in *The Daytona Beach Morning Journal* and appeared on the same page next to the missing airmen article. It reported the following information:

Members of the Tallahassee Civil Air Patrol yesterday reported recovering a strange paper balloon from the top of a tall pine tree where they saw it land Saturday. CAP men engaged in a search for a missing plane spotted the object drifting along about 25 miles an hour near the Tallahassee airport. CAP Col.

Wally Schanz, State Aviation Director, reported the location of the tree in which it landed. The next morning, a CAP cadet shinnied up the tree and pulled it down. It was a hot air balloon apparently made of rice paper over a wire frame. The paper was in panels of white, green and blue. Attached to it were streamers of white, green and red paper. It contained no writing or markings. In the inside, there was a wire bracket for a heating element. The interior was badly smoked but there was no indication of what type of fuel was used to provide hot air to raise the balloon. It is being turned over to military authorities.

In review, the CAP is a semi-military volunteer organization supervised and administered by the Air Force and trained to assist in emergencies. The balloon was first sighted on September 13 when it landed in a tree. Its location was reported and it was retrieved the following day. The strange balloon was discovered the day after two Air Force jets disappeared. Had the CAP men been searching for Lt. Jones' missing jet fighter or the lost observation jet when they found the balloon? Did something unreported occur in the Tallahassee area on September 12 that linked the balloon to the missing jets? This story raised more questions than it answered.

Another story called "Mystery Object Frightened His Cattle" was reported in *The Daytona Beach Morning Journal*. This article also appeared on the same page as the "Odd Balloon" story in Tallahassee. It reads:

Floyd Brown, a milker at the Everglades Experiment Station, said yesterday "a large red lighted object" scared some cattle he was trying to milk early Sunday. Brown told civil defense authorities he went out to milk the cows about 4:30 a.m. and saw "a large red lighted object" over the barn in the trees, about 100 feet above the ground. The lighted object settled down to within about 40 feet of the ground with a whistling sound and the cattle bolted, he declared. Then the object moved off. Brown said he rounded up the cattle and was just driving them into the barn. When the object appeared, again the cattle bolted. The milker was alone at the time.

Belle Glade is on the south side of Lake Okeechobee. This object was "100 feet above the ground in the trees," which precluded it having been a conventional aircraft. Brown also said it settled to within 40 feet off the ground, which I interpreted to mean hovering downward from 100 feet. No mention was made of engine noise or any sounds associated with conventional aircraft. This object appeared again after having moved off the first time. This is not behavior exhibited by a meteor, but instead is consistent with controlled maneuvers made by a craft with intelligent guidance.

The search for the Starfire continued on Monday, shifting to the Gulf of Mexico. The last piece of information I found occurred on Wednesday. This was two days after fishermen had reported hearing shouts while fishing, and six consecutive days of search for Jones. I found no

142

further newspaper reports on the search. However, General Benjamin Chidlaw told Jones' family the search had continued for eight days.

The military's story about the missing airmen was filled with blatant inconsistencies, time gaps, and vague explanations. The families of the two airmen, and the media were actually given misinformation by the Air Force. My research indicates that the story told by the USAF concerning the disappearance of Jones and DelCurto was partially fabricated. The communications from the Air Force to the next of kin and news services were not all outright lies though.

Instead, they were fragments of truth, fragments that did not mesh to form a logical timeline or a coherent set of facts. The military's story had too many holes in it and did not make sense.

The Starfire's disappearance spread so quickly throughout the media, that the Air Force did not have time to prepare a sufficiently believable cover-up story. It is also worth noting that when I was corresponding with several Florida newspaper archivists who were sending me articles, several of them called me and had raised points of inconsistencies contained in the news releases!

Runways at MacDill AFB in Tampa, Florida

CHAPTER FIFTEEN

CASE: 52-9-12-4

To this day, the two flyers and their F-94B Starfire jet have never been found. Second Lt. John A. Jones Jr. and Second Lt. John S. DelCurto simply vanished off the face of the earth without a trace. For more than 50 years, they were forgotten about by most and their families never had closure. I will never forget the moment that I found Second Lt. Jones memorial head stone marker at the cemetery located in Ocala, Florida in the summer of 1999. I found it after researching this story for about seven years.

At first, I was excited because I found it, and then I became sad. As I looked down at the head stone that was over grown with grass and weeds, I knelt down and cleaned them away from the stone marker. I brushed away the sediment from the face of the stone and a chill ran through me when I saw the date of Jones' death carved in stone. The date of his death was the day that he vanished on "September 12, 1952." Not the day he was officially declared dead by the Air Force on "22 October 1952."

IN MEMORY OF
JOHN A. JONES, JR.
FLORIDA
2D LT. US AIR FORCE
NOV 12 1928   SEPT 12 1952

As I stared at the memorial, John Jones Jr. became more than just a name that I had read about in a few newspaper articles and reports. I felt very sad as I put a small American flag into the ground next to his long forgotten and neglected memorial. I then thought, "John, if only I could talk to you, I would have a lot of questions to ask!" I needed some answers to the many questions about this incident.

When Stanton Friedman visited the National Archives in 2005 to research the declassified Air Force accident reports he focused on 1952. Friedman requested, received and looked through the 1952 aircraft accident documents. The Air Force recorded aircraft accidents for each month that included statistical documentation, which contained fighter aircraft accident information.

Friedman went in search of the September 1952 statistics documents and discovered they were all removed from the file.

Shortly after, I discovered that the once classified the Air Force's reports of Major "Aircraft Accidents of 1952" had been declassified by the government. "The Directorate of Flight Safety Research," located at Norton Air Force Base in San Bernardino, California, documented these original reports. These reports were recorded on 16 mm microfilm reels from, the "Department of the Air Force – Air Force Research Historical Agency – Maxwell AFB, Alabama." I quickly contacted Stanton T. Friedman and told him about the declassified reports. In turn, he contacted the microfilm archivist in charge of the Air Force reels. Friedman called me back and said the Jones and DelCurto case was verified and contained on it, according to the microfilm representative. Stanton T. Friedman then sent for the reel, received it and sent it to me in Florida. Finally, I had the case report in my hands and was anxious to review it.

I scanned the reel and the incident involving Second Lt. John A. Jones Jr. and Second Lt. John S. DelCurto was indeed on the microfilm. Furthermore, this incident was only one case out of eleven known cases that were documented on September 12. The Jones and DelCurto case was recorded by the USAF as case number "52-9-12-4." It was the fourth major accident documented of the eleven recorded for that day.

When I looked through the eleven case files, the first thing that I noticed was that two major aircraft accident cases were removed. The two files missing were case numbers three and five. These were the cases just before and after the Jones and DelCurto incident case. There is no reference at all to these two missing cases; they are simply absent from the microfilm. There is not one page of documentation for either one of these cases... they are gone! The only way I knew that both cases were missing is they are listed in sequential order and the case numbers jumped. These two cases were actually pulled and put into another higher classification than the others that were already considered "restricted."

Why were both cases "52-9-12-3" and "52-9-12-5" removed from the major Aircraft Accidents for September 12, 1952? What was contained in each of the cases that the USAF does not want the public to see? How many aircraft were involved in each of these major accident reports and what kind of major accidents were they? *Moreover, were there any more September 12, 1952 cases removed after the last known case, the eleventh case that was recorded as the "52-9-12-11" accident case? We would never know because there would be no way to track and identify any cases after the last listed case. An ingenious way to remove documents from the record without leaving a trace of evidence, there would be no sequential case numbers to compare after the eleventh accident case! Once again, official 1952 Air Force aircraft accident documents for the month of September were missing. How many jet fighter accidents and disappearances really occurred on September 12, 1952?*

Another major jet accident that occurred on September 12, 1952 that involved Tyndall AFB was not documented in the "Aircraft Accidents For 1952" files. *The Tampa Tribune* documented this incident on September 13, 1952. The information appeared in the article, "Pilot Bails Out, Lands Safely After MacDill Hears Distress Call." It states that, "The pilot of a jet observation plane ran into technical trouble during a training flight today [September 12], and bailed out after heading the plane in the direction of The Gulf of Mexico." The pilot of the jet was said to have, "radioed in to his base at Tyndall that he was setting the controls so the jet would come down far out in the Gulf."

Why is this accident not documented by the Air Force? Was the incident one of the two cases that were missing from the eleven known September 12 documented cases? Regardless, this major accident is not documented. *The Tampa Tribune* article that disclosed this incident also stated the following information about the pilot in this incident: "His name wasn't learned immediately." I have never found the follow-up story about this pilot at all. This major accident was forgotten about long ago.

The Jones and DelCurto incident was not forgotten about. Even though this incident *never* made headlines across the country, the Florida press heavily documented it. It does not surprise me that this case was finally declassified after more than a half century. I personally believe that if the case had not been declassified and made available to the public, it would have raised more suspicion because the U.S. government had become aware of my research from the manuscript of the original 2004 printing of this book.

I then transferred the entire case report to paper so I could read it. Then I read and reviewed the case # "52-9-12-4" involving the mystery of the lost jet and its crew. It was more than 65-pages long. Sixty-five pages of some of the most convoluted information I have ever read. The information set forth in the Jones and DelCurto incident was comparable to the Air Force's meteor and "Flatwoods Monster" explanation for that same night. Whoever concocted the explanations given about the "Flatwoods Monster" Incident, probably wrote the script for the Jones and DelCurto story.

Of course, the documents in the case did not refer to flying saucers or UFOs. That would have made it too obvious and easy to link the lost jet together with the UFO events that night. I had never expected that there would be any reference to UFOs or saucers in the Jones and DelCurto documents. After I reviewed this case many of my questions were finally answered, but several more questions arose. The intentions of the Air Force in this particular incident were blatant and obvious. The information that appears in this accident report involved a massive COVER-UP. Moreover, I will say that it was covered up very poorly.

These two flyers were allegedly on a "routine weather training mission" according to Colonel BT. Kleine of Tyndall AFB. Air Defense Commander Benjamin Chidlaw stated that what occurred next, "When the weather deteriorated all aircraft were recalled and instructed to proceed to Moody AFB."

As I read and reviewed the 65 pages of declassified documents and found that, several documents in the case file were not there. There were several chosen extracts from other documents included but not the entire reports. Included in the 65 page report were Air Force forms, a preliminary report, the AF Aircraft Accident report, statements and aircraft information, to name a few. Also included were the very important transcripts for two "Board proceedings" conducted by "The Aircraft Accident Investigating Board." The first meeting occurred on "29 September 1952" and the second on "3 October 1952." Both board proceedings were held at Tyndall AFB in Panama City, Florida.

The Directorate of Flight Safety Research located at Norton Air Force Base in San Bernardino, California, received information on aircraft accidents as they occurred. Their officials decided whether if their personnel would conduct the investigation or those of a local base. Author Alfred Goldberg explains this in, "A History of the United States Air Force: 1907-1957." He states, "Directorate personnel actually investigated only a small percentage of the USAF major accidents, selected because they involved new aircraft, indicated new accident trends, or presented unusual technical difficulties."

I extracted information from these documents where information was given. I then formed a detailed timeline of the incident. I compared information from several different documents and reports and pieced them together. I also compared and cross-referenced the information contained

146

in these 65 pages with the telegrams and letters sent to the pilot's brother shortly after the incident occurred. In addition, I utilized the Florida newspapers that followed the Jones and DelCurto incident. The earliest of these articles were quite valuable as they contained the first information about the incident from the initial September 12, 1952 USAF press conference in Tampa, Florida.

By utilizing, the information contained in all of these sources I was able to put together a complete time line of events according to what the USAF said happened. The incident involving the disappearance of Jones & DelCurto still does not add up according to the USAF version. The declassified documents are more convoluted than the press information and the information contained in the Air Force telegrams and letter sent to the pilot's brother.

I will point out the many inconsistencies in the Air Force's story. The USAF officially stated, "The primary cause of this accident was the pilot failed to keep himself oriented at all times while on instruments." The convoluted time line of events tells a different story, which indicate Jones and DelCurto were not on a "routine weather training mission" on September 12, 1952.

Some of the most pertinent information I found useful in this case was extracted from the two board proceedings held at Tyndall AFB in Tampa. Documentation for the first board meeting states the following, "1. The Aircraft Accident Investigating Board convened at 0830 hours, 29 September 1952 in the Wing Conference Room at Tyndall Air Force Base, Florida for the purpose of investigating a major aircraft accident involving F-94B, NO. 50-819A piloted by 2nd Lt. John A. Jones, Jr. To date the aircraft and crew are still missing."

The six men from the board involved were, "Major Peter E. Pompetti, the acting board president, 3 members; Major Roderick E. McCaskill, Major Wesley I. McKee and Major Joseph E. Wisby. Also present were, "Medical member, Captain Leo Jivoff and the recorder Captain John L. Armour." Pompetti said the purpose of the board meeting was said to be "strictly fact-finding."

During this investigation, the board questioned three key Tyndall persons involved in this incident. They were Capt. Phillip P. Harrison, flight instructor of "B" flight, 1st Lt. Robert A. Dunn, Tyndall AFB approach control officer and Captain Oran E. Need, weather officer. After these individuals were questioned on Monday, September 29, 1952, the board decided it needed "additional evidence." Documentation states it would be "necessary in order to reach a comprehensive conclusion in this case." Subsequently, a second meeting was scheduled four days later on Friday, "3 October 1952." The Aircraft Accident Investigating Board reconvened on Friday and interviewed an additional Air Force witness; the Approach Controller who was on duty in Tyndall AFB tower, his name S/Sgt. Ernest S. Bolen.

During both meetings that week, each man was called before the board for questioning, administered the oath and testified before the board. Major Pompetti used the same basic opening to each man before the questioning commenced. He stated, "The purpose of this board is strictly fact-finding. It is not punitive in any sense of the word. We are here to read the testimony in file and to listen to other testimony, which might not be covered in the statements; to delve into the circumstances surrounding this accident and try to reach a conclusion, which might prevent accidents of this nature from occurring again. Do you understand?"

It is interesting to note that the only individual who was *not* asked, "Do you understand" was the flight instructor, "Captain Harrison." On several occasions throughout the two board proceedings, Major Pompetti and his men had trouble getting straight answers from the Tyndall AFB men. Numerous times, when the board members asked them direct questions, they only received very vague answers. The Tyndall AFB men involved in the Jones and DelCurto incident were blatantly evasive with several of their answers, when asked direct questions.

It is obvious that the persons at Tyndall AFB, as well as several others involved in this incident from other bases and locations had been silenced. After I analyzed and dissected the transcripts of these two board meetings, I found several inconsistencies in the story. It was obvious that the Aircraft Accident Investigating Board was frustrated with many of the answers it received.

Subsequently, because the first board meeting was so convoluted, a second meeting had to be scheduled later that Friday to reach a conclusion about the incident. I believe, and it is obvious, that the Aircraft Accident Investigating Board was in the dark during the first "fact finding" meeting on that Monday; they were the outsiders. Something happened behind closed doors at Tyndall over the next four days until the second meeting, which caused a complete turnaround in the case, ending it swiftly. Interestingly, the first three Tyndall men who were questioned during the September 29 meeting were *not* recalled for questioning during the October 3 meeting!

By separating, comparing and cross-referencing all of the information I had concerning the incident, the inconsistencies continued to build up. The blatant lies and outlandish cover-ups began to surface as well. The Air Force had presented an illogical case. Tyndall AFB was the headquarters of the Advanced Interceptor, 3626 Fly Tng-Gp. (AI) Tyndall AFB, FL. Jones had his wings and DelCurto was in training at the time they disappeared. The jet that the two flyers were flying was a Lockheed F-94B Starfire, "No. 50-819A," the second Starfire jet in the series.

Lockheed F-94B Starfire All-weather Night-fighter

The F-94B Starfire preceded the F-94C and 357 were ordered by the USAF and put into operation. This jet was an "All-weather night-fighter" and carried a two-man crew, a pilot and rear-seat radar observer.

During the first few months of 1951, the new F-94B Starfire jet interceptors began to arrive at several American Air Force bases and put into service. The B-model Starfire, an improved version of the F-94A, had received numerous internal improvements. This included a larger hydraulic system, a better pressurization system, and new gyroscopic instruments, including a Sperry Zero Reader. It also received new 230-gallon fuel wing tip-tanks, which were centrally mounted, unlike the earlier "A" model's under-slung wing tanks. The F-94B Starfire jet fighter had a total fuel capacity of 648 gallons and a range of 1,079 miles.

The F-94B was armed with four .50 caliber M-3 machine guns, each allocated with 300 rounds of ammo, which protruded slightly from each of the gun ports. They were mounted just beneath the Hughes E-1 Fire Control System radar, which was located behind the radome and coupled to the AN/APG-33 radar system. The F-94B had a maximum speed of approximately 600 MPH and a maximum service ceiling of 47,000 feet.

Lockheed F-94A Starfire All-weather Jet Interceptor in Flight

In April of 1951, the first F-94 Starfires were utilized during the Korean War. Four FEAF squadrons of the 68 FIS at Itazuke Air Base, Japan, flew F-94A and B model Starfires to provide air defense for American facilities in Japan and Okinawa.

Throughout the war, Starfires dropped over 1,000 tons of

bombs on Korea during night interdiction sorties. They were also utilized to intercept enemy planes that were attacking American B-29 bombers on night missions.

Lockheed F-94B Starfire All-weather Night-fighter in Flight

The F-94 Starfires were also utilized in the defense of the United States during the Cold War era of the early 1950s.

This was especially true as the F-94 Starfires based in America during that time were frequently used on intercept missions against UFOs, more commonly known as "flying saucers."

To this day, the two flyers and their F-94B Starfire jet have never been found. Second Lt. John A. Jones Jr. and 2nd Lt. John S. DelCurto simply vanished off the face of the earth without a trace on September 12, 1952.

They have been forgotten about by most and their disappearance has never been officially explained. The USAF does not know where these two airmen are…or do they?

Occasionally, I will visit 2nd Lt. Jones memorial head stone marker at the cemetery located in Ocala, Florida. Yes, some of us remember and some want us to forget!

CHAPTER SIXTEEN

THE TRUTH?

The United States Air Force Dictionary gives the following information, "Tyndall Air Force Base. An AF base at Panama City, Florida, named for Lieutenant Frank B. Tyndall, a WW I fighter pilot, killed in 1930." As I was researching this case and writing this book, I often wondered; what questions would Lt. Tyndall have asked if he were present at those two "Aircraft Accident Investigating Board" meetings? How would this fighter pilot have handled the situations as they unfolded? Would Lt. Tyndall have believed the testimonies that were being told to the board? Now, ask yourself the same questions as you read the following declassified information.

POINT 1: THE ADDITIONAL JETS INVOLVED

The first point to raise in this incident; there was no mention to the press at the original press conference, that Lt. Jones was flying with "three other jets." It was presumed that he was flying alone. The only mention of the additional aircraft involved was sent to the Jones family. The recently declassified documents now state, that Jones and DelCurto were said to be part of the "B" flight with five other jets. All six jets were said to be F-94B Starfire all-weather interceptors, on a "local weather proficiency flight." The first segment of this incident involves the actual take-off time of the six Starfires from Tyndall AFB. They were said to have departed Tyndall AFB between 1:47 p.m. and 2:26 p.m. CST. Lt. Jones and DelCurto were documented as the fourth jet to depart the base at "1408C," 2:08 p.m. CST in jet # 0819.

POINT 2: AIRCRAFT OF "B" FLIGHT WERE NOT RECALLED
BECAUSE OF DETERIORATING WEATHER

On September 13, 1952, Tyndall sent a teletype of their "Preliminary Report of a Major Accident" to several USAF bases. The Directorate of Flight Safety Research at Norton AFB received one of the reports. Contained in the declassified documents was a letter from the Office of the Inspector General at Norton AFB, California to Tyndall AFB.

In this letter, the Executive Director of Flight Safety Research, Lt. Col. Warlick, asked seven questions in reference to the Jones/DelCurto Incident. It stated, "req fol info" [request following information]. The letter was dated "16 September 1952." Two questions of interest are as follows:

Question #5, "Description [of] weather deterioration from takeoff time until recalled to Tyndall?"

Question #6, "What was forecast weather and why were aircraft not recalled sooner?"

On the following day, "17 Sept 1952" Tyndall AFB sent a teletype to Norton AFB with answers. Question #5 was answered, "Aircraft were not recalled, were holding and letting down on IFR [Instrument Flight Rules] clearances under control of Tyndall Approach Control." Question #6 was also answered. It stated, "1500 BN 8000 overcast 2 miles rain; all aircraft were on IFR clearances and under control of Tyndall Approach Control."

I will now show the four previous statements made by the USAF between September 13 and September 17, 1952:

1). Sept 13, 1952. 8:54. Preliminary Report Of A major Accident AFHQ Form O-309..."When weather started to deteriorate, all aircraft were recalled"

2). Sept 13, 1952. 9:04. Teletype of Preliminary Report Of A Major Accident..."When weather started to deteriorate all aircraft were recalled."

3). Sept 15, 1952. 3:27 p.m.
MacDill Western Union Telegram. General Benjamin W. Childlaw - Commanding General ADC – Ent AFB, Co. MacDill..."When the weather deteriorated. All aircraft were recalled and instructed to land at Moody."

4). Sept 17, 1952.
Letter from "B. T. Kleine Colonel, USAF Commanding. HQ 3625th FTW - Tyndall AFB (Advanced Interceptor)..."When the weather started to become near our minimum, all of the aircraft were called to come back to the field."

It is obvious that Norton AFB officials were obviously puzzled by the explanations that Tyndall AFB officials presented and wanted some answers. Why did Tyndall AFB officials release four prior false statements? What were the officials at Tyndall AFB trying to conceal? How many other false statements were made by Tyndall AFB officials?

POINT 3: INFORMATION REVEALS TYNDALL AFB LOSES POWER AS JETS PREPARE TO LAND

The truth has been revealed that the six jets were not recalled because of deteriorating weather. What was said to have occurred next, as the first of six jets prepared to land at Tyndall AFB, is questionable. Tyndall AFB Flight Instructor Capt. Harrison stated the following information on Sept. 29 to the Aircraft Accident Investigating Board members, "About an hour after the first one got off they were all at altitudes on top and working assigned quadrants of range; it came for approach times and one of them was already making his approach. About that time, Tyndall range went off the air. Immediately several called in and said their radio compass was out and all they could hear was static. I advised them the range was off the air."

Captain Harrison gave the following information in his statement dated, "23 September 1952." In this document he states, "No difficulties arose until Tyndall Range went off the air. At that time about three ships called for steers; one was Lt. Jones in aircraft #819."

The Report of AF Aircraft Accident reported the following information in "Section O. Description of Accident." It stated, "Tyndall radio range went off the air at 1440 C and was off until 1445 C. During this time, Lt. Jones called for a D/F steer back to the station."

The following information appeared in the Tyndall AFB teletype, "Preliminary Report of a Major Accident" dated Sept. 13. It stated, "When jet acft started letting down procedures Tyndall Range went off the air. It was off the air from 1440 to 1445 CST" [2:40-2:45 CST].

Norton AFB official Lt. Col. Warlick asked the following in his "16 September 1952" letter to Tyndall AFB officials, "Reason Tyndall range went off air." On "17 September 1952," the following day Tyndall answered, "AACS power maint. Personnel were making a power change-over CH in order to test the emerg power. The emerg power did not take over and the radio range went off the air until the tower operators called in and ADV the power maint personnel to reset the commercial power."

The "Airway and Air Communications service" at Tyndall AFB actually claimed to have tested their emergency power while the six jets of "B Flight" were preparing to land. They claim that the emergency power failed to go on and their "radio range went off the air" for five minutes. The power maintenance personnel were supposedly contacted by the Tyndall tower operators and advised to reset the commercial power. This scenario as presented by Tyndall AFB is absurd. Power Maintenance personnel do not pull the plug on an air force base and make a "changeover" so they can "test the emergency power," whenever they feel like it. This would be a very dangerous practice. A test of this nature would have been scheduled with the entire base. A surprise power outage could have had catastrophic results especially when a group of six F-94 Starfire jets was preparing to land. This explanation does not seem plausible.

During this time in 1952, the US government was anticipating a Soviet nuclear assault by long-range bombers. Tensions ran high and air force bases were on a 24-hour alert to scramble jet fighters toward any airborne intruders. Was it common practice during the Cold War, for base commanders to allow their Power Maintenance personnel to perform unscheduled power changeover tests? Did Tyndall AFB actually allow such risky and dangerous actions to take place? Tensions were high enough at these bases without the addition of any other surprises, like cutting your power unannounced.

How many other equipment malfunctions actually occurred on that day besides the "radio range" power loss? Was the power loss at Tyndall AFB really caused by an unscheduled power changeover test? Captain Harrison explained the following information when he was questioned by Major Pompetti and board members, "Q. How long was the [Tyndall AFB] range off the air - Do you know? A. It was off the air long enough for them to finish one pilot up from penetration and bring another one all the way down. Why did the board ask Harrison, "Do you know?" Harrison was the flight instructor and should have known. It seems the board was becoming more suspicious evident by their sarcasm?

Pompetti also asked, "Q. How many ships at one time were they working? A. About three." Capt. Harrison also told the board, "The man [pilot] who was making a letdown was brought in using D/F. The next man was brought in all the way with D/F."

The pilots of these jets actually made visual landings with the aid of Tyndall AFB directional finder to guide them in. The pilots used VFR/Visual Flight Rules procedures. The visibility in the Tyndall AFB area was good at that time, so the aid of instruments or IFR/Instrument Flight Rules was not necessary. Approach Controller 1st Lt. Dunn actually stated in his signed "Certificate" that the first two jets "cancelled their instrument flight rules" plans.

At this point in the incident, the first two F-94 jets of B-Flight were brought down and landed at Tyndall AFB, they were "AF-1332" and "AF-0867." Four jets remained in the air, including Jones and DelCurto in jet "AF-0819." Captain Harrison said the following in his statement, "By this time the weather was getting a little bad (light rain) so I decided to send the top four ships in the stack to their alternate [Moody AFB]."

Captain Oran E. need, The Tyndall AFB Weather officer on duty that day was questioned by Major Pompetti and the board. He stated the following information about the four jets that did not land at Tyndall. Captain Need stated, "After 1500 C [3:00 p.m. CST] there was not much doubt in my mind—but what they would have to [do is] make IFR letdown at the home terminal, Tyndall or cancel and go to their alternate." Captain Need then made this statement contradicting Capt. Harrison's decision to land the four jets at Tyndall using IFR, "In my opinion, I could not see why the pilots could not clear IFR [Instrument Flight Rules]."

Why didn't the jets land at Tyndall AFB using their Instrument Flight Rules? Why did Captain Harrison redirect the four jets away from Tyndall AFB because of "light rain"? Even the Tyndall AFB weather officer could not understand "why the pilots could not clear IFR." Was there another reason that flight instructor Captain Harrison redirected the four jets toward Moody AFB in Valdosta, GA?

Actual Photograph of F-94B Starfire "AF-0867"

POINT 4: CONVOLUTED STATEMENTS FROM TYNDALL TOWER
THE COVER-UP BEGINS TO UNRAVEL

At this point in the incident, I cross-referenced information between flight instructor Capt. Harrison, Tower Approach Control Officer, 1st Lt. Dunn and Approach Controller S/Sgt. Bolen. Harrison stated the following, "At this time #819 was not over the station so I told the Tower Officer [1st Lt. Dunn], who was working with him on D/F to direct him [Jones] to his alternate when he got back over the base, which he did. Capt. Harrison explained this segment further to Major Pompetti and the board members, "#819 [Jones] was not back over the station at that time. About five minutes later they [approach controllers] got him over the station."

Harrison also told them, "When Lt. Jones got back over the station, he was at 29,000 ft and acknowledged he was proceeding to his alternate [Moody AFB]."

Tyndall AFB Approach Controller, S/Sgt. Bolen told a different story to Major Pompetti and the board members. The board asked the following question which was answered by Bolen, "Q. Do you feel sure in your mind that the aircraft [0819] was ever actually over the station before he [Jones] departed Moody—that he actually departed from Tyndall to Moody? A. I can't say."

Capt. Harrison continued his version of the incident and told the board the following, "I asked Lt. Dunn to tell #819 [Jones] to pick up a heading of 075° to Tallahassee and when over Tallahassee, to contact Moody D/F on 'D' channel and call for a homer. Tyndall Approach Control Officer Dunn stated the following to the board concerning this section of the incident, "Q. Did you relay instructions to #819 [Jones] to depart to his alternate [Moody AFB]? A. yes sir. Q. In these instructions, was he instructed to report to Moody D/F over Tallahassee? A. Not that I remember."

It is obvious that flight instructor Captain Harrison was not on the same page as his men. Why was Captain Harrison telling a different version of the incident from what the two approach control operators told? Were these statements involving this segment of the incident a fabrication? Was the entire scenario involving this incident a complete fabrication?

POINT 5: CONFLICTING INFORMATION CONCERNING JONES REDIRECTION DEPARTURE TIME TO MOODY AFB

There are two different times in the 65-page report for Lt. Jones redirection departure time to Moody AFB. This was the point in time when he was sent to his alternate base, while flying over the Tyndall AFB area. The "Report of AF Aircraft Accident" states Jones' time of redirection at 3:35 p.m. It states, "It is assumed that 0819 departed Tyndall AFB at 1535 with 289 gallons of fuel on board."

On the contrary, a signed "CERTIFICATE" by 1st Lt. Dunn, Approach Control officer states, "Pilot asked for a VHF/DF steer to the [Tyndall] field and was brought back over the field at 29,000 [ft] and instructed to go to his alternate at approximately 1525 [3:25 p.m.]." Why is it, the Air Force *"assumed"* the information that they used in this segment of the incident? Why is there a ten minute differential between these two documents for the same event? Was the time 3:25 p.m. or was it 3:35 p.m.? This is a big difference when piloting a jet fighter!

Was this just another hapless mistake on the part of the Tyndall Tower controllers when logging their times, or just a sloppy mistake in record keeping? On the other hand, was the USAF intentionally trying to confuse the times and facts contained in the official documentation of this incident? Whatever the excuse may be, it is obvious that they could not keep track of their story—or their jet!

Harrison explained what allegedly occurred next, "In the meantime we contacted Moody. They were alerted and had already worked one aircraft sent over there. Others were on their way; there were three already gone. Lt. Jones was the last one. Now Jones and DelCurto were allegedly en route to Moody AFB in Valdosta, GA. That was the last we heard of him for a while until we heard him calling Moody Approach Control on 'B' channel. He [Jones] was coming in clear at that time."

1st Lt. Dunn explained what happened next while in front of the board during his questioning, "Q. Did the person who was monitoring D/F in Tyndall Tower [or working D/F], did they hear

0819 calling Moody D/F for a steer over Tallahassee? A. I heard him calling Moody on 'B' channel."

The board then made an inquiry about the time and asked, "Q. When you first heard him ask Moody for a steer do you know what time it was? A. Somewhere around 1600 [4:00 p.m. CST] — I can't be sure." Why was Lt. Dunn unsure of the time at this point?

Lt. Jones should have reached Moody AFB in about fifteen minutes from Tyndall AFB. After an approximate twenty-five to thirty-five minute time lapse, the pilot was finally heard over the airwaves. At approximately 4:00 p.m. CST, Jones and DelCurto were still en route to Moody and had not landed yet. Where were the airmen during this time they were overdue and what were they doing? Why had they not landed yet?

The board questioned Lt. Dunn further. The following transpired:

Q. At any time during this incident did you or anyone else instruct #819 to switch to 'D' channel?
A. No-not to my knowledge.
Q. Was there some reason for not switching to 'D' channel?
A. No – I don't know of any reason for not switching to 'D' channel. [Note: There was contact with jet)
Q. The reason I asked the question is because it is obvious from the statements in file that at approximately 1600 [4:00 p.m. CST] this thing was reaching emergency stages, yet we evidently did not go to emergency frequencies. My question is why?
A. There I think it is the pilot's responsibility to go to D channel if he considers himself emergency."

When Jones and DelCurto were overdue, and not heard from between twenty-five and thirty-five minutes later, were they actually on another mission? Is this why there was a delay in their arrival time at Moody? Furthermore, what was the reason that Lt. Jones did not go to an emergency frequency? Was it because he did not consider himself in an emergency? Was Jones really lost at 4:00 p.m.?

POINT 6: THE TRUTH ABOUT THE RADIO COMPASS

Jones and DelCurto proceeded toward Moody AFB to attempt a landing. At this point in the incident, the pilot was in radio contact with tower controllers at Tyndall AFB.

Another Air Force base that was monitoring the situation intervened. MacDill AFB in Tampa stepped into the picture and attempted to assist the pilot. MacDill's RDF named Homer, a high frequency radio directional finder had tracked Lt. Jones and DelCurto. *The Panama City News Herald* stated the following information on September 14, 1952, "MacDill operations told him [Lt. Jones] to attempt a landing at Valdosta, GA. and gave him a fix…failure of a radio compass was believed to be the cause of the pilot's non-compliance with the order directing him to land in Valdosta."

MacDill AFB Public Information Officer Captain Mitchell stated the following at the Sept. 12, 1952 press conference in Tampa, "First inkling that the craft was in trouble came when the pilot called Tyndall Air Force Base. He was directed to land at Valdosta, GA [by MacDill] but for some reason, failed to comply with orders."

The MacDill Public Information Officer also said, "The plane was apparently lost and Air Force officials speculated that its radio compass failed." They said this may have been the reason Lt. Jones "failed to comply with orders" to land.

At this point in the incident, at approximately 4:00 p.m. CST, the USAF "speculated" that the radio compass had malfunctioned. During this time, the Tyndall AFB tower operator was in contact with the pilot of the supposedly lost jet. Captain Harrison then stated, "We were reading him very weakly."

The first radio compass information released by the USAF at the September 12 press conference actually was not speculative. Captain Harrison revealed the truth about the condition of the Starfire's radio compass on September 29 to Major Pompetti and the board. **Harrison was asked the following question, "Q. Did he [Lt. Jones] mention any malfunction of the radio compass after the [Tyndall AFB] range went back on the air? A. *No sir.*"**

A failed radio compass *was not* the factor "of the pilot's non-compliance with the order directing him to land in Valdosta." At this point in the incident the Air Force stated, "The plane was apparently lost." Could the weather over Moody AFB in Valdosta, GA, have been a contributing factor to Jones being "apparently lost"? Captain Need, the Tyndall AFB Weather Officer on duty during the incident, stated the following information to Major Pompetti and the board:

"Q. Did the forecast at Moody change any from what you forecast it to be during the period from the time the aircraft were flying?
A. It never changed to IFR. It did get very light rain, visibility remained 10 mi., VFR weather, ceilings remained the same. I believe that appears on the clearance."

The weather over Moody AFB was not bad at all, only "very light rain." There was a ten-mile visibility the pilots that preceded Jones to Moody AFB "never" had their orders "changed to IFR." Because there was a ten-mile visibility, the pilots were able to bring in their jets and land visually without instruments. These pilots used "Visual Flight Rules" because the weather was not a deterrent factor. When Lt. Jones "called Tyndall AFB" and was "directed to land at Valdosta, GA," what was the reason he "failed to comply with orders to land"?

The "Medical Report of AF Aircraft Accident" document explained what occurred next, "He [Jones] called Tyndall Approach Control and was given a VHF/DF steer to return to TAFB [Tyndall AFB]."

POINT 7: TALLAHASSEE AIRPORT STEPS INTO THE PICTURE

Captain Harrison explained this segment, "Tyndall started giving him [Lt. Jones] steers since #819 couldn't read Tyndall, instructions were being relayed to Tallahassee tower." Harrison told Major Pompetti that "By working through Tallahassee Tower, which was able to read him, [Lt. Jones could not hear Tyndall AFB, but could hear Tallahassee Airport tower], we [Tyndall tower controllers] relayed headings and steers for him and Tallahassee relayed back information which Lt. Jones had to give."

Tallahassee Airport intervened and allegedly became the go-between communicators for Lt. Jones and Tyndall AFB tower controllers. Why were two USAF bases with the most advanced state-of-the-art equipment unable to communicate with their jet, yet a small airport in Tallahassee was able to have full communications with Lt. Jones?

What occurred approximately fifteen minutes later at 4:15 p.m. CST was never released to the public or to the brothers of the two flyers in 1952.

POINT 8: 2ND LT. JONES DECLARES AN EMERGENCY

At 4:15 p.m. CST, pilot 2nd Lt. Jones declared an emergency to Tyndall AFB tower controllers. This information was found in the 65 page case file in an "Extract from Air Rescue Service Report." This report was sent to "Maxwell AFB, dtd 24 Sept. 52 (to headquarters, Fifth Air Rescue Service), from Tyndall AFB, Panama City FL." It states, "At approximately 1615 C [4:15 p.m. CST]. 12 September, 819 [Lt. Jones] called Tyndall Tower and declared an emergency."

Five days later after Tyndall AFB wrote this letter addressed to Maxwell AFB, Capt. Harrison answered the following question, addressed to him during the first board proceeding, "Q. Did the pilot at any time declare an emergency? A. No sir." What was flight instructor Captain Harrison trying to hide from the board? The cover-up continues to unravel. Why did Lt. Jones declare an emergency at 4:15 p.m.? Why is there no record of what occurred at 4:15 p.m. that prompted Jones to declare an emergency? What occurred at 4:20 p.m. CST and afterward is the most convoluted segment of this incident?

B. T. Kleine, Colonel USAF commanding, Tyndall AFB stated the following in a letter to Lt. Jones brother, "He indicated that he was not sure of his position at 4:20, however, the Tyndall radio directional finding gave him a steer to Tyndall Air Force base."

The following information was contained in the "Report of AF Aircraft Accident" document, "At 1620 [4:20 p.m.] Tyndall Tower heard 0819 [Jones] calling Moody on channel 'B' and took a fix on him."

The report goes on to state, "The inbound steering to Tyndall AFB was 318-degrees." The following information concerning this segment of the incident transpired at the board meeting between Major Pompetti and S/Sgt. Bolen, "Q. [Pompetti] When you heard 819 calling Moody, after that you were able to hear transmissions, were they loud and clear or work?

Tyndall AFB CPS-6 Radar Antenna

A. [Bolen] They were very weak to start with. When he received our first steer of 318-degrees, from that point on - his volume would increase until it was four by four." [NOTE: A four by four course refers to a radio range that beams on-course signals in four different directions.]

S/Sgt. Bolen also told the board that, "Tallahassee advised they were reading 819 loud and clear. Tyndall Tower relayed 318-degree steer through Tallahassee Tower. The aircraft acknowledged steer through Tallahassee." There is not one word of information in the 65 page case report of Lt. Jones location at 4:20 p.m. when Tyndall "took a fix on him."

At that time, Tyndall actually knew where the jet's location was. Why is there no information in the Air Force records about Lt. Jones location at 4:20 p.m.? Was the pilot really lost at that time or were the two airmen of jet 0819 on yet another mission? Why were Tyndall AFB officials being evasive?

POINT 9: FUEL CONSUMPTION OF JET #0819

At 4:20 p.m. CST, the USAF stated that Lt. Jones F-94 Starfire had "94 gals. of fuel left." The "Report of AF Aircraft Accident" document stated the amount of fuel that the jet had when Lt. Jones supposedly was redirected to Moody AFB at 3:35 p.m. It states, "It is assumed that 0819 [Jones] departed Tyndall AFB at 1535[3:35 p.m. CST] with 289 gallons of fuel aboard." By using these Air Force quotes, the following information can be formulated.

Tyndall AFB supposedly redirected Lt. Jones toward Moody AFB after he departed the Tyndall AFB area at 3:35 p.m. CST. At 4:20 p.m. CST, Lt. Jones was supposedly lost and redirected back toward Tyndall AFB. Tallahassee tower relayed information back and forth between Tyndall tower and the jet.

During that 45-minute time span between 3:35 p.m. and 4:20 p.m. CST, Lt. Jones jet used 195 gallons of fuel. Captain Harrison gave the following information in his statement dated "23 September 1952." He said, "The alternate I named was Moody AFB, Georgia. A distance of 139 nautical miles [160 statute miles] and would take 190 gallons of fuel from [Tyndall AFB] deck to reach if it were necessary."

Colonel B. T. Kleine stated the following information in his "17 September 1952" letter to Lt. Jones' brother, "all of the aircraft were called to come back to the [Tyndall AFB] field. Supervisory personnel in the Central Tower advised John and three other aircraft to go to Moody Air Force Base about 15 minutes north of Tyndall."

By combining Capt. Harrison's information together with Colonel Kleine's information, an F-94B would consume 190 gallons of fuel over a distance of 160 statute miles in about 15 minutes, from Tyndall AFB to Moody AFB. The September 17 Tyndall teletype stated, "1620 CST [4:20 p.m. CST] pilot called in with 94 gals." The "Report of AF Aircraft Accident" document stated, "0819 had 94 gals. of fuel left. This information was relayed by Tallahassee Tower because 0819 could not read Tyndall Tower." Lt. Jones jet consumed almost the same amount of fuel — 195 gallons, yet he was in the air for 45 minutes between 3:35 p.m. and 4:20 p.m. CST. How was Lt. Jones Starfire able to stay in the air for 45 minutes on approximately 15 minutes worth of fuel? Why did the USAF have to assume that #0819 had "289 gallons of fuel onboard" at 3:35 p.m.?

At 4:20 p.m. CST, Lt. Jones was in an emergency situation over land and just northwest of Tyndall on a 318- degree bearing. According to Tyndall Tower controller S/Sgt. Bolen, Jones had acknowledged the 318-degree steer from Tallahassee Tower from Tyndall Tower. S/Sgt. Bolen stated the following, "At this time tower contacted Jacksonville control and advised of the situation. Also called Florida State Police to patrol the area between Tyndall and Apalachicola vicinity." S/Sgt. Bolen also stated, "Jacksonville had alerted rescue facilities."

POINT 10: LT. JONES DECLARES ANOTHER EMERGENCY

One minute later at 4:21 p.m. CST, Tyndall AFB relayed a message to Tallahassee Airport who in turn contacted Lt. Jones. The "Report of AF Aircraft Accident" document stated the following, "At 1621C [4:21 p.m.] a second bearing of 320-degrees was given by Tyndall AFB."

The Tyndall AFB "Direction Finding Log" also disclosed more information of what occurred at 4:21 p.m. CST. At that time, the log recorded that Lt. Jones had declared another emergency. The D/F log states, "A/C IDENT-0819. COURSE - 320. TIME - 1621. REMARKS - EB EMER. [Emergency]."

This was the second emergency declared by Jones in six minutes. The first was at 4:15 p.m. CST. At approximately 4:21 p.m., Tyndall tower controllers were steering the jet on a 320-degree course toward their base when the emergency was declared. Lt. Jones was actually on a southeast trajectory near Tyndall AFB when the USAF said he declared the emergency situation. What occurred between 4:21 p.m. and the supposed last contact with the jet at 4:42 p.m. is an absolute travesty. Lt. Jones and Lt. DelCurto never landed at Tyndall AFB, overshot the base, and continued proceeding southeast.

The two flyers passed over the area between Tyndall AFB and just west of Apalachicola. This is the stretch of coastline where S/Sgt. Bolen referenced when the Tyndall Tower allegedly "called Florida State Police to patrol area between Tyndall and the Apalachicola vicinity." Jones and DelCurto never attempted to crash-land nor did they attempt to ditch their jet and eject along this stretch of land. They continued proceeding southeast, passed over the coastline, and then proceeded out over the Gulf of Mexico.

Why did Jones and DelCurto not land at Tyndall AFB? Tyndall Tower had supposedly contacted the Florida State Police. The police were informed to patrol between Tyndall and the Apalachicola vicinity for the jet if it went down along that stretch of coastline. Tyndall Tower controllers therefore must have instructed Lt. Jones to make an emergency landing or ditch between those two points! Why did Jones not attempt a crash-landing or attempt to ditch his plane and eject with DelCurto along the coastline between Tyndall AFB and Apalachicola? Did Jones really declare an emergency at 4:21 p.m. because he was preparing to put the jet down? Why did Jones continue proceeding southeast over the Gulf waters with only about 90 gallons of fuel left?

POINT 11: THE WEATHER

Jones and DelCurto were on a northwest to southeast trajectory, proceeding across the Gulf of Mexico, when Tyndall changed their bearing back to 318-degrees. The "Statement of Weather Officer," by Oran E. Need, Captain USAF gave the following information. On 26 September 1952 Captain Need stated, "This is our stability chart valid for today, 12 September 1952, which shows very unstable air over the entire local area, state of Florida and most of Georgia and South Carolina, with the flow being from SE to NW. We expect thunderstorm activity over that entire area and shower activity.

At 1230C, 12 September, Suntan, which controls the radar operations at this base [Tyndall], is painting solid thunderstorms from 35 miles SE of the station due East for 120 miles throughout the entire SE quadrant approximately 120 miles." Captain Need also stated, "The greater percent of the weather is well to the south and southwest of your alternate, which is Moody, and will not affect your alternate since the flow is to the NW."

Jones and DelCurto were actually flying through and into the direction of the oncoming weather. Why didn't Tyndall AFB controllers turn Lt. Jones around and redirect him back toward their base? Why did Tyndall let the two airmen proceed across the Gulf waters when the jet was low on fuel? Lt. Jones continued to proceed southeast across the Gulf waters when another Air Force base intervened into the situation, MacDill AFB in Tampa.

The very evasive Captain Harrison answered the following question when asked by Major Pompetti and the board, "Q. At what time did MacDill start working him [Jones]? A. I would say it must have been around 1625 [4:25 p.m. CST] because we were giving him, [Lt. Jones] steers through Tallahassee on 'B' channel. All of a sudden he switched to 'C' channel – someone else was working him."

1st Lt. Dunn also made this statement in his signed certificate; "Aircraft switched from 'B' channel to 'C' and started working MacDill." Captain Harrison was also evasive and vague when he made his official "statement" on "23 September 1952" concerning this incident. He also forgot that he answered "No Sir" to the board when he was asked, "Did the pilot at any time declare an emergency?" His statement concerning this segment of the incident when MacDill took over is as follows. Harrison stated the following:

Tyndall started giving him 'steers' since #819 couldn't read Tyndall, instructions were being relayed by Tallahassee Tower. At this time, the tower alerted Jacksonville control of the emergency. About this time, McDill (sic) AFB started working #819 and the Tyndall tower was unable to read any further transmissions from #819. What happened after this time was relayed to Tyndall Tower from McDill (sic) AFB." [End Statement]

Signed Phillip P. Harrison - Captain, USAF.

Besides First Lt. Dunn's questionable answer, concerning the time that MacDill took over and began to steer Jones, there is no official documentation recording the time. Another document contained within the 65-page case file states the following information, "Extract from Air Rescue Service Report, Maxwell AFB, dated 24 September 1952." It states:

A). "819 was given steer of 318-degrees to Tyndall, no time." [No time entered on the log for steer given].
B). "At approximately the same time, MacDill AFB also gave him a steer of 120-degrees to MacDill, no time logged for the steer."
C). "At 1635C [4:35 p.m.], MacDill gave 819 a confirmed class 'A' steer 104-degrees to MacDill; at 1637C [4:37 p.m.], a second bearing of 112-degrees was given."

The information contained in these extracts is very odd. The B. Information extract gives no time for the first MacDill steer of 120-degrees. The information contained in the C. extract does not even recognize the first steer of 120-degrees.
Captain Harrison told Major Pompetti this segment of the incident that concerned MacDill's takeover from Tyndall AFB, "By working through Tallahassee Tower, which was able to read him, we relayed headings and steers for him [Lt. Jones] and Tallahassee relayed back information which Lt. Jones had to give. MacDill then started working since he seemed to be closer to them.
Air Defense Commander, General Chidlaw stated the following in his Western Union telegram to Lt. Jones brother on Sept. 15, 1952, "The Tyndall Tower was directing him to MacDill AFB FLO, which was the nearest base." Tyndall AFB Colonel B. T. Kleine stated the following in his letter, "The Tyndall radio directional finding gave him a steer to Tyndall AFB. MacDill Air Force Base directional finding [Homer] was able to pick up John's voice and gave him a steer also." Captain Harrison stated, "MacDill started working him [Jones] since he seemed to be closer to them?"
MacDill tower controllers gave Jones his first steer when he was only 100 miles southeast of Tyndall. In contrast, the jet was 145 statute miles northwest of MacDill in Tampa. Why didn't they redirect the flyers back to Tyndall field, which was closer?

160

Captain Harrison said in his statement, "The alternate I named was Moody AFB, Georgia, a distance of 139 Naut. miles [160 statute miles] and would take 190 gallons of fuel from the [Tyndall] deck to reach."

Once again, by using Harrison's numbers in this statement to approximate fuel consumption and distance, I ask; how could Lt. Jones Starfire have reached MacDill AFB in Tampa from Tyndall AFB, approximately 245 statute miles away, on about 94 gallons of fuel? Lt. Jones jet would not have even come close to reaching the half waypoint across the Gulf of Mexico to MacDill in Tampa.

Furthermore, the jet was said to have disappeared approximately 70 miles northwest of MacDill AFB, an area approximately 175 miles away from Tyndall. On September 13, *The Tampa Tribune* article reported, "MacDill said the fighter could have been anywhere up to 70 miles northwest of Tampa at the last radio report." MacDill Public Information officers stated, "The plane's position at the time of the last message was unknown, except that it was northwest of Tampa and probably within 70 miles of here [Tampa]."

Lt. Jones jet obviously had more than 94 gallons of fuel left at 4:20 p.m., shortly before he crossed out over the Gulf waters near Apalachicola on his 318-degree bearing. The "Direction Finding Log" shows the "course" for "0819" at "1631" or 4:31 p.m. CST was still "318."

According to the Air Force map that illustrates the four-plotted steers that MacDill gave the jet, the point nearest to MacDill is the number "4" steer. This plotted location of the jet indicates that it was approximately 70 miles northwest of MacDill. This indicates the farthest point that the jet reached along its southeast flight path toward Tampa on its 318-degree bearing given by Tyndall AFB.

On the map, I illustrate an arc that represents the 70-mile point from MacDill AFB, in Tampa. Why is the time at this point documented by the Air Force as 4:35 p.m. CST? The jet allegedly flamed-out at 4:42 p.m. CST. Furthermore, the previous steer, the number "3" steer, is documented at 4:41 p.m. CST. This plotted location indicates the jet at a point approximately 80 miles northwest of MacDill later, six minutes later. The number "2" steer, just before the number "3" steer, documents a time of 4:37 p.m. CST at a distance of 90 miles away from MacDill in Tampa. The plotted points indicate the following information:

A). **Plot 4**. When Jones was nearest to MacDill AFB along his southeast trajectory, approximately 70 miles from Tampa, he turned back northeast at 4:35 p.m. CST. (104-degree steer).

B). **Plot 2**. Lt. Jones proceeded approximately 20 miles northwest of MacDill to an area about 90 miles away from Tampa at 4:37 p.m. CST. (112-degree steer).

C). **Plot 3**. Jones then redirected southeast once again and proceeded 10 miles. Four minutes later, at 4:41 p.m. CST the pilot was approximately 80 miles from MacDill in Tampa. (109-degree steer).

Why was Lt. Jones going back and forth when he should have been continuing toward Tampa to land at MacDill AFB? Why did he redirect away from Tampa at 4:35 p.m., when this was the nearest he came to the base and the coastline? Moreover, Jones' 318-degree bearing was never aligned with the direct path to MacDill in the first place!

Even those outside Military and Aviation institutions are obviously aware that the shortest distance between two points is a straight line. This logic however was not employed on this fateful day when the airmen and their craft vanished.

THE FOLLOWING MAP SHOWS AN OUTLINE OF THE LOST AIRMEN'S FLIGHT PATH

THE LOCATIONS OF THE FOUR AIR FORCE BASES AND AIRPORT INVOLVED IN THE INCIDENT ARE LISTED BELOW:

A). MOODY AFB - VALDOSTA, GEORGIA
B). TALLAHASSEE AIRPORT, FLORIDA
C). TYNDALL AFB - PANAMA CITY, FLORIDA
D). MACDILL AFB - TAMPA, FLORIDA
E). EGLIN AFB - VALPARAISO, FLORIDA

A map displaying the steers that MacDill gave is identified as "mission 5-C-9-12 SEP 52 — (SUSP)" is as follows, [NOTE; MacDill is spelled incorrectly]:

1. "steer of 120 degrees given by McDill – 1" [no time logged]
2. "steer of 112 degrees given by McDill – 2" [4:37 p.m. CST]
3. "steer of 109 degrees given by McDill – 3" [4:41 p.m. CST]
4. "steer of 104 degrees given by McDill – 4" [4:35 p.m. CST]
   "bearing of 318 degrees given by Tyndall"

NOTE: The 318-degree bearing given by Tyndall AFB was the southeast trajectory that Jones followed out over the Gulf of Mexico.

On the map, the 318-degree bearing is represented by the solid line between C. Tyndall AFB and number the #4 point, the 104-degree steer given by MacDill AFB.

This map also shows all the locations for the four steers, 1, 2, 3 and 4 along the solid line, the 318-degree bearing line. This solid line shows the plotted first steer, 1. "steer of 120 –degrees given by MacDill" to Lt. Jones.

The location of the first steer; 1. Steer of 120-degrees that was given by MacDill AFB is 100 statute miles southeast of Tyndall AFB. This point is actually less than half the distance between C. Tyndall AFB and D. MacDill AFB.

The broken flight path line on the map illustrates a direct flight path from C. Tyndall AFB, in Panama City to D. MacDill AFB in Tampa. The distance along this flight path is approximately 245 miles.

2nd Lt. Jones' Final Flightpath with Inset of Actual USAF Map

Solid line represents LT. Jones actual flight path across the Gulf of Mexico. Broken Line represents LT. Jones alleged direct flight path across the Gulf of Mexico

A. Moody AFB Valdosta, GA
B. Tallahassee Airport FL
C. Tyndall AFB Panama City, FL
D. MacDill AFB Tampa, FL
E. Eglin AFB Valparaiso, FL

The following information comes from the transcript between an inquiring Board member and Approach Controller S/Sgt. Bolen:

Q. Did you ever hear 819 transmit to MacDill on any channel?
A. I did not.
Q. Did anyone else in the [Tyndall] tower?
A. Not to my knowledge.
Q. At this time, you were on B channel!
A. D/F was still on B channel. The aircraft was advised by Tallahassee tower. I believe Lt. Dunn received that transmission on C.
Q. From the aircraft?

A. Yes-from the aircraft. MacDill then gave the aircraft a steer of 109-degree to a point of nearest land.

Q. Where did you get that information?

A. That was given [to] me by Tallahassee Tower. That was all the contact with the aircraft. We had several advisories at the time from their operations–Captain Gillette and Captain Harrison – as to emergency procedure to be given [to] the aircraft. I relayed information to Tallahassee and MacDill to attempt contact or transmission in the blind to 819."

POINT 12: LT JONES AND THE EMERGENCY FREQUENCY CHANNEL - "D" CHANNEL

The Aircraft Accident Investigating Board asked First Lt. Dunn the following question that concerned the emergency "D" channel. "Q. At any time during this incident, did you or anyone else instruct #819 to switch to 'D' channel? A. No – Not to my knowledge," answered Dunn.

S/Sgt. Bolen gave a contradicting statement concerning the "D" channel situation. Major Pompetti and the board asked the following questions of S/Sgt. Bolen concerning the "D" channel, "Q. There was no advice to him [Lt. Jones] to switch to D channel? A. He had only switched to D channel once and there was no contact at all. Q. Who told him to go to D channel? A. I'm not sure who told him as we were unable to contact the aircraft. Q. Did you hear this yourself or did someone tell you about it later? A. No. It was over plan 62 [plan 62, a term used in Military Air Transport Service to Designate a Specific Communication System for transmitting messages regarding the movement of aircraft]. There was no conversation addressed to me. I heard people talking among themselves—Tallahassee Tower and others. I am not sure who they were. Q. They mentioned for him to go to D channel and he never heard them? A. Right. B. Channel was the best working frequency at Tyndall that day."

Approach Control officer 1st Lt. Dunn, and approach controller S/Sgt. Bolen were in the same control room at Tyndall tower during this time. Yet both men gave different information about Lt. Jones being advised to switch to the emergency "D" channel. Why were those two controllers unaware of what was going on with their own jet? Why it that these highly trained men were unaware of the situation in their own control room? Moreover, who were the other people involved in this incident that Bolen was unable to identify? Why didn't S/Sgt. Bolen make an inquiry to the "others" and find out whom they were? He said, "I am not sure who they were."

Were the unknown people involved in the incident who were said to have advised Jones to switch to "D" channel fabricated by S/Sgt. Bolen? At this point, in the incident I ask; was Lt. Jones actually in an emergency situation or was he involved in another situation? Why didn't Jones declare an emergency at the point when he was flying back and forth over the Gulf of Mexico?

POINT 13: JET #0819- THREE FLAME-OUT TIMES

Captain Harrison explained the flame-out segment of the incident to the board and stated, "When he got low on fuel, I gave instructions to turn him 90-degrees toward land and when he reached 5,000 ft, bail out. That was the last we heard." There were actually three recorded times that Lt. Jones jet was said to have flamed-out. These times were all contained in the 65-page case file report. They were recorded as 4:34 p.m., 4:37 p.m. and 4:42 p.m.! The entire list of this documentation is as follows:

1). 4:42 p.m. Extract from Flight Service Center – Daily Operational Log, Maxwell AFB. Date: 12 September 1952, **"At 1642 pilot stated he had just flamed out and was preparing to bail out."**

2). 4:34 p.m. Airways and Air Communications Service - 1922 AACS Squadron, Tyndall AFB, FL. Date: 12 September 1952, **"1634 A/C [aircraft] flamed out."**

3). 4:34 p.m. Tyndall AFB Telegram—Preliminary Report of a Major Accident – Aircraft Missing. Date: Sep 13 – 9:04, **"Pilot said he had flamed out at 1634."**

4). The official "Report of AF Aircraft Accident," actually gave two different times that the jet flamed out within their same report. 1). 4:34 p.m., "Section – General Information. Missing Aircraft Report. Hour and Time Zone: **1634 CST**. Duration of Flight since last takeoff: 2 + 26." [2 hours + 26 minutes=2:08 CST until **4:34 p.m. CST**]. 2). 4:42 p.m. CST "Section O. Description of Accident: MacDill D/F heard him say at 1642C that he flamed out and was at 15,000 ft., still in weather and preparing to bail out." **"4:42 p.m. CST."**

5). 4:34 p.m. CST. Medical Report of AF Aircraft Accident, "Time of Accident. 1634 CST. **"At 1634 he reported a flameout."** Length of use: 2:30 Hrs." [2 hours +30 minutes].

6). 4:42 p.m. Extract from Ltr. to Flight Service Hq., Washington, D.C., from Flight Service Center, Maxwell AFB, dtd 16 September 52. "At **1742E**, the pilot stated that he had a flameout and was preparing to jump."

7). 4:34 p.m. Tyndall AFB Telegram – Ref 11 - #9/47z. 17 September 1952. "1620 CST P/T called in with 94 gals, **flamed out at 1634 CST.**"

8). 4:37 p.m. AACS, Tyndall AFB – "CERTIFICATE" by 1st Lt. Robert A. Dunn, Approach Controller. 18 Sep. 52. "Overheard pilot to say **he 'flamed-out' at 1637."**

9). 4:42 p.m. Extract from Air Rescue Service Report, Maxwell AFB, dtd 24 Sept 1952. **"At 1642C, 819 reported out of fuel** at 15,000 ft IFR."

10). 4:42 p.m. Letter. HQ 3625 FTW – Tyndall AFB. Joseph E. Wisby – Major USAF Flying Safety Officer. "The accident occurred on 12 September 1952 at approximately **1642 hours** Central Standard Time."

Why were there three different times stated for the jet's flameout? The alleged flameout was caused because of the jet being out of fuel, which could only occur once. Why was the USAF unable to keep track of their story? How much of this story was a fabrication and when did the jet allegedly flameout? Why did Major Pompetti and the board fail to address the matter concerning the three different times during their two meetings?

The following information was released at the Sept. 12 press conference in Tampa shortly after the jet vanished, "The last radio sound indicated the disabled craft was down to 8,000 ft," Captain Mitchell said. The time was 5:42 p.m. [EST/4:42 p.m. CST]. Captain Mitchell also stated, "The plane was apparently lost, and Air Force officials speculated that its radio compass had failed."

Captain Harrison was asked the following question by the board, "Q. After he called 'Flame-out,' did you get another call from him? A. No – the only information we got was from MacDill. I believe they were the last to hear from him at 8,000 ft." It is very interesting to note, that at the end of flight instructor Captain Harrison's questioning he was asked. "Q. Would you care to voice your opinion as to what brought about this accident?" "A. No Sir." Harrison answered. Here, Harrison's reply is evasive.

Why didn't Harrison care to voice his opinion as to what brought about the accident? He was the flight instructor in charge of the "B flight" that day and should have known every move being made. Captain Harrison should have known what brought about the accident and been able to voice an opinion. That is, unless he was actually covering up what had actually occurred!

Furthermore, I ask, was Captain Harrison being evasive when he wrote his "Statement," which concerned the times involved in the Jones and DelCurto incident? These are some of his quotes for you to judge:

1. "At that time."
2. "at that time"
3. "by this time"
4. "At this time"
5. "At this time"
6. "About this time"
7. "after this time"

At any time, did Captain Harrison know what was going on during this incident? The following quotes, which were taken from Harrison's answers during the "September 29 board meeting," are uncharacteristic of a man who played such an important role in the incident. They are listed below:

1. "About that time"
2. "at that time"
3. "About this time"
4. "at that time"
5. "At one time"
6. "I cannot remember exactly…"
7. "I think he based it…"
8. "At one time we found him [Jones] where he was…"
9. "I don't know…"
10. "I don't remember"

Was flight instructor Captain Harrison hiding the truth from Major Pompetti and the board during his questioning? Harrison was not the only one who gave the runaround to Pompetti and the board members during the first board meeting. 1st Lt. Dunn gave the following answers. They seem very indistinct and inappropriate for an Approach Control officer:

1. "Not that I remember."
2. "There must have been"
3. "I can't be sure"
4. "I would say it must have been around"
5. "No–not to my knowledge."

When the Investigating Board re-convened on October 3, 1952, they interviewed Approach Controller, S/Sgt. Bolen. The following quotes were taken from Bolen's answers when the board questioned him during this second fact-finding meeting.

His vague answers are listed below:

1. "sometime later..."
2. "At this time"
3. "No sir – I do not remember."
4. "I am not sure..."
5. "I could not say."
6. "Not to my knowledge."
7. "I am not certain."
8. "I am unable to say."

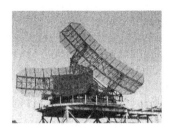

These three men, Harrison, Dunn and Bolen, were all in the Tyndall Tower during the Jones and DelCurto incident. Judging from their quotes, do they seem like sincere honest answers, or were these men hiding something that involved a cover-up? Why were these three men being evasive? Did the Air Force fabricate the Jones and DelCurto incident as a cover story and coerce the Tyndall Tower men into using it to hide the truth? Would the Air Force go to the extent of fixing all of their official reports to cover-up another story? Would this explain all the inconsistencies in their documentation of this incident?

Why did the Air Force have such a difficult time in keeping track of their story concerning the missing aviators? Did the Air Force silence everyone involved in this incident? Why were there only three men from Tyndall AFB questioned by the Aircraft Accident Investigating Board, when so many people were involved? More people being questioned meant more inconsistencies. Would the Air Force also go to the extent of doctoring up Lt. Jones military records and actually degrading the missing pilot?

The "Medical Report of an Individual - Involved in AF Aircraft Accident" talked about Jones in the "Personal Factors (pilot or crew member only)" section of their report. John Jones graduated from "Advanced Single - Engine Pilot Training Course" on May 10, 1952 at Vance AFB, OH. He went to Moody AFB for "jet transition training" then reassigned to Tyndall AFB for "All-Weather Jet Interceptor Training." This document states, "At the time of the accident total time was 290:30 hrs." The "Report of AF Aircraft Accident" document states the "Total Pilot Hours" at "292:55," a time difference of two hours and twenty-five minutes.

The "Medical Report of an Individual" states, "He had approximately 2:45 hours of weather time," while the "Report of AF Aircraft Accident" states, "Total 1st pilot Instrument Weather Hours-5:10." This is a time difference of three hours and five minutes. The "Medical Report of an Individual" states that Jones had "56 hours" of flying time in "jet-type aircraft." The "Report of AF Aircraft Accident" states, "Type and model 1st pilot experience in similar aircraft: T-33A – 52:00 and F–80B – 4:55" hours. This is a total of 56:55 hours, a time difference of 55 minutes from the other report.

The "Medical Report of an Individual" states that Jones had "70 hours of hood time." The "Report of AF Aircraft Accident" document states Jones hood times, including weather and hood times as, "21:35, 26:45, 25:00" for a total of 73:20 hours; a time difference of 3 hours and 20 minutes from the other report. Why these inconsistencies in Jones' flight record? Which documented times are correct? Moreover, are any of these documented times correct or were they all tampered with?

The "Report of AF Aircraft Accident" document states in the "General Information" section; "HOUR AND TIME ZONE" of the accident was "1634 CST" or 4:34 p.m. CST. In another section of the document, "Description of Accident" it states, "MacDill D/F heard him say at 1642C [4:42 CST] that he had a flame-out and was at 15,000 feet, still in weather and preparing to bail out." These two times, which are contained in the same document, show a time difference of 8 minutes for the same accident.

The "Report of AF Aircraft Accident" document states the length of the flight as follows, "Duration of Flight since last takeoff: 2 + 26 [2 hrs = 26 minutes]." The "Medical Report of AF Accident Report" states, "Length of use: 2:30 Hrs [2 hours/30 minutes]," a time difference of four minutes. Medical examiner, Captain Leo Jivoff, wrote the following in Lt. Jones "Medical Report of an Individual" that was dated "8 Oct 52." Jivoff states, "Early in the accident flight he [Jones] was faced with an emergency situation requiring the use of the pitot heat button. He did not know where it was and was told by another student via radio."

First off, was Captain Jivoff possibly trying to type the words "pilot heat button"? Secondly, Lt. Jones was allegedly unable to find this "pilot heat button" when he was faced with an emergency situation early in the accident flight. Lt. Jones did not declare his first emergency until "1615C [4:15 p.m.] when he called Tyndall Tower and declared an emergency...two hours and eight minutes into his flight." His flight only lasted another 18-26 minutes longer, depending on which AF document is used as reference. In reality, Lt. Jones was near the end of his flight when he declared his first emergency situation, not "Early in the accident flight."

Furthermore, why is there no record of this "emergency situation" that supposedly occurred during the early part of Jones' flight? Why was this point not raised at the investigating board proceedings? Thirdly, what was the emergency situation that arose, which required the use of the "pitot heat button"? The only other emergency situation occurred five minutes after the first emergency. It was documented at 4:21 p.m. CST.

Point #4 involves the "student" who allegedly told Jones "via radio" where the "pitot heat button" was during the alleged emergency. Who was this "student" and why is there no record of the "student" in any Air Force documents and no record of a name?

Was this entire statement by Jivoff a complete fabrication to degrade Second Lt. Jones to make him appear incompetent? The "Medical Report of An Individual -Involved in AF Aircraft Accident" was written by Jivoff and dated "8 Oct 52." This document was actually dated five days after the final Aircraft Accident Investigating Board proceeding ended.

Also contained in this report within the "Personal Factors" section of this document is information about Lt. Jones background and progress. The Air Force made the following statement about Lt. Jones, "He was a quiet, retiring individual who always kept himself in the background and did not mix with other pilots...He never visited the officers' club and preferred going to movies alone. No one knew him well." The Air Force also stated, "The impression of his [Jones] fellow students was that he was always visibly tense and apprehensive of flying and that he lacked self confidence."

The Air Force documented the unsubstantiated impressions of fellow students who portrayed Jones in a negative manner even though "no one knew him well." Why was the Air Force documenting degrading accounts from unnamed sources about Lt. Jones? Furthermore, if Jones was "apprehensive of flying," then why was he in the USAF flying planes and jets?

The Air Force also gave the following unsubstantiated account of Lt. Jones. One fellow student who knew him for 15 months and had been through pilot training with him said, "I wouldn't fly with him. He was uncoordinated, tense, responded poorly in emergencies and could not make decisions. He was even tense in B-25 aircraft and would grip his hands so tightly on controls that his knuckles would be white." Once again, the USAF made allegations about Lt. Jones incompetence as a pilot by using unnamed sources…students.

Why did the USAF intentionally go out of their way to degrade Lt. Jones and repeatedly make accusations about his flying? Why did the USAF permit Lt. Jones to fly aircraft if he was so incompetent? This same document also gives accounts of Lt. Jones flying progress during the previous days leading up to his last flight. It includes information about his other flight missions including "interceptor missions in B-25" aircraft and his F-94 transition flights. The Air Force continually showed Lt Jones' weak points in this document and actually stated, "This officer verbalized less than the average student but had expressed dislike for jet fighter aircraft."

The Air Force even stated the following assertion; "On the day before the accident he verbalized his doubts in his abilities to fly the [F-94B] aircraft." This statement seems absurd. Who were the persons that Lt. Jones allegedly verbalized to, when he made these statements?

The Air Force gave a summary of Lt. Jones progress during these days prior to his disappearance. It states, "The following is an instructors' summary of pilots' progress, 'This student had difficulty on landings with the F-94. He tried to force the aircraft on the runway [8 September 1952], which resulted in a hard landing, porpoising and ran off the runway damaging the tire on the aircraft. He was given a check ride in the T-33 [trainer jet] and it was unsatisfactory due to his poor judgment and his inability to think ahead of the aircraft. He was given another check ride, the following day, which was satisfactory, and it was recommended that he be given more transition in the F-94. He was transitioned again and completed eight very satisfactory traffic patterns and landings.'"

On September 11, the day before Jones and DelCurto vanished the following was said to have occurred, "On 11 September 1952 subject officer was given a check ride in a T-33 because of unsatisfactory performance on the previous day. At this time he completed 8 transition landings satisfactory." The Air Force also stated what was said to have happened on September 12, 1952. This report states, "On the day of the accident, during B-25 interceptor mission pilot [Lt. Jones] again was noted to be slow in executing commands and demonstrated other weaknesses (i.e. 'range weak, could not hold altitude, let heading drift, airspeed control weak')."

According to the "Report of AF Aircraft Accident" document, the "primary Duty Assignment" of Lt. Jones was a "Stu Plt (Grad)," student pilot graduate. His "Organizational Assignment" was Hq ADC, Ent AFB, Colorado." Second Lt. John DelCurto's "Organizational Assignment" was "ARTC, CTAF, 3626 Fly Tng Gp (AI) Tyndall AFB Fla. This translates as follows, Air Training Command, Crew Training Air Force - 3626 Flying Training Group (Advanced Interceptor) Tyndall Air Force Base Florida.

It seems very odd that there is *not* one word in the 65-page report case file about DelCurto's participation during the incident. Jones and DelCurto were both members of the "3626 Flying Training Wing-Advanced Interceptor," yet there is no mention of DelCurto's involvement in any of the Air Force documents. The "Medical Report of an Individual - Involved in AF Aircraft Accident" concluded the following, "It appears that this officer's [Lt. Jones] relative incompetence, apprehension and inability to handle emergency situations were the prime factors in this accident."

Medical Officer Leo Jivoff, Capt. USAF, stated the following in the "Medical Officer's Recommendations" section of Jones,' "Medical Report of AF Aircraft Accident." He stated, "Recommend that student pilots be screened prior to an assignment to high performance jet aircraft performing All Weather Interceptor Mission in attempt to remove 'minimum satisfactory' students and those apprehensive of this type aircraft and mission." What was the type of mission was Jones actually involved in? Was 2nd Lt. John A. Jones Jr. actually a "minimum satisfactory" pilot as stated by the USAF? Were the prime factors in the Jones and DelCurto accident caused by Jones "relative incompetence," apprehension, and inability to handle emergencies?

Right up to the day that Jones and DelCurto vanished, the USAF claimed that Jones had several unsatisfactory flight performances. The Air Force made several unsubstantiated degrading statements about him and portrayed him in a very negative way. The Air Force made it appear as though Lt. Jones was struggling right up to the day he stepped into the cockpit with DelCurto. Jones was also said to have "verbalized his doubts in his abilities to fly the [F-94B] aircraft on September 11, 1952 on the day before the accident."

The Air Force made the following assertions in this case report:

A. "This officer [2nd Lt. Jones] verbalized less than the average student but had expressed dislike for jet fighter aircraft."
B. The following is an instructor's summary of Jones' progress, "This student had difficulty on landings with the F-94. He tried to force the aircraft on the runway [8 September 1952], which resulted in a hard landing, porpoising and ran off the runway damaging the tire on the aircraft."
C. "On the day before the accident he verbalized his doubts in his abilities to fly the [F-94B] aircraft."
D. "On 11 September 1952 subject officer was given a check ride in a T-33 because of unsatisfactory performance on the previous day. At this time he completed 8 transition landings satisfactory."
E. "On the day of the accident, during B-25 interceptor mission pilot [Lt. Jones] again was noted to be slow in executing commands and demonstrated other weaknesses (i.e. 'range weak, could not hold altitude, let heading drift, airspeed control weak')."

I now ask the following questions about this convoluted incident:

1). If Jones was a "minimum satisfactory" pilot who doubted his own abilities to fly the F-94, and also having problems, why was he put into the cockpit with a student radar operator with less experience?

2). Why was trainee 2nd Lt. DelCurto in the cockpit with 2nd Lt. Jones instead of a skilled flight instructor who's job it is to transitions student pilots, especially student pilots who are said to be having difficulties?

3). Why is there no mention in the 65-page Aircraft Accident report concerning radar observer 2nd Lt. John DelCurto's participation in this disastrous incident? The USAF dictionary defines the job of a "radar observer," and states, "He ordinarily operates radar equipment to obtain information relevant to navigation, interception, search or bombing." Del Curto, the onboard radar observer of this jet, was a key figure in its navigation, yet the Air Force never talked about his involvement in the incident at all.

When, the Oct 3, 1952, Aircraft Accident Investigating Board meeting ended, the members of the Norton AFB investigating board had finally reached their "conclusions." They reached these conclusions "after a discussion of all evidence in file and all testimony," according to official transcript. Their two conclusions appeared in the official "Report of AF Aircraft Accident" document in the "CONTRIBUTING CAUSE FACTORS" section. It explains the two following factors, which contributed to the cause of the Starfire's disappearance on September 12, 1952:

170

1. Pilot failed to exercise proper emergency facilities available to him.
2. Tyndall Tower failing to properly advise the pilot to declare an emergency and go to the emergency channel "D" channel.

Here both Lt. Jones and the Air Force controllers on the ground were deemed incompetent. The accident report's "FINDINGS" section states, "The primary cause of this accident was that the pilot failed to keep himself oriented at all times while on instruments." Did the USAF actually use Second Lt. John A. Jones Jr. as the scapegoat? The Aircraft Accident Investigating Board ended their investigation with the following recommendations. The transcript stated:

RECOMMENDATIONS:

1. That this accident be brought to the attention of all pilots, informing them that in case they were confused on orientation and their status of fuel was such as to place them in emergency condition, they should not hesitate to go to 'D' channel and declare an emergency.
2. The emphasis be placed on using the radio compass in the loop position to overcome the effects of thunderstorm activity and/or static.
3. That the Tower personnel be reminded that in case of an emergency or suspected emergency that the pilot be advised to utilize his emergency procedures, specifically switching to 'D' channel and also advising him of further navigational aids that may be utilized by him."

The "AUTHENTICATION" section was signed by the members of the board at the end of the report, but there was a discrepancy. In this section, there is a *rebuttal* area, where conclusions can be refuted. The following two segments were marked off in boxes:

"1. X. Personnel Responsible for this Accident have been offered opportunity of Rebuttal."
Here, in section one, the word **"tower"** was typed in above the word "personnel."
Also marked was, "X. Rebuttal Statement attached."
"2. Personnel Responsible Not Available Because of: X. Death."
"X. Other (Explain)" The following words were typed- in, "**Missing - Presumed dead.**"

The "REBUTTAL STATEMENT" was submitted to the Air Force by Captain Vickers. It is dated, "6 October 1952," and signed, "A. J. Vickers - Captain, USAF - Tower Officer-In-Charge." His rebuttal was in reference to the second item listed of "CONTRIBUTING CAUSE FACTORS," which states, **"2. Tyndall Tower failing to properly advise the pilot to declare an emergency and go to the emergency channel "D" channel."**
Captain Vickers rebuttal statement reads, "Reference item 2 under Contributing Cause Factors on AF Form 14, at the time was ascertained that an emergency existed [and] the aircraft was not within range of the Tyndall Towers Transmitter. Furthermore, declaration of emergency rests entirely with the pilot, and his usage of radio frequencies is to be determined by existing conditions. If his emergency can be satisfactory handled on a frequency other than "D" channel, his channel of first contact is normally used."
In closing, Vickers stated, "At the time Tyndall Tower heard #819 calling Moody Approach Control, contact was attempted with the aircraft with no success. After this time, further contact was made through relay of Tallahassee Tower and in such condition, it is felt that all traffic be held to a minimum to lessen error in relay." In his rebuttal letter, Captain Vickers does not give

any times to use as reference points that would indicate Lt. Jones' location. He only states the following, "At the time" and then states, "After this time." It is obvious that Capt. Harrison, 1st Lt. Dunn and S/Sgt. Bolen all spoke the same evasive language as Captain Vickers, the Tower officer-in-charge. All four-tower men were fluent in this evasive "time" tactic-speak. Why did all of them intentionally avoid stating the locations and times of the jet during this incident?

Did the Air Force contrive the timeline of events in this incident to make it appear as though Jones was lost? Jones *did* declare two emergencies that were documented by the Air Force. The first emergency occurred at 4:15 p.m. CST. The second emergency occurred at 4:21 p.m. CST. The USAF never disclosed the jet's locations during those times either. If they had pinpointed the jets' locations along with the times, it was over those specific areas that would have shown their timeline as incorrect. Is this the reason Captain Harrison didn't care to give his opinion as to what brought about the accident? Is this the reason he made a ludicrous statement like, "at one time we found him where he was." This sounds like a Yogi Berra remark, *not* the statement of an officer!

On "5 January 1953," Vickers' rebuttal was granted by command of the "chief of staff," via a letter to the "Commanding General, ATC-Scott AFB, Illinois." This letter opens by stating, "Reference is made to the major aircraft accident involving F-94B, serial # 50-819A, which occurred on 12 September 1952. Wreckage of the aircraft has not been located to date." In part it also states, ***"This office does not concur with the [Directorate personnel of the Aircraft Accident Investigating Board's] finding of Tyndall Tower failing to properly advise the pilot to declare an emergency and go to the emergency (D channel), as a contributing excuse factor to this accident. This factor has been deleted as a contributing cause to this accident."*** The letter is signed, "Thomas C. Marbin – Major General US Air Force – Acting Deputy Inspector General."

When this "Contributing Cause Factor" was over-ruled and deleted from the official record, there was only one contributing cause, factor remaining, "1. Pilot's failure to exercise emergency facilities available to him." Unbelievably, Tyndall Tower was cleared of being incompetent and the full blame was put on Second Lt. John A. Jones Jr. It was easy to blame it on the dead man, who couldn't defend himself!

In closing this chapter, I would like to mention two documents that have reference code tabs attached to them. These documents are labeled "RE-1 1342." Both documents are signed with the initials "ASA" and do not bear any other identifying name on them. What are interesting in both of these documents are the handwritten notes that appear on them signed by "ASA."

The first document is a "BASIC CODE SHEET" and states, "CHECKED BY: 3 November ASA." In the "CAUSE FACTOR" section of this document, a handwritten note appears, "Failed to declare emergency." This note references the contributing factor said to have caused the accident. The other document containing a handwritten note by *"ASA"* appears on "Accident Information Checklist." It states, "For accident no. 52-9-12-4." Checked off on the first list is "FIGHTER." Three headings state, "DATE-CHECKED BY DATE" and handwritten under them is "11/26-ASA-1 DEC." The second checklist is titled "SUBJECT."

The section here that was checked off states, "Supplemental Accident Information." Just below this section at the bottom of the page is the area designated "REMARKS." The following handwritten note appears in that area, "Upon receipt of Command Correspondence determine whether or not re-evaluation of accdt [accident] is appropriate—Make final decision. *ASA.*"

What is the name of the bearer with the initials *ASA* and what is the person's responsibility? Why did ASA make the remark about questioning the evaluation of the Jones & DelCurto accident? Did these two airmen die in vain? Finally, I ask, why are there several missing documents in this Aircraft Accident Report and why were they deleted from the case file?

CHAPTER SEVENTEEN

THE UNCHARTED FLIGHT

On Wednesday, September 24, 1952, CIA Director of Scientific Intelligence, H. Marshall Chadwell, sent a memorandum to the Director of Central Intelligence, G. Walter Bedell Smith. This memorandum was in reference to recurring UFO sightings and incidents across the United States. The four-page memo was declassified in April 1977. It is quoted in part below:

1). "Recently an inquiry was conducted by the Office of Scientific Intelligence to determine whether there are national security implications in the problem of unidentified flying objects, i.e. flying saucers."

2). "The public concern with the phenomena indicates that a fair portion of our population is mentally conditioned to the acceptance of the incredible. In this fact lies the potential for the touching-off of mass hysteria and panic."

3). "In order to minimize risk of panic, a national policy should be established as to what should be told to the public regarding the phenomena."

Considering this memo was dated only five days after the airing of the "Flatwoods Monster" segment on the, *We The People*, TV show; there seems to be a definite connection in reference to these three memo points. Now, consider the following memo point in reference to the September 12, 1952, Jones and DelCurto incident, "A worldwide reporting system has been instituted and major Air force bases have been ordered to make interceptions of unidentified flying objects."

The account the Air Force had given concerning the Jones and DelCurto case of September 12, 1952 was incomplete and illogical. This case was filled with lies, discrepancies, convoluted timelines, and incorrect storylines, which left large gaps in the incident. The story made absolutely no sense at all and did not add up. The routine weather training mission that Jones and DelCurto were said to have been on is an implausible story.

This incident was a blatant cover-up, which was implemented by Tyndall AFB officials and carried through by higher-up United States Air Force officials. With my extensive research and the help of several others, including tower controllers, radar men, and pilots, we used all my collected information to recreate the entire incident. I plotted the location points that involved each segment of the incident on to several different Florida and Georgia maps. Then, I transferred all of this information on to my primary master map. Next, we recreated the entire scenario of events and filled in the missing gaps of the story.

My assistants and I have concluded that the flyers disappearances were not attributed to a flameout, bad weather conditions, being lost or to pilot error. Contrary to the Air Forces conclusions, we conclude that the jet and crew vanished as the result of a conflict with UFOs, when they attempted to "shoot them down."

This incident triggered a nationwide crisis that night and evolved into a series of events that ended up in Flatwoods, WV. It was also the beginning of what became a modern-day War of the Worlds. The Jones and DelCurto incident was the first of a sequence of events that evening that caused the three mid-Atlantic UFOs to be fired upon by U.S. military forces.

In his 1973 book, *Aliens From Space*, Donald Keyhoe made the following statement in reference to UFOs vulnerability to jet fighter armaments in the 1950s. He stated:

In the late 1950s, as a number of futile U.S. chases mounted, some pilots were convinced that the UFOs were immune to gunfire and rockets. Several intelligence analysts believed the aliens might be using some negative force linked with gravity control to repel or deflect bullets and missiles. But the top control group disagreed. In a special evaluation of U.S. and foreign reports, they found evidence that UFOs were not invulnerable. Some had been temporarily crippled, apparently from power or control failures, and a few others had been completely destroyed by strange explosions. In one or two cases, it appeared that missiles or rocket fire could have been the cause.

The events on September 12, 1952, which involved damaged UFOs that fell from the sky was one such case that showed UFOs were vulnerable to jet fighter firepower. Based on my extensive research into this missing jet case, the following scenario that I present is a feasible explanation for the events that occurred that day, on September 12, 1952.

The Air Force's contrived and pitifully covered-up version of this incident does not make sense, is illogical and does not fit the time line of events as they stated. Unlike the convoluted scenario that they presented to the public, my version of the incident disputes their incongruous version. Until more evidence is found, documents are released or one of the participants in this incident comes forward to tell the *truth*, I now present another perspective into case, "52-9-12-4."

Air Force Bases and Naval Air Stations in Florida and South Georgia

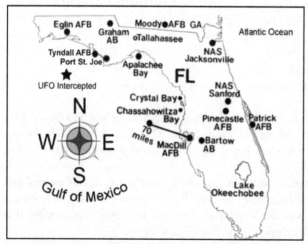

The Jones and DelCurto incident unfolded off the coast of Florida over the waters of the Gulf of Mexico. The events on September 12, 1952, unfolded shortly before 2:08 p.m. CST. Several southeast Air Force bases tracked sixteen UFOs on their radar screens flying several miles above the Gulf of Mexico waters, south/southwest of Tyndall AFB.

The 16 UFOs were separated into four groups, with each group consisting of four objects. All the UFOs were surveying the Florida panhandle coast, while moving high above the Gulf waters.

These Air Force base radars formed a radar-net that surrounded the Gulf of Mexico area. Radar net is defined as, "a network of radar installations set up to detect aircraft entering a defined airspace." Furthermore, these USAF base radar installations formed a "warning net," defined as "any system of communications set up to give warning of aggressive enemy movements, esp. enemy aircraft."

In addition to these nearby Air Force bases, the Jacksonville Naval Air Station, on the east coast of Florida, was also tracking the groups of unidentified objects. These UFOs were within and over the restricted boundaries of the Air Defense Identification Zone. Any aircraft that intends to enter the United States through one of these zones, in this case it was a coastal ADIZ, is required to file a flight plan. This flight plan would have been filed with the Military Flight service or the Civil Aeronautics Administration. If pilots did not file a flight plan or did not follow their flight plans in these ADIZ areas, jet fighters would have intercepted them. Several radio contacts were attempted by the Air Force to establish contact and verify the identification of these unidentified aircraft. There was no response.

Within minutes, all southeast Air Force bases and Naval Air Stations were on alert. The USAF Air Defense Command headquarters at Ent AFB in Colorado Springs was simultaneously informed. The ADC "yellow warning light" flashed on. Simultaneously, the large "warning bell" sounded, thereby alerting ADC officials unknown aircraft were being detected at that time.

The locations where these UFOs were situated above the Gulf of Mexico, near Tyndall AFB justified a full air defense readiness, declaration by the ADC. At that point, Ent Air Force Base officials contacted the White House, alerting President Harry Truman, the Commander in Chief. President Truman quickly contacted Robert A. Lovett, Secretary of Defense, and the National Security Council. Simultaneously, the Joint Chiefs of Staff were alerted and all defense forces throughout the entire eastern United States were put on "red alert."

Three Florida Air Force bases began to deploy combat air patrols over and near their bases. Two were from the panhandle, Tyndall AFB in Panama City and Eglin AFB in Valparaiso and the third was the west coast's MacDill AFB in Tampa. During this "red alert" situation, time was of the utmost essence. Fighter pilots and radar operators dashed to awaiting jet fighters to race aloft after unknown targets. Tyndall AFB scrambled six F-94B Starfires into the air between 1:47 p.m. CST and 2:26 p.m. CST. It was during this red alert that pilot 2nd Lt. John A. Jones, Jr. was paired into a waiting F-94B Starfire with radar operator trainee 2nd Lt. John S. DelCurto.

The commanders at Tyndall AFB, headquarters of the Advanced Interceptor "3626 Fly Training Group," used the best fighter aviators they had available at that time. With no time available, to access or assign duty to who would be most qualified for the mission - jet fighters were scrambled into the air.

The time elapsed when Jones jet departed at 2:08 p.m. CST until he was supposedly lost at 4:20 p.m. CST was two hours and twelve minutes. From this time until Jones' F-94 jet supposedly has, a flameout en route to MacDill AFB at 4:42 p.m. CST was another 22 minutes. One minute later at 4:43 p.m. CST, the last radio noise was heard from the jet and the jet disappeared. The total time of Lt. Jones and Lt. DelCurto's flight was two hours and thirty-five minutes. Following the storyline, the four groups of UFOs continued moving at very high altitude above the Gulf of Mexico.

The movements of the UFOs were being monitored by Air Force radar on the ground as well as Ground Control Intercept Stations along the Gulf coast. The UFOs continued to ascend but stayed just above the ceiling range of the climbing jets that were being guided toward them. Shortly afterwards, the four groups of UFOs spread out into different directions toward the coast.

The six jets now patrolling the skies and searching for these UFOs were in constant radio contact with ground radar controllers, who kept the jets informed. Suddenly, one group of UFOs began to descend as they moved closer to the Florida panhandle. The fourth object from that group ceased its descent and circled above the three companion ships.

The remaining three groups of UFOs stayed just above 50,000 feet, above the reach of the jets and began to hover in place. The three objects that had descended to a lower altitude had reached a "Warning Point." This is defined as, "Any point which when reached gives warning that a critical moment or action is to follow." The warning given upon reaching the designated warning point of a restricted area is called a "Warning Order." This is defined as "A preliminary notice that another order or action is to follow, designed to allow time for making plans and preparations." Meanwhile, Tyndall AFB had sent up another Combat Air Patrol of four jets over their base.

Tyndall AFB as well as the pilots of the four nearby interceptors issued a "Warning Order" to the three descending UFOs. The warnings went unacknowledged. At that point, another major concern arose. The airspace this group of UFOs was nearing was close to Eglin AFB. This Air Force installation operates the Air Proving Ground Command (APGC). The mission of the Air Proving Ground, Eglin AFB, is the operational suitability testing of all Air Force aircraft and equipment. This includes the development of tactics and techniques for the tactical employment of this equipment. This installation conducted many top-secret aircraft tests and experiments from many of its base area test sites. The installation was heavily restricted to air traffic and required many special air traffic rules upon any craft entering its air spaces. Besides the concern that the UFOs could be extraterrestrial, there was the possibility that they were advanced Soviet aircraft, planning an aerial assault against U.S. bases.

Shortly afterward, while still descending, the three UFOs passed into the service ceiling height area where the jets were capable of flying. Immediately, three nearby patrolling Tyndall jets moved in and issued another "Warning Order" to the objects that continued to descend. Once again, there was no response. I will now reiterate the words, "'shoot them down' if they refuse to land." While the other three Tyndall jets were tracking and flying near the other groups of UFOs, Tyndall officials ordered the other three jets to intercept the three descending objects. They had been considered possible enemy aircraft and probably hostile. Just before 2:40 p.m. CST, GCI guided the jets toward the three unidentified aircraft. Final warnings were issued by the pilots with no response. The jet fighters then approached their descending targets to "shoot them down."

F-94B Starfire

The UFOs were sighted in the distance as the pilots closed in on their targets. The objects were identified as not being Russian aircraft. They were recognized as being unconventional and unknown crafts; they were oval and sphere-shaped and approximately 20-30 feet in size with a smooth, metallic-like skin. The objects were not sleek saucer-shaped objects but very large and cumbersome, similar in comparing a Greyhound bus to a Ferrari sports car.

The three F-94s moved toward their targets. Seconds later, the jets had the UFOs locked on their radar systems, closed and then fired upon them. The UFOs scattered as the F-94B jets unleashed a barrage of cannon fire that blanketed the sky. Simultaneously a strange vibration filled the air and sky lit up. Seconds later, one of the objects took a direct hit, exploded, and then caught on fire. Sparks erupted and showered the sky and the object began to fly erratically. Simultaneously, the three jets pulled out of the fray but something was wrong.

The two nearest jets had been hit by an unknown wavering shock. The pilots immediately contacted Tyndall AFB's tower through a static transmission. The messages however, were not positive. F-94 jets #1332 and #0867, the two nearest the UFOs, had developed electrical difficulties with some of their onboard systems. The jets were acting erratically and had intermittent problems with their instruments and radar systems. The jet pilots told Tyndall tower about the strange powers that the objects possessed and informed them these UFOs did not possess the agility of a saucer-shaped craft.

Tyndall tower controllers immediately ordered the two damaged and struggling jets back to base as the combat air patrol pilots listened in on the airwaves. These UFOs possessed a propulsion system that produced an anti-gravity field. This field was generated by an onboard power source unlike any known system. The field, an electromagnetic-type field actually surrounded the UFOs. This field had adverse affects on any electrical systems at close range, but moreover, the power systems of these objects also acted as weapons systems.

The anti-gravity field of the intercepted UFO was damaged by the jets firepower, causing it to lose power, fly erratically and drop in altitude. It was in desperate need of electrical power and needed a source to regenerate itself. Moments later, the damaged object being escorted by another UFO descended, as the third object ascended back into the sky. With no time to waste, the destination of the damaged object became Tyndall AFB. Meanwhile, all three jets were also en route to Tyndall as the two damaged jets struggled through their descent. Tyndall tower men watched their scopes as the two UFOs descended and approached the base on northeast headings.

They were unsure if the base was being targeted for an attack. The tower advised their jets to remain above the objects in their stack formation. Minutes later, the damaged UFO and its escort approached Tyndall AFB and started their final descent. Stunned officials sounded the warning siren as pandemonium broke lose. Vehicles filled with heavily armed guards scrambled across the field and followed the two objects as they passed across the base.

The damaged UFO then hovered over a giant generator as it struggled to stay airborne. A strange device was lowered and it absorbed energy into its electrical power system. The other UFO hovered over the base between the approaching guards and the damaged UFO to safeguard the area. The power drainage caused Tyndall's radio range to go off-line. Power maintenance personnel tried switching over to emergency power, which was also already incapacitated. As personnel scrambled to overcome the problem, the tower operators contacted the power maintenance crew and told them to try resetting the commercial power.

Near the UFOs, a strange electrical vibration intensified throughout the area. This stalled the approaching vehicles and shocked the guards who backed off. Officials were aware of the damaging electrical powers the objects possessed but were unaware if they possessed any deadly armaments. If these objects did have deadly weapons and chose to use them, Tyndall AFB could become the scene of a raging battlefield. At this point, there was another major concern; would the other objects hovering above and along the Florida coastline descend upon the base? To complicate matters, three aircraft were descending to land at Tyndall Field and two were damaged. The guards were ordered to stand down and not to fire at the objects until further notice.

This segment of the incident involving the power loss was stated in the "Preliminary Report Of A Major Accident," dated 13 September 1952. It states, "When jet aircraft started letting down procedures Tyndall Range went off the air. It was off from 1440 to 1445 CST." [2:40 p.m. to 2:45 p.m. CST]. The official "Report Of AF Aircraft Accident" stated, "Tyndall Radio Range went off the air at 1440C and was officially off until 1445C." During this time, Lt. Jones called for a D/F steer back to station. In an official statement by Captain Phillip P. Harrison, Flight Instructor of the 3625 Interceptor Training Squadron dated September 23, 1952, he said, "No difficulties arose until Tyndall Range went off the air. At that time about three ships called for steers, one was Lt. Jones in aircraft #819 (F-94B, AF-50-0819)."

The explanation of the power loss was detailed in the Air Force document dated 12 September 1952. Ref 11 #9/47z explained, "AACS (Airway and Air Communication Service, Tyndall AFB) power maintenance personnel were making a power change-over check in order to test the emergency power. The emergency power did not take over and the radio range went off-the-air until the tower operators called in and advised the power maintenance personnel to reset the commercial power." This explanation seems both unlikely and dangerous, that a power changeover to test emergency power would occur during a flight operation with three jets "letting down procedures."

As Jones and the two damaged craft were letting down their jets heading for Tyndall AFB, they proceeded to radio the tower. As previously stated, on September 29, 1952, the first board proceeding was held at Tyndall AFB in the Wing Conference Room. Six members of The Aircraft Accident Investigating Board were present including acting president, Major Peter E. Pompetti. Major Pompetti spoke to Capt. Harrison at length. Capt. Harrison explained, "It came for approach times and one of them (Jet #1332) was already making his approach. About that time (2:40 p.m. CST), Tyndall range went off the air. Immediately several [pilots] called in and said, their radio compass was out and all they could hear was static. I advised them that the range was off-the-air." This was the time, when the UFO hovering over the base, between 2:40 and 2:45 p.m. CST, was draining the power.

During this time when the Tyndall Radio Range went off the air, Tyndall tower using radio "D/F," Radio Direction-Finding; the act or process of determining the direction from which a transmitted signal originates, hence, a method for establishing the bearing or position of an aircraft, guided in the three jets. The three jets were being guided by this method because Tyndall's Range being off-air enabled them to utilize their IFR, or Instrument Flight Rules. IFR is the collection of rules in AF directives, which govern flight procedures under "instrument conditions."

The jets on-board radio compasses would not function during off-air times. Capt. Harrison also stated, "Several of them [pilots] called for directional steers...Lt. Jones called for a steer and there were a couple more. The man who was making a letdown was brought in using DF." This was aircraft #1332.

Just after 2:45 p.m. CST, the damaged UFO began to ascend a short distance away from the base. The escort craft began to follow. The power for the radio range was switched to commercial. About 2:47 p.m. CST, the two UFOs ascended to a higher altitude, but the damaged craft was still unstable as it struggled to climb and attempted to leave the atmosphere. At 3:00 p.m. CST, Tyndall radar continued to track the UFOs slow ascent.

During this time, Tyndall officials had learned the UFOs were vulnerable to their jet's firepower. They had also become aware that the propulsion systems of these unknown objects were somehow generated by electricity or, electrical power. Subsequently, officials at Tyndall had realized when a craft was hit it would suddenly lose power, quickly go down and need to regenerate. Meanwhile, Tyndall was in communication with officials at the Pentagon; they updated them of the unfolding situation in Florida and informed them about the electrical propulsion systems of these UFOs. The Pentagon then contacted the experts at the "Air Technical Intelligence Center," located at Wright-Patterson AFB and gave them this propulsion system information. Quickly, the officials at ATIC began to analyze this important information.

178

Furthermore, the "Top Brass" in the Air Force wanted the damaged UFO before it could escape and gave explicit orders to capture it if possible. Tyndall tower contacted the three jets on combat air patrol with orders to intercept it. They also contacted Lt. Jones and redirected him toward the other three fighters.

At this time, all three jets were positioned above the two UFOs, the damaged one and its escort. The three combat air-patrol jets descended as Jones was vectored toward them. Minutes later, Jones joined formation as Ground Control Intercept began to guide the fighters toward the UFOs. The pilots were informed that the UFOs could wreak havoc on their electrical systems at close range with some kind of unknown weapons system. They were warned to keep their distance. Separating into pairs, two jets targeted the damaged UFO while the other two targeted the escort craft. As GCI vectored the jets toward the UFOs, onboard radar observers picked up the targets on their scopes.

The four jets closed in, diving toward the UFOs. Jones and his wing mate closed in on the damaged object. The two pairs of jets both flew toward their designated targets. The escort object changed its course onto a head-on collision course and proceeded toward two of the jets. The jets and the escort object headed at each other and not planning to play chicken, the jets fired at the UFO then broke away. The object avoided this strike, dove below the jets, and sharply banked and set a course for the other two jets.

The escort UFO dove toward them as they closed-in on the damaged and struggling object. However, the approaching UFO did not reach the area in time and the damaged object was hit by the cannon fire from the two attacking F-94s. Meanwhile, the two jets that had engaged with the escort UFO only moments earlier were experiencing electrical problems. At this time, Tyndall ordered all four jets back to base. Colonel B. T. Kleine stated the cover story in his letter, "When the weather started to become near our minimums, all aircraft were called to come back to the field."

Meanwhile, the now severely damaged object turned away from the coastline and headed southwest in the opposite direction of its pursuers. The escort UFO then followed the damaged ship; its condition was deteriorating and it was having trouble staying airborne. As the objects were making their escape, F-94, #1332 was approaching Tyndall to land. The Direction Finding Log dated 12/9/52 stated that while "1332 was on a course of 314 degrees at 1447/2:47 p.m. CST." Remarks were stated that a "BE EMERG" was declared during the jet's approach. This emergency was declared because the UFOs were still in vicinity of the base.

The first jet approaching Tyndall field did not land until nine minutes later…after declaring its emergency. An Airways and Air Communications Service document dated September 18, 1952 and titled "Certificate" states, "AF1332, F-94…cleared for approach at 1445 (2:45 p.m.). Cancelled instrument flight rules flight plan at 1456 (2:56 p.m.)." To avoid a confrontation, the approaching jet was diverted away from Tyndall for nine minutes, which is how long it took the UFOs to be out-of-range.

Capt. Harrison continued his statement by speaking of the next jet to land…F-94, AF-0867. He stated, "The next man was brought in all the way with D/F." The Direction Finding Log dated 12/9/52 stated that this jet was "cleared for approach at 1540 (3:04 p.m. CST). Cancelled IFR flight plan at 1512 (3:12 p.m. CST)." Meanwhile another UFO re-entered the picture. This was one of the three objects involved in the original confrontation when the damaged UFO was initially hit. After that exchange, it ascended to a higher altitude hovering unnoticed above Tyndall, observing the fray. No longer on the sidelines, the third UFO began its descent back toward the panhandle coastline. Tyndall AFB had just scrambled four jet fighters toward the damaged UFO and the escort object accompanying it. The intent of this third object was to keep the scrambled jets away from the two retreating UFOs by heading them off. GCI was guiding the four jets. As the jets met this new threat, they knew that the UFO seemed vulnerable to their firepower but possessed an advanced weapon system. The onboard radar observers on the F-94s carefully guided their pilots toward the incoming ship despite the risks.

A little wiser and more prepared for round two, these F-94s planned to fire at their targets at a distance a little farther away. They intended to riddle the sky with .50 caliber rounds, then immediately pull out of range to avoid the UFO's strange shock wave force. Unfortunately, the pilots also found out the full effects of the armaments they were now up against when they fired upon them. The energy from this shock wave could fry their jet's electrical system and incapacitate them if they received a direct hit. An indirect hit could damage the aircraft or temporarily disable it and stun them.

Another form of defense the UFOs utilized was a devastating high-intensity energy beam. Upon direct contact, the beam engulfed the target and completely disintegrates it. These weapons though, had a major drawback; they would drain the power of their craft if used repeatedly over a short time. This would lessen the strength and range of their weapons and slow down the craft.

The striking jets closed on the third UFO and blasted a round of cannon fire at it. The object banked, narrowly escaped being hit and struck one of the jets trying to bypass it with a shock wave. It was a direct hit; the jet was incapacitated and fell out of the sky. The remaining three jets scattered after the horrified pilots saw what had just occurred. Shortly thereafter, the jets attempted another interception. As they fired their cannons, the third UFO retaliated, fired its high-intensity beam and engulfed one of jets, instantly disintegrating it. Seconds later, cannon fire was shot again at the object by the remaining two F-94 jets. They missed it.

Meanwhile, the damaged UFO and the craft escorting it headed southwest out over the Gulf waters and decelerated. Traveling out over the Gulf waters could be fatal for the damaged and struggling craft should it go down. As the damaged craft struggled to stay airborne, it ceased its ascent over the Gulf of Mexico to assess its damage and stopped heading further southwest. At that point, Air Force officials tracking the UFO's movements believed they might have been regrouping for a retaliatory attack. Eglin AFB directed their four CAP jet fighters toward them.

Meanwhile, the first four jets, including Jones' jet were in contact with Tyndall tower. The two damaged F-94 jets informed Tyndall that they were still struggling with their electrical systems, which were intermittently malfunctioning. Tyndall AFB controllers guided all four jets toward their base to attempt landings. Jones and his wing mate were stacked above the two damaged jets and they all continued toward Tyndall field.

In the meantime, Tyndall tower was simultaneously in contact with the two remaining jets in battle with the third object that was descending toward the base. Tyndall redirected Jones and his wing mate back toward the descending UFO to assist the two remaining jets in overcoming it. Just as Jones and his wing mate arrived into the air battle area, the two jets had been disintegrated. They attempted to intercept the third object as Jones wing mate fired his remaining ammunition but missed his target in a desperate attempt to overtake it. The UFO bypassed the two jets and continued descending as the two jets were ordered to return to Tyndall immediately.

At this point, a major concern had arisen. The UFO was still descending and heading for Tyndall in addition to the last two jets that had sustained electrical problems. During the Aircraft Accident Investigating Board proceedings, flight instructor, Capt. Phillip P. Harrison stated, "Lt. Jones called for a steer and there were a couple more. The man who was making a letdown was brought in using D/F [pilot of AF-1332]. The next man was brought in all the way with DF [pilot

180

of AF-0867]. At about this time the weather was getting bad with light rain. I had been instructed if there were any rain showers to send them to their alternate. So at this time I told Lt. Dunn on Approach Control, to send the top four ships in the stack to [Moody AFB] the alternate."

Lt. Jones and the other three jets were never actually recalled back to Tyndall AFB because of bad weather. The first two jets ahead of Jones and the other three jets had already landed ahead of them, before the "light rain" started. Colonel Kleine, USAF commanding, from Tyndall AFB stated in a letter to Lt. Jones brother, dated 17 September 1952, "When the weather started to become near our minimums, all aircraft were called to come back to the field."

This statement contradicts Capt. Harrison's statement of September 29, 1952. Colonel Kleine then states: "Supervisory personnel in the control tower advised John and three other aircraft to go to Moody Air Force Base about fifteen minutes north of Tyndall." Colonel Kleine neglected to say that there were actually six jets and two of them had already landed at Tyndall Field before Lt. Jones and the three others.

Colonel Kleine made it appear as though the bad weather was the factor that caused Tyndall AFB personnel to call the jets to come back to the field. The weather was not a factor. At this point, two jets were struggling with their electrical systems, another jet was out of ammunition and Lt. Jones was the last behind the group and low on ammunition, as they proceeded to their home base. In the meantime, Tyndall officials had alerted Washington officials, Air Force and Navy officials, and briefed them about the devastating weapons that these UFOs possessed. Soon after, Air Force experts at the "Air Technical Intelligence Center" were contacted again and given this information about the UFO's powerful weapon systems. Immediately, they began to analyze it!

Meanwhile, the damaged UFO hovered erratically, had trouble staying airborne, and continued to lose altitude. The decision to make an emergency landing along the Florida coastline was inevitable. The damaged object and the escort object accompanying it stopped, turned and redirected. They proceeded on a northeast trajectory over the Gulf of Mexico toward the coastline behind the descending third UFO. Meanwhile, four combat air patrol jets from Moody AFB had been vectored southwest toward the area of the three descending UFOs. Simultaneously, the Eglin jets also headed southeast toward them. At that point, Air Force bases encompassed the three UFOs with jets closing in on them from different directions. Another confrontation with Air Force jets could prove fatal for the damaged UFO if it were hit again.

Shortly after, all three of the UFOs, including the damaged one, grouped together and descended. They proceeded northeast toward the Florida Panhandle so the damaged one could make an emergency landing. As the Four Eglin jets headed toward the three objects from the northwest and four Moody jets approached from the northeast, the entire situation changed. The remaining groups of thirteen upper-level UFOs hovering high in the atmosphere began to descend and take control of the situation.

The descending objects separated and spread out in a shotgun pattern, moving into strategic positions toward other military installations. As they fanned out in different directions, they formed an aerial blockade around their damaged craft. The UFOs maneuvered and cut off several access points of the military jets. Some UFOs moved into strategic Air Force operating areas and actually neutralized several airfields from scrambling any further jets.

Their main objective was to protect the damaged craft from being destroyed or captured by the Air Force. The main objective of the Air Force was to destroy these objects before they invaded the United States.

Within moments of their descent, these UFOs jammed communications of the AF bases and naval air stations. The UFOs neutralized or made temporarily useless the following military installations. They are arranged in a clockwise order starting from an area just south of the Apalachee Bay:

1. Tyndall AFB, Panama City, FL. Flight paths neutralized, jets intercepted & airfields neutralized.
2. Eglin AFB, Valparaiso, FL. Flight paths neutralized, jets intercepted & airfields neutralized.
3. Pensacola Naval Air Station, FL. Flight paths neutralized, jets intercepted &airfields neutralized.
4. Brookley AFB, Mobile, AL. Flight paths neutralized.
5. Craig AFB, Selma, AL. Flight paths neutralized.
6. Gunter AFB, Montgomery, AL. Flight paths neutralized.
7. Maxwell AFB, Montgomery, AL. Flight paths neutralized.
8. Lawson AFB, Columbus, GA. Flight paths neutralized.
9. Graham AB, (5 miles north of Marianna), FL. Flight paths neutralized.
10. Bainbridge AB, Bainbridge, FL. Flight paths neutralized.
11. Dobbins AFB, Marietta, GA. Flight paths neutralized.
12. Turner AFB, Albany, GA. Flight paths neutralized.
13. Robins AFB, Macon, GA. Flight paths neutralized.
14. Spence AB, Spence, GA. Flight paths neutralized.
15. Moody AFB, Valdosta, GA. Flight paths neutralized & jets intercepted.
16. Hunter AFB, Savannah, GA. Flight paths neutralized.
17. NAS Jacksonville, Jacksonville, FL. Flight paths neutralized.
18. NAS Sanford, Sanford, FL. Flight paths neutralized.
19. Pinecastle AFB, Orlando, FL. Flight paths neutralized.
20. Patrick AFB, Cocoa, FL. Flight paths neutralized.
21. MacDill AFB, Tampa, FL. Flight paths neutralized & jets intercepted.

The first Air Force bases descended upon and neutralized were Tyndall AFB and the main runways of Eglin. During this time, one of the descending UFOs actually encountered a jet observation plane near the coast. Tyndall had dispatched this jet toward the Gulf of Mexico to survey the area and look for survivors. The UFO did not fire at the jet but got close enough to cause its electrical system to malfunction.

This is when the "jet observation plane ran into technical trouble." The pilot saw the object coming toward him, and considering the problems it had caused with the jet's electrical system, "bailed out after heading the plane in the direction of the Gulf of Mexico." Shortly thereafter, the pilot landed near Tyndall AFB and the UFO continued toward Tyndall AFB and circled over their airfields. Another UFO that had descended near the coast dropped in over Eglin and circled over the main runways. These strategic maneuvers prevented jets from scrambling into the air after the damaged UFO.

Meanwhile, every military radar installation in the southeast was tracking the thirteen descending UFOs. They also tracked the first three UFOs, including the damaged object, which was quickly losing altitude and heading toward Florida. It was feared the objects might attack, crash-land into a populated area, or make a kamikaze maneuver into a nearby Air Force base.

In the meantime, the third UFO left the damaged craft and the other escort object and headed toward the four incoming Eglin jets to head them off at the pass. The intentions of this object were not to destroy the jets but only to stop them from advancing. Because the Eglin fighter pilots were not aware of the UFO's strategy, the first jets fired upon it and missed. Seconds later, the UFO retaliated and destroyed them. The remaining jets were hit by an indirect shock wave and were damaged. They were ordered back to Eglin, told to land at one of the smaller fields, and guided in.

The third UFO then continued to descend over the Gulf of Mexico and followed the jets back toward Eglin AFB. Shortly after the jets landed, the UFO descended over another area of that large base and circled other airfields. At that point, Eglin AFB actually had two UFOs hovering over their airfields to thwart off any more jets that may have been scrambled.

Meanwhile, across the Gulf, MacDill AFB had vectored four CAP jets northwest toward Tyndall through a rainstorm. Four UFOs from above detected the four MacDill jets. The four UFOs descended through the clouds and rain. Two of these UFOs moved to the west of Crystal Bay and the Chassahowitzka Bay coastline over Gulf waters. They were positioned to form a horizontal blockade where they could make lateral movements across the Gulf of Mexico. Simultaneously, the two other UFOs headed toward the west coast of Florida.

The intentions of the two objects over the Gulf waters were to prevent the MacDill jets from going any further northwest. The Air Force interpreted this as an offensive strategy. These UFOs were above U.S. restricted airspace and deemed enemy invaders. While tracking the UFOs, one pair of jets moved toward one UFO, while the other pair of jets headed toward the second UFO. The UFOs continued to descend, moving into the jets' flight paths. The jets continued on their intercept bearings to overtake and bypass the UFOs. The first jets opened fire on the UFO in front of them; they missed. The UFO retaliated with fire, destroying the two jets. Seconds later, the second pair of jets closed in on their target and fired, narrowly missing it. This UFO attempted to shock wave the jets but missed a direct hit. The two jets were partially hit though and flying so erratically they did not pose a threat anymore. The two pilots struggled to control their jets. They retreated to MacDill AFB where one jet crash-landed and the other landed safely.

Meanwhile, the Air Force and Navy scrambled more fighters from MacDill AFB in Tampa, Pinecastle AFB in Orlando, Sanford NAS in Sanford, and jets from Patrick AFB in Cocoa. Radar stations discovered that two of the UFOs were moving toward populated areas. One UFO circled high above Ocala in the clouds, while the other hovered in the Inverness area, forming a north-south aerial blockade against the jets. The military could not afford aerial battles over populated areas. They did not know if the UFOs would strike civilians. Another concern was how many more UFOs there were in a position to descend upon Florida. The northwest bound jets from the central and west coast of Florida were recalled, as well as the jets moving over the Gulf from MacDill. At that point, the situation along the west coast had turned into a standoff.

The Air Defense Headquarters in Colorado and Air Force Headquarters officials at the Pentagon were flooded with calls from southeast officials. Meanwhile, pandemonium was raging, and it was far from being over. Military installations were being neutralized throughout the southeast as well as all the flight paths leading into the Gulf of Mexico. Within moments, nearly the entire southeast United States would be neutralized, rendering military installations helpless.

In the meantime, the four F-94B jets that were approaching Tyndall for landings could not touch down because the descended UFO had neutralized the base. This UFO had cut off their airfields and was circling over and above the base. Jet fighters were not capable of getting off the ground and the four incoming F-94 jets were unable land. Jones was approaching Tyndall with his wing mate who was out of ammunition as the other two damaged jets flying below them struggled with their electrical problems. Tyndall personnel including Capt. Harrison analyzed the situation along the coastline southwest of their base. The two damaged jets and the jet depleted of its arms were then redirected to their alternate landing base, Moody AFB in Valdosta, Georgia.

Jones and DelCurto were also contacted with new orders. They were instructed to assist the four Moody jets in the interception of the damaged UFO and the remaining escort UFO. Jones and DelCurto then redirected their jet. As the four Moody fighters headed toward the damaged object and its escort, they were tracked coming in.

The escort object descended, redirected toward the four jets and attempted to intercept them as they neared. The first pair of jets closed and fired upon the escort object, which deftly outmaneuvered their barrage of gunfire. The object quickly retaliated against the jets, and disintegrated them. The other two Moody jets immediately broke off their attack. They banked away, reorganized and then prepared to intercept the escort UFO from another approach.

In the meantime, the damaged craft approached the Florida panhandle on a northeast trajectory across the Gulf in flames. It decided against Tyndall AFB as a power source and looked for another source along the panhandle coast. It descended, dropped off radar and then passed over the St. Joseph Peninsula. The flaming object proceeded toward the coastline as Tyndall towermen watched it descend out in the distance and disappear from sight. The damaged UFO flew over the coast near Port St. Joe and began to decelerate to prepare for its landing near some power lines. The craft struggled to hover atop the trees, made its final descent inland between Mexico Beach and Port St. Joe, southeast of Tyndall AFB and finally landed.

During that time, the Air Force was unaware of the object's exact location but knew it was near the coast and just southeast of the base. It became apparent, because of the damaged craft's trajectory, that it had been forced to make an emergency landing.

The primary objective of the Air Force was to now locate the downed craft until it could be reached by ground forces and retrieved.

Officials ordered contingents of men to gather arms and explosives and prepare to advance to the area in vehicles in an attempt to retrieve the object. Their first obstacle was to get off base without being noticed by the UFO circling over Tyndall AFB.

The "strange paper balloon" that was found drifting along near the Tallahassee airport by the Tallahassee Civil Air Patrol "where they saw it land in a tall pine tree" now enters the scenario. This "hot air balloon" was "apparently" not positively "made of rice paper over a wire frame." Inside of the so-called balloon was a "wire bracket for a heating element." The interior of the balloon was "badly smoked." Furthermore, "there was no indication what type of fuel had been used to provide hot air to raise the balloon." This odd balloon was "being turned over to military authorities" because the balloon was directly related to the craft that landed.

When the UFO had been damaged, the electrical field around it was broken, which was directly related to its anti-gravity and propulsion systems. When the object was forced to land, it landed near the power transmission lines, which were located along the coastline of the Florida panhandle. This object had to regenerate by drawing electricity from a power source. The "odd balloon" was the conductor used by the craft to draw electricity to itself.

When the damaged UFO landed near the power transmission lines, it launched the electrical conductor balloon into the air. When the balloon neared the power transmission lines, the electrical flow of energy was transferred within and through the balloon conductor back to the object. The UFO could recharge itself. Meanwhile, Lt. Jones' wing mate and the two damaged F-94s were directed away from Tyndall to Moody AFB in Georgia.

At this point during the incident Captain Harrison explained, "In the meantime, we had contacted Moody. They were alerted and had already worked one aircraft sent over there." This aircraft was F-94, #0842. Harrison then stated, "Others were on their way."

The other jets that were on their way were #0851 and #0849. The AACS at Tyndall AFB stated the following in a certificate dated 18 September 1952, "AF 0842 F-94 …landed 1535C (3:35), AF 0851 F-94 …pilot advised to go to his alternate at approximately 1520C (3:20), AF 0849 F-94, [Tyndall AFB] was unable to contact aircraft. Jacksonville control advised aircraft was working Moody D/F station." This document does not show landing times for the last two jets sent to Moody. Furthermore, Tyndall AFB was unable to contact the last jet; Jacksonville control line had actually informed Tyndall tower that Moody AFB was guiding the jet back to their base. Captain Harrison then stated, "There were already three gone. Lt. Jones was the last one…and acknowledged he was proceeding to his alternate."

In turn, the four jets were redirected and vectored toward their alternate field, Moody AFB. The official AF Accident report stated, "It is assumed that 0819 [Lt. Jones] departed Tyndall AFB at 1535 (3:35 p.m. CST) with 289 gallons of fuel." In an official statement given by Capt. Harrison, he said, "#819 said his fuel was 289 gallons and that his altitude was 29,000 ft. I gave him a course of 075-degrees to fly to Tallahassee, FL and told him to contact Moody AFB D/F on 'D' Delta when he got over TAL. The tower took care of his clearance. He [Lt. Jones] acknowledged these instructions and it was assumed that he was proceeding to his alternate."

The official AF Accident report also stated, "The instructor in the tower, Capt. Harrison advised Tyndall Approach Control to send 0819 [Lt. Jones] to his alternate, Moody AFB, when he got back over the station. Capt. Harrison advised 0819 to depart for Tallahassee radio on a heading of 075-degrees and to contact Moody D/F when over Tallahassee, on D channel for a steer."

At the AAI board meeting, Major Pompetti asked Capt. Harrison if one of the Ground Approach Controllers had acknowledged Lt. Jones calling Tyndall upon reaching Tallahassee. Pompetti asked Harrison, "Does he [Ground Approach Controller] remember if #819 [Lt. Jones] reported or called over Tallahassee as he was instructed?" Harrison answered, "I don't remember whether he [Ground Approach Controller] said he [Lt. Jones] was over Tallahassee or not."

Approach control operator, 1st Lt. Robert A. Dunn told a different story when he was questioned by Major Pompetti at the AAI board meeting. Major Pompetti asked Lt. Dunn the following, "Q. Did you relay the instructions to #819 [Lt. Jones] to depart to his [Moody] alternate. A. Yes, Sir. Q. In these instructions, was he instructed to report to Moody D/F over Tallahassee? A. Not that I remember," answered Lt. Dunn. It is evident by the statements that this incident was a convoluted mess and officials seemed to have *selective memory*. Why was everyone unaware of Lt. Jones location? I believe these towermen actually knew where the pilot was. Jones was in communication with Tyndall AFB and was being tracked on radar.

How could they not know where Lt. Jones was? Why were Captain Harrison and Lt. Dunn unable to remember what occurred? In the meantime, the two remaining Moody fighters had regrouped and attempted to intercept the escort object again. A fierce battle ensued as the UFO warded off yet another intercept by the jets. By keeping their distances, the jets survived this confrontation, passed out over the Gulf waters, ascended, and regrouped for another attack.

Meanwhile, in Ohio, intelligence officials at ATIC had come to some conclusions about the power source of these UFOs. They concluded that the source of power, which generates the crafts propulsion systems are electricity produced by an onboard generator system. An anti-gravity field that is based on the principals of electro-magnetism also surrounds their ships. In other words, the ships are surrounded by an electromagnetic field, which creates their own anti-gravity environment. When this electromagnetic field is disrupted by firepower, the anti-gravity field is broken, which also causes a loss of power and causes the craft to descend or fall to earth.

Intelligence theorized that the UFO's armaments might also have a major drawback. When their high-intensity attack beam is repeatedly utilized, it will probably drain the power from their craft. This would lessen the range and strength of the weapon and drain the power from its propulsion system, which would subsequently slow the craft down. The ATIC officials quickly called Tyndall officials and briefed them with this information. Tyndall officials contacted other nearby military installations involved in the situation over the Gulf and made them aware of this information. Quickly, word was also conveyed to the fighter pilots. Simultaneously, ATIC officials had also contacted several top-ranking intelligence officials in Washington, D.C. about their findings.

Meanwhile, Tyndall tower officials contacted Jones and gave him new orders. He was told not to head into the air battle of the escort object and the two remaining Moody jets. Moody AFB had just scrambled four more fully armed jet fighters toward the air battle area to attempt an intercept against the escort UFO. At this point, Second Lt. Jones was reordered to the Port St. Joe area where the damaged object was seen going down and told to find it. Tyndall radar operators steered Jones and DelCurto to the coastline. As the jet descended and approached the area, the pilot looked for the downed UFO with orders to immediately radio its location so ground forces could find it. Jones was also ordered to attempt an air strike to assure the object stayed down.

Jones and DelCurto kept descending; they saw the damaged object on the ground. The pilot took notice of the odd balloon that was connected to the power lines. They radioed back to Tyndall AFB, reporting the object and its location. Tyndall responded by telling the pilots to take out the balloon and and/or the power lines and try to separate the balloon from the craft. During the time the damaged craft was grounded, it was continuously absorbing electricity through its conductor to regenerate itself.

The jet approached and fired at the downed object and the odd balloon. Simultaneously, the UFO fired back. A barrage of gunfire soared through the air in the vicinity of the object and ground throughout the area. As .50 caliber bullets hit the power lines, they were instantly set ablaze, damaging the balloon. After completing their successful air strike mission, pilot Jones and DelCurto departed the area and radioed Tyndall AFB.

Meanwhile, the ground contingents were alerted of the downed object's location. Hurriedly, they split up and headed southeast toward the target area on separate paths. As the ground forces left the base, the UFO hovering over Tyndall tracked one of the groups of men. It moved in the direction of the contingent, descended toward their vehicles and fired in their vicinity in an attempt to stop them from advancing. The object circled back and forth between Tyndall's airfields and the advancing contingents in an attempt to neutralize them, which proved to be a difficult task. The contingents continued to advance southeast on different courses while the patrolling UFO relocated and circled the airfields to intercept any jets that may have been scrambled.

In the meantime, Tyndall AFB control tower personnel ordered Jones to proceed to Moody AFB. At this point, Lt. Jones was advised by Tyndall AFB tower personnel to go to Moody AFB, the alternative landing field because their armaments were nearly depleted. They advised that Jones should not enter the battle against the UFO because Moody AFB had already vectored two fully armed jets toward this area. Meanwhile, the escort UFO had overcome the two relentless Moody jets engaged in battle against it.

The next objective for this UFO was to neutralize nearby Moody AFB, but two more jet fighters had already been scrambled. The escort UFO headed northwest toward Moody AFB and the pair of incoming Moody jets. A confrontation was inevitable. Second Lt. Jones had informed the incoming Moody jets of the exact location of the downed object.

Within minutes, the Moody jets were about to strike at the escort object headed toward them in an effort to bypass it and continue after the downed object. The two Moody jets were vectored by CGI toward the UFO. Moments later, the radar operators had the object on their scopes and directed their pilots toward their target. The pilots took control and shortly after approached the UFO and closed on it. The jets fired at the UFO with rapid gunfire from the fixed gun armaments and gunfire blanketed the sky. The UFO evaded the onslaught by pulling up and away and then banked away and passed over the nearest striking jet and disintegrated it. The remaining jet pulled away and climbed to an even higher altitude to escape the UFO.

Likewise, the UFO maneuvered and climbed in the opposite direction away from the jet. Once again, the remaining jet received orders to attempt an intercept on the UFO, which had positioned itself between the downed object and the jet.

Meanwhile Lt. Jones and Lt. DelCurto were vectored toward Moody AFB, bypassing the air battle area after their air strike against the downed object. During this time between 3:35 p.m. and 4:00 p.m. CST, they were allegedly flying by Tallahassee en route to Moody AFB. There was an elapsed time of approximately twenty-five minutes. During this time, Captain Harrison made this statement to Major Pompetti, "That was the last we heard of him for a while until we heard him calling Moody Approach on 'B' channel. He was coming in clear at that time."

Approach control officer, Lt. Dunn told Major Pompetti what occurred next, when he was questioned:

Q. When you first heard him [Lt. Jones] ask Moody for a steer, do you know what time it was?
A. Somewhere around 1600 [4:00 p.m. CST] I can't be sure.
Q. Did you at any time ask him to switch to the 'D' Channel?
A. No. I did not.
Q. At any time during this incident, did you or anyone else instruct #819 to switch to "D" channel?
A. No—not to my knowledge.
Q. Was there some reason for not switching to "D" channel?
A. No, I don't know of any reason for not switching to "D" channel. (NOTE: There was contact with jet.)
Q. The reason I asked the question is because it is obvious from the statements in file that at approximately 1600 [4:00 p.m. CST] this thing was reaching emergency stages, yet we evidently did not go to emergency frequencies. My question is why?
A. There I think it is the pilot's responsibility to go to "D" channel if he considers himself in emergency.

At this stage of the incident, Lt. Jones did not declare an emergency because he simply was not in an emergency situation at this juncture. Furthermore, the electromagnetic field of the UFO hovering over Tyndall AFB was the cause of the airwave communication problems. Meanwhile, Jones and DelCurto were en route to Moody AFB to land when Jones contacted Tyndall Tower. MacDill AFB in Tampa who was monitoring the situation overheard him.

At that point, MacDill tower controllers intervened. What occurred during the time that MacDill made their takeover was documented in *The Panama City News Herald* on September 14, 1952. In an article titled, "Flyers Hunt Tyndall Pair" it states, "McDill (sic) operations told him [Lt. Jones] to attempt a landing at Valdosta, GA and gave him a fix…Failure of a radio compass was believed to be the cause of the pilot's non-compliance with the order directing him to land in Valdosta [Moody AFB]."

USAF explained what allegedly happened at this point in the incident. MacDill AFB public information officer Captain Mitchell stated the following at the Sept. 12, 1952 press conference in Tampa, "First inkling that the craft was in trouble came when the pilot called Tyndall Air Force Base. He was directed to land at Valdosta, GA [Moody AFB] but for some reason, failed to comply with orders to land."

This portion of the incident is an Air Force fabrication. Jones had not notified Tyndall by radio that he was unsure of his position. Since he was in radio contact with Tyndall tower, why didn't he also explain why he could not contact Moody AFB? Why did the Air Force have to speculate that Lt. Jones radio compass failed?

Furthermore, why did Jones fail to comply with orders to land at Moody? Major Pompetti questioned Captain Harrison about Lt. Jones' onboard radio compass. The question as to whether the radio compass was functioning was answered. Furthermore, the question as to whether there was contact between Tyndall AFB and Lt. Jones at this point was also answered. Major Pompetti asked, "Q. Did Lt. Jones ever mention any difficulty with the radio compass, other than the [Tyndall] range going off the air, after the range went back on?" Captain Harrison replied, "A. At one time, when we found him where he was I instructed the tower operator to have him [Lt. Jones] check the slave compass against the magnetic compass and we never did get a satisfactory reply. We were reading him very weakly and could not make out exactly what he said." Pompetti asked, "Q. Did he mention any malfunction of the radio compass after the [Tyndall] range went back on air?" Captain Harrison answered, "A. No sir."

Lt. Jones approached Moody AFB to land his jet, but there was trouble on the ground. Two of the three jets that Tyndall tower redirected to Moody ahead of Jones had just crashed. The two damaged jets that were struggling with their electrical systems had approached Moody erratically and upon touching down, crashed, caught fire, and tied up the airfields. At that point, it was not possible for Lt. Jones to land. Jones and DelCurto were given orders to go into a holding pattern and await further instructions. At this time, while the aviators were circling near the base in their holding pattern, they were said to be lost and unable to contact Moody tower. While Jones kept the jet in a holding pattern and awaited his landing orders from Moody tower, there was a change in events.

The "medical report of AF Aircraft Accident" document explains this section of the incident as well. It states, "He [Jones] called Tyndall Approach Control and was given a VHF/DF steer to return to TAFB [Tyndall AFB]." At this point in the incident, Jones and DelCurto were supposedly being steered back toward Tyndall AFB in Panama City. The airmen had been listening via radio to the transmissions of the lone Moody airmen who were about to go into a one on one battle against the escort UFO. The Moody jet ascended and was about to attempt another intercept against the UFO. The jet went into a dive, approached the object and locked on to it. As gunfire careened through the sky, the object veered away fired and missed as the two veered away from each other at blinding speed. The jet continued to dive, maneuvered past the UFO and headed toward the downed object. The UFO then turned and reversed positions and headed toward the jet.

When Jones and DelCurto were said to be returning to Tyndall AFB, they were actually en route to assist the lone Moody AFB jet that was about to go one on one against the UFO. They kept in constant radio contact with Tyndall AFB tower controllers, who were directing the two flyers toward the air battle of the UFO and the remaining Moody AFB jet. Colonel B. T. Kleine's September 17, 1952 letter should have stated that the Tyndall radio directional finding had given Jones a steer in the direction of the air battle to assist the lone Moody jet, which was at odds against intercepting the UFO. The time was approximately 4:00 p.m. CST. While Jones and DelCurto were en route toward the air battle area, the UFO was attempting a diversionary maneuver to divert the jet away from the downed object sitting near the power lines.

Jones proceeded southwest as the UFO continued toward the Moody jet, the Moody pilot informed Jones that he believed the object was closing in on him to strike. This pilot decided to counter maneuver and go after the UFO. The pilot completed a wingover and dove directly toward the object. As the Moody jet approached the UFO, it struck first and fired.

The object maneuvered away from the diving jet, and fired back. With blinding speed, the jet veered away unharmed. It headed toward the UFO again. The fighter pilot fired and once again missed the target. Simultaneously, the UFO fired, hitting and disintegrating the jet. Jones and DelCurto continued southwest having heard what had just occurred. The UFO turned toward Moody AFB, wanting to neutralize that base before any more jets could be scrambled.

Moody AFB runways were ablaze from the jet fuel of the two crashed jet fighters. Ground crews were still trying to clear the twisted metal wreckage so they could safely scramble more jets as a fiery carnage raged across their fields.

Jones and DelCurto were redirected on a northwest heading around and away from the UFO. Its intention was to descend upon Moody AFB to prevent any more jets from being scrambled. The Air Force's intention however, was to have Jones avoid a deadly confrontation, then redirect him back toward the Panama City area and go after the downed object again. Jones continued on his northwest heading as the UFO continued in the other direction on a northeast heading toward Moody AFB.

At approximately 4:15 p.m., Lt. Jones declared an emergency; this time he actually was lost and had requested directions toward Panama City. During the Aircraft Accident Investigating board proceedings on 29 September 1952, Major Pompetti asked Capt. Harrison the following, "Q. Did the pilot at any time declare an emergency? A. No sir." This answer was an outright lie.

The following information appeared in the Extract From Air Rescue Service Report, Maxwell AFB dated September 24, 1952. [To Headquarters, Fifth Air Rescue Service] from Tyndall AFB and contradicts Harrison's answer. It stated, "At approximately 1615C [4:15 CST] 12 September 1952, 819 [Lt. Jones] called Tyndall Tower and declared an emergency, lost, and five minutes fuel left."

When Jones declared his emergency, he was temporarily lost. He became lost when Tyndall controllers redirected him away from the UFO, not because he had five minutes of fuel left as the Air Force stated. Lt. Jones actually needed directions back toward the Panama City area. The jet did not allegedly flameout until 4:42 p.m. CST, which is a time lapse of twenty-seven minutes later, not five minutes. The emergency information contained in the preceding extract sent to Maxwell AFB by Tyndall only contained a partial truth!

At approximately 4:15 p.m. CST, the situation took a turn for the worst at Moody AFB in Valdosta, GA. As jet fighters hit the runways to take-off, the UFO descended upon the base and began to circle the airfield. The object fired toward the ground near the jets. Supervisory personnel ordered their tower controllers to keep their jets grounded. At this point, if the jets attempted to take-off, it would have been like shooting ducks in a barrel. The jet pilots on the ground preparing to scramble were contacted and told not to take-off.

To complicate the situation, the electromagnetic fields of the objects that hovered over the two bases had disrupted the Air Forces airwave communications. Simultaneously, Tyndall redirected Jones back south through Tallahassee tower controllers and toward Panama City.

At this point, Tyndall AFB tower controllers directed the jet over the Florida panhandle through Tallahassee Airport. This F-94 Starfire was being tracked on radar throughout the state. The USAF and the two aviators realized the situation had now taken a turn for the worse and was hopeless. The flyers' options had run out. Jones and DelCurto, aware of their dire situation, were actually trapped between both bases and unable to land at either one. Moreover, military ground forces were unable to reach the damaged object and the Air Force was concerned it would escape before they reached it.

Documents from the case reported information about Lt. Jones fuel capacity at 4:20 p.m. CST. A September 17 teletype from Tyndall to Norton AFB stated, "1620 CST pilot called in with 94 gals." The "Report of AF Aircraft Accident" also stated, "0819 had 94 gals of fuel left." This information was relayed to Tallahassee Tower because 0819 could not read Tyndall Tower. Approach Controller S/Sgt. Ernest S. Bolen explained the following to Major Pompetti, "Tallahassee advised they were reading 0819 loud and clear. Tyndall Tower relayed 318-degree steer through Tallahassee Tower. The aircraft acknowledged steer from Tallahassee." The Tyndall "Direction Finding Log" recorded the time of their 318-degree steer at, "TIME-1620 (4:20 p.m.)."

S/Sgt. Bolen continues, "At this time, Tower contacted Jacksonville control and advised of the situation. Also called Florida State Police to patrol area between Tyndall and Apalachicola vicinity. MacDill then got in contact with the aircraft on another channel and Jacksonville control had alerted rescue facilities."

The situation that Tyndall AFB had alerted the Jacksonville control about was an emergency. At 4:21 p.m. CST, Tyndall AFB relayed a message to Tallahassee Airport who in turn contacted the fighter pilot, Lt. Jones.

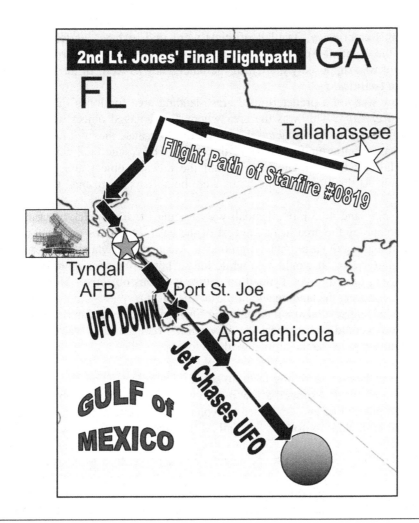

The "Report of AF Aircraft Accident" document stated the following, "At 1621 C [4:21 p.m.] a second bearing of 320-degrees was given by Tyndall AFB." The Tyndall AFB "Direction Finding Log" also disclosed more information of what occurred at 4:21 p.m. CST. At that time, Lt. Jones had declared another emergency. The "D/F log" states, "A/C IDENT - 0819. COURSE - 320. TIME-1621. REMARKS - EB EMER. [Emergency]." This was the second emergency declared by Jones in six minutes.

The first was at 4:15 p.m. CST. What supposedly occurred next was the most convoluted segment of this entire incident. Although Lt. Jones had declared a second emergency at 4:21 p.m., the USAF never disclosed the location of the supposedly lost jet at 4:20 or 4:21 p.m. The coordinates were never given and the information concerning this segment of the incident is vague in details. This was obviously never disclosed because it would have raised too many questions concerning the validity of this incident. Jones and DelCurto were actually northwest of Tyndall AFB, and proceeding on a southeast trajectory toward it.

The jet was supposedly being steered back to Tyndall AFB with just over 90 gallons of fuel remaining, back into the area where they were redirected away from because of supposedly bad weather. During this emergency, Tyndall officials were said to have alerted the Florida State Police to patrol the Tyndall-Apalachicola area according to tower controller S/Sgt. Bolen. Jacksonville control was supposedly alerted of the emergency as well. In turn, they were said to have alerted rescue facilities.

This emergency was *not* a predetermined crash-landing area for Jones' jet though. *This was the Air Force's cover story.* This was the area where the damaged object was down along the coast. Military officials actually contacted the State Police because they did not want civilians in the area if there was an opportunity to retrieve the object. The rescue facilities were contacted in case a situation did rise between the Starfire and the downed object and the airmen needed emergency attention. At this point, all the bases were being covered to hide the outcome of this event.

Between 4:21 p.m. and 4:25 p.m., Tyndall was steering Lt. Jones back toward Panama City and ordered him to survey the area just southeast of the base. Jones was told to find the downed object, fire upon it and make sure it stayed grounded. Meanwhile, Tyndall's ground forces were advancing slowly to the area. It would be a while longer before the area could be reached. Jones flew southeast passing directly over Tyndall on course with this objective. Moments later the jet passed over the St. Joe area, the landing site of the downed UFO.

The jet descended and several small smoldering fires could be seen, damped out by the falling rain. Billowing smoke could be seen near the power lines, rising from a black and burnt area on the ground near a utility pole. As the airmen made a closer pass, they noticed that the downed craft was gone!

They passed over the area searching for it, to see if it had relocated nearby. Jones followed the power lines and the object was spotted a few miles away. Once again, the object had its balloon apparatus aloft at a power line and continued to replenish its electrical power. As the jet, headed toward the downed craft, Jones informed Tyndall AFB of the craft's exact location and told them he was going to attempt an air strike. Seconds later, the downed craft lifted off, disconnecting from the balloon's umbilical cord that was connected to the power line. Moments later the balloon separated from the power line and drifted away into the sky. Rather than risk another air strike that could permanently disable it, the craft began to flee and fired at the maneuvering jet but missed.

Jones quickly banked the Starfire, put the jet in a dive and chased the fleeing UFO toward the Florida coastline. As the UFO picked up speed, it continued to ascend, with Jones in hot pursuit. If not for Jones and DelCurto, the damaged UFO would have been able to charge itself to full capacity.

Instead, the weakened UFO was unwillingly forced to deal with a jet that was desperately trying to take it down. Jones closed the gap on the UFO as it neared the coastline just west of Apalachicola on a southeast trajectory. Shortly after, the damaged object passed out across the Gulf waters with Jones and DelCurto in hot pursuit and following right behind it.

At 4:25 p.m., MacDill intervened once again and began steering Jones and DelCurto. The following segment concerns this point in time of the incident. Tyndall Approach Control Officer, 1st Lt. Dunn was asked by Major Pompetti, "Q. At what time did MacDill start working him? A. I would say it must have been around 1625 [4:25 p.m. CST] because we were giving him steers through Tallahassee on 'B' channel. All of a sudden, he switched to 'C' channel—someone else was working him."

First Lt. Dunn also made this statement in his signed certificate; "Aircraft switched from 'B' channel to 'C' and started working MacDill." When Capt. Harrison was questioned by Major

Pompetti and the board concerning this segment of the incident, the following conversation transpired:

Q. When did MacDill D/F take over?
A. We [Tyndall] did not have any way of telling exactly when they took over. We got information from Tallahassee and they just notified us MacDill was working him [Jones] and we discontinued giving steers.
Q. Can you tell us how long this aircraft was following Tyndall's D/F from the time they regained contact with him?
A. I would say about five minutes or longer. When we first made contact with him again through Tallahassee Radio, I made inquiry about fuel and he had 94 gallons."

Tyndall AFB Colonel B. T. Kleine stated the following in his letter, "The Tyndall radio directional finding gave him a steer to Tyndall AFB. MacDill Air Force Base directional finding [Homer] was able to pick up Jones' voice and gave him a steer also." Air Defense Commander, General Chidlaw stated the following in his Western Union telegram to Lt. Jones' brother, on 15 September 1952, "The Tyndall tower was directing him to MacDill AFB FLO, which was the nearest base." Capt. Harrison told Major Pompetti this segment of the incident concerning MacDill's takeover from Tyndall. He said, "By working through Tallahassee Tower, which was able to read him, we relayed headings and steers for him [Jones] and Tallahassee relayed back information which Lt. Jones had to give. MacDill then started working him since he seemed to be closer to them."

What did Capt. Harrison mean in his statement that MacDill was working with Lt. Jones "since he seemed closer to them"? As Lt. Jones passed over the Florida panhandle coast on a 318-degree bearing, just southeast of Tyndall AFB, he was *not* on a direct flight path to MacDill AFB on the West Coast. The pilot's bearing was actually about ten degrees west of the direct flight path to Tampa.

Subsequently, when MacDill AFB gave Jones his first steer, the jet was only 100 miles from Tyndall in Panama City and 145 statute miles from their base in Tampa. Lt. Jones was *not* closer to MacDill AFB at this point. Moreover, the jet would have had less than 90 gallons of fuel left, only enough to get the two airmen part way across the Gulf waters to Tampa. The actual scenario; they never had any intentions of going to MacDill AFB when they passed over the Florida coastline.

Furthermore, Jones actually had more fuel than what the USAF stated; this was the Air Force's cover story. Jones was not lost and low on fuel. He was actually in hot pursuit of a fleeing UFO. The damaged UFO started to overheat as it sped away from the jet. This forced the object to slow down. The shell of the craft was burning up and it could not risk flying any faster. If the damaged object did not decelerate as it traveled further south over the Gulf of Mexico waters, it would deteriorate even further and be unable to get back to the coast. Meanwhile, the Starfire was in afterburner and consuming a large amount of fuel. Jones kept a watchful eye on his fuel gauge to avoid the same problem of being unable to reach land. Jones continued to accelerate and began to close the distance between them, as both aircrafts proceeded farther out over the Gulf waters.

The overheated object flew erratically to compensate for its loss of speed, trying to outmaneuver the jet. This strategy caused the damaged craft to lose control slightly. Jones pursued the object and guided his Starfire toward his erratic moving target with the assistance of DelCurto. Jones followed the object then got a momentary lock-on it and fired. However, the UFO had decelerated, pulled abruptly out of the fray, reversed direction and avoided the gunfire. The damaged object quickly ascended into some clouds and disappeared. After their failed intercept over the Gulf, the nearest base at this point was actually MacDill AFB. As Colonel B. T. Kleine explained, "MacDill Air Force Base directional was able to pick up John's voice and give him a steer also."

As Jones and DelCurto proceeded further southeast, MacDill radar officials alerted the flyers that the UFO had now started pursuing them. The aircraft's ammunition was nearly depleted as MacDill officials continued to steer the jet southeast. Controllers advised Jones and DelCurto to redirect their flight course and proceed toward Tampa and put their wheels down. The UFO continued to trail the Starfire, intending to follow it back to MacDill from a distance and from a higher altitude. It slowly descended, keeping the jet below and in front of it, trying to prod it to a lower altitude until it reached the coast and landed.

Meanwhile at MacDill, the combat air patrol jets continued to circle their base in anticipation of an aerial attack. However, the CAP jet fighters were not vectored toward the incoming UFO. MacDill officials believed doing so would result in deadly results for Jones and DelCurto. There were still two UFOs hovering north of Tampa along the coastline that could maneuver and attack at any moment. Any jet fighters maneuvered toward the direction of the damaged UFO might prompt attack by the two additional UFOs on the Starfire. An attack at this point could have proved disastrous for all of the jets. The situation had developed into a dangerous standoff. Frantic MacDill radar controllers advised the flyers to immediately direct toward the coastline and to continue descending. The pilot and navigator were still aware that the UFO was still following behind them, forcing them to fly at a lower altitude. Jones and DelCurto believed they were being maneuvered for an intercept attempt.

At 4:35 p.m. CST/5:35 p.m. EST, Jones and DelCurto were in afterburner, trying to outrun the UFO approximately 80 miles northwest of MacDill AFB. They were in radio contact with MacDill radar controllers who were tracking both the jet and UFO. Again, the flyers were ordered toward Tampa and told to attempt a landing at MacDill. The UFO continued to trail the Starfire while descending in altitude.

Jones was fully aware of the descending UFO's position and simultaneously descended. Both aircraft continued southeast toward the coast, cutting in and out of clouds and rain. Jones continued to drop in altitude, but had no intention of leveling off and proceeding to MacDill AFB. He contacted MacDill tower and made controllers aware that he intended to go after the object. A reverse maneuver would put the Starfire onto a northwest heading toward the object. Ground Control Intercept could guide the jet fighter onto an intercept course at the damaged UFO, since the jet had enough ammunition left to attempt one more good strike.

Jones then put the Starfire into a steep climb and ascended back up into the heavens. As the jet soared through sky, he quickly redirected it and completed a renversement. The jet was now on a northwest heading and the UFOs intent to trail the jet had failed. MacDill GCI guided Jones and DelCurto onto a direct intercept course toward the oncoming UFO. The Starfire soared through the air as DelCurto guided the jet toward the object. The autopilot was coupled with the jet's radar. As the two aircraft neared one another at blinding speed, the Starfire obtained a lock-on onto its target. The UFO accelerated, went into a dive and then changed direction as cannon fire blanketed the sky and partially hit the diving object, which burst into flames.

The damaged object did not go down and struggled to pull out of its dive as the Starfire continued heading northwest, completely out of ammunition. The damaged object slowly pulled out of its dive but was having trouble-attaining altitude as it continued southeast being tracked on radar. MacDill then radioed the flyers and told them that the object was still airborne. At 4:37 p.m. CST/5:37 p.m. EST, Lt. Jones contacted MacDill and alerted them that even though he was out of firepower, there was one remaining offensive maneuver to attempt. "Ramming" as defined by the USAF, "In air combat, an act or instance of deliberately flying or crashing into an enemy aircraft, engaged in only as a tactic of last resort." Jones and DelCurto had decided against proceeding to MacDill to land and opted to go after the UFO.

Their plans were to set the jet on to a collision course at the object and to eject from the jet before impact. The pilot began his renversement to go back south and maneuvered the Starfire into a wingover. Colonel Kleine should have made the following statement in his September 17 letter, "Shortly afterward, Jones said that he and DelCurto had decided to engage with the UFO and ram it." General Chidlaw should have stated the following in his September 15 telegram, "He informed MacDill AFB that they were going to attempt to ram the UFO."

General Chidlaw's September 17 telegram should have explained, "Immediately thereafter John completed a renversement and proceeded on a southeast heading after the damaged UFO to ram it." MacDill AFB began to direct the two flyers onto a course to approach the damaged object in a lead-pursuit intercept attack. Meanwhile the fleeing UFO had burst into flames as it continued southeast over the Gulf waters. Its power supply had diminished and the object needed to locate power lines where it could land and replenish its energy. At this point, the damaged object opted to go near the populated west coast area and did it want to risk going anywhere near MacDill AFB who still had their jets on combat air patrol. It redirected and proceeded on a northwest course toward the Florida Panhandle with the intention of landing in an isolated area to recharge.

At this point, both aircraft had reversed their flight headings and were now proceeding toward each other. MacDill alerted Jones that the UFO had just reversed its course away from the West Coast area and was now headed northeast in their direction. The UFO proceeded back north in the direction of the oncoming and diving F-94 Starfire, while struggling to keep its altitude steady. It flew erratically in an attempt to turn away from the jet and shake it.

The UFO then accelerated in an attempt to fly below the diving jet and continue past it heading north in the opposite direction away and from it. At 4:41 p.m. CST/5:41 p.m. EST, MacDill gave Jones a steer toward the northbound UFO flying below them. At 4:42 p.m. CST, MacDill guided the jet on an intercept course and Jones brought the jet down to an altitude of 15,000 feet. The jet continued to proceed toward the object in a dive, as the UFO tried to pass below it in the opposite direction. At this point, the jet supposedly had a flameout. Colonel B. T. Kleine stated, "Shortly afterward, he [Jones] said he had a flameout at 15,000 feet."

The Tampa Daily Times reported the following on September 13, "Lt. Col. Rosenblatt base operations officer [MacDill AFB], said the last coherent radio contact with the plane disclosed the pilot had engine trouble at 15,000 feet over the Gulf." It also gave the following information about the Starfire, "an Air Force jet plane last heard from at 5:42 p.m." *The Tampa Tribune* reported the following information about the flameout, quoting the same time as *The Tampa Daily Times*, "Earlier MacDill Air Force Base at Tampa reported a jet fighter has been unheard from since it radioed it was out of fuel at 5:42 p.m. [EST/4:42 p.m. CST.]"

The Tampa Tribune also reported the following, "The pilot was unable to give his exact position, and MacDill said the fighter could have been anywhere up to 70 [nautical] miles northwest of Tampa at the last radio report." According to the USAF version, the Starfire had a flameout. I compiled the following list of events in sequential order, as given by the USAF. I used the 4:42 CST flameout time because the official report had stated it three times. The list follows:

1). The Starfire radioed that it was out of fuel at 4:42 p.m. CST.
2). The pilot had engine trouble at 15,000 feet over the Gulf.
3). The Starfire had a flameout.
4). The flameout occurred at an altitude of 15,000 feet over the Gulf of Mexico.
5). The pilot was in radio contact with MacDill AFB when he notified them of the jet's flameout.
6). Jones was unable to give MacDill AFB tower his exact position.
7). The last coherent radio contact from the pilot occurred at 4:42 p.m. CST.
8). The last coherent radio contact from the pilot disclosed the jet was at 15,000 feet.
9). The jet had not been heard from since it radioed that it was out of fuel.
10). MacDill AFB said the Starfire could have been anywhere up to 70 miles northwest of Tampa at the last radio report.

According to the USAF version, when Jones reported the jet's flameout at 15,000 feet, the Starfire descended 7,000 feet. At 4:43 p.m. CST, the last radio sound heard from the jet indicated that it was down to 8,000 feet.

The UFO accelerated and began to flame up into an inferno. It swerved and tried to avoid the jet, which was now descending and heading in its direction. Jones and DelCurto proceeded at the object with the assistance of MacDill GCI and then achieved a radar lock-on shortly after. The pilot put the engine into afterburner, flashed through sky, and headed directly at the UFO. The object veered away from the descending jet and tried to avoid a mid-air collision but was too slow to out-maneuver it.

The Starfire continued to approach the object to ram it and showed no sign of turning away. The swerving UFO began to accelerate while redirecting its heading northeast. This maneuver proved ineffective. The descending Starfire closed on the UFO in afterburner and still locked-on to ram it. As the Starfire closed on the object and the flyers were about to eject, the object hit the jet with a tremendous shock causing its electrical system to go haywire and malfunction, blowing the circuit breakers. The jet was fried and the stunned airmen were knocked unconscious as the jet dove at the damaged UFO. At that point, there was complete radio fadeout and contact was lost.

The F-94 B Starfire cut through the air like a javelin as it approached the damaged object. Sadly, the "ramming" technique chosen by the two flyers had unwillingly turned into a kamikaze mission. Seconds later, at 4:43 p.m. CST, the UFO fired on the approaching jet, which vanished in a blinding flash. Air Force personnel on the ground were unaware if the crew had bailed out of the jet. Radar operators tracking this incident only knew that the jet had disappeared from their radar screens.

This segment of the incident agrees with the original statement made to the press, by MacDill AFB Public Information Officer Captain Paul Mitchell. On September 13, *The Tampa Daily Times* reported that Mitchell stated, "The last radio sound indicated the disabled craft was down to 8,000 feet. The time was 5:43 [4:43 p.m. CST]." MacDill base operations officer, Lt. Col. Charles A. Rosenblatt, stated the following: "There was complete radio fadeout at 5:43 [EST/4:43 CST] at about 8,000 ft. Standard procedure is for the crew to bail out."

The damaged UFO continued toward the Florida panhandle coastline and transmitted a call to the other UFOs hovering throughout the southeast. It notified them that its power was nearly drained and it desperately needed to land and regenerate. Meanwhile, the MacDill AFB combat patrol jets patrolling the base were ordered to stay over the vicinity of Tampa and not to pursue the object over the Gulf of Mexico. Very slowly, the damaged UFO proceeded across the Gulf and received instructions to land near the Apalachee Bay area, south of Tallahassee, where it could recharge its nearly depleted system. The damaged object continued to burn-up as it descended en route to its destination to make a landing.

Meanwhile, President Truman and Washington officials were being informed of the unfolding events throughout the southeast, including the recent Jones and DelCurto incident. Air Force bases along the Florida coast also alerted them that military radars were still tracking the damaged UFO. During this time, Air Force officials from Tyndall AFB also informed Washington that it was inevitable the damaged UFO was going to land again to recharge. Here, the government had another opportunity to attempt to capture the damaged craft once it landed; but how long would it be on the ground was another question.

Government officials were fully aware that Air Force and Naval Air Stations along the Gulf of Mexico were still neutralized as well as military flight paths leading to the Gulf waters and were furious. Brookley AFB and Pensacola NAS already had their flight paths into the Gulf of Mexico neutralized by a UFO hovering off the coast and were out of the picture. Jet attacks through corridors over populated areas to reach the damaged object were ruled out. Upon landing, this object had to be kept on the ground until it could be retrieved.

Air Force officials jointly devised a plan to utilize fighter planes from their Alabama bases. They would head southwest toward the Florida panhandle coastline and then proceed out over the Gulf of Mexico west of Pensacola NAS. The planes would then redirect east and head toward the area where the object was descending toward the Apalachee Bay coastline. If they reached the area, they would attempt an air strike. The planes from Alabama were deployed shortly after and headed toward the Gulf waters along the southern Alabama coastline. However, as they neared the coast to flank around Brookley AFB there was a sudden change in events.

While en route, their movements were being tracked. As they neared the coast to proceed across the Gulf, an object that hovered over the Gulf near Brookley AFB and two objects that patrolled the coastline near Pensacola NAS and Eglin AFB descended and moved into strategic positions. The UFO out over the Gulf waters south of Brookley AFB turned inland toward the Alabama coastline and moved northwest as the two other objects shifted west as backup. The first object continued northwest, passed over Mobile Bay and did a flyby over Brookley AFB.

It then descended on the city of Mobile, and began to circle the area. Moments later, for fear of negative repercussions on Mobile, the entire attack plan was aborted, as the heavily armed UFO continued to patrol over that densely populated city. The planes then headed back to Alabama.

Meanwhile, at about 5:45 p.m. EST/6:45 p.m. EDT, the damaged UFO continued to descend

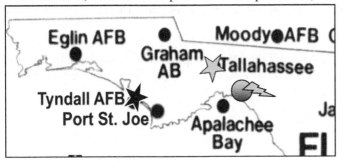

as it proceeded northwest and neared the Apalachee Bay coastal area. The object continued to descend over the Gulf toward the panhandle coast as Tyndall officials tracked it until it dropped below radar to the southeast of their base. At this point, they realized the object needed power and knew its objective.

Simultaneously, radar controllers at Tallahassee Airport tracked the UFO as well. They also had a visual on the flaming object as it neared the coast southeast of them only a short distance away. Moments later, the object passed over land, decelerated and headed for the power lines along the coast and prepared to land.

Tallahassee Airport officials knew the approximate area where the object was going to land near the coast and notified Tyndall AFB officials of the location. In desperate need of electricity, the damaged UFO headed toward the power lines and transformers along the panhandle coastline. Tyndall officials immediately contacted the contingents of heavily armed ground forces who were in the Port St. Joe area. The ground forces were ordered to redirect toward the Apalachee coast area in an attempt to reach the relocated object. Moments later, they headed east. The cat and mouse game continued in the densely wooded Florida swampland.

Wrapping up the events up to this point, the UFOs that descended on the southeastern United States on September 12 had actually originated from one main large craft, a Mothership. This enormous craft was a carrier, or Mothership, capable of holding and transporting many smaller crafts. It was positioned over the southeastern Unites States, high above the outer atmosphere of the earth, known as the exosphere. The Mothership hovered in space and had dispatched the sixteen smaller crafts toward Earth. These crafts made atmospheric entries and observed the Florida panhandle coastline; they were on an aerial reconnaissance mission to examine military installations throughout the southeast. When three of these crafts descended toward the Gulf, jet fighters intercepted them. One of the UFOs was hit and damaged, and it sustained a major power loss. It was unable to ascend out of the earth's atmosphere and reach the Mothership.

When the Air Force attempted to intercept the damaged object again, the remaining UFOs descended to protect it and the situation escalated. Jets were lost, several were damaged, and many were recalled back to their bases. Moreover, military installations and flight paths were neutralized.

During this entire event, the United States military was the aggressor. During battle, the UFOs had used their armaments only in retaliation after being fired at first. During these air battles, the United States military became fully aware of the objects maneuverability's and advanced armaments. When intelligence analyzed the information about the UFOs, they were correct when they concluded the UFOs were generated by an electrical propulsion system. Furthermore, they were correct when they theorized that repeated firing of their armaments would drain their power and slow them down. Therefore, the more power used, the less powerful their arms were!

The UFOs had another disadvantage, they were also large, cumbersome and when their power drained, they became less agile. The UFOs still overcame the jets even when they were outnumbered by a ratio of 4 to 1 because of their devastating powers, yet they were vulnerable to the armaments of Air Force jet fighters. During these air battles, the American jets were the slugger going up against the boxer.

However, the jets also had another major disadvantage; while they were trying to outmaneuver the UFOs, the entire area was being monitored by the Mothership hovering high above the Gulf of Mexico. This craft was directing the objects below it and keeping them informed of the jet fighters' maneuvers during these air battles.

198

The UFOs Descended from a Mothership

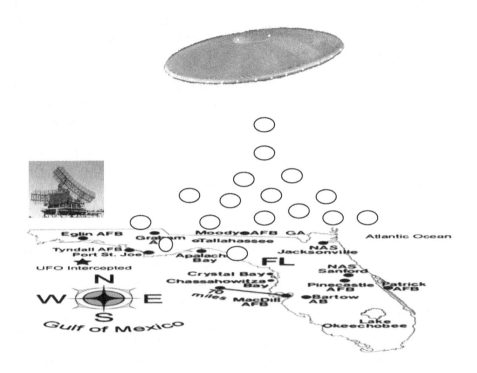

CHAPTER EIGHTEEN

TARGET FLATWOODS

The damaged UFO continued to descend and landed near the power lines along the Apalachee Bay coastline at approximately 5:55 p.m. EST/6:55 p.m. EDT. In the meantime, the Mothership that was positioned over the Gulf off the Florida coast, had headed northeast over the United States toward the mid-Atlantic region. The downed and damaged object then launched another balloon-type apparatus toward the power lines at the transformer and began to charge itself as ground forces headed toward it.

Meanwhile, the Mothership proceeded northeast above the atmosphere and passed high over Virginia. It then flew over Delaware, continued south of New Jersey, and passed out over the Atlantic Ocean. The Mothership continued northeast over the Atlantic, stopped and located about 90 miles off the coast of New Jersey. It positioned itself near the 39-degree latitude/73-degree longitude mark, an area approximately 200 miles east of Washington, D.C. The time was approximately 6:00 p.m. EST/ 7:00 p.m. EDT.

This craft's position, which was directly east of the nation's Capitol, was not a coincidence; it was the area where the three flight paths of the damaged mid-Atlantic UFOs converged near the 39-degree latitude/73-degree longitude point. This was the area where the three mid-Atlantic objects were actually dropped from their Mothership.

The three objects made their atmospheric descents into this area shortly after 7:00 p.m. EDT. This descent into the atmosphere just east of the Capitol and into the radar net of the Atlantic ADIZ was an assertive tactic to make their presence known to Washington officials. The intention of the three UFOs was not to attack Washington; they could have already done that by descending on the city. Their objective was to warn Washington officials to keep away from their downed craft in Florida and to leave it alone. The "pilots" of the UFOs knew their damaged craft sitting in Florida needed more time to regenerate before it could lift off again.

Meanwhile, radarscopes along the east coast and mid-Atlantic coastline had picked up the three descended UFOs. Immediately, the Pentagon was notified. In a "situation room" at the Pentagon, conversations went back and forth between the Secretary of Defense, the National Security Council and the Joint Chiefs of Staff as the situation escalated. These military officials did not interpret the appearance of these objects as a warning to back off from the downed craft in Florida. They interpreted their blatant appearances as a threatening maneuver to attack Washington, D.C. Again, President Truman was immediately contacted at the White House and notified of this recent situation. Upon receipt of this information, the President demanded to be taken to the Pentagon immediately and was quickly ushered out.

Enroute to the Pentagon, Truman, the Commander in Chief, was updated about the unfolding UFO events off the east coast as well as the grim situation in Florida. Upon entering a "situation room," an infuriated President Truman spoke with Defense Secretary Robert Lovett, members of the Joint Chiefs of Staff and the National Security Council about his tactical options. Subsequently, a stern Mr. Lovett advised President Harry Truman that an all-out air assault against these objects is inevitable and the UFOs should no longer compromise the United States. All of President Truman's military advisors agreed as well.

An enraged President Truman calmed down, analyzed the situation and considered his options. He pondered, looked around the room at his advisors and then nodded, yes to them.

Truman then ordered the Air Defense Command and Navy to send up combat patrol jets around the Capitol area to form a perimeter around the city. Frontline jets were also ordered to patrol the coastline over the mid-Atlantic waters to the east of Washington, D.C. President Truman then ordered nearby east coast Air Force bases and Naval Air Stations to scramble their jets after the UFOs over the Atlantic Ocean. Within minutes, interceptors, including rocket-bearing jets, guarded the Capitol area and coastline. An unyielding President Truman stared across the room at his advisors. I cannot help but echo the words stated by President Truman in 1949, *"It is much better to go down fighting for what is right than to compromise your principles."*

Meanwhile, intelligence officials at Wright Patterson AFB had contacted the "situation room" at the Pentagon. The experts at ATIC told the President that the most vulnerable area of the crafts is actually their underside. If this area of the craft's anti-gravity field is disrupted, the gravitational pull that balances it between the magnetic poles is immediately lost, which will cause it to fall toward the earth. The weak spot of the UFOs had been found! Immediately, the word went out to every east coast Air Force base and Naval Air Station and all pilots are informed about their enemy's vulnerable underside area. The fighter pilots are told to attempt their interceptions from below and fire at the belly of the crafts if possible.

At approximately 7:05 p.m. EDT, U.S. jet fighters were en route to intercept the objects ninety miles off the coast, with orders to *"shoot them down."* The nearest Air Force bases that scrambled jet fighters toward these objects are as follows:

1. McGuire AFB. Wrightson, New Jersey - 90 miles away
2. Dover AFB. Dover, Delaware - 120 miles away
3. New Castle AFB. Wilmington, Delaware – 135 miles away
4. Stewart AFB. Newburgh, New York – 175 miles away
5. Andrews AFB. Camp Springs, Maryland– 193 miles away
6. Westover AFB. Chicopee Falls, Mass. – 205 miles away
7. Langley AFB. Hampton, Virginia – 220 miles away
8. Otis AFB. Falmouth, Massachusetts – 235 miles away

The following four Naval Air Stations scrambled fighters:

1. NAS New York. New York - 120 miles away
2. NAS Willow Grove. Pennsylvania - 140 miles away
3. NAS Patuxent River. Maryland – 180 miles away

4. NAS Norfolk. Virginia – 220 miles away

President Truman then ordered additional jet fighters into action over the United States. These jets also began combat air patrols near the vicinity of Washington, D.C. to further protect its citizens and government officials. Within minutes, the Capitol area was fully guarded. These jet fighters were dispatched from the following installations:

1. Bolling AFB. Washington, D.C.
2. Andrews AFB. Camp Springs, Maryland
3. Quantico Marine Corps Air Station. Quantico, VA.
4. NAS Patuxent River. Maryland

The United States Navy had the duty to patrol the Potomac River area, which included the District of Columbia. On duty in this area were the Potomac River Naval Command and the Severn River Naval Command. The best jet fighters the Air Force, Navy, and the Marine Corps possessed at that time are as follows:

AIR FORCE
1. *Thunder Jets* a) F-84E b) F-84G

2. *Sabre Jets* a) F-86D b) F-86E c) F-86F

3. *Starfires* a) F-94B b) F-94C

NAVY
1. *Banshees* a) F2H-2

2. *Cutlasses* a) F7U-1 b) F7U-3

3. *Sky Knights* a) F3D

4. *Panthers* a) F9F-2 b) F9F-3 c) F9F-5

MARINE CORPS
1. *Panthers* a) F9F-2 b) F9F-3

The above jets I have listed were the superior jet fighters during that time of the various models of aircraft possessed by the United States military. Three of these jet fighters were armed with powerful twenty-four 2.75-inch rockets nicknamed the "Mighty Mouse." These rockets had a greater range than aircraft machine guns, which made them more deadly. They served as an optional weapon on the F7U-3 Cutlass were standard-issue on the F-86D Sabre Jet and came equipped on the Air Force's newest aerial defense innovation, the F-94C Starfire.

The other jets that I listed were also armed with powerful weapons. The Air Force jets carried multiple .50 caliber cannons and the Navy and Marine jets carried 20 mm machine guns that could deliver thousands of rounds of fire. The F-84E jet fighter armed with six .50 caliber cannons was also capable of carrying wing loads of thirty-two 5-inch HVARs (High Velocity Aircraft Rockets). In combination, all of these military jet fighters had the capability to deliver devastating firepower against airborne enemies. Shortly after, East Coast Air Force bases and Naval Air Stations vectored their jet fighters after the UFOs being tracked on radar.

The pilots knew that these objects were vulnerable to the cannon firepower of their jets and were aware of their opponent's weapons. The fighter pilots received strict orders to keep a safe distance from them and to be extremely cautious. Unlike the aerial battles over the Gulf, this situation would be very different. Several of these jet fighters were armed with rockets, which included the 2.75-inch rockets nicknamed, "Mighty Mouse," preparing to go into battle. On September 13, 1952,

The Boston Globe reported this unusual incident that involved jets on September 12, 1952. This incident took place over Rhode Island, about forty miles from the coastline and read:

Unidentified Jets 'Buzz' R.I. Town

Residents of the Tarklin section were thrown into near panic today when two unidentified jet planes "buzzed" the area. According to complaints they roared 30 feet above the ground at one time. Raymond F. Cahill, town Civil Defense director, said he would report the incident to Army and Air Force authorities at the New Haven [CT] filter center.

Mrs. Cyril Bruineel of Tarklin Road reported it was only a "miracle" that her house wasn't hit by one or both of the jets. She said the planes flashed by at lightning speed almost at rooftop level, barely missing telephone wires. The woman said she threw herself flat on the ground during the "buzzing" and that terrified farm animals kept up a noisy chatter for 45 minutes. Another Tarklin woman, Mrs. James A. Starck, of Barnes road described the experience as "harrowing." She said it appeared as though the planes would crash into houses or trees at "almost any second."

This article informs us of a highly unusual episode that occurred over Rhode Island that involved two jets. In 1952, the only American jets flying over the United States were jet fighters. The article states the aircraft were "two unidentified jet planes." The nearest Air Force base to the Tarklin area was "Westover Air Force Base," in Chicopee Falls, Massachusetts. This base is located about 55 miles northwest of Tarklin and home of the 4707th Defense wing, 60th Fighter Interceptor Squadron.

These two jets were almost certainly Sabre Jets from Westover AFB. These jets would not be flying at such a low altitude under normal circumstances as to endanger the lives of innocent American civilians. Their very low altitude would indicate they were flying well under radar to go undetected from an enemy, a military term called, "In the weeds." Nevertheless, why were the two jets fighters flying at such a dangerously low altitude and where were they going "at lightning speed"? The unusual circumstances of this event led me to believe they were scrambled on an intercept mission...into the Atlantic ADIZ!

Ground Control Intercept stations along the coast guided the jets toward the unidentified objects. Minutes later, the first intercepting jets from McGuire AFB had reached the vicinity of the UFOs. Within seconds, these jet fighters had unleashed an aerial assault against them. Moments later, the UFOs retaliated with return fire and destroyed the nearest striking jet. As jets and UFOs scattered across the sky, the remaining jets prepared for another attack as several more fighters arrived from Dover AFB and NAS New York and entered the air battle.

A full-scale air battle was underway and the sky was covered with dozens of 2.75 rockets and thousands of rounds of gunfire. The UFOs started firing against the striking jets. Some were destroyed while others had their onboard electrical systems temporarily jammed causing malfunctions. Additional fighter planes then arrived from McGuire AFB and fired at the UFOs, unleashing a barrage of cannon fire. The UFOs shocked nearby planes and fighter pilots struggled with their aircraft's electrical systems. Some were recalled and returned to nearby bases. Seconds later, a wave of jets from New Castle AFB arrived. The New Castle jets, also heavily armed with rockets had salvoed them at the UFOs as they attempted to strike at the swarming jets. The UFOs were becoming weaker and slower as their weapons drained their power sources. During this episode, one of the UFOs had been separated from the other two crafts, becoming a primary target. While jets continued their relentless fire on the other two UFOs, jet fighters from NAS Willow Grove arrived into the battle and fired at the objects.

Dozens of jet fighters swarmed throughout the air battle, launching Mighty Mouse rockets, HVARs and firing countless rounds of cannon fire. The singled out UFO became a target and was overwhelmed with relentless firepower. It managed to temporarily paralyze a closing jet, but more and more kept striking and attacking. The relentless jet fighters fired at the UFO from every angle and direction then quickly pulled out and away. The long-range rockets were a surprise to the intruders and the repeated firing of their weapons at the striking jets was starting to take its toll. Their weapons were getting weaker as their electrical systems were being depleted. Subsequently, the UFOs were starting to slow down.

The rocket-bearing jets had an advantage in this particular air battle while the cannon- bearers followed up during several attacks. Jet fighters continued to barrage the lone UFO with rocket and cannon fire and the sky looked like a hailstorm. This onslaught was a success. At approximately 7:20 p.m. EDT, the object was hit by several rockets followed by a barrage of cannon fire.

The electrically charged gravity field surrounding the object exploded like a fireworks display as sparks flew in every direction and covered the sky. The damaged UFO instantly lost altitude, went into a rapid dive and then burst into flames as it careened through the atmosphere. The two remaining UFOs withdrew from the air battle and attempted to return to the safety of the carrier ship hovering high above the atmosphere. Their attempt was futile though; several jet fighters had surrounded the entire area, cut off their access points to the Mothership and continued to fire mercilessly upon them.

Meanwhile, the damaged object headed southeast toward the coastline when a pair of patrolling combat air patrol Navy jets chased it and attempted an interception; they fired on it, but were not successful. One of the pursuing Navy jets continued after the object, fired on it again and hit it. As sparks flew in every direction, the Navy banked away in the opposite direction. The blazing object lost altitude but refused to go down in the Atlantic waters below. It continued on its southeast heading toward the east coastline and passed over the Delaware coastline minutes later.

Meanwhile, NAS Patuxent River and Stewart AFB jets had reached the air battle area and began to fire on the two other UFOs. The remaining jets, which had run out of ammunition, headed back to nearby Air Force bases, but additional fighters from the east coast were being scrambled into service. The entire air battle area was again swarming with maneuvering jet fighters firing on the two crafts. The UFOs attempted to shock some of the striking jets, but the jets kept their distances. The objects also fired at them but only managed to put one more down as the jets kept redirecting, closing, firing and quickly breaking away.

At approximately 7:35 p.m. EDT, the two UFOs attempted to ascend and reach the Mothership high above them. Before they could reach their destination however, they were attacked by yet another wave of jet fighters from Andrews AFB. One of the objects managed to outmaneuver the onslaught of firepower, but the other object was caught by a barrage of rockets, hit and exploded.

This damaged UFO became the second victim of the jet fighters. Sparks fell like rain as it headed northwest toward land at about 7:36 p.m. EDT. This object had also sustained more damage than the first damaged UFO; it suffered damage to its gravity field as well as its structural shell. The damaged object didn't go down though, and continued to fly northwest at a tremendous speed in a dive. The UFO flew north of several combat patrol jets positioned along the east coast, tried to avoid them but a pair of patrolling Navy jets gave chase after it. The intercepting jets closed on the object, fired on it with cannon fire, hit it and quickly banked away. The UFO exploded, burst into flames and continued to dive as it headed northwest toward the east coast engulfed in flames, still refusing to go down.

Meanwhile, the third object was involved in a lone raging confrontation with jet fighters over the Atlantic and desperately sought to ascend to the Mothership when jets from Westover AFB arrived into the air battle area. In the meantime, while these fast-paced events unfolded over the mid-Atlantic, another series of events had simultaneously developed over the southeastern United States at 7:36 p.m. EDT.

In Florida, ground forces continued east after the damaged object that was still recharging. Shortly after, several vehicles of armed men approached the UFO to disable it. Even though the damaged object was not fully charged and up to par because it was heavily damaged, the object had enough power to fly and possibly attempt to exit the atmosphere. The object rapidly lifted off and finally left Florida soil. The remaining UFOs neutralizing the southeast military installations made their exit as well and ascended out of Florida with it. The military retrieval had failed.

Meanwhile, off the mid-Atlantic coast over the Atlantic Ocean, yet another UFO had descended from the carrier ship as jet fighters from Langley AFB and NAS Norfolk reached the battle and began to fire. This jet-shaped UFO made its atmospheric descent into the air battle to assist the third object, but arrived too late. At 7:40 p.m., Otis AFB jets arrived into battle from above and joined the Westover jets that were now swarming the third object while keeping a safe distance from it. These fighters then launched an all-out devastating bombardment of rockets and cannon fire that blanketed the sky and hit the UFO, which failed to retaliate.

The crafts gravity field exploded around it while rockets caused severe structural damage to the body. Sparks covered the sky, fire engulfed the UFO and it immediately dropped in altitude then went into a dive. It changed its heading and then proceeded due west toward the east coast. The blazing UFO continued to descend, leveled off and then was attacked by a merciless onslaught of firepower from another pair of pursuing jets. Sparks and pieces exploded from the object as it wobbled and continued to descend but failed to go down. The severely damaged UFO headed on a western heading…directly toward Washington, D.C.

In the meantime, the second damaged object that had been hit about five minutes before had already crossed into Delaware. The first damaged UFO was continuing on its southwest heading over Virginia, nearing Roanoke. It was approximately 7:40 p.m. EDT and all three mid-Atlantic objects had been damaged. They are as follows:

1. The Virginia/TN #1 Object
2. The Baltimore/WV #2 Object
3. The Washington/Flatwoods #3 Object

Meanwhile, the jet-shaped UFO was still in air combat with jet fighters. While the jet fighters were trying to intercept this UFO, the three damaged objects headed farther west. All of the UFOs that had departed Florida were heading toward Washington, D.C., making the capitol their target. This red-alert crisis had gone out of control and was escalating toward total disaster.

Aviators had perished, numerous jets had fallen, and an enemy with frightening potential had made base 90-miles off the coast of the United States above the atmosphere. Moreover, there were also three damaged UFOs inevitably going down in the United States. In the following ten minutes, between 7:40 and 7:50 p.m. EDT, United States government officials had to make the biggest military decision in history; when the three mid-Atlantic UFOs were damaged over the Atlantic and forced down, they all took different flight paths...toward the United States!

The Virginia/TN #1 Object proceeded southwest. It had sustained a minimal amount of structural damage. However, it was unable to travel at maximum speed because its gravity field was damaged. The Baltimore/WV #2 Object flew northwest, having sustained significant structural damage. The Washington/Flatwoods WV #3 Object flew due west toward the east coast. It had suffered the most severe structural damage to its body and had the slowest rate of speed.

The three damaged UFOs were spreading out in a fan-like pattern. Their objective was to reach and threaten key government locations including military installations. Each UFO had a different geographical target:

1). **The Virginia/TN #1 Object** headed southwest and targeted the Oak Ridge National Laboratory in Tennessee.
2). **The Baltimore/WV #2 Object** flew northwest and targeted Wright Patterson AFB.
3). **The Washington/Flatwoods #3 Object** headed due west and targeted Washington, D.C.

The three damaged UFOs chose these strategic targets to get the attention of Washington officials and to intimidate them into withdrawing their jets from the Atlantic air battle. Looking back, before this mid-Atlantic battle began; the main concern of the UFOs was to get their damaged craft out of Florida. When southeast military forces became relentless in trying to capture it, the Mothership situated above the Gulf of Mexico near Florida relocated, flew toward the mid-Atlantic, and positioned itself high over the Atlantic Ocean in the Atlantic ADIZ, about 90-miles from the east coast. Moreover, this area is approximately 200-miles east of the Capitol.

The Mothership then released the three crafts into the atmosphere of the Atlantic ADIZ, which

were quickly tracked by military radars. This blatant maneuver was actually a warning to government officials to back off from their downed craft in Florida. This warning did not work! Washington officials deemed this action as a maneuver to attack the Capitol and the military aggressively attacked them. Subsequently, the three UFOs over the Atlantic Ocean were intercepted and shot down.

The first damaged UFO, the Virginia/TN #1 Object, undoubtedly intended to neutralize the Top-Secret, Oak Ridge National Laboratory. Targeting ORNL would surely be an extreme action that would clearly indicate a message to Washington officials to back off the downed craft in Florida. ORNL was no secret to the UFOs. Sightings had occurred there for many years.

Edward Ruppelt made the following statement in his book; "UFOs were seen more frequently around vital areas to the defense of the United States. The Los Alamos-Albuquerque area, Oak Ridge, and the White Sands Proving Ground rated high. Strategic Air Command bases and industrial areas ranked next." During this time, both the FBI and USAF wanted to downplay all UFO sightings because they were directly responsible for the security of these installations, and the seemingly at-will breaches were becoming an embarrassment to J. Edgar Hoover.

The second damaged UFO, the Baltimore/WV #2 Object, proceeded toward Dayton, Ohio, with the intention of neutralizing Wright Patterson AFB. Washington officials had not yet realized the intentions of these two damaged crafts proceeding inland.

In Florida, the grounded craft struggled to ascend and shortly thereafter, discovered it was still unable to climb out of the atmosphere. Simultaneously, the rest of the southeast UFOs ascended with it. They exceeded an altitude above the reach of any jet fighters that may have gone after them and then headed north. Meanwhile, the damaged ship, being escorted by four other objects led the way flying at high altitudes in the upper atmosphere.

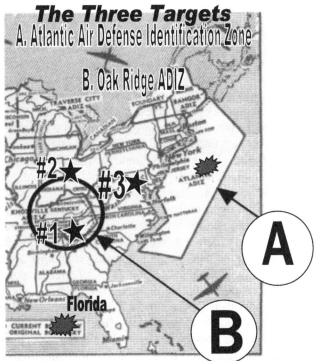

Air Defense Identification Zones

#1. Oak Ridge National Laboratory
#2. Wright-Patterson AFB
#3. Washington, D.C.

The intentions of all these objects were to drop in over the Capitol and several surrounding areas. This strategic maneuver actually involved a main plan and an optional plan. Depending how the government handled the unfolding situation would determine how and when these plans would be implemented. The "*main plan*" was for the UFOs to descend over the Capitol and other nearby areas in a blatant aerial display. This barefaced maneuver would certainly make their presence well known and would easily enable military radar stations to track them and their movements.

If this threatening maneuver worked, it could possibly pressure military officials into withdrawing the jets from the mid-Atlantic air battle, their combat patrol jets from the mid-Atlantic coastline as well as the jets around the Capitol area. Then, the situation would be over!

The "optional plan," if officials didn't order their jets to be withdrawn from the Atlantic air battle and the combat air patrol area near the mid-Atlantic coast, the UFOs would descend along the east coast waters and attempt to open a path for the incoming westbound damaged craft. This plan would result in an air battle with combat patrol jets along the coast, which would ultimately continue into the Washington, D.C. area until; the flight corridor was completely cleared and unobstructed.

If complications developed, and the damaged ship went down during a confrontation, one of several other descending UFOs would be there to extract it. The third damaged UFO, the Washington/Flatwoods #3 Object, targeted Washington, D.C. while being tracked on radar as it descended toward the east coast; additionally, it also wanted to pressure officials to withdraw jets from the Atlantic air battle. As this third damaged object continued west toward the coast, its crew was contacted and made aware that several more ships from the south were enroute to Washington, D.C. and surrounding areas. Meanwhile, the coastal combat patrol jets continued to guard the east coast as the damaged object approached the mid-Atlantic United States.

In the meantime, several jet fighters had focused their attention on intercepting the last mid-Atlantic UFO, the jet-shaped object. Jet fighters swarmed around the UFO and continued to mercilessly fire upon it. The UFO was trapped and unable to reach the Mothership hovering above as waves of incoming jets kept going after it.

Meanwhile, the third damaged object continued to descend toward Washington, D.C. on a direct flight path and showed no sign of turning away. This was the point, when Washington officials had 10- minutes to decide the fate of America and possibly the world. In the meantime, the Mothership was high over the Atlantic, and dropped yet another object from its hull.

This UFO was another jet-shaped UFO object, the #2 Jet-Shaped UFO. The #2 Jet-Shaped Object did not drop into the air battle area though, it descended and flew west, high above the patrolling jets near the coast then flew south of Washington, D.C. This object was traveling at tremendous speed at a high altitude toward West Virginia. Its mission was to locate an isolated area for the incoming damaged "Flatwoods Monster" craft to make an emergency landing.

Should the damaged ship reach the chosen area, it could attempt to make repairs, try to depart the area unseen and relocate to an area near power lines where it could regenerate itself and leave. The emergency landing area to be chosen for this incoming damaged ship had to be located to the west of Washington, D.C. but along its direct western flight path.

Moreover, the area had to be situated far inland and away from any Air Force bases, which could impose any further threat to it. The area also had to be situated at a high altitude where the damaged ship would have clear access to land, especially if it was flying erratically. The location had to be a very high plateau, which was cleared and void of trees. Subsequently, the damaged ship's crew was contacted and informed that the beacon drop plan had been implemented.

The #2 jet-shaped UFO quickly continued toward central West Virginia to drop the homing device. Washington radar stations and Ground Observer Corps stations continued to track it but officials were unsure of its intentions. This maneuver around Washington, D.C. might have been a flank attack against the Capitol. This maneuver may also have been a plan to bypass Washington, D.C. and proceed toward Oak Ridge, Tennessee or Dayton, Ohio. In any event, this UFO had complicated the ongoing situation for a group of concerned Washington officials. Additionally, they had to decide how to handle the unfolding situation of the third incoming damaged craft.

Meanwhile, the #2 Jet-shaped Object flew south of Washington, D.C., passed over southern Maryland and northern Virginia en route to West Virginia. Several people sighted the #2 Jet-Shaped Object as it passed over Virginia. *The Baltimore Sun*, September 13 (UP) article, subtitled "Like A Flaming Jet," stated, "Persons throughout Virginia saw what they variously described as a 'big star,' a 'flying saucer' and something 'like a flaming jet plane.' They said it ranged in color from pale yellow to greenish and reddish and was noiseless." It was also said to have, "moved from east to west." As this so-called flaming jet plane continued west, it was sighted over Harrisburg, VA, twenty miles from the West Virginia border. *The Ohio Columbus Citizen* reported on September 13 in an article titled, "Fireballs Shower City Area," that "Residents in Harrisburg, VA reported a 'cigar-shaped' object trailing blue-green flame [which] streaked across the sky."

Meanwhile, the southwest-bound object was still heading toward Oak Ridge and was nearing Roanoke, VA. The northwest-bound object en route to Dayton, Ohio had just passed over the Delaware coast and the third damaged mid-Atlantic object was over the Atlantic Ocean and heading directly toward Washington, D.C.

In the meantime, the entire southeast group of UFOs was high above Georgia, quickly moving up the coast toward Washington. The Ground Observer Corps and radar stations were tracking the Virginia/TN #1 Object heading southwest. As reports of the UFO's location were being forwarded to Washington and the ADC, military officials were quickly plotting its flight path. Shortly after 7:40 p.m. EDT, Washington officials realized this UFO's projected flight course was Oak Ridge, Tennessee. It was only 240 miles away from its designated target!

Meanwhile, the Baltimore/WV #2 Object, engulfed in flames, decelerated and descended over Baltimore at approximately 7:46 p.m. It buzzed the city at a "very low" altitude. It then accelerated to a higher altitude, blazed past Baltimore and continued northwest. During this time, Washington officials still had not withdrawn their jet fighters from the air battle area over the Atlantic Ocean ADIZ. Unbeknownst to these same officials, the group of sixteen UFOs from Florida was still headed northeast toward them high above the atmosphere going undetected.

Simultaneously, the #2 Jet-Shaped UFO had reached central West Virginia. At about 6:55 p.m. EST it flew over Flatwoods and chose the mountaintop plateau on the Fisher Farm for the emergency landing location. This jet-shaped UFO, according to witness A. M. Jordan, "proceeded across the sky, then halted suddenly [and] seemed to fall rapidly toward the hilltop." This was the point when the UFO dropped a homing device on the plateau for the damaged object to follow.

The jet-shaped UFO then quickly departed the area. This particular drop area in Flatwoods, West Virginia was by no means a randomly chosen site for the emergency landing. The state of West Virginia has no Air Force bases located within its borders. Several of the nearest ones are located in other surrounding states that encompass West Virginia. As the damaged object proceeded on its due west trajectory after passing over Washington, D.C., it actually "threaded the needle" of USAF bases around it. During this time, the object continued to descend along its flight path at a low altitude, which made it virtually impossible to track on radar as it headed toward Flatwoods. Moreover, it could go undetected to avoid any potential jet interceptions.

Furthermore, Flatwoods being the geographical center of the state, was an ideal location to make an emergency landing because there were no nearby USAF bases. Consequently, there were no nearby Air Force bases to scramble jets after the damaged object while in the air or after it landed. Moreover, it would be nearly impossible for the Air Force to find the object from the air in this mountainous region once it was down, especially at night. The following USAF bases encompassed Flatwoods, WV and listed in a clockwise order starting from the north. I have also listed the approximate distances from each Air Force base to Flatwoods:

1. Greater Pittsburgh Airport, PA; base for the 71st Fighter Interceptor Squadron, F-86 Sabre Jets -125 miles north of Flatwoods
2. Olmsted AFB., PA- 240 miles northeast of Flatwoods
3. Andrews AFB., MD- 200 miles east of Flatwoods
4. Bolling AFB., Washington, D.C.-195 miles east of Flatwoods
5. Langley AFB., VA-. 250 miles southeast of Flatwoods
6. Pope AFB., NC- 255 miles south/southeast of Flatwoods
7. Shaw AFB., SC- 320 miles south of Flatwoods
8. Donaldson AFB., SC-280 miles southwest of Flatwoods
9. Godman AFB., KY- 280 miles west/southwest of Flatwoods
10. Clinton County AFB., OH- 170 miles northwest of Flatwoods
11. Wright Patterson AFB., OH- 205 miles northwest of Flatwoods

Meanwhile, the Mothership contacted the crew of the damaged westbound object, which was headed toward Washington, D.C. They were notified that an emergency landing area had been found and the homing beacon device was dropped. The crew of the damaged ship notified the Mothership that its propulsion system was damaged and drastically deteriorating. The occupants of the crew did not know if the craft would be able to regenerate itself if it reached the designated landing area safely. Subsequently, there was a chance that they might be stranded.

Meanwhile, the first five UFOs that had departed Florida were in contact with the Mothership as they headed northeast over Georgia. One of these ships was the damaged object that was downed in Florida and unable to ascend out of the atmosphere. They continued northeast and departed Georgia, then flew over South Carolina at a high altitude, but the damaged ship was losing altitude quickly. The damaged Florida object was experiencing problems again, began to flame-up and started to overheat. It was in dire condition, continued to descend and began to fly erratically. The five objects were ordered to immediately change their flight paths away from the Washington, D.C. area and make their way to West Virginia instead.

The downed Florida object had become such a major concern that the Mothership felt it safer to redirect it toward the relatively unpopulated woods of Braxton County with its escort ships. This damaged craft was in no condition to travel to Washington, D.C. and assist with the plans to descend over the Capitol area. If a battle ensued this object would not be able to fight. They already had a severely damaged object headed west toward Washington, D.C. and two more within the United States. At this point another plan was implemented, a rendezvous and rescue mission. In the meantime, the occupants of the westbound object, the Washington/Flatwoods #3 Object were notified of this rescue plan in progress.

The damaged Florida object continued to lose altitude as the five objects continued northeast over South Carolina. The four UFOs passed over Florence, South Carolina when the damaged object began to rapidly descend in flames. The damaged object notified the three others that it was going down and looked for an isolated area to land. The others hovered near the South Carolina/North Carolina border and waited. Moments later, the damaged object streaked out of the sky, headed towards the wooded area of a farm and crash-landed.

The Morning News of Florence described what occurred in a September 13, 1952 article, "Meteor Hunt Today - Fifty Ton Object Seen Falling Near City." It stated the following information about the crash-landing:

A search by ground and air will begin this morning for remnants of a meteor believed to have fallen north of Florence last night. The meteor thought to be "four to five feet in diameter" and weighing possibly 50 tons was reported to have fallen on farmland near the residence of Smith Barnes on the Douglas Street Extension. The Civil Aeronautics Administration Office here reported the meteor was observed in Raleigh, Fayetteville, Lumberton and Fort Bragg. A woman in Mars Bluff was also reported having seen it.

Barnes said the object, first glowing red and then flaring brilliant white as it approached the ground, moved earthward at a 45-degree angle. It made no noise but lighted up sides of trees indicating it might have fallen in woods about 1,000 feet from the Barnes home. The highway patrol conducted an initial investigation but found nothing. The CAA spokesman said two local fliers, Freddie Higgins and [illegible] Fowler, plan to conduct an air search today. The highway patrol and Barnes also will search afoot.

This supposed meteor had descended and then landed on the farm, yet it did not cause a sonic boom or make an impact pit in the ground. It this object was indeed a huge meteor, it would have caused a noticeable sonic boom, which would have caused a severe shock wave as well as a huge impact pit which would have leveled the entire area. This object did not observe the characteristics of a meteor because it was not a meteor; it was a damaged UFO. The reason that "nothing" was found in the area was because this object had taken off shortly after it had landed.

Shortly after the object crash-landed, it cooled down, ascended out of the area, headed northeast and rendezvoused with the other four objects over the border in North Carolina. The five UFOs sighted over North Carolina actually had a specific task when they descended upon the state. These objects were on a search and rescue mission, their target area – Flatwoods, West Virginia; they were the five North Carolina Rescue Objects.

The first three objects descended over North Carolina at approximately 6:50 p.m. EST and proceeded on northwest trajectories toward Flatwoods, West Virginia. The damaged object descended over Lumberton and proceeded north. The second object also descended into the Lumberton area and the third object descended into the airspace over the Winston-Salem area.

The two additional objects, the #4 North Carolina and the #5 North Carolina Rescue Objects had different objectives in this rescue mission. The #4 North Carolina Rescue Object descended over the area of Flatrock, North Carolina, located along the North/South Carolina border. This area is approximately 25 miles northeast of Greenville, South Carolina, home of Donaldson AFB, 18th Air Force. Moreover, this base is situated along the Oak Ridge National Laboratory, ADIZ perimeter and serves as protection for this security sensitive installation. Even though this UFO descended into the ORNL ADIZ just north of Donaldson AFB, it was not intercepted!

The last UFO, the #5 North Carolina Rescue Object, hovered high over North Carolina and watched over the area of Pope AFB, Fort Bragg, undetected. At this point, both objects hovered over North Carolina to thwart off any possible offensive maneuvers against the three northwest bound objects and guarded them while over this area. The #5 Object hovered out of sight when the other objects descended and positioned itself to the east of them. It guarded the area as a backup role in this rescue mission and then descended over Lake Waccamaw about one hour later. Upon its descent, it headed northwest and passed over Elizabethtown, Fayetteville, Fort Bragg, continued over Raleigh and northeast of that city. It was sighted by witnesses to the northeast of Raleigh by several residents from Rocky Mount and Arcola. The remaining 11 southeast objects continued north toward the Washington, D.C. area above the atmosphere and completely undetected by radar.

Meanwhile, the first three northbound objects that descended over North Carolina had picked up the signal of the homing device on the farm in Flatwoods and began to follow it. Upon their descents, several witnesses throughout North Carolina began to report sightings as the three UFOs flew in unison over the state and continued toward their destination in Flatwoods. The #4 North Carolina Rescue Object that hovered over Flat Rock, left the area, headed north and flanked the three objects to the west as they flew toward West Virginia. The fifth object redirected, then flew southeast toward the North Carolina coast and positioned itself as a beacon for the damaged ships to follow out later.

Meanwhile, Ground Observers throughout the mid-Atlantic were calling in the sighting of the Baltimore/WV #2 Object. Washington area radars were simultaneously tracking it, for it was still ablaze as it neared Cumberland, MD. At that point, military intelligence had projected the object's flight path and calculated that it was en route to Wright Patterson AFB in Dayton, Ohio. Every military official involved was well aware of the possible consequence.

President Truman was then alerted by several military sources and informed that the third damaged UFO they were tracking from the east was nearing the coastline. It was descending and still on a western trajectory toward Washington, D.C. Then, Truman was notified that radar installations were tracking several UFOs, which were heading toward the Washington area from the south. Nearing the Washington area, they blatantly descended and made their presence known.

Shortly after, these objects arrived over Washington, D.C. and nearby states, maneuvered into position, and descended further. They stopped, then hovered and waited above the service ceiling ranges of the combat patrol jets. Now, Washington officials wondered whether the Capitol and other surrounding areas were going to be attacked from the sky above. At this point, key targets of an aerial assault would have been the Capitol and nearby military bases.

President Truman and the National Security Council, including Secretary of Defense Robert Lovett, discussed the options with the Department of Defense. A quick decision had to be reached regarding the withdrawal of the jet fighters from the air battle over the Atlantic. Between a rock and a hard place, President Truman, as Commander in Chief of the Armed Forces, finally gave the order to withdraw the jets from over the Atlantic Ocean air battle area.

Shortly after, the jets withdrew, but the front line jets guarding the east coastline from a possible enemy strike on the Capitol were still on combat air patrol. Suddenly, the UFOs hovering over the Capitol and other areas began to descend slowly. Truman was once again alerted by nearby radar stations. The President being concerned with a possible assault by the descending UFOs instructed the frontline combat air patrol jets to withdraw from the east coastal region. The incoming damaged UFO was not to be intercepted. Shortly after, it passed west over land.

Meanwhile, the combat air patrols over and near the immediate area of Washington were not ordered to withdraw. They were ordered to intercept the incoming UFO only upon receiving direct orders. Truman would have to decide whether to give these orders as the situation unfolded. If Truman gave the order to intercept the UFO coming toward Washington, what course of action would the two UFOs heading toward Oak Ridge and Wright Patterson take? If President Truman ordered the incoming damaged UFO taken down it would have inevitably crashed near Washington.

To attack this incoming UFO would probably mean catastrophic outcome, considering that several UFOs were hovering over Washington and might descend and strike against the jets, nearby bases and the city. By approximately 7:51 p.m. EDT, the jets off the mid-Atlantic coast had disengaged from battle against the Jet-shaped UFO and headed back toward their bases. The large Mothership contacted all three damaged westbound UFOs and ordered them to abort and cease their progression toward their targets. The first Jet-shaped UFO had departed the air battle area and proceeded back toward the Mothership. Moments later, the Mothership proceeded due west toward the coastline, out of sight, and headed toward Washington, D.C.

Previously, the Air Force had sent combat air patrols into the perimeter of the Oak Ridge Air Defense area from three separate bases, which formed a triangulation net pattern around ORNL. The three Air Force Bases were Dobbins AFB in Marietta, GA, Godman AFB in Louisville, KY, and Donaldson AFB in Greenville, SC. The patrolling jets within this highly restricted area were ordered not to make any aggressive maneuvers toward the UFO. They were instructed to only intercept it upon receiving direct orders from their base superior commanders. Additionally, Wright-Patterson AFB had also put up jets around their perimeter in anticipation of an attack.

Meanwhile, the Virginia/TN #1 Object had been called off from the Oak Ridge National Laboratory. It began to decelerate to find a location to land. It had already traveled approximately seventy miles into the Oak Ridge Air Defense area. At about 6:55 p.m. EST, this UFO landed just across the Tennessee border in Arcadia, about 110 miles northeast of Oak Ridge without any incident. The Baltimore/WV #2 Object that had targeted Wright Patterson AFB in Dayton was over Morgantown, WV, when it was called off. It began to decelerate and sought an area where it could land.

The third mid-Atlantic damaged object was the "Flatwoods Monster" ship. It was engulfed in flames and approached Washington on a due west course. The nearby Washington area jet fighters on combat air patrol around the Capitol and other areas had not yet been ordered to withdraw. This strategy was deemed as an offensive maneuver against the damaged UFO.

Still hovering above the atmosphere, the Mothership craft continued west, headed toward Washington, and reordered the other two westbound objects toward their original designated targets again. Seconds later, the Virginia/TN #1 Object, which had just landed in Arcadia, took off and once again proceeded toward Oak Ridge. Simultaneously, the Baltimore/WV #2 Object, which was searching for an area to land near Morgantown, continued toward Ohio. When this object started toward Dayton once again, the residents of Fairmont sighted it. *The Charleston Daily Mail* reported; "About 40 persons in the Fairmont area said the object looked like a spotlight with a greenish tail and was traveling from 100 to 500 miles per hour."

Military radar installations had again begun to track the Virginia/TN #1 Object. Washington officials were immediately alerted that it was moving toward Oak Ridge again. Nearby military installations also alerted them that the UFOs being tracked on radar over Washington, D.C. were now descending upon them. President Truman had to decide if he should let the damaged flaming UFO get closer to Washington, D.C.

If Truman let the incoming UFO through to Washington, what would it do upon arrival? Would it bypass Washington and go farther west, or would the damaged object execute the worst-case scenario? If President Truman let the UFO through, would it land in the city in front of thousands of witnesses, or would it attack Washington and destroy it? On the other hand, if Truman struck at the object as it approached DC and the craft went down in the city, it could kill many civilians and the Capitol could be attacked from above as well. If that happened, the President of the United States would have to tell the American public that the government had known that extraterrestrial aircraft were visiting earth. Moreover, if Truman did choose to strike at the incoming object, what would happen if the other two objects continued on to Oak Ridge and Dayton?

Equally important were the series of events that unfolded above them. The UFOs that were hovering over Washington, Virginia and Maryland continued descending as the Mothership neared the Washington area. If the nearby combat air patrol jets were not withdrawn, the Washington DC area could be the scene of a raging full-scale air battle.

Truman and his military advisors held the fate of the nation in their hands. With only minutes remaining to make a decision, Truman decided to call off the jet fighters on Combat Air Patrol. Then all he could do was hold his breath, wait and pray as the object headed toward Washington, D.C. Shortly after, at about 8:00 p.m. EDT, the damaged "Flatwoods Monster" ship passed over the northern part of Washington. *The New York Times* called this object the, "Flame over Washington." This UFO actually buzzed Washington as it passed over the heads of "jittery Washingtonians." When *The New York Times* reported the incident, the reporter wrote, "The blazing object moved horizontally across the heavens and came 'awfully low.'" This is the UFO that I designated, the Washington/Flatwoods #3 Object.

The Mothership passed high over the Washington area overseeing the situation and then contacted the Virginia/TN #1 and the Baltimore/WV #2 Objects. They were immediately called off from their targets because the "Flatwoods Monster" ship had passed over Washington, D.C. without incident. The Virginia/TN #1 Object redirected its southwest heading after traveling another 35 miles toward Oak Ridge. It headed east over Rogersville, Tennessee. One witness was "Sam Miller of Rogersville [who] reported a ball of fire resembling a meteor passed over there about 7 p.m. heading east. Miller said it 'looked like a full moon with a tail on it.'"

The Baltimore/WV #2 Object was called away from Dayton, Ohio also. It was engulfed in flames and burning up, traveling at near maximum speed. This damaged craft slowed and searched for a spot to land. It could not land immediately as it was over a heavily populated area near Columbus, OH. The craft redirected northeast and flew directly over Columbus, heading for the northern West Virginia panhandle. Shortly thereafter, it passed over Zanesville. *The Columbus Citizen* reported CAA officials at Port Columbus concurred with Zanesville CAA officials in describing the phenomenon as "probably a meteor shower."

The Columbus Citizen also reported, "In Zanesville, CAA officials at the [Zanesville] Municipal Airport said an army pilot at 10,000 feet reported what looked like a burning plane." What the pilot actually saw was the damaged UFO engulfed in flames. A distress call was made to the Mothership and the damaged UFO was instructed to land in an isolated area near an easily recognized landmark and wait for assistance. As the damaged object headed toward the West Virginia panhandle, it followed the signal of the Wheeling-Ohio County Airport in Wheeling, WV. Upon reaching their airspace, "One pilot said the object nearly clipped the wing of his aircraft." After this near mid-air collision, the UFO redirected on a southern heading and searched for an area to land. Shortly after, it landed a few miles away in the area of Oglebay Park. Meanwhile, the Washington/Flatwoods #3 Object was following the homing signal to Flatwoods.

Simultaneously, the three North Carolina rescue ships were traveling more than twice as fast toward Flatwoods being followed by their back up, the #4 object. At this point, the "Flatwoods Monster" ship was west of Washington, D.C. and passing over Virginia. It was reported, "A pilot en route to Wheeling from the east reported sighting the object from the vicinity of Front Royal, VA." This pilot had actually sighted the Washington/Flatwoods #3 object. He noted that it was "tremendously large" and "seemed to disappear in a bunch of sparks."

It was flying erratically at a low altitude and was having trouble staying airborne. This object was literally burning up and the farther it traveled, the more damaged it became. It had to slow down so it would not crash before reaching its rendezvous point in Flatwoods.

In the meantime, military officials had ordered combat air patrols into the air around all major military installations throughout the country. These fighter patrol jets were ordered not to make any offensive maneuvers toward the UFOs. Radar operators had sighted the three rescue ships over North Carolina proceeding northwest. Military officials finally realized that all this UFO activity was a rescue mission in progress. Washington officials decided that the safest and most logical way to proceed with such an incredible situation was to leave it alone.

In the meantime, at about 7:00 p.m. EST, the three North Carolina Rescue Objects were sighted passing above the Appalachian Mountains in Virginia as the #4-rescue ship flew northwest and flanked them to the west. It was reported, "Persons in southwest Virginia saw at least three flashing objects that were described as meteors." After these three objects passed over Virginia on northwest trajectories, they crossed over the southern West Virginia border and passed over Monroe County and then Summers County. Shortly after, they flew over Greenbrier County and continued onward toward Flatwoods to rendezvous with the incoming damaged craft.

The three North Carolina Rescue Objects continued north and passed over Nicholas County then crossed over the border into Webster County. The next county they would fly over would be Braxton County. Meanwhile, the #4 object continued to pace the three objects as it continuously flanked them to the west at a high altitude. When the three objects passed over into Webster County on their northern flight path, they were seen. I met and spoke to the witnesses about this sighting. At first, I received an email letter from a man who lived in Gauley Mills, West Virginia back in 1952, and now resides in Florida. This witness, Mr. Frank Woods, contacted me after had he listened to me on a talk radio program.

He wrote, "I was listening to George Noory's program and heard Linda Moulton Howe talking about Frank Feschino." He stated, "I thought you might like an eyewitness account of the 'UFOs' of 1952." Mr. Woods wrote me the following letter and explained, "I was a teenager in the eighth grade, living in Gauley Mills, Webster County, West Virginia on the night of the 'Flatwoods Monster' incident. Gauley Mills is a small town located approximately 25 miles southeast of Flatwoods. He stated, "I, with two or three other playmates saw three bright lighted objects streak across the sky in a northerly direction. It was about 7:00 p.m., shortly after supper." Several adult witnesses also saw these three objects as well.

Mr. Woods stated what they thought about the lights, "Adults who saw the 'UFOs' (not called that at the time) said they were meteors." He then gave the following information, "They were close together in a triangular formation. We were too young to determine the altitude of the objects. Airliners did not fly across that part of the state, so it was uncommon to see anything larger than a piper cub. We dismissed the sighting until the next couple of days; *The Charleston Gazette* had run front-page pictures of the 'Flatwoods Monster.'" In closing, Mr. Woods added, "I was not exactly sure where Flatwoods was located, except it was near Burnsville and Sutton and I knew where these towns were."

Shortly after receiving this information, I phoned Mr. Woods. He had no idea how the three objects he saw that night fit into the timeline of events that took me years to figure out. I asked him if we could meet and talk further about what he had seen. He agreed to meet me and we arranged a meeting in Orlando, Florida.

A couple of weeks later, I met Mr. Woods and he talked further about his sighting. As usual, I brought along a pencil and sketchpad. As we talked, I drew sketches and took notes about the incident. I was very adamant about knowing the direction that these three objects were headed. Mr. Woods explained to me "a boy growing up in the woods of West Virginia had to know his directions." He said it was "second nature."

By using "mountain ranges" and "rivers" as landmarks in the vicinity, as well as the location of the sun, one would be accustomed to directions. Mr. Woods was very distinct and detailed in his descriptions. He told me these three objects were "very bright" and "not small like stars."

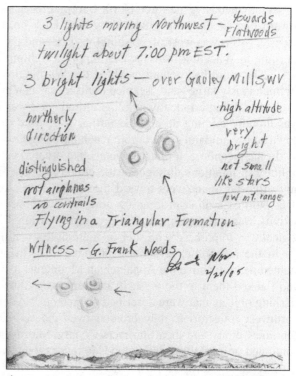

He stated, "They were not airplanes, or jets—there were no contrails." He added, "They were large." He told me, "They were heading North/Northwest at a high altitude," and "flying in a triangular formation when they passed over Gauley Mills, WV." I drew sketches, and witness Frank Woods signed and dated the information I

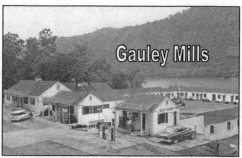

had written accompanying the drawings. The location of this incident, Gauley Mills, was then plotted on my master map along with the flight paths.

At that time, none of the three rescue ships knew the location of the damaged ship, nor did the Mothership, since it had descended to such a low altitude and was having difficulty transmitting. Meanwhile, the three objects entered over Braxton County from the south, followed the homing signal and continued to fly north toward Flatwoods. Moments later, they were joined by the #4-rescue object as they all flew into the Flatwoods area. However, it had received word from the Mothership that it was needed in the Wheeling area where the Baltimore/West Virginia #2 object had gone down. The #4 North Carolina Rescue Object was needed to participate in yet another search and rescue mission and departed the area on a northwest heading.

At about 7:05 p.m. EST, the #1 North Carolina Object, the damaged ship, had reached Flatwoods and was desperate to land. The other two objects following it arrived shortly after and began their search for the "Flatwoods Monster" ship. Meanwhile, as the "Flatwoods Monster" ship

216

headed west, navigating had become treacherous. About 80 percent of West Virginia lies in a plateau region of towering mountain ridges and narrow valleys. East of this plateau is rolling countryside. The mountains of West Virginia had now become the enemy as it struggled to stay in the air and began losing the signal of the homing beacon device.

The lead ship, the damaged #1 North Carolina Rescue Object, worked its way north toward the homing device, descended below tree level and flew over the Fisher Farm. It passed over the mountaintop on the rear of the property to rendezvous and land with the other damaged craft, the Washington, D.C./Flatwoods #3 object.

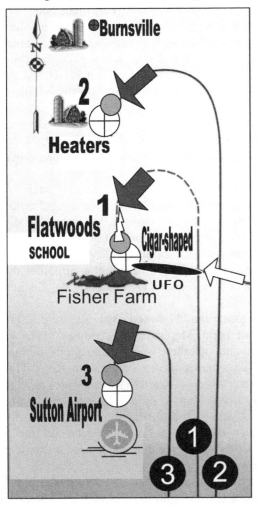

There was a major problem though; the "Flatwoods Monster" craft had not arrived in Flatwoods yet. Within moments, the northbound rescue ships engaged in a low-altitude grid-pattern search and looked for the damaged craft in the likely event it crashed in the nearby vicinity.

The damaged ship flew over the Fisher Farm. The second had flown to the north of Flatwoods and passed over the town of Heaters, while the third object flew south of Flatwoods over the nearby Sutton Airport and began its search there.

Each of these objects eventually made U-turns and then swept back to the south at low altitudes. Meanwhile, the incoming damaged westbound ship, unable to contact its comrades, was still on its way to the rendezvous point on the farm and was over the Monongahela National Forest area.

The overheating ship struggled, decreasing its speed and had difficulty following the signal as it passed over the mountainous terrain. It veered off its direct course to Flatwoods and headed toward northern Braxton County. At about 7:15 p.m. EST, the "Flatwoods Monster" ship passed over Elkins, WV, engulfed in flames and continued west. Several residents in Elkins reported seeing this fiery object pass over them on a western heading.

The three rescue ships desperately continued their search for the ship. I was able to distinguish the different flight paths of the 3 North Carolina Rescue Ships with the information I had compiled:

1). The #1 North Carolina Rescue Object was damaged and on fire when it passed over the Bailey Fisher mountaintop with the intentions of landing.

2). The #2 North Carolina Rescue Object went five miles north of Flatwoods and passed over the town of Heaters.

3). The #3 North Carolina Rescue Object flew just three miles south of Flatwoods and passed over the Sutton Airport.

Investigator Gray Barker reported this information in his September 1953, Vol. 1, No. 1 issue of the Saucerian. Barker interviewed Mr. Hoard, who had seen an object pass over the Fisher Farm and stated, "Mr. Hoard said he'd be glad to tell me everything he saw. At approximately 7 p.m. [actually 7:15 p.m. EST], he had gone out in his front yard to feed his chickens. His attention had been drawn to a fiery object coming over the horizon, though in a slightly different direction than the others reported. It had not landed but had gone across the sky. It went over the Bailey Fisher cistern and it was about here (he pointed to a location in line with his house) that a piece of fire broke off it. As it neared the horizon, toward the Sutton Airport, it exploded and went out."

This incident puzzled Barker because he thought this object was the "Flatwoods Monster" ship. This object reported by Mr. Hoard was actually the damaged #1 North Carolina Rescue Ship. It flew over the farm searching for the downed ship as to rendezvous with it and then land. Barker also stated, "And if Hoard were in his yard at the time, why did he not see the amazing occurrences on the nearby hilltop, easily within his view?" There was a reason that Mr. Hoard did not see "the amazing occurrences" that involved the "monster" encounter on the nearby hilltop; it *was not* the "Flatwoods Monster" ship.

Meanwhile, the #2 North Carolina Rescue Object was five miles north of Flatwoods over Heaters searching for the downed object. During one interview with Mrs. May, she said, "Jerry Marples from Heaters called the sheriff's office and said there was a flying saucer coming down behind the hill in Flatwoods."

Investigator Ivan T. Sanderson also reported the UFO sighting over Heaters. He said, "A bright globular object was seen passing fairly slowly through the sky at low altitude and at the same time as the others, slightly to the east of the settlement known as Heaters. This was allegedly seen by several people along a line to the southeast and to a point about due east of Sutton." In this episode, the craft was leaving the vicinity after making its sweep of the area.

Sanderson also reported a "similar object was said to have passed over Sutton airport at the same time." This craft was the #3 North Carolina Rescue Object called the "shooting star," which was sighted over Winston-Salem and then seen Mount Airy.

These three North Carolina rescue ships did not locate the "Flatwoods Monster" ship at the designated rendezvous area on top of the Bailey Fisher Farm. Moreover, the condition of the #1 North Carolina Rescue Object was also worsening and although there was still enough daylight to continue circling and sweeping the area, it would have drawn further attention to them. This attention, they did not need. Subsequently, the three objects were ordered to leave the area and the damaged North Carolina object needed to find another area to land.

In the meantime, the severely damaged craft, the "Flatwoods Monster" ship, continued to fly west. The craft struggled to stay airborne, had difficulty following the homing beacon and finally reached northern Braxton County. It slowed down, made a 45-degree turn and headed south over State Route 5, a main artery that led south toward Flatwoods.

The UFO flew above State Road 5 to avoid the treacherous mountains that surrounded it and passed south over the town of Burnsville, located about ten miles north of Flatwoods. The craft flew over that town just above tree level and continued south while moving through the valley of the surrounding mountains above the road. The UFO then passed over Heaters, six miles south of Burnsville. Here, State Route 5 intersects State Route 4, the main artery that leads south.

The damaged object then began to follow State Route 4 on its southern heading between the mountains. The craft continued to follow the signal on the farm and neared Flatwoods, now only four miles away.

The Damaged Craft Flew South over State Route 4 above Flatwoods

Shortly after, the damaged UFO passed over the Flatwoods border. Upon reaching Flatwoods, the object struggled to stay airborne and veered away from the safety of the road below it. The craft went slightly off course and headed for a mountain that was directly in front of it, and then burst into flames as it barely cleared the top of the mountain.

Moments later, while proceeding south, it passed over the town and then flew over the Flatwoods Elementary School playground, where a group of boys was playing football. The object then turned east, passed over State Route 4 and continued to follow the homing signal toward the Fisher Farm mountaintop. It barely cleared the treetops as it passed over the Fisher Farm where the homing device was located on the back of the property.

The damaged craft followed the signal to the back of the farm, descended and landed on the grass in the wide-open field on the mountaintop at approximately 7:24 p.m. EST/8:24 p.m. EDT. The damaged object sat aglow on the mountaintop, severely overheated and in dire need of assistance, awaiting the three rescue ships. As the minutes passed, the situation became very grim. The occupant of the damaged craft had missed the rendezvous with the rescue ships by a matter of minutes and had missed its opportunity to make an escape. The ship was not in flames, but its interior was extremely hot. The propulsion system inside the craft was severely damaged.

It was still glowing from the friction damage it had sustained from burning off plasma while traveling through the atmosphere. The craft's outer shell was also severely damaged from the missile and gunfire it had received. The pilot of the ship needed to move the ship off the mountaintop to a less conspicuous location.

It lifted off and moved into the pasture of a nearby valley. At approximately 7:30, the craft landed in a grassy field near the bottom of the sloping valley. Extreme heat caused by the damaged and leaking propulsion system radiated throughout the craft's cabin. The generator was barely producing power and the communication system was barely functioning.

A few minutes later, communication was established with the Mothership. A faint signal revealed that the pilot had reached the beacon on the mountaintop. The occupant was notified that the first rescue mission had been aborted, but another rescue mission would be underway shortly after dark. The alien was told to stay near the ship and beacon, so it could be found.

The occupant departed its ship to the cooler atmosphere outside the craft. When this tremendous creature emerged from its ship, it was wearing a metallic-like space suit. This space suit, which resembled a small shuttlecraft, was capable of hovering and was maneuverable. However, it was severely damaged. The alien hovered toward the ground in its battle-damaged suit and descended over the grass. Its main objective was to head for cover where it could not be seen.

The "Flatwoods Monster," then traveled across the open field and up the slope of the valley and maneuvered toward some nearby woods for cover. It spewed oil from its damaged suit, leaving behind a scarred trail in the grass caused by the force of its propulsion system.

Upon reaching the crest of the valley, the "Flatwoods Monster" hovered to a level grassy area. It traveled a short distance through some tall grass and brush and then hovered across a narrow dirt path bordering the woods blowing rocks and dirt aside. The hovering alien then positioned itself next to a large oak tree at the outskirts of the woods along the dirt path. It then settled to the ground and concealed itself. The being went undetected and waited to be picked up by the second rescue party.

Journalist Evert Clark stated the following information when he visited Flatwoods to write his story, "Editor Bob Earl and Advertising Manager Creel Cornwell of the weekly *Democrat* in Weston, 40 miles to the north, did some investigating too "Just as Mr. Earl and Mr. Cornwell were leaving Flatwoods, a little girl brought them a slip of paper on which a man had sketched four tear-shaped objects, one behind the other." Editor Bob Earl and Advertising Manager Creel Cornwell of the Weston *Democrat* reported to Clark, "She said he said he saw them in the sky about the time the fireball and the saucer went over, but we didn't get to talk to him. We were in a hurry to catch a train." From this information, it is apparent that these UFOs were the four North Carolina Rescue Objects that had flown into the Flatwoods area, the fourth one being called away shortly after its arrival.

Meanwhile, the damaged #1 North Carolina Object had difficulty flying. It did not leave the area with the other two North Carolina rescue ships that had already ascended out of Braxton County. The craft continued to struggle and was having trouble staying airborne; its propulsion system was in dire need of electrical power.

The craft needed to find a power source at some location where it could land and regenerate but before it found a source, it crashed nearby. In Flatwoods, Mr. Hoard saw this fiery object, circling over the back mountaintop of Fisher Farm. After it left the farm, the object flew south toward the airport and a piece of fire fell from it. Then, I discovered information about this object, which had also crashed in the Flatwoods area that night. Mrs. May had actually informed me about this second object that went down just outside of Flatwoods. It had crashed in Holly, an isolated, wooded area about five miles southeast of the Sutton Airport. This object was undoubtedly the #1 North Carolina ship, forced to make a temporary stay in Braxton County.

By plotting the Holly point on a map, this nearby site accounts for the second damaged object that went down in the Flatwoods vicinity. It was previously seen flying toward the area of the Sutton Airport, continued south and then landed nearby in Holly. It cooled off, departed the area, then redirected southwest and left the region. Next, it was reported in Braxton County again when it crash-landed in the community of Sugar Creek located along on the Elk River.

On Monday September 15, *The Charleston Daily Mail* reported the story, "Braxton Folks Divided Over Visitor." It stated, "Woodrow Eakle [sic] of Duck along the Braxton-Clay line was traveling toward Flatwoods as the aerial phenomenon made its appearance. He reported to Braxton County Sheriff Robert Carr a small airplane had crashed against a mountainside. A later search failed to disclose any remnants of the wreckage or persons." Investigator Ivan T. Sanderson spoke with several witnesses. Mr. Sanderson said of the object after interviewing Woodrow Eagle, "He saw a flaming object, which he thought from his army experience to be a small Piper Cub plane, shoot over a saddle to his left, cross the main road, the river, and the rail line beyond, and crash into the wooded side of a steep hill immediately to the south."

Another witness "who lived on a farm above the road, had that night seen the flaming object come around the low hill opposite him, horizontally and below its crest, making a neat turn and then go into the valley where Mr. Eagle said he saw it crash. He described it as a 'flaming bucket with a tail.'" A man who lived in Sugar Creek said this to Sanderson, "He and others had been puzzled by the smoke that hung about the face of the hill in question on the evening of September 12, and remarked that there had been 'a strong smell of woods burning.'" Woodrow Eagle reported the crash at Sugar Creek to the Braxton County Sheriff's Department.

This was the first call that Sheriff Carr and Deputy Long responded that involved a supposed plane crash. When the lawmen arrived in Sugar Creek, they did a visual scan of the area and found no signs of an airplane wreck because the object had already relocated to a secluded area.

Feschino at the Banks of the Elk River in Sugar Creek where the UFO Crashed

This craft had actually crashed into a hillside along the Elk River, then lifted up, and landed on a mountaintop, where it could not readily be seen from the valley area below. It then cooled down and rested shortly before it was able to take off again. Ivan Sanderson and four other men investigated the landing site at Sugar Creek.

The "Flatwoods Monster" ship landed on the Bailey Fisher Farm about the same time that the #1 North Carolina Rescue Object had crashed in Sugar Creek. Shortly thereafter, yet another plane crash was reported about eight miles southwest of Sugar Creek along Elk River in Frametown. This so-called plane crash was actually the crash landing of the damaged #1 North Carolina Rescue Object, after it departed Sugar Creek.

Gray Barker reported this incident in Vol. 1, No. 1, of the Saucerian. He said, "A Piper Cub plane, an excited hitchhiker was reporting, had crashed into a hillside near Frametown and was burning. He had seen it from a car from which he had received a 'lift,' then driven to the first available phone to report this incident." Barker added, "Sheriff Carr and a deputy [Burnell Long] rushed the seventeen miles to the scene but could find no trace of the burning plane." Again, this damaged UFO was thought to be a downed airplane!

In my car, I retraced this same route as stated by Barker and also traveled the same seventeen-mile distance along Route 4. The trip from police headquarters to the scene of the crash placed me about two miles west of the Frametown line. This was the approximate area where the hitchhiker witnessed the alleged airplane crash. I noted a mountain in the nearby area that I believe to be the hillside referred to by this witness. It was across the Elk River from Route 4 where I was parked; this area was clearly inaccessible without a boat. When the sheriff went to the site, he did not find a downed airplane because the object had already taken off again.

While the sheriff was searching for the downed aircraft at about 8:15 p.m. EST, Cecil Rose, the Braxton County sheriff's office jailer, received the call from Mrs. May, who reported the "monster" incident in Flatwoods.

The next report of a UFO occurred about nine miles southwest of Frametown in the Duck Creek area along the Elk River. This was the next area where the #1 North Carolina Rescue Object was sighted. It is interesting to note that after the damaged object left the Holly area it followed the Elk River. It is evident that this damaged object flew above the river as it navigated between the mountains for safety reasons as it proceeded out of the area looking for a power source. The UFO sighting that occurred over Duck Creek was from an automobile along Route 4.

Mrs. May explained what happened, "I heard a man and wife were driving through Duck [Creek] when they saw the thing. She was scared to death and in the hospital for about two days."

I then asked Mrs. May, "Why did the lady have to go to the hospital?" She answered, "She thought it was a plane on fire, at first." I then asked her, "What was it that scared her so badly?" She answered, "It was one of those things flying around Braxton County that night." She added, "I heard it flew above their car." I discussed with Colonel Leavitt the Duck Creek incident involving an automobile. The following conversation transpired:

Frank: "Now, could you explain about the craft that flew over the automobile and what happened with that? Now that's never been documented?"
Leavitt: "No, it's never been documented, but it has been said from other people what happened. They [Witnesses] just said the [UFO] shut its engine off and they couldn't it get started again. Then when it [UFO] left, they went on up the road."
Frank: "And the engine just started up again?"
Leavitt: "Yeah. Well, they started it up."
Frank: "But while the craft was over the top of it, the engine went completely dead?"
Leavitt: "Yeah, that's what they said."
Frank: "Was that the same night the [Fisher Farm] crash happened here?"
Leavitt: "Yes. It was on the same night."
Frank: "Do you remember what part of town that was in?"
Leavitt: "Well, it was [pauses]; do you know where Duck Creek is? (Waving hand) It was back this way."

According to my timeline and research, this was the last time the damaged #1 North Carolina Rescue Object was seen in Braxton County. This object was the same UFO that was intercepted earlier near Florida and once again had difficulty flying. Furthermore, it was the UFO that 2nd Lt. John Jones and 2nd Lt. John DelCurto had confronted, intercepted and subsequently shot down!

Feschino in the Duck Creek Area where the UFO was Seen

CHAPTER NINETEEN

DESCENDING GUARDIANS

Project Blue Book led the public to believe that the single "Washington area meteor of 12 Sep." was the cause of all the sightings over the Washington area. I probed more deeply into the Project Blue Book files, hoping to find further information that would explain the discrepancies between these sightings. What I found were more documents that reported several additional UFO sightings made that evening. These documents included several Project 10073 Record Cards, numerous ATIC compilation reports and Tentative Observers Questionnaires. These reports all referred to several objects seen around 8:00 p.m. EDT. These sightings occurred on September 12, over the areas of Washington, Virginia, Maryland, and Pennsylvania.

ATIC explained away the numerous sightings that night within a Project 10073 Record Card and stated, "One of numerous Wash. DC area reports of 12 Sept. meteor." I combed through all the Project Blue Book reports and documents and put them into a comprehensible order. The most difficult task I had was separating the multiple sightings; the number of sightings reported does not directly correspond with the actual number of objects. I categorized the numerous sightings of the objects by their times, locations and descriptions. This took several years to organize.

I arranged all the information, picked out the most relevant facts, and constructed a chart comparing these objects. I was able to establish the number of objects seen over the Washington, Virginia, Maryland, and Pennsylvania areas around 8:00 p.m. I arranged the objects in order by the times of their appearance. I gave each object a designated number because so many of them were sighted around 8:00 p.m. EDT.

Based on my research of the sightings; there were two waves of UFOs that passed over the eastern United States that evening. The first wave of UFOs passed over the mid-Atlantic coastline shortly before 8:00 p.m. EDT. They were the first three damaged objects that fanned out over the United States.

The second wave of UFOs was positioned over designated areas over Washington, D.C., Virginia and Maryland. They prepared to descend and assist the incoming damaged object as it proceeded west toward Washington, D.C. When the damaged UFO flew toward the Washington, D.C. area, twelve UFOs descended to protect it. While some descended over the Capitol, several actually formed a perimeter and followed the damaged craft west.

These UFO sightings were actually recorded in an Air Force document by "THE INSPECTOR GENERAL USAF - 4th DISTRICT OFFICE OF SPECIAL INVESTIGATIONS - BOLLING AIR FORCE BASE." This "SEP 13 1952" document "24-0-220," an Air Force "SPOT INTELLIGENCE REPORT" stated; a "Duty Officer" at Andrews AFB, "Lt. John K. Wales," was contacted by Navy "Commander ELLINGTON" at the "Ana Costa NAS," near Bolling AFB in Washington, D.C. The report states Lt. Wales reported that Commander Ellington, "had received calls from eleven (11) persons between the hours of 2000 [8:00 p.m.] and 2015 [8:15 p.m.] in which calls 'flying saucers' were reported." This report also details the sighting of a UFO made over Arlington, Virginia. Witnesses there reported they "had observed an unidentified flying object over their homes at approximately 2000 hours" or 8:00 p.m. EDT.

Lt. Wales then contacted "the OSI Agent" at Bolling AFB and informed him of the series of sightings over the area. The Air Force also reported, "As a result of these calls, Navy plane 51257 which was approaching the Air Station was ordered to remain aloft to look for any unusual objects." The document also states, "The pilot reported that he had observed an object which appeared to be a falling star." Here, the UFO sightings were taken seriously enough to keep a Navy plane in the air to reconnoiter the area for UFOs reported by concerned local citizens!

In contrast, a witness from Washington, D.C. who also saw the alleged single meteor recorded the following statement in Blue Book. It demonstrates the confusion that arose regarding the single meteor story when it appeared in newspapers. He said, "From newspaper accounts of other observers in the Washington area there was a very wide variation in the size, color and direction the object was traveling, which *assuming* they saw the same object as we did indicates the observation[s] of many people are unreliable in many respects." They weren't all the same object!

This statement reflects the outcome of the U.S. government's disinformation plan at work. They give out false information or a lack of information to the public through the media, which causes mass confusion and subsequently discredits the UFO eyewitnesses.

To discredit the single meteor explanation, I used several different portions of important information from Blue Book and extracted key testimonies from many of the eyewitness, "Tentative Observers Questionnaires.

Officials sent out these Air Force forms to witnesses upon request. Each UFO questionnaire was of a standard format, which contained thirty different questions pertaining to a UFO sighting.

The questionnaires were completed by the eyewitness and then sent back to the Air Force at ATIC for their officials to review, comment on and finally evaluate.

Object #	TIME EDT	Location Direction	color	shape	Description
#1-UFO	8:00pm EDT	WDC.-SW.	yel.-white		Ball
#2-UFO	8:00pm	WDC-West	Green		slightly-oblong
#2B UFO	8:00pm	McLean.VA.	Green-Wh.		oval w/ pink
	SECOND SIGHTING of #2 object - WDC. west to McLean VA.				
#3-UFO	8:00pm	WDC-SW to west	Greenish-blue w/red trailer		Balloon-shaped & size of onion+ dirigible
#4-UFO	8:00pm	WDC "zoomed to the west"	white to red w/green tail	NO Report of Fire "ZOOMED"	exploding plane soundless rocket
#5-UFO	8:00pm	Arlington VA. West-NW.	Green Ball Type		Ball - little flattened
#6-UFO	8:00pm	WDC- south-SW	bluish-yellow yel.tail-fringe		flaming ball
#7-UFO	8:01pm	WDC - Georgetown	light-Green flame color		plane on fire + size & shape of fuselage of plane
#7B-UFO	8:02pm	WDC - Georgetown	white to red Green at tail	"GLIDING"	plane on fire
	SECOND SIGHTING of #7 object over Georgetown is #7B				
	SECOND SIGHTING was - "GLIDING towards the northwesterly direction"				
#8-UFO	8:03pm	WDC	silvery-white red-orange tail		spherical shape- white ball
#9-UFO	8:03pm	Fairfax, VA. Lt commander USN- Aviator	Greenish-wh. white rim		slightly oblong
#10-UFO	8:04pm	District Heights Maryland	Bright Blue Green-white in center. tail-blue grn		size of an automobile This thing was being flown
#11-UFO	8:05	Beltsville Maryland	light blue Lt blue tail		large round thing
#12-UFO	8:10pm	Alexandria Virginia	yellowish- white		round front- tapered to a point

224

This illustrated graph represents the sightings of those various UFOs that descended over three states between 8:00 p.m. and 8:10 p.m. EDT. It is obvious that these sightings were not attributed to a single meteor!

These twelve different UFOs had dispersed over Washington, D.C., Virginia and Maryland. They were sighted by witnesses as they descended then flew on western headings. I have designated the 12 objects as "Rescue Objects." Much of the reconstructed and reenacted storyline of events that occurred on that evening are based on the following actual Blue Book UFO reports.

Rescue Object #1. Source: Tentative Observers Questionnaire. A man and wife saw the #1 Object at 8:00 p.m. EDT as they were driving their car along Western Avenue in Washington, D.C. The man filled out the questionnaire. His wife called his attention to the object "thinking it was fireworks." They were looking "southwest" in the sky and "the object appeared solid." The witness said, "It gave off a yellowish-white light" and there was "no sound audible."

The question was asked, "Was this the first time that you have seen an object like this? Yes, although many meteors have been observed but none as intense as this one or that appeared to travel as slowly." This witness also stated it looked "like an auto headlight but somewhat more yellowish." The couple was looking to the "southwest" when the object disappeared from their sight. When this witness initially contacted PROJECT BLUE BOOK and reported his sighting, ATIC documented the following, he stated, the "Object was shaped like a ball with light radiating from it...tail was almost as bright as object itself." This object actually passed over Washington, D.C. from the "northeast" and continued "on a southwest trajectory before it disappeared."

Baltimore, MD is located to the northeast of Washington DC where another description of this object was previously made. A previously mentioned September 13 Baltimore Sun article gives the following information, "Not since Baltimore, with the rest of the world, first began to read about flying saucers several years ago, has anything approached so close to what locals considered the 'real thing' made its appearance here. The first excited call came in a few minutes after 8 p.m. [EDT] And they kept up for more than an hour...to Herman Rosenthal, when he first saw it swinging 'treetop height' near his home in 2700 block of Spring Hill Avenue, it looked, at first like a 'plane on fire.' He soon realized that it was no plane however. 'But it was that big.' he said." He described it as a large, sun-colored ball with a tail.

Rescue Object #2. Source: Witness Compilation Report & Tentative Observers Questionnaire. A witness from 21st Street NW, Washington, D.C. saw the #2 Object at 8:00 p.m. EDT. While calling his girlfriend, he "saw a bright green light through the window" from his eighth-floor apartment. He "first noticed a plane circling for a landing." After the "plane disappeared from view" the witness said he, "saw a green light where the plane was and it dove toward the ground. It sort of leveled off and disappeared." The witness described this UFO as a "solid object" that was "slightly oblong" in shape. He stated the object emitted a "bright-green light" and said the object was traveling "toward the west." The length of time the object was seen was "8 seconds." This would have been a near record for a meteor sighting! However, unlike a meteor, this object leveled off after making a dive toward the ground. The eyewitness also noted that the object had "no tail."

Another description of this object was made to the west in McLean, VA by a fifty-year-old male who worked for the Army. This sighting occurred while he was traveling in his car with his wife. This witness stated:

The object looked like an oval Roman candle descending at the speed of a passenger plane until it suddenly disappeared, leaving for a second the black or gray outline of an arrow or rocket, which could have been either an object or smoke. It was a greenish white light as I first saw it. My wife who was with me agrees with the above but adds that she would include pink in her description of the object.

The witness also stated, "The object was no more than 2,000 feet above the ground." A question asked, "How far was it from you?" The witness answered, "Near enough for us to debate stopping the car for fear of what might happen when it landed." The witness also answered the following question in the questionnaire, "In your opinion, what do you think the object was and what might have caused it?" The answer, "I don't know."

This object was close enough to the witness that he actually saw what it was, and was scared it was going to land near them. There was no sonic boom noted, even though he stated it was only about 2,000 feet above the ground. This object also suddenly disappeared or dematerialized, like so many of the objects seen earlier. It seems unlikely that a witness who worked for the United States Army would have been afraid of a meteor.

Rescue Object #3. Source: Tentative Observers Questionnaire. The #3 Object was seen from the corner of Massachusetts Avenue and 39th St. NW, Washington DC, at 8:00 EDT. This witness saw the object disappear from the "southwest to west" direction as he was driving a car through a residential neighborhood. He said it was "greenish-blue with a red trailer," and noted that there was, "no sound." The witness said the UFO was about "as big as a dirigible" and stated that he had "no idea" what it was. The Air Force witness compilation report initially stated it looked "onion shaped" with a streamer tapering gradually. The color was, "bright light green with a yellow-red tail." The object appeared to be "heading northwest." The observer also said the object, "seemed to be traveling remarkably slow."

Once again, this object did not demonstrate the characteristics of a meteor. The most striking description besides the size of this object was that "it seemed to be traveling remarkably slow." If this dirigible-sized object was a meteor that disintegrated that close to Washington, D.C. then every person in the city would have heard a sonic boom and felt its percussion. The witness answered the following Blue Book question, "In your opinion what do you think the object was and what might have caused it?" The witness stated emphatically, "I haven't the faintest idea."

Rescue Object #4. Source: Tentative Observers Questionnaire. The #4 Object was seen over the Capitol by a couple at 8:00 p.m. EDT in the presence of their two children. This UFO sighting was made from "the banks of the Potomac River, near the Lincoln Memorial." The witness, a fifty-three-year-old wife who filled out this questionnaire stated, "Our family was watching the sky-sunset and airplanes going toward the airport." The witness was looking to the south when she "first saw the object," and saw it "disappear to the west." The woman said it "looked transparent" and then added that it had, "changed size, color and brightness." The following descriptions were also given, "SOUND- none," and reported its color as a, "Blazing white, with red, then green tail." Its size was described as "about the same as a small airplane."

The observer said the striking points about this object were "its sudden appearance in the sky as though from nowhere." The witness was shocked by "the suddenness of its disappearance over the hills, but as though it had burned out in the sky before it could have possibly landed. Just appeared, zoomed toward the opposite horizon moving very fast like a comet's flash or a rocket, but soundless, and then just couldn't be seen. I personally thought it might be a non-lethal guided missile." This object was of the cigar-shaped type UFO, which was commonly seen in the 1950s.

The most interesting part of this woman's statement concerning the object's appearance was "its sudden appearance as from nowhere." Again, these unidentified and unconventional objects seemed to be materializing and dematerializing. The witness answered the following question in the questionnaire, "In your opinion what do you think the object was and what might have caused it?" This witness stated, "Can't imagine what it was."

Rescue Object #5. Source: Witness Compilation Report. The #5 Object was seen at 8:00 p.m. EDT from Arlington, VA. While driving in a convertible with top down, the witness "saw a luminous green ball type object. A little flattened with a short orange-yellow tail." The Object was sighted "toward the west." The observer stated it "looked similar to a Roman candle if seen at close range. Could not judge distance or speed. No sound." The witness also stated the object was seen for "5 seconds" and it was "on a west-northwest heading until it disappeared behind a hill."

This UFO was also recorded by "THE INSPECTOR GENERAL USAF-4th DISTRICT OFFICE OF SPECIAL INVESTIGATIONS-BOLLING AIR FORCE BASE." This document, a "SPOT INTELLIGENCE REPORT" stated, "SUBJECT: Unidentified Aerial Object-Observed Over Arlington, Va. on 12 September 1952-FLYOBRPT." OSI officials at Bolling received this report from "Special Agent PHILIP WILSON of the Federal Bureau of Investigation." Agent Wilson reported that witnesses in "Arlington had observed an unidentified aerial object over their homes at 2000 hours." One witness stated, "The ball of light had a very short tail, flying at approximately 500 feet without any sound of propulsion. She said that the object was much slower than a conventional type of aircraft could fly and remain aloft…it disappeared behind some trees."

Rescue Object #6. Source: Witness Compilation Report. The #6 Object was sighted at 8:00 p.m. EDT from the vicinity of the "National Guard Armory" in Washington, D.C. The report gave the witness' description as, "One flaming ball, bluish in color, yellow in fringe." The witness also said it was, "falling toward earth." The UFO had a "tail" that was described as "yellow" in color. From the location of the witness, the object out in the distance "looked smaller than a baseball." The observer's point of observation was near the National Guard Armory, "facing south-southwest." He said the object was "heading in the direction of the National Airport."

It is clear that even though these six sightings were made at 8:00 p.m. EDT, they were definitely not the same object. There are far too many discrepancies regarding the shapes, colors, directions of flight and movements made by these witnesses for all of the 8:00 p.m. sightings to have been one object, an alleged meteor.

Rescue Object #7. Source: Witness Compilation Report. The #7 Object was seen from Georgetown at 8:01 p.m. EDT. The Object was described as "about size and shape of fuselage of plane. Light green in color and glowing incandescently." The witness stated, "It looked at first like a plane on fire." He said the, "color varied from green to flame color toward tail, almost giving it a teardrop shape." There was no mention of the object's disappearance. The observer said his sighting lasted for "about five seconds."

Another "Georgetown" witness described this same object. He said it was "no more than 500 feet in the air." Its color was described as, "White turning to red and green at the tail." The witness said, "It made no noise." This witness also described the object's movement as it descended along its flight path over Georgetown. He stated that the "object" was "gliding toward the ground." The "Washington area meteor" according to Blue Book stated its speed as "27 miles per second" in a very non-gliding fashion. This particular UFO was another one of the cigar-shaped objects.

It was also noted to have "disappeared in the sky with a flash," which indicates it may have actually dematerialized. The #7 Object and the #4 Object were very similar in their descriptions, as both were elongated UFOs and both thought to be planes on fire. Both of these UFOs descended from the sky approximately one minute apart and proceeded in different directions. The descriptions of these two objects are nearly identical to the description of the "jet-shaped" or cigar-shaped UFO previously seen over Flatwoods by A. M. Jordan. This #7 object was actually the same UFO that dropped the homing beacon on the Fisher Farm mountaintop.

Rescue Object #8. Source: Project Blue Book Teletype & Record Card. The #8 Object was sighted at 8:03 p.m. EDT over Washington, D.C. The report is as follows:

FM HQ USAF WASHDC [From-Headquarters-U.S. Air Force-Washington DC]
TO JEDEN Commanding General Air Defense Command [Ent Air Force Base, Colorado]
JEDWP Chief, Air Technical Intelligence Center [Wright-Patterson Air Force Base, Ohio]
JEPLB CG TAC LANGLEY AFB VA
JEPLB Commanding General-Tactical Air Command [Langley Air Force Base, Virginia]

Presently on duty as security officer, JCS reports the following flying object sighting. Spherical effect appearing as a ball spinning clockwise. Reddish orange tail protruding from brilliant silvery-white ball with brilliance of phosphorous. Tail about half-length of diameter of object. Observed at 2003 [8:03 p.m.] for two seconds falling with trajectory like Roman candle. Object observed at angle of 40 degrees altitude moving in north-northwest direction. Size about two-thirds that of moon on bright night when moon is at 75 degree angle. Looked as if it might be about 3 miles away and would fall on outskirts of D.C. Brightness seemed whiter than sun. Further observation prevented by mass of buildings and woods. Observed from position in front of 2641 Conn Ave, N.W. Facing 2606 Conn. Ave. N.W. Source has plotted map-showing angles of observation in his possession.

The following information comes from the 10073 Record Card of that report. It states, "One of numerous Washington, D.C. area reports of 12 Sept. meteor." Furthermore, the conclusion stated, "Was astronomical-meteor." It is hard to believe that Project Blue Book logically concluded this object was the "12 Sept. Meteor." This is even more unbelievable considering that the Pentagon [HQ USAF WASHDC] contacted Ent AFB, Wright-Patterson AFB and Langley AFB. In 1952, Ent AFB was the headquarters for the Air Defense Command (ADC). It seems inconceivable that the Pentagon would have contacted all of these key Air Force bases with regard to a "meteor."

Rescue Object #9. Source: Tentative Observers Questionnaire & Project 10073 Record Card. The #9 Object was sighted at 8:03 p.m. EDT over Fairfax, VA. Enclosure 3 is a questionnaire completed by, "LCDR [Lieutenant Commander—blacked out] USN [United States Navy], following his telephonic report of a sighting to this office." The Lt. Commander stated, "I was sitting at the dinner table facing the window when the object flashed by the window." He said the object looked "solid" and the object gave off "a greenish-white light." The observer further stated the color was, "white rim about a greenish-white core" and there was "no sound." The actual size of the object as he saw it was the size of a "basketball." The witness was looking "southwest" in the sky when the object disappeared. He described the object as, "slightly-oblong" and said it was, "moving in a horizontal path over ground." He reported that the object had, "no tail or sparks." He also noted it displayed a "solid incandescent outline."

The questionnaire asked, "In your opinion what do you think the object was and what might have caused it? I don't know. The newspaper said it was a meteor, but it had no tail and was not falling and was larger than any meteor that I ever saw." This witness, like many of the other witnesses, questioned the Air Force's meteor explanation. The Project 10073 Record Card for this case read, "Local newspaper reported object as meteor. Duration of sighting was only 3 seconds and observer was in poor position." Once again, Project Blue Book had two informative points to comment on about this sighting!

The 10073 Record Card also stated the witness was "source-Naval Aviator (Lt. Cmdr)." It seems that even though this witness was a Navy aviator, Project Blue Book officials did not consider him a credible witness.

Rescue Object #10. Source: Tentative Observers Questionnaire. A man from District Heights, MD, sighted the #10 Object at 8:03 p.m. EDT. This sighting was made "in the residential section of the city." The witness was "on [his] porch facing SSW," when he noticed the object. In response to the questionnaire, he stated these answers to the following questions:

How did the object look? <u>Solid</u>
Give off smoke? <u>Yes.</u>
Did the object give off light? <u>Yes</u>
What color was the light? <u>Bright blue-green</u>
Sound? <u>None audible</u>
Color? <u>Very white in center to blue green on edge</u>
Which of the following objects is about the same size as the object you saw? <u>Automobile</u>
How did the object disappear from view? <u>Gradually</u>
What direction were you looking when the object disappeared? <u>West</u>
How long was object seen? <u>11 or 12 seconds</u>
Clouds? <u>Clear sky (very)</u>

The witness said that the object, "disappeared below horizon in west," and stated the, "entire object was a constant very bright glow traveling at steady rate." A question was asked, "In your opinion what do you think the object was and what might have caused it?" The eyewitness answered, "This is your job. I have seen many meteors. This was not one—much too large. It was not an image or reflection." The witness then added, "The object's trajectory was constant in a swooping arch following the curvature of the earth and eventually going behind the horizon. It didn't fall toward the earth."

The testimony this witness gave at the end of the report was even more convincing. He wrote:

For a person with limited knowledge about things of this nature, I can give an opinion that may be of too little value. I do not know what it was I saw and will insist on what it was not. I have seen meteors, and the newspapers will have a hard time telling me I was looking at a meteor on 9/12. Maybe it sounds good to persons who didn't see the object. This thing was being flown. Picture for yourself a jet plane going over and into the horizon. Now set it on fire to a bright glow and have it travel 3 times as fast, covering the same trajectory in 1/3 the time. Does it look like a meteor? In summarization, this may sound as though I am inferring some fraud in the reports given to the public. Perhaps responsible parties believe they are true and the best information available, but did they see the thing on 9/12?

This report was obviously written by a man who was very adamant of what he saw and was not afraid to tell the U.S. Air Force his opinion. The lone fireball meteor theory became weaker the more questionnaires and reports I read.

Rescue Object #11. Source: Witness Compilation Report. The #11 Object was sighted over Beltsville, MD, at 8:05 p.m. EDT. The witness report said the object looked like "a large round thing resembling a child's ball." It was said to have looked, "like a moon with a tail." The witness said it was traveling about "the speed of a plane." When he first observed the object, it was "very high but heading toward the ground" in the direction of "the plant at Industry Station," in Beltsville, MD. Note, this object was descending on a trajectory "heading toward the ground."

Did this alleged meteor change its course to avoid impacting the earth? The report said, "The source was unable to give a direction of flight but said it was "toward the west." The report also informed of another witness, "Second observer at same time and place was Mr. [blacked out], an employee at Bolling AFB." This particular object was seen northwest of Washington, D.C. at 8:05 p.m., five minutes later than the first six objects seen over Washington, D.C.

Rescue Object #12. Source: Witness Compilation Report. The #12 Object was sighted from Alexandria, VA, at 8:10 p.m. EDT. The witness "saw a yellowish-white, very bright light about one-half the size of a full moon." The witness said the object "had a vaguely rounded front with a tail about twice the diameter and tapering to a point." It was reported, "The object made no sound." The report also stated, "Observer was at home facing southwest and saw object through open window in house. Traveled west in a straight line." The object was seen "for 3 seconds."

This second wave of UFOs was a group of twelve rescue objects that were positioned over three states, Washington, D.C., Virginia and Maryland. In military terms, they were the extraction team. If the incoming damaged "Flatwoods Monster" craft had gone down, these twelve objects would have been available to take control of the situation and extract it out of the area.

When the damaged craft proceeded west toward the Capitol and neared Washington, D.C., they descended between 8:00 p.m. and 8:10 p.m. EDT. These twelve "Rescue Objects" formed an aerial perimeter around the damaged UFO and protected it from being intercepted over the Washington area. They followed the damaged craft as it flew west over the Capitol without incident and followed it until it was safely west of Washington, D.C. The twelve "Rescue Objects" then ascended back in to the sky and out of sight. The damaged object continued west, flew over Virginia, West Virginia and then landed in Flatwoods, about 25-minutes later.

During this situation, there was another rescue object involved, "Rescue Object #13." It hovered high above Olmsted AFB, in Middletown, Pennsylvania as sentry for about an hour until 9:07 p.m. EDT. The #13 Rescue Object then descended, passed over the base and then departed shortly thereafter. Based on my years of research data, timelines, and the understanding of military strategy, the following scenario fits the chronological order of events that led up to the 8:00 p.m. EDT sightings that night.

These thirteen rescue objects were eleven of the sixteen UFOs that had neutralized the southeastern military installations. The "Flatwoods Monster" ship that was engaged in an aerial battle over the Atlantic Ocean was damaged and headed west toward the coastline enroute to Washington, D.C. At that point, the group of sixteen objects that departed Florida was passing over North Carolina. Three of these sixteen UFOs went on to Flatwoods, West Virginia to rendezvous with the "Flatwoods Monster" ship; they were the North Carolina Rescue Objects.

The fourth and fifth North Carolina rescue objects hovered over North Carolina near the vicinities of Pope AFB and Donaldson AFB, to guard against any potential military aggression toward the three other North Carolina objects. The #4 North Carolina Rescue Object then descended over Flat Rock, just north of Donaldson AFB. It proceeded north and followed the three rescue ships over Virginia towards West Virginia then flew to Ohio. The #5 North Carolina Rescue Object stayed behind and did not follow the others. It positioned itself as a beacon near the southeast coast of North Carolina and transmitted a signal for the damaged UFOs to follow back out along an escape corridor. It also patrolled the skies over North Carolina, securing this corridor.

The remaining eleven UFOs headed toward the Washington, D.C. area. They arrived shortly after, spread out and moved into their strategic positions over Washington, D.C., Virginia, Maryland and Pennsylvania. The two jet-shaped objects dispatched from the Mothership then moved into position with the other eleven UFOs. The extraction mission, was now in order, and involved thirteen crafts. Twelve of them waited over three states, began to descend, stopped and watched over their designated areas. The thirteenth object hovered high out of sight over Pennsylvania as sentry while the situation unfolded.

Meanwhile, as the damaged Flatwoods ship approached the east coastline, the combat patrol jets between the east coast and Washington, D.C. were withdrawn, but the combat patrol jets surrounding the Capitol as a last line of defense were not withdrawn. Consequently, the twelve observing UFOs began to descend to lower altitudes and tracked on radar by Washington National Airport, Andrews AFB, Bolling AFB and other nearby Navy installations. If President Truman had not withdrawn the patrolling combat patrol jets around the Capitol area, all thirteen UFOs would have descended to very low altitudes in order to clear the area for the incoming damaged ship. Subsequently, if there had been a confrontation along the damaged ship's flight path as it neared Washington, D.C. and it crashed, these UFOs would have extracted it.

As the damaged ship neared Washington, D.C., President Truman finally gave the order to withdraw the patrolling combat air patrol jets surrounding the Capitol. Moments later, the jet fighters withdrew, the corridor to the Capitol was opened, and the damaged UFO passed over Washington, D.C. without incident. This damaged UFO was called, "The Flame Over Washington." Shortly after, twelve of the thirteen ships descended upon Washington, D.C., Virginia and Maryland as the Mothership watched the situation unfold high above the Capitol.

After the twelve "Descending Guardians" dropped from the skies over three states, they proceeded west at low altitudes. This was a deliberate and direct maneuver to follow the damaged craft until it was away from the Capitol area and secure it from any potential jet intercepts. Subsequently, hundreds of American citizens were later told they had seen meteors! The "Rescue and Extraction Mission" that involved the 12 "rescue objects" ended at 8:10 p.m. when the west bound "Flatwoods Monster" craft was considered to be a safe way distance from Washington, D.C. Every one of the twelve objects involved in this mission ascended back up into the sky and disappeared no later than 8:10 p.m. EDT.

During that ten-minute time though, there were also other UFO sightings reported over eastern Ohio and the northern panhandle of West Virginia. At 8:05 p.m. EDT, two different objects were seen in two different locations in eastern Ohio. One object, which resembled "an enormous skyrocket," was sighted in the area of Freeport and Tappan Lakes. Another object that resembled "the shape of a frying pan" was sighted from Lafferty, OH, also at 8:05 p.m. The Freeport and Tappan Lakes areas are approximately 35 miles northwest of Wheeling, WV. Lafferty, OH is located approximately 18 miles almost due west of Wheeling.

The Columbus Citizen reported yet another incident that occurred approximately 50 miles west of Freeport, "Mt. Vernon State Patrolmen said they received a report at 7:05 p.m.[EST/8:05 p.m. EDT] from G. S. Gallopy of Danville [OH], reporting a 'plane on fire going down.' He said the crash seemed to be near Millwood, 12 miles east of Mt. Vernon. Patrolmen said no crash could be found, however." Shortly after, at 8:06 p.m. EDT another UFO sighting occurred, not in Ohio but over West Virginia in the northern panhandle. This sighting was made over West Liberty, WV, which is about ten miles northwest of Wheeling, West Virginia.

The Times Leader reported this sighting, "W. A. Garrison of West Liberty reported seeing an object that looked like 'a Roman candle' flash over his home and at 8:06 it headed southwest." The information concerning the 8:06 sighting over West Liberty was also in The Wheeling Intelligencer. The headlines on September 13, "Mystery Lights Zip Through Skies Here Stirring Mild Furor—Flashing Light Believed Caused By 'Low' Meteors."

These articles reported objects thought to be airplanes, blazing objects, meteors, and flames that appeared in the skies over eastern Ohio and the northern WV panhandle. In reality, they were actually UFOs. Furthermore, some of the objects were sighted over those areas before 8:10 p.m. EDT. So, where did they come from and why were they there? The "Rescue and Extraction Mission" that involved the twelve UFOs, which descended over Washington, Virginia and Maryland to follow the "Flatwoods Monster" west, did not end until 8:10 p.m. EDT. At that time, the "Flatwoods Monster" was a safe distance away from the Capitol enroute to Flatwoods, WV and the mission ceased.

However, at least three of those twelve "Rescue Objects" had redirected their flight paths northwest and ascended out of the Washington, D.C. and Virginia areas before the others. Those three ships, which departed first, were not following, assisting or searching for the "Flatwoods Monster" craft along its western flight path toward West Virginia. They actually headed northwest for an all together different reason; they were on an entirely different mission with yet another agenda. Between 8:05 p.m. and 8:10 p.m. EDT, the first three objects that departed the Washington, D.C. and Virginia areas began to descend over eastern Ohio and northern West Virginia on yet another rescue mission!

Earlier, when the damaged northwest bound craft, the Baltimore/WV #2 object, was called away from its target, Wright-Patterson AFB, it slowed, redirected and changed to a northeasterly path. It then followed the beacon signal being transmitted from the Wheeling-Ohio County Airport and continued northeast toward the northern West Virginia panhandle. Shortly after, it passed over Columbus and Zanesville in Ohio, en route to the panhandle. Moments later after passing over the state of West Virginia, the damaged UFO nearly hit a passenger plane as it approached the area of the Wheeling-Ohio County Airport. The UFO quickly redirected south over the panhandle, looked for an isolated area to land and then touched down in Oglebay Park.

When this craft was damaged over the Atlantic Ocean by jet fighters, one of its occupants was severely injured and burned. When it proceeded toward Dayton, OH, the condition of this damaged ship had deteriorated. The object overheated so severely that the living conditions inside the cabin of the damaged ship became nearly unbearable; in order to survive, the injured alien was dropped off into the cooler atmosphere of the earth and was to be picked up later.

Subsequently, a distress call was made. The numerous sightings of these objects in eastern Ohio and northern West Virginia were actually rescue ships that were looking for the stranded occupant of the damaged Baltimore/WV #2 object. At 8:05 and 8:06 p.m. EDT, the first rescue ships descended into eastern Ohio, but there were some major problems with the rescue mission. They did not know the exact location where the damaged ship had went down. The Times Leader reported the 8:05 p.m. sightings with the headline, "Authorities Probe Flashes in Area Skies—Strange Lights Observed Over Four States." It stated the following:

Civil Aeronautics Authority officers were still trying to find an explanation today for a flurry of bright flashes seen in the skies of eastern Ohio and three other states by hundreds of people the previous night shortly after 8 p.m. Switchboards of law enforcement officers, newspapers and airports were swamped with calls last night with reports of the meteor-like flashes that appeared over Washington, Pittsburgh, and Virginia, as well as above the Ohio valley. The U.S. Naval Observatory at Washington said the reports 'sounded like a typical meteor,' but the most persistent report in eastern Ohio was that a plane had crashed in the Freeport-Piedmont Lake area. O. C. Frantz, Martins Ferry postmaster, said he and two other post office employees, Roy Lucas and Dave Smith, were fishing in Piedmont Lake when a flaming object appeared in the sky at 8:05. The men first thought it was a 'flying saucer' but said it looked like an enormous skyrocket. It was big enough to be a plane they said, and they thought later it might have been a bomber or large passenger plane.

The Patrol investigated the report, but could find no evidence of a plane crash. Other reports of the flashing objects all confirmed the time at 8:05 last night. Three cheerleaders from Lafferty High School told the Times-Leader that what they saw a flying saucer appearing at the same time [8:05]. The girls, Nancy Azallion, Madelyn Calovini and Seania Bayat, said they were practicing cheers at the high school when an object 'the shape of a frying pan,' appeared. It was very white and bright and had sparks shooting from the tail, the girls said. They saw it come from east to west and disappear over a hill in the west—in 30 seconds. Carol Santini, a former Lafferty cheerleader, incidentally in town had also reported a similar object.

This UFO described as "the shape of a frying pan" over Lafferty, Ohio was seen for "30-seconds," far too long of a sighting to have been a meteor. Previously, it was seen over Flatrock, NC. This UFO was actually the #4 North Carolina rescue ship that descended as back up over North Carolina. It headed north and followed the three North Carolina Rescue Objects over Virginia, into Flatwoods, WV, then ascended and headed toward the northern West Virginia panhandle area. It then proceeded into Lafferty, Ohio, about 18 miles due west of Wheeling and was sighted there at 8:05 p.m. At that time, the search for the downed alien had begun.

Another UFO was sighted in Ohio at the same time, 8:05 p.m. *The Wheeling Intelligencer* reported, "The Brookside station of the Ohio highway patrol last evening received a number of calls from eastern Ohio points concerning the strange visitor in the sky. One of these reported it was seen in the vicinity of Piedmont and Tappan Lakes." This other object, sighted at 8:05 p.m. was said to have "looked like an enormous skyrocket." This UFO was another rescue ship that had descended into eastern Ohio, which was part of the search and rescue mission.

I then studied, reviewed and dissected the reports of the other objects seen that night throughout the country and compared them. It seems this object was the same ship sighted over several other locations across the country at different times. This UFO, which was described as a "skyrocket" was actually sighted over the following five locations:

1). Harrisonburg, VA. It was reported, "Residents in Harrisonburg, VA, reported a 'cigar-shaped object trailing blue-green flame' [that] streaked across the sky." This object had just previously left the air battle area over the Atlantic Ocean.

2). Har, West Virginia. Witness Donald Morrison saw an "elongated object" about "45-feet long" near Flatwoods, WV. It looked like a "propane tank" and was flying very low, just about tree top level.

3). <u>Flatwoods, WV.</u> When this object reached Flatwoods, Mr. A. M. Jordan saw it. After interviewing Jordan, Gray Barker said, "Evidently it came from over the horizon from the southeast as he was sitting on the porch. It proceeded across the sky, then halted suddenly, seemed to fall rapidly toward the hilltop [of the Fisher Farm]." This object had dropped the homing beacon, ascended and headed west out of Flatwoods. The object then rendezvoused with the Mothership that was hovering high above Washington, D.C.

4). <u>Georgetown, Washington, D.C.</u> This object was then sighted over Georgetown at 8:01 p.m. EDT. It was the #7 Rescue Object that descended from the Mothership with the others. Again, it was sighted over Georgetown at 8:02 p.m. EDT during its flight. The witness stated the, "Object looked like a plane on fire at first, and then like some sort of flare gliding toward the ground in the general direction of the Lee Memorial." It flashed and "disappeared" over the Capitol and was seen minutes later over Ohio.

5). <u>Freeport, OH</u> - (Piedmont Lake area) at 8:05 p.m. EDT. After this object "disappeared" at 8:02 p.m. over Georgetown, it then reappeared over eastern Ohio. At 8:05 p.m., "a flaming object appeared in the sky."

The Elongated Jet-shaped Object with No Appendages

The UFO that these witnesses saw over eastern Ohio was the #7 Rescue Object descending into the area. The description of this #7 Rescue Ship seen across the country that night was also similar to the description given of the #4 Rescue Ship. Both of these UFOs were described as being elongated and shaped like a rocket or a wingless aircraft. The #7 Object was reported to be a much larger craft than the #4 Object though.

These elongated wingless objects were also well documented by the USAF. Some of these objects appeared in *Flying Saucers: An Analysis of the Air Force Project Blue Book Special Report No. 14.* Some of the elongated wingless UFOs that appeared in this report were categorized in the report as "Cigar Shape – Cases IV and V." The first listed was "Case IV (Serial 4599.00)"; "two cigar-shaped objects" that "both had an exhaust at one end" were sighted on July 19, 1952. The second listed was "Case V (Serial 0565.00 to 0565.00)" multiple sightings made from "DC-3" aircraft by pilot, copilot and a passenger. These sightings occurred on "JULY 24, 1948." Drawings also accompanied the two reports.

These objects were almost identical to the descriptions of the elongated wingless objects, which were sighted on September 12, 1952. I own a copy of the drawing made by Mr. A. M. Jordan, who saw the wingless jet-shaped UFO over Flatwoods. His drawing and description of the UFO he saw is nearly identical to the UFO sighted by the DC-3 pilot on July 24, 1948. I also own the Donald Morrison drawing that resembles the cigar-shaped objects in both cases. These UFOs were frequently seen throughout the early to mid 1950s.

The other object sighted at 8:05 p.m. was over Lafferty, Ohio. This object was a flying saucer described as "the shape of a frying pan." I would classify this UFO as a disc-shaped object with a tail. This UFO's description was almost identical to another well-documented UFO sighting in *Flying Saucers: An Analysis of the Air Force Project Blue Book Special Report No. 14.*

Mt. Vernon State Patrolmen recorded the third UFO sighted over eastern Ohio at 8:05 p.m.. They had "received a report at 7:05 p.m.[EST/8:05 p.m. EDT] from G. S. Gallopy of Danville [OH], reporting a 'plane on fire going down.' He said the crash seemed to be near Millwood, 12 miles east of Mt. Vernon."

The three UFO's sighted at 8:05 p.m. in eastern Ohio were the first rescue objects that had descended into those areas. They are as follows: 1. The Lafferty flying saucer, 2. The Freeport cigar-shaped UFO, 3. The Millwood flaming object that resembled a plane. These objects were all sighted to the west of the Ohio River but there was a problem. The area where the occupant was dropped off was to the east of the Ohio River near Oglebay Park Resort.

The Times Leader reported an 8:06 p.m. rescue attempt, "W. A. Garrison of West Liberty reported seeing an object that looked like 'a Roman candle' flash over his home and at 8:06 it headed southwest." The mid-Atlantic rescue ships were sighted between 8:00 p.m. and 8:10 p.m. before their initial extraction mission was called off at 8:10.

I re-examined the mid-Atlantic sightings that occurred before the 8:06 p.m. West Liberty, WV sighting that resembled a "Roman candle." The following mid-Atlantic "Rescue Objects" were reported to have had similar characteristics said to resemble a Roman candle; A.) #1 Rescue Object, Washington, D.C. 8:00 p.m.: "thinking it was fireworks." B.) #2 Rescue Object, McLean, VA 8:00 p.m: "The object looked like an oval Roman candle." C.) #5 Rescue Object, Arlington, VA 8:00 p.m: "Looked similar to a Roman candle."

I re-examined the directions that these three objects were said to be heading. Only one of these objects was noted to be heading in a direction toward West Virginia's northern panhandle. The Virginia witness to the #5 Rescue Object said it was moving "north-northwest." This UFO was the craft that proceeded north-northwest to West Liberty, WV. This area is just northwest of Oglebay Park, where the damaged Baltimore/WV #2 Object had landed earlier and dropped off the injured occupant from the craft. The #5 Rescue Object, which flew over Virginia, was actually the first rescue ship to search for the stranded being in West Virginia.

The other three UFOs were searching in eastern Ohio. A later sighting in Frankfort, OH appeared to be a plane on fire, falling from the sky. The *Columbus Citizen* reported, "Fireballs Shower City Area: Meteor Fall Blamed Cause of Scare." The article stated, "In Chillicothe, patrolmen said a Frankfort [OH] man reported a burning plane falling north of town about 8:30 p.m. No plane could be found they said." This article also named two other locations of "what appeared to be a plane crash" in the areas of Mt. Vernon and Chillicothe, Ohio.

The Chillicothe sighting was another one of the rescue ships. This UFO landed about 30 miles northwest of Clinton County AFB in Wilmington. This UFO had strategically positioned itself between this Air Force base and the Wheeling, WV search area. This maneuver was a warning to the military officials to stay out of area.

Throughout the night, witnesses in eastern Ohio and northern West Virginia saw fireballs, flaming objects, blazing objects and alleged planes on fire. For nearly two hours, several UFOs descended and made desperate attempts to locate the injured and stranded being in West Virginia. In some of these episodes, the craft actually landed and witnesses thought they were plane crashes. *The Wheeling Intelligencer* reported that their "editorial room was also swamped with calls between eight and ten o'clock [EDT] from residents on both sides of the river."

First Rescue Objects
Nearest to Oglebay Park

Mystery Lights Zip Through Skies Here Stirring Mild Furor

•Pittsburgh

'Balls Of Fire' In Pittsburgh

Ohio

8:05 p.m. **Freeport**

8:05 p.m.

Lafferty

15

Martins Ferry

Bridgeport

16

WOC Airport

West Liberty

8:06 p.m.

17

Glenwood

Triadelphia

Eastern Ohio

Bellaire

18

WV

PA

19

Fayette County
Markleysburg•
Uniontown

20

☆ Sighting Locations of #2 Balt./WV Object

15. St. Clairsville, OH.
16. Wheeling-Ohio County Airport, WV.
17. Oglebay Park, WV. (LANDED)
18. Wheeling, WV.
19. McMechen, WV.
20. Proceeded SW to Parkersburg, WV.

Two of the rescue objects were the elongated wingless jet-type #4 and #7 objects that emitted flames from their crafts through their propulsion systems. Those aircraft looked similar to a plane on fire when they descended. Some of the other objects produced tails of various colors while passing through the earth's atmosphere. These tails were produced by the "plasma phenomenon."

236

This is caused by extreme heat surrounding the energy field of a craft while passing through the earth's atmosphere at tremendous speed.

On September 14, The *Wilmington Delaware Sunday Star* reported, "'Balls of Fire' in Pittsburgh'- Jittery Citizens Report Planes in Flames over Wide Area." In part, it stated, "Civil Aeronautics Administration officials at Wheeling, WVa, Pittsburgh, and Zanesville, O., were deluged with calls reporting great numbers of aircraft plunging from the skies in flames."

The *Evening Standard* newspaper of Uniontown, Pennsylvania reported numerous sightings over the Fayette County area, which is south of Pittsburgh. Their September 13 headline read, "FLYING SAUCERS IN DISTRICT ONCE MORE – Reports of Sighting the Discs Coming in From All Sections; Some Citizens Jittery." It reported the following information, including objects going down near homes:

Flying saucers have again been reported over Fayette County with most persons who profess to have seen them setting the time yesterday between 8:00 and 8:30 p.m. Reports of sighting the "saucers" have streamed in from all corners of the county and surrounding district.

A call was received this morning from Mrs. John Collins, Confluence Road. She reported having seen what looked like a "ball of fire" about twice as long as it was wide fall near a neighbor's house. At first, she stated, "It looked like it was about to hit a house but as it neared the ground it seemed to go out. Other reports received in Uniontown stated that the saucers were seen in Franklin Township, Smithfield, from the Jumonville Methodist Training Center, Smock, Greensboro as well as Uniontown. Another report received here this morning came from Mr. and Mrs. George Dodson, Bitner. They stated that while sitting on their front porch shortly after 8 p.m. yesterday, they saw a round light in the sky. A call from Markleysburg by Mrs. Myers revealed that her husband saw a bright light fall from the sky into the woods near their residence.

The Sandusky, Ohio *Register Star News* also reported the following headline, "FALLING METEOR STARTLES OHIOANS," which was datelined, "COLUMBUS, Sept. 13 (INS)." It reported the following information:

The State Highway Patrol said today its stations throughout Ohio were flooded with calls Friday night that a "burning plane" and "balls of fire" were streaking across the sky. The mystery seemed cleared up, though, with statements from aerial experts of the Civil Aeronautics Administration that the spectators saw a falling meteor of great brilliance. The same spectacle was reported by veteran sky watchers in Washington, D.C., West Virginia and Pennsylvania.

This biased, ill-informed article explains the numerous UFO sightings were attributed to a single "meteor of great brilliance." It explains that, "statements from aerial experts of the Civil Aeronautics Administration" had reached this conclusion! The *Intelligencer* stated the following information in its September 13 article concerning a late night sighting, "The CAA office at Stifel Field, Wheeling-Ohio County airport received a call late last night from a Martins Ferry man who claimed to have seen what looked like a light plane afire crash to the ground between the transmitters of radio stations WHLL and WKWK atop Glenwood Heights."

Glenwood Heights, in the Wheeling area, is approximately 15 miles southwest of the Oglebay Park area where the injured alien was left off from the damaged Baltimore/WV #2 craft. This maneuver was a final effort by one of the rescue objects to find the stranded being. This object landed at Glenwood Heights at a high point where it could be easily sighted. In all probability, this object was one of the elongated wingless ships. Obviously, the craft that landed on the hill between two radio towers was capable of taking off again. Since no plane or wreckage was found, the flaming aircraft must have been an unconventional-type aircraft.

The Times-Leader also reported the following in its September 13 article, "All witnesses agreed that the blazing objects, planes, meteors, rockets or whatever zoomed horizontally and awfully low."

On September 13, *The Boston Globe*. Boston, Massachusetts, stated in part, "Four States 'Bombarded' by Meteor-Like Objects. Pittsburgh. (UP) Authorities sought an explanation today for the flurry of meteor-like objects sighted over four states that caused jittery citizens to report airplanes plunging from the skies in flames…Descriptions of the weird spectacle varied widely but all witnesses agreed the blazing objects moved horizontally and 'awfully low.'" This two-hour episode, thought by many to be a meteor shower, finally ended when the search and rescue mission was abandoned at around 10 p.m. EDT/9 p.m. EST.

Meanwhile, in Flatwoods, the "Braxton County Monster" had encountered Mr. May and the boys on the farm. At about 8:05 p.m. EST, it boarded its craft after being sighted. While preparing to depart the Fisher Farm, it contacted the Mothership over the Capitol. The damaged craft needed to relocate to a nearby area before the locals threatened it. Moreover, the damaged ship was not capable of regenerating. Because its power was nearly depleted, it could not go far. This would probably be its last transmission. Shortly after taking off, the craft gained enough altitude to rise above the hills and mountains. It picked up momentum and rose out of the valley.

There was only one witness, who saw the "Flatwoods Monster" craft depart the Fisher Farm that night. Mrs. May talked to me about this witness, "This editor from Webster Springs was over there [at the sheriff's department] when I called. And he got in the car and he went down Monkey Row [local nickname for Salt Lick Road] and he saw the thing up there, the light, and he went upon [sic] the field trestle (a railroad bridge located in back of the Fisher Farm) and stood up there and watched it. And he said it went down a little grade like this (gesturing downward motion) and he said it went around and around and took off and went to the airport. It turned and then went right back down the river."

Just southwest of the Sutton Airport is the small town of Little Birch. *The Charleston Gazette* reported the following incident on September 14, "Residents of Little Birch reported seeing a fiery object flash overhead shortly after the 'monster' was reported. It was conceded that the 'monster' may have climbed in its 'ship' and taken off again shortly after his untimely visit." According to all my research, timeline, and plotted points, this analogy was quite accurate.

The craft then changed direction and headed northwest toward Frametown. This incident was documented in the *Braxton County Democrat*, September 18, 1952. The article by J. C. Dean told about a fiery object that had landed on a mountaintop in Frametown. One week after the incident occurred, investigator Sanderson went to the home of Mr. Dean in Frametown. Sanderson said that Mr. Dean reported an, "aerial object had crashed or landed on a nearby farm" in Frametown. Ivan T. Sanderson continued, "Mr. Dean received us most courteously and informed us that a craft had landed on an overgrown and isolated field atop a hill known as James Knoll or Knob but that, although seen by the two young James boys, it had not been investigated because it had been regarded as a fireball." Shortly before, another witness had seen this object, prior to it crashing.

In 2009, while in Flatwoods for an event, I met a man from Frametown, Mr. Randy James, who introduced me to his mother. Mrs. James had come forward to tell me about a UFO, she saw passing over Frametown on September 12, 1952. Randy James and his Mom are actually of the James family, which the Knoll was named after. On that night, Mrs. James, a young woman, was with her family when she saw the "thing" that "flew over Frametown," near James Knoll. It was just after dark. She explained that the object "was red" in color, and "it was flying low." The witness saw it clearly, as it passed over the nearby mountains, and didn't know what it was.

This object was *not* a fireball meteor. It was actually the damaged UFO, which crash-landed on James Knob atop a field. James Knoll is located in a very mountainous and isolated region in Braxton County. It has a wide-open field on top, a good location for a damaged ship to land where it could not be easily reached. James Knoll was a perfect location for an emergency landing. My research shows, this was the last known location where the damaged ship was seen that night.

Four States "Bombarded" by Meteor-Like Objects

Flashing Meteors Scare Residents In Three-State Area

Fireballs Shower City Area

Meteor Fall Blamed As Cause of Scare

'Balls Of Fire' In Pittsburgh

Jittery Citizens Report Planes In Flames Over Wide Area

Pittsburgh, Sept. 13 (U.P)—Author

Authorities Probe Flashes In Area Skies

Strange Lights Observed Over Four States

CHAPTER TWENTY

EXIT-NORTH CAROLINA

I was able to trace the flight paths of the following ships:

   A. The three damaged mid-Atlantic objects.
   B. The jet-shaped UFO.
   C. The five southeastern North Carolina Rescue Objects.

The following list indicates the locations where these nine UFOs were last seen that night.
A. **The three mid-Atlantic UFOs**

   1. The damaged Virginia/TN #1 Object was last seen airborne and traveling east over Elizabethton, TN.
   2. The damaged Baltimore/WV #2 Object was last seen over Bluefield, WV.
   3. The damaged Washington/Flatwoods WV #3 Object was last seen crashing into James Knob in Frametown, WV.

B. **The one jet-shaped UFO**

   1. This object was last sighted over Flatwoods.

C. **The five southeastern North Carolina Rescue UFOs**

   1. The damaged #1 North Carolina Rescue Object was last seen airborne over an automobile in Duck Creek, WV before it departed the area.
   2. The #2 North Carolina Rescue Object was last seen airborne over Heaters, WV. It also ascended into the upper atmosphere.
   3. The #3 North Carolina Rescue Object was last seen airborne over the Sutton airport. This ship also ascended into the upper atmosphere.
   4. The #4 North Carolina Rescue ship, a backup ship, was a "flying saucer." It was reported over Flat Rock, NC. It was then sighted over Virginia with the other three NC rescue ships as it headed north. It flanked the 3 objects to Flatwoods and then flew to Lafferty, OH.
   5. The #5 North Carolina Rescue Object was a backup ship, last seen near the Raleigh, North Carolina area. Later, it acted as a beacon ship along the North Carolina coastline.

Of the nine UFOs listed above, four were damaged; the three mid-Atlantic objects and the #1 North Carolina Rescue Object, which was intercepted by jet fighters over the Gulf of Mexico, waters earlier. I closely examined the characteristics that these four ships displayed. The ships were all described as having been on fire at one point or another during their flight paths and had crash-landed. While in flight, these ships were seen emitting sparks, had pieces fall off of them, exploding, and hurling off fragments, to name a few.

After the ships initially landed, they were seen airborne several times afterward, except for one ship. The only ship I could not find an extended flight path for was the "Flatwoods Monster" ship.

It remained on James Knob in Frametown and that is where its flight path ended. The other three damaged ships were seen airborne heading out of each of the states where they had landed. Two were departing West Virginia and one was departing Tennessee.

Upon examining the Project Blue Book case files, I found additional reports of objects sighted after 7:00 p.m. EST. These reports all relate to two separate incidents reporting three separate objects. They were sighted at 7:45 p.m. EST/8:45 p.m. EDT, and 8:03 p.m. EST/9:03 p.m. EDT.

The 7:45 p.m. EST incident involved the sighting of two UFOs that were flying together in unison. The second incident at 8:03 p.m. EST involved the sighting of a single object. Moreover, all three of these UFOs were seen near the Greensboro, NC area. In examining the eighteen-minute time span between these two incidents, it is clear that these objects were undoubtedly the three damaged ships making their departures out of the country. Greensboro was actually a designated departure point along the escape route; the same area that the #1 and #2 North Carolina ships passed over when they flew toward Flatwoods, West Virginia, about an hour before.

Meanwhile, the #5 North Carolina Object, which stayed behind over North Carolina was hovering near the coastline just south of Lake Waccamaw. It had positioned itself as a beacon and transmitted a homing signal for the damaged crafts to follow to the coast and rendezvous with the Mothership and get picked up. In the meantime, the damaged objects had been contacted and made aware of this rescue operation. They headed to the Greensboro area so they could exit the state along a southeast corridor toward the coastline of North Carolina. [See map on page 238].

The first UFO sighting at 7:45 p.m. involved two of the damaged objects that were unable to make atmospheric ascents. These two objects were the Virginia/TN #1 Object and the #1 North Carolina Rescue Object. This incident was recorded in a Project Blue Book Tentative Observers Questionnaire by a Greensboro woman. She reported that two objects flew one in front of the other in unison and were "close to ground." The lead object was described as a "huge light." It was flying in front of and "attached" to a "fiery ball in rotation" as if it were towing the fiery object.

Shortly before this Greensboro incident, another similar incident involved two objects flying together in unison. It was made over Ward, WV. *The Charleston Daily Mail* article, "2-in-One Meteor Seen Over Ward," reported the story. Witness Mr. Blount said, "It appeared to be two balls of fire, one over the other, with a connecting tail." These alleged meteors were actually the damaged Baltimore/WV #2 Object and the #1 North Carolina Rescue Object. The Baltimore/WV #2 Object had lost power and had trouble staying airborne over West Virginia. It already landed on the outskirts of Charleston twice trying to get to safety, before it landed in nearby Cabin Creek.

At some point between Charleston and Ward, West Virginia, the Baltimore/WV #2 Object had made a rendezvous with the #1 North Carolina Rescue object. The damaged #1 North Carolina object had just departed Braxton County after regenerating its power supply then headed southwest toward Charleston. When these craft made their rendezvous, they connected in midair so the #1 North Carolina Rescue Object could transfer energy to the failing Baltimore/WV #2 Object. This process is similar to the procedure of airplane in-flight fueling.

During this process however, the damaged Baltimore/WV #2 Object began to overheat and caught on fire, igniting the #1 North Carolina Rescue Object. Subsequently, the Baltimore/WV #2 Object was forced to land again. It then went down in Cabin Creek, West Virginia, just southeast of Ward. The #1 North Carolina Object, now low on power, continued on a solo flight and departed West Virginia. It struggled on a southeast trajectory toward the Greensboro, North Carolina area, so it could travel the escape corridor and make its rendezvous near the coastline.

During that time, the last damaged ship that was unaccounted for, the Virginia/TN #1 Object, had reentered the scene. It was last seen headed east over Elizabethton, TN, approximately 120 miles northwest of Greensboro. As the fleeing, damaged #1 North Carolina Rescue Object continued southeast and got closer to Greensboro, it was in communication with the damaged Virginia/TN #1 Object and tracking it from the west. As they reached the Greensboro area, the Virginia/TN #1 Object intercepted the #1 North Carolina Rescue Object and the two crafts linked together. Moments later, energy was successfully transferred and they continued on their journey.

Minutes later, both of these craft moved over Greensboro, North Carolina at a low altitude heading southeast. During this episode, the Virginia/TN #1 Object was described as "a huge light flying in front of a fiery ball," which was actually the #1 North Carolina Rescue Object. The two damaged objects continued to follow the signal of the beacon ship, passed over Lake Waccamaw and reached the coastline shortly after. Then, they waited for the Mothership to pick them up.

Eighteen minutes later, at 8:03 p.m. EST, Project Blue Book reported another incident near Greensboro, North Carolina. According to my research, this was the last damaged ship, the Baltimore/WV #2 Object that had previously landed in Cabin Creek, West Virginia to cool down.

It was last seen heading south across the southern West Virginia border over the town of Bluefield. When the Akron Astronomy Club saw the Baltimore/WV #2 Object earlier, it was described as "egg-shaped with a smaller radius in front." Later, when the object was sighted over Charleston, WV, a witness said he "saw sparks for a moment." Afterward, when it was seen over the skies of Greensboro, it was reported as "trailing red sparks." The ship was in dire straits.

The following is a record of the incident in Project Blue Book, called a "Flying Object Report." The report states:

One oblong fiery object, whitish glow trailing red sparks was observed from B-25 aircraft, 20 miles south-southwest of Greensboro, North Carolina by Captain [blacked out]. Special Investigations Unit Bolling AFB, Washington. Object observed for approximately 15 seconds, object disappeared going north very fast. Altitude of B7-25 [B-25] was 2000 feet, air speed 215 MPH. Time of sighting 12/2003 [12 September/8:03 p.m. EST].

During this time, the #5 North Carolina Rescue Object, which was waiting for the last damaged ship, the Baltimore/WV Object, was still positioned near the coastline. It was contacted by the damaged craft and told that an airplane was flying nearby and it may need assistance, as its intentions were unknown.

The beacon ship quickly descended over the state towards Greensboro to assist the damaged ship. It descended over Lake Waccamaw and flew northwest towards the Greensboro area where the B-25 plane was approaching the damaged object. If a confrontation unfolded, this rescue ship could defend the damaged object by intercepting the airplane, which could also include drastic measures if deemed necessary. The #5 North Carolina Rescue Object swiftly flew northwest toward Greensboro to assist the Baltimore/WV #2 Object.

Moments later, as the rescue object was flying over Fayetteville, it was contacted by the damaged craft and notified that nearby aircraft was not an interceptor plane. This aircraft was actually a slow moving plane, probably doing reconnaissance, and did not seem to be a threat to their craft. Regardless, the rescue ship continued toward Greensboro until it received further word from about the unfolding situation. The damaged Baltimore/WV #2 Object passed near Greensboro, NC on its southeast flight path, redirected north and accelerated when the B-25 came near it. The damaged craft descended, continued north, moved away from the B-25 plane, and then redirected its flight path southeast. The damaged craft then contacted the #5 North Carolina Rescue Object that was flying just west of Raleigh and called off the intercept; it was now safe.

Moments later, the rescue object ascended from the Raleigh area, redirected southeast and headed back toward the coastline. The damaged UFO, in communication with the rescue object, continued to follow its homing signal and trailed it back to the coast. Shortly after, the rescue object passed south over Lake Waccamaw and reached the coast. It stopped and situated itself near the coastal Atlantic waters with the other two damaged objects that were circling nearby.

The damaged ship continued southeast toward the beacon ship, finally reached the coastline and joined the awaiting ships. Meanwhile, the large Mothership that was over the Washington, D.C. area was relocating southeast toward North Carolina. It was contacted by the three damaged objects and the #5 North Carolina Rescue Object and notified that they were all together. This segment of the mission was a success. Moving high above the atmosphere, the Mothership continued southeast toward the North Carolina coastline for the rendezvous.

Upon reaching the North Carolina coastal area, the Mothership situated itself a few miles off the coastline over the Atlantic Ocean and notified the waiting ships. It then descended low into the atmosphere as the three damaged ships and the rescue object flew over the Atlantic waters to meet it. Shortly after, the Mothership picked up the four objects and the rendezvous mission was a complete success. The large craft then ascended and headed north on yet another mission. The next mission, another rendezvous mission, involved the placement of two crafts over two different strategic locations, Delaware and Maryland.

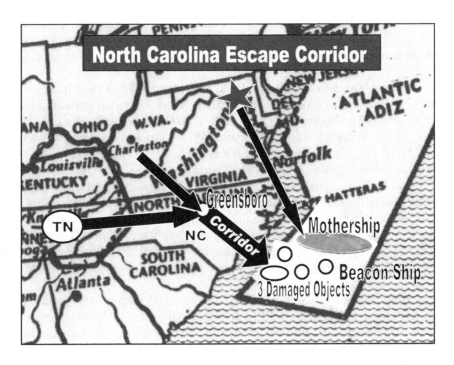

CHAPTER TWENTY-ONE

THE LAST SEPTEMBER 12 SIGHTINGS

The next sighting of a UFO occurred over Middletown, PA. An Air Intelligence Information Sheet, a Project 10073 Record Card and Action Synopsis Sheet explained the sighting. A civilian observer saw this UFO at 8:07 p.m. EST/9:07 p.m. EDT over Olmstead AFB. The following information was contained in the "AIR INTELLIGENCE INFORMATION REPORT" dated, "16 September 1952." It states:

[Name blacked out] an employee of this base reported seeing an unidentified flying object while at work at 0107z [8:07 p.m. EST/9:07 p.m. EDT] on 12 Sept 1952. Mr. [blacked out] described the object as a bright white light that looked like an automobile headlight at a considerable distance. The light moved in a straight line from the southwest to the northwest and disappeared behind a tree. Its speed was described as "slower than an airplane." The light was visible for "three or four" minutes, but Mr. [blacked out] reported that during this time it dimmed "considerably" for a period of approximately five seconds after which it regained its former brilliance. No exhaust or sound was noted. There were no local aircraft in the air at the time. Weather was clear with twelve miles visibility, winds calm.

Mr. [blacked out]'s estimate of the length of observation discounted astronomical phenomena such as meteors. Although no sound was heard and he maintained that the object did not resemble an aircraft, the object's speed and level flight strongly suggested the possibility of an aircraft.

The bright light sighted over Olmstead AFB at 9:07 p.m. EDT bore a striking similarity to an earlier sighting. Olmstead AFB was also the location where an earlier sighting of a UFO took place at 3:35 A. M. EDT on September 12, 1952. In both Olmstead AFB cases, the reports stated an object changed brightness while being observed. Was it just another coincidence that this was the second UFO seen flying near Olmstead AFB that day?

It is interesting to note, "There were no local aircraft in the air at the time." Yet, at the end of this report they said, "The object's speed and level flight strongly suggest the possibility of an aircraft." In the "Project 10073 Record Card," the U.S. Air Force stated its conclusion as "possibly aircraft." It is also interesting to note that in the Air Intelligence Information sheet report, the Air Force stated, "This office can offer no definite explanation of the sighting." This sighting was put into a synopsis report by Olmstead AFB, stamped "ACTION." This case did not receive an "Unknown" evaluation, even though the Air Force officials at Olmsted AFB could not explain the sighting.

On the contrary, by utilizing my timeline of events and map-plotted points, this sighting indicates that this object was actually a UFO. It was actually the #13 "Rescue Object. This UFO hovered high over Olmsted AFB and kept a watchful eye over the events that unfolded around the Capitol area, between 8:00 p.m. and 8:10 p.m. EDT. Olmsted AFB, only being located 90 statute miles directly north of Washington, D.C. was an ideal location to observe, direct and interact if needed.

Furthermore, from a military stance, this UFO also kept a watch over the entire area, in the event that the damaged "Flatwoods Monster" craft attempted to depart West Virginia. Approximately one hour after the damaged craft passed over Washington, D.C., the #13 object finally descended. At 9:07 p.m. EDT., it descended and dropped directly over Olmsted AFB, made a blatant low-level appearance, and then disappeared. More than one hour had passed and the damaged craft and crew were still missing in the mountain state of West Virginia.

The next sighting occurred over Allen, Maryland, one hour and twenty-three minutes later. Project Blue Book heavily documented this case, and recorded the sighting as "Unknown" case #2077. The witnesses, Mr. And Mrs. Kolb made their sighting report to the Baltimore, MD Ground Observer Corps Filter Station at 9:30 p.m. EST/10:30 p.m. EDT. They also reported the sighting to the 647th AC & W ["'Aircraft Control and Warning'...as in *AC & W facility, installation, system, unit."*] in Manassas, VA. Subsequently, a teletype report from the 647th AC & W was sent to two Air Force bases and the Pentagon. This document stated:

Object was round with streamers, flashing greenish-white light, with a red rim. Moving at about 2,000 feet and under observation about 35 minutes. Visibility was 10 miles. No aircraft were detected with radar; however, low-level emissions were sighted.

Soon after, the 647th AC & W made this report; it was teletyped to the ATIC at Wright-Patterson AFB. Upon receipt, it was hand-stamped "ACTION." Shortly afterward, a follow-up report was completed. This report was an "Air Intelligence Information Report." This two-page report was also copied and sent to ATIC Project Blue Book for evaluation. The document read:

SUMMARY: a report received at 0245z [9:45 p.m. EST] 12 September 1952 from the Baltimore Ground Observer Corps Filter center stating that an unconventional flying object had been sighted at 0230z [9:30 p.m. EST]. Object was round with streamers, flashing green, white light with red rim, moving mid-Atlantic at approximately 2,000 feet. Object was observed through field glasses for a period of thirty-five minutes during which time the red rim around the object grew fainter and object faded altogether. A check of the area of reported sighting was made by this station using all electronic equipment available and no targets were detected.

After ATIC reviewed this report, a handwritten note was added in the margin, disregarding the possibility the object was a low-level mission being conducted, "wind 90 degrees [arrows indicating direction] = could not be a weather balloon. No split [arrow indicating direction]."

After Project Blue Book officials analyzed this report, they gave their final evaluation on the sighting of the Allen, Maryland object. This was recorded in a Project 10073 Record Card, "Comments: Does not coincide with regular releases in area...Conclusion: Unknown."

The Baltimore GOC Filter Station thought this UFO seen over Allen, Maryland was crucial enough to have contacted an Aircraft Control and Warning Squadron. The 647th AC & W Squadron Air Intelligence Information Report stated a check was made on all electronic equipment available, and no targets were detected. After receiving this report at 9:45 p.m. EST and checking for the object on radar, they were unable to find it and the object appeared in the sky for another "twenty minutes."

I plotted the Allen, Maryland UFO on a map and realized it was actually surrounded by USAF bases and Naval Air stations at all points except over the Atlantic Ocean.

This was not a coincidence. This UFO had actually positioned itself over Allen, Maryland in the middle of the following military installations:

1). NAS Patuxent River, 35 miles west of UFO
2). Dover AFB, Delaware, 65 miles NE of UFO
3). Andrews AFB, Maryland, 75 miles NW of UFO
4). Bolling AFB, Wash, DC, 80 miles NW of UFO
5). NAS Quantico, VA, 85 miles NW of UFO
6). Langley AFB, VA, 90 miles SW of UFO
7). NAS Norfolk, VA, 100 miles SW of UFO
8). NAS Oceana, VA, 105 miles SW of UFO.

After the Baltimore GOC station reported this UFO, the military was unable to detect the object because it was hovering under radar. The UFO was positioned at such a low altitude that radar was unable to pick it up. At this point, the 647th AC & W squadron did not scramble jet fighters after it. In turn, they contacted the Pentagon, Wright-Patterson AFB, and ENT AFB!

The Allen, MD UFO was Sighted for 35-minutes at a 2,000-foot Altitude

Why did the Air Force and Navy leave this UFO alone and not attempt to intercept it? Military officials knew of its presence and left it alone, but why? This UFO did not position itself in the middle of these military bases to go undetected. It actually wanted to be seen, hovering at an altitude of 2,000 feet for 35-minutes. The craft was round, with white light and a red rim. It was "flashing green and blinking." It also had "streamers" flowing from its body. Meanwhile, the story continued to unfold elsewhere!

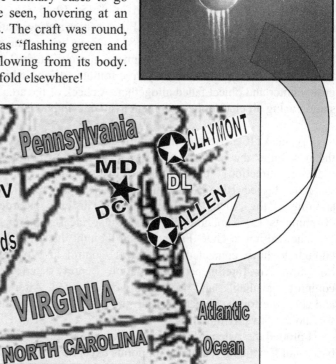

Approximately 108 miles northeast of Allen, MD, another UFO was sighted in Claymont, DE hovering at 2,000 feet. *The Wilmington Journal* printed an AP article from Baltimore dated September 13, 1952, titled, "Fiery Object in Sky Stirs 'Saucer Reports' in 4 States." It stated, "Several persons living in the vicinity of Claymont called State Police and the weatherman at New Castle Airport last night inquiring about 'the spinning tops in the sky.'"

The Wilmington Morning News printed another story about these sightings. The headline read, "Flashing Meteors Scare Residents In Three-State-Area." It stated, "They had seen what they described as a spinning top in the skies north of Wilmington. (The object resembled a spinning top in shape, which remained in one position and did not travel through the skies.) Paul Ridgeway said it appeared to be about 2,000 feet in the sky." Its size was said to be, slightly smaller than a dirigible."

However, the bold actions of these two crafts, which were so near to Washington, D.C., did not prompt interceptions against them. Government officials were actually well aware of the two UFOs and just backed off because the objects had strategically positioned themselves north and south of the Capitol at low altitudes. In this situation, the top-shaped object and the other round object over Allen, MD had a motive; they had both acted as beacons. If the damaged Flatwoods ship had departed West Virginia, it would have had the option to move toward either one of these beacons. The same beacon tactic was used over North Carolina earlier that night, when the three damaged objects followed the #5 North Carolina Rescue Object to the coast and were subsequently picked up by the Mothership over the Atlantic Ocean.

In this episode, the large top-shaped craft over Delaware was actually the Mothership that had descended over the Claymont area. Earlier, when it departed the coastal area near North Carolina, this huge craft flew north. It passed over Allen, Maryland and dropped off a beacon craft over that area, then flew to Delaware. It then descended to 2,000 feet and waited to pick up the damaged "Flatwoods Monster" ship if it came toward the eastern seaboard. A projected flight path from Braxton County to either of these beacons would have taken the object around Washington, D.C.

In this situation, the UFOs had made their presence well known and stayed below the radar's tracking capabilities. If the damaged object attempted to reach either UFO, both of them were near enough to the Capitol to strike the city if jet fighters attempted to intercept it. This was a strategic maneuver! This would have made it impossible for the United States military to track any striking maneuvers made against the country.

The Mothership was said to be "slightly smaller than a dirigible"

Graf Zeppelin

In this situation, Washington, D.C. officials definitely knew something was going on and perhaps the two UFOs were a part of a rescue plan. Just prior, installations across the country were tracking and reporting the three damaged objects, which were sighted across the country.

These two low-hovering UFOs were actually awaiting the damaged "Flatwoods Monster" craft, yet military officials did not know if a rescue mission was the motive or if the objects were positioned to attack!

About three hours after the object was seen over Allen, a Teletype was sent from U.S. Air Force headquarters to the Pentagon, Ent AFB, Wright Patterson AFB, and Langley AFB.

The following statement was made, "One Navy pilot over Patuxent River, MD, and one Air Force pilot over Greensborough [sic] NC reported seeing shooting stars at about the same time of the sightings." According to the teletype, the U.S. Navy pilot reported this sighting to the Pentagon. Why did a Navy pilot report seeing shooting stars to the Pentagon? It seems that the teletype was forwarded to three Air Force bases because the Pentagon was aware these alleged "shooting stars" were actually UFOs. This Navy report was the first hint of a cover-up, foreshadowing the "single meteor theory" that would be given.

It is hard to believe that the U.S. Air Force could explain away all the sightings that night with their single meteor theory. The public accepted Washington's explanation in 1952, but looking at the evidence today, we see that the single meteor explanation fails to explain much of anything. Furthermore, not one word about any of these sightings appeared in Edward Ruppelt's 1956 book!

The final UFO sighting that occurred that night was in Braxton County, in Flatwoods, over the Bailey Fisher Farm. Investigator Gray Barker discovered the story and reported it in the Saucerian Vol. 1 No. 1. Barker reported, "I often puzzle over one account I drove fifty miles to obtain. It was said that Bailey Frame of Birch River, had been on the scene, and had witnessed a rocket ship take off from the hill. I found him in a tavern at Birch River, where he hastily denied most of the report, but did say he had seen a strange object in the sky after the 'monster' incident."

Barker added, "It was a large orange ball, he said, flattened on top, from which jets or streams of fire shot out and down around the sides. It circled around in the sky, and was seen from a small valley at Flatwoods, near the hilltop, where Bailey Frame had driven half an hour after hearing about the matter. After circling for fifteen minutes, it suddenly left at great speed toward the Sutton airport." Barker also said, "This, I thought, was most important. For it filled an important gap—the exit of the 'monster.'"

Barker explained the following episode involving Bailey Frame. "He said he'd be glad to meet me at a restaurant that evening, drive to Flatwoods with me, and take me to the exact spot where he had seen the thing. He did not show up. I was not greatly impressed by the report anyway." Barker was obviously not impressed because the sighting of this object and its description did not fit the profile of the "Flatwoods Monster" ship.

Barker had hoped that this was "the exit of the 'monster'" ship. The "Flatwoods Monster" ship was described to me as elliptically shaped, not round. Witnesses Jack Davis and Freddie May both described the incoming damaged ship to me in a rather detailed manner. Their descriptions of the object did not sound like or match Mr. Frame's description nor did it fit the time frame.

The Rescue Ship Circled the Fisher Farm for Fifteen Minutes

The object spotted circling the mountaintop of the Fisher Farm was actually a later sighting of a rescue ship. It was making a last-ditch effort to find the downed craft and its occupant. This would explain why the object circled the hilltop of the Fisher Farm for fifteen minutes.

From Mr. Frame's description of the object's circling flight pattern in the sky, it appears that it was intently searching the area. I re-examined the shapes and descriptions of the 8:00 p.m. rescue ships seen over the mid-Atlantic and found a striking resemblance to one of the objects.

The #5 UFO, which was witnessed flying over Arlington, VA, was a nearly identical match to Mr. Frame's UFO sighting in Flatwoods. Frame described the shape of the object he saw as a "large orange ball…flattened on top." The Arlington, VA witness described the object as "a luminous green ball-type object, a little flattened with a short orange tail." The reason for the color differences is that the object seen by Frame was hovering and emitting jet streams of fire, reflecting against the body giving it an orange appearance.

In both sightings, the witnesses described the object as being round and having a flat side. These two objects were the only two described as ball-shaped with a flat side. Furthermore, the Arlington area sighting at 8:00 p.m. EDT and the West Liberty, WV sighting were both said to resemble a Roman candle while in flight. From the descriptions reported it seems that this particular object was seen over three separate locations throughout the night!

Gray Barker said that Bailey Frame had "driven half an hour after hearing about the matter." He did not give the time that Frame heard about the incident. According to my research, Frame's sighting occurred after A. Lee Stewart, Jr. and the sheriff left Mrs. May's house in Flatwoods between 10:30 and 11:00 p.m. The object had headed toward Flatwoods, called by the homing beacon. It followed the beacon signal to the Fisher Farm and circled over its several acres.

James Knoll in Frametown, West Virginia

Nevertheless, the occupant named the "Flatwoods Monster," was stranded in Frametown atop James Knoll and was unable to transmit any messages from its overheated ship.

After the rescue object circled the Fisher Farm for fifteen minutes, it departed. Trying to locate the damaged ship at night in the mountains of West Virginia without any communications had been virtually impossible. All search and rescue attempts had ceased.

The beacon UFO over Maryland and the Mothership over Delaware then ascended and departed into the upper atmosphere. The Mothership rendezvoused with the beacon ship near the coast and then picked it up. It headed northwest, hovered back over Washington, D.C., and positioned itself out of sight from the population below. Meanwhile, the rescue objects that had abandoned their search of their two stranded comrades over eastern Ohio and through out West Virginia, rendezvoused with the Mothership over the Capitol and waited!

CHAPTER TWENTY-TWO

TWO STRANDED IN WEST VIRGINIA

On September 13, 1952, Washington officials congregated behind closed doors at the Pentagon into the wee hours of the morning and frantically discussed cover stories to tell the American public. They were also aware that at least one downed extraterrestrial was probably stranded in West Virginia from the night before and had no idea what was going to unfold next.

Mr. and Mrs. Smith of the "CSI" group reported a "flying saucer" sighting had occurred in Flatwoods during the early morning hours of September 13, 1952. They stated, "At 6:30 the next morning, the director of the Board of Education saw a flying saucer take off, not far from his house, and immediately reported it to the Sutton newspaper." It is significant to address this UFO sighting in which the object was described as a "flying saucer" and its motive.

On September 12, the night before, the #4 North Carolina Rescue ship was called a "flying saucer." It was first reported over Flat Rock North Carolina when it descended into the "Oak Ridge ADIZ." It was then sighted over Virginia with the other three NC rescue ships as it headed north, flanking the 3 objects to Flatwoods, West Virginia. Then, the "flying saucer" flew on to Lafferty, OH to participate in a search and rescue mission, which was called a "meteor shower."

This early morning UFO sighting in Flatwoods, which involved a "flying saucer" that took off, was undoubtedly another effort to locate the stranded "Flatwoods Monster" and its craft. Moreover, it is apparent the searching craft, called a "flying saucer" was the same one sighted the night before over various locations. Later that Saturday morning, September 13, 1952, while newspapers around the country had released articles about the strange phenomenon of the previous night, nobody was fully aware of the aftermath.

The "Flatwoods Monster," the occupant of the craft described as the "Flame over Washington," was stranded in Frametown, atop James Knoll. Moreover, the occupant of the damaged Baltimore/WV ship was still awaiting rescue near Oglebay Park. The occupant of this craft did not make its presence known until Monday night, September 15.

When this occupant was sighted in Wheeling on Monday night, it was also called a "monster." It had been stranded in the area since Friday night, when it had been dropped from its craft because it had sustained injuries. The area where the creature was sighted was the Vineyard Hill Housing Development, approximately five miles from Oglebay Park. On Tuesday, September 16, 1952, the following article appeared on the front page of *The Wheeling Intelligencer*, "Powered by Suggestion? ' Monster' From Outer Space Arrives Here Via 'Saucer.'" It reads:

"Bashful Billy," the monster from outer space and southern West Virginia, arrived in Wheeling by flying saucer yesterday and promptly set tongues wagging and telephones burning. Even the Wheeling police prepared to call out all space cadets. Telephones of *The Wheeling Intelligencer* and city police kept humming last night as anxious residents attempted to confirm rumors, but in true Hollywood style, the monster apparently vanished without pausing to light a single cigarette with his fiery breath.

One call to the *Intelligencer* office asked if it was true that the horrible burned body of a woman was found at Vineyard Hill and that, a city policeman was burned mysteriously about the arm. Since no members of the department are equipped with Buck Rogers' rocket guns, Lieutenant

Murphy declined to assign men to the area. "The only green-eyed monster I ever heard of was a jealous woman," Detective Howard Millard said.

Callers also reported that an unpleasant odor was produced by the monster, who evidently hasn't heard of chlorophyll since he's newly arrived on this planet, and police admitted there was something smelly about the way the rumor was started from no apparent source. Lieutenant Murphy said undoubtedly the rumors were caused by over-active imagination following yesterday's *Intelligencers* story of an outer-world monster, reportedly spotted in the woods near Sutton, W. Va.

The Wheeling monster must have been a "Bashful Billy," however, as none of the people who called the *Intelligencer* or police had actually seen the fugitive from fairyland, but were merely passing on reports from people who had talked to people who had talked to people who had heard about the Vineyard Hill Frankenstein. Meanwhile three disbelievers of the flying saucers story had a change of mind last night when they reported seeing a 'ball of fire' soar through the heavens to the west, just outside of Independence, Pa. Ernest Mitchell, of 1038 Capline Street, William Downey, who lives at the Wheeling Country Club, and Katherine Meyers, of Barnesville, Ohio, were returning to Wheeling from Aspenwall last night after visiting Downey's brother when they sighted the object.

"We were watching an airplane from the Independence Airfield when the ball of fire zoomed over the horizon." Mitchell said, "And then it was gone in no time at all." Mitchell's statement was verified by Miss Meyers, who said the object was seen between 7:30 and 7:45 o'clock [EDT] headed due west. "I've been watching every night since I first heard of flying saucers and I've never seen one, until tonight that is," Downley said. All three described it as a plain ball of fire, quite small, and said it wasn't trailing sparks.

Powered by Suggestion?
'Monster' From Outer Space Arrives Here Via 'Saucer'

"BASHFUL BILLY."
Green-Eyed Monster From Mars

This witty and sarcastic newspaper article was actually filled with a lot of valuable information, much of it very close to the truth. It was reported, "One caller to the *Intelligencer* office asked if it were true that the horribly burned body of a woman was found at Vineyard Hill and that a policeman was burned mysteriously about the arm."

Further reports about this Wheeling city police officer were made to the police department. Their response was, "Police Lt. John P. Murphy reported similar calls pertaining to an injured policeman, and in one incident was asked to send a patrolman to Vineyard Hill for guard duty. Lieutenant Murphy declined to send a man to the area."

I ask; when the Wheeling Police Department received such a large number of calls, why did Lieutenant Murphy allegedly refuse to send a police officer to the Vineyard Hill area? Even if the calls were only rumors and Lt. Murphy placed no credibility in the story, it is the police department's duty to protect and serve its citizens.

It is surprising that Wheeling Police Department officials stayed at their office answering phone calls instead of going out to Vineyard Hill to talk to their concerned citizens. Was this the truth or did they actually respond to the calls?

I find it odd that Detective Millard saw fit to mock one of the callers with the comment, "the only green-eyed monster I ever heard of was a jealous woman." Had the Wheeling Police Department already responded to the call, and knew quite well what was happening at Vineyard Hill? Was it a rumor or a fact that an officer had "been burned mysteriously about the arm"? If this was a fact, had the officer been dispatched to Vineyard Hill to respond to the calls about a "green-eyed monster"? It was also noted in this article that, "Callers reported an unpleasant odor was produced by the monster."

The *Fairmont Times* newspaper also carried the "Bashful Billy" story on September 16, 1952. The overactive imaginations of Wheeling area readers who read about the "Flatwoods Monster" incident was said to have caused the "Green-Eyed Monster" story, otherwise known as "Bashful Billy." This article reported the "monster" nicknamed "Bashful Billy," was a "10-foot monster from another world" and was "gas-breathing." These descriptions were actually the truth!

Green-Eyed Monster Again Reported on Loose in State

WHEELING, Sept. 15 (U.P.)—The gas-breathing, green-eyed monster of West Virginia again was reported on the loose tonight.

Telephone calls from anxious residents of the Vineyard Hill housing project flooded switchboards at the police department and the Wheeling Intelligencer asking for confirmation of rumors that the "10-foot monster from another world" was roaming about their community.

Police said one person asked if it were true that the "horribly burned body of a woman" was found on Vineyard Hill and whether a policeman had been burned mysteriously about the arms.

Detective Howard Millard, who declined a request for a patrolman to stand guard duty at Vineyard Hill, said:

"The only green-eyed monster I ever saw was a jealous woman."

Police blamed the rumors on the active imaginations of newspaper readers who read stories about a fire-breathing monster with BO gadding about the woods near Sutton Friday night.

Now consider the following questions; was the body of a "horribly burned woman" found at Vineyard Hill, or was this the cover story for what was actually found? If a body had been found, was some attempt made to ascertain the identity of the victim? Under these circumstances, why didn't police authorities try to establish whether the victim in question was involved in an accident or a homicide? Why is there no follow-up story or death record about this alleged dead woman?

252

Did an officer respond to the call and have to handle a burnt human body? On the other hand, had he been exposed to the body of a burnt extraterrestrial that caused his injury? Cover stories aside, I believe there were sightings of an extraterrestrial being in that area.

Moreover, it was actually discovered dead. That would explain why the Wheeling police gave no public statement about already having responded to the calls by sending an officer to the area. The officer in question would have responded to the reported calls of the "monster" sighting.

This is another scenario of that incident, unlike the newspaper reported. After reaching Vineyard Hills, the officer actually found the burnt extraterrestrial body of an occupant from the damaged Baltimore/WV #2 ship. The alien sustained severe injuries while onboard its craft during a direct confrontation with USAF jets on Friday night. When the living conditions inside the craft became intolerable, the craft landed. The cooler atmosphere outside the ship was the alien's only chance of survival. Subsequently, the alien was dropped off in Oglebay Park.

After the being was dropped off in Oglebay Park, several rescue ships searched in vain for approximately two hours to recover the injured and stranded being. The rescue ships that repeatedly descended to the earth looking for their comrade were labeled a "meteor shower."

On the contrary, there is no official documentation for this "meteor shower." For three days, this injured being waited alone in the West Virginia woods near Wheeling to be picked up, and then died.

Shortly after, the extraterrestrial was found dead by persons from Vineyard Hills. It is quite interesting to note a "gas-breathing" reference was made of the "Monster" in the *Fairmont Times* September 16, 1952 article. Moreover, an "unpleasant odor" was also reported in *The Wheeling Intelligencer* article, "Callers reported an unpleasant odor was produced by the monster."

The unpleasant odor "produced" by the "monster" was actually a gaseous exhaust, which was emitted from the propulsion system of the alien's hovercraft vehicle! A stench was also present on the Fisher Farm in Flatwoods during the "Braxton County Monster" incident and sickened the witnesses. This odor had lingered on the farm for some time. It was described as "sulfur."

After the body was discovered, a call was then made to the Wheeling Police Department. The witnesses escorted an officer to the area. The officer approached the horribly burned body. The officer was himself burned when he was exposed to the body and metallic suit, apparently sustaining injuries to one or both of his arms because of the contact. This burn was more than likely a type of radiation burn that was later described as "mysterious."

Shortly thereafter, the West Virginia State Police were notified of the incident as well as officials in Washington. The area where the body was discovered was cordoned off and the body was quickly removed from the scene. During that time, in Vineyard Hills, rumors started circulating about the "horribly burned body of a woman" having been found. This was the cover-up story. It was told to the Wheeling residents that had seen or heard of the "monster."

Another point to bring up regarding the "green-eyed monster" comment made by Detective Millard; The September 15, 1952, *Wheeling Intelligencer* article that Lieutenant Murphy cited, "Monster from Space Roaming West Virginia Hills," did not refer to a green-eyed being or "monster." How did Detective Millard learn about this detail? He obviously heard this description from someone who contacted the police department, either a witness or another police officer! Additionally, the *Fairmont Times* September 16, 1952 newspaper article that said the being was a "10-foot monster from another world" seems to have actually reported the truth of the matter!

On Wednesday, September 17, *The Wheeling Intelligencer* printed yet another article mentioning a "monster." This article refers to two Ohio sightings on Tuesday night, September 16. The following is a complete quotation of the entire article, "Bashful Billy Plagues Patrol" It stated:

Reports of a roving monster, which have been coming in from various sections, shifted to Ohio last night, much to the discomfiture of the State Highway Patrol at Bridgeport. At about 9:30, a boy telephoned to headquarters and said: 'Yes, I saw the thing. It was from 10 to 15 feet tall and had a green body and a red head. It was spitting flames from its mouth.' Another call came from a man in Bellaire who said his grandchildren were 'almost scared to death' by something they had seen but their descriptions were vague. The names of the callers are not known.

Were these roving so-called "monsters" actually another search and rescue group, which were trying to locate their injured and stranded comrade? More than likely, they were! (See map on page 236 for the two locations).

What really happened to the being nicknamed "Bashful Billy" will never be fully known. However, it seems that the alien never made it off this planet alive. A military retrieval operation to obtain the dead alien body was most likely handled in a similar manner to the Roswell, NM area crash retrieval operation of July 1947.

Meanwhile, the fate of the "Flatwoods Monster" stranded in Braxton County awaiting rescue in Frametown was quite a different story. The outcome of that incident resulted in a successful rescue on the night of September 13, the day after its ship went down.

CHAPTER TWENTY-THREE

RESCUE MISSION COMPLETED

The UFO events of September 13th continued into the late afternoon of the day. Interestingly, the first recorded Blue Book sighting of September 13, 1952, actually occurred right over the heads of USAF officials in Washington, D.C. It was recorded in a Project Blue Book "Flying Object Report" and a "Project 10073 Record Card." These two documents explained what happened on that afternoon. Furthermore, the UFO was reported as a "SAUCER."

This UFO episode occurred over "Washington, D.C." at "LOCAL: <u>1630</u>" or 4:30 p.m. EDT. The first document, a "FLYOBRPT" originated from the "HQ USAF WASHDC." It was sent to the following USAF bases: the "Commanding General-Air Defense Command-Ent AFB Colorado," the "Chief ATIC-Wright Patterson AFB-Ohio," and the "Commanding General-TAC-Langley AFB-VA." Upon receipt, Blue Book stamped it, "ACTION." It states the witness had, "RPTD SAUCER OVER CENTER WASHINGTON D.C. PENNA AVE AND 10TH ST." It also added, "MOVING SLOWLY SE EST 100 MPH IN VIEW 30 TO 45 SECONDS." The UFO had, "NO WINGS, SILVER COLOR AND GLOWED, NO VAPOR TRAILS, WEATHER CLEAR."

According to the Project 10073 Record Card, the UFO was reported by a "civilian" who described it as a "circular shape" and having a "silver color." The document states the, "TYPE OF OBSERVATION" was a "Ground Visual." The Record Card also recorded the length of the observer's sighting, "LENGTH OF OBSERVATION: 30-45 seconds" and states the object was on a "SE" heading. This report did not receive an evaluation; the witness did not fill out the entire report and the sighting was considered to have "INSUFFICIENT DATA FOR EVALUATION."

This daring and blatant maneuver by a "SAUCER" over the Capitol in broad daylight was a forewarning to Washington officials of things to come later that day! Yes, the UFOs were back!

In 1955, the president of the Flying Saucer Research Institute, Paul Lieb, wrote a story entitled "The West Virginia Monster." This story was a narrative told to Mr. Lieb by witness, George Snitowsky, who told about his encounter with a UFO and an alien in Frametown, WV on September 13, 1952. It was published in *Male* magazine in July 1955. I was amazed by the article's content. The evidence is overwhelming that there was a direct connection between this incident in Frametown and the incident in Flatwoods. These two towns are about 17-miles apart.

In December 1993, I sent Mr. Snitowsky some of my Braxton County UFO research material and expressed my interest in his story. Shortly afterward, I received a signed postal receipt for the material I had sent him. I then contacted George in New York by telephone. He acknowledged that he was the witness interviewed by Paul Lieb and that indeed the story was true. As we talked, I took notes about the incident including a description of the being that he saw that night.

After our conversation, I asked George if he would work with me and possibly do a taped interview. George told me that he publicly told his story once, and preferred not to deal with the negative repercussions again. I respected his request and did not push him further. Most of what Mr. Snitowsky told me appeared in the 1955 article by Paul Lieb. The following information is from that article as told to Mr. Lieb by George Snitowsky.

George Snitowsky, his wife, Edith, and their eighteen-month-old son had traveled from Queens, New York, to visit a relative in Cincinnati, Ohio. After a three-week vacation, they left Ohio and began their drive back to New York. The Snitowsky couple had not been in a hurry, so they visited small towns and enjoyed the scenery along the secondary roads. Dusk approached as George drove into Braxton County. It was about 8:00 p.m. EST on September 13, 1952.

This quiet and peaceful sightseeing trip through the mountains was about to turn into a night of absolute terror. The Snitowsky's automobile inexplicably stopped and they were stranded along the roadside. George Snitowsky said, "According to the map, we were in Braxton County, WV somewhere around Frametown and Sutton." Several attempts to start the engine failed. It seemed the car battery was dead which was odd. Snitowsky stated, "It was a relatively new battery and there had been no indication that it was running down."

As George continued trying to start the car, the fresh mountain air became filled with a sickening odor, something "like a mixture of ether and burnt sulfur." Immediately George jumped from the car and raised the hood, thinking the engine was burning. He found no problem with the engine.

As the odor worsened, the baby began to cry uncontrollably as he lay in a small crib in the back seat. George got back into the car and closed all the windows, as the odor grew stronger. By that time, it was getting dark and George did not want to leave his wife and baby alone in the car while he sought help.

Suddenly, the car was bathed in "a dazzling flash of light with a wavering, unsteady beam." The light was emanating from a wooded area bordering the road. The diffused light was described as "a soft, violet hue, blinding to the eyes." George opened the window to get a better look. It had become difficult to see because the area had now become engulfed in a cloudy haze. When he opened the car window, this dusty, cloudy haze filled the car, causing everyone to gag. A nauseating stench made them sick to their stomachs. The poor baby was crying uncontrollably. George said at that point, "I didn't know what the hell was going on."

George got out of the car to investigate the light in the distance. He walked toward the light, and after only a few steps, he was overcome by the odor and vomited heavily. As he tried to regain his balance, he gazed down into the woods at the light source. Off to the side of the road, the ground sloped down into a valley and George was able to look between some trees. What he saw was only the beginning of the nightmare into which they had stumbled. About "200 or 300 feet away behind a few trees", there was an object that George described as "some kind of luminescent spheroid." He stood gazing at the object in disbelief, trying to comprehend what he was seeing. As George neared the object, trying to get a closer look, he became sicker from the stench permeating the air.

Upon closer examination he said, "It was like a frosted street lamp a couple hundred times enlarged." This large spheroid was not sitting on the ground, but "it seemed to float on one end, moving slightly back and forth." Walking closer to the spheroid, George became more nauseated from the odor that still filled the air. He walked about half the distance to the floating object when he became hot. George then felt a strange "tingling sensation" coursing through his body. Despite these adverse conditions, his curiosity overcame him and he moved closer to the spectacle. After taking only a few more steps, George Snitowsky felt a sensation he described as feeling like "thousands of needle-like vibrations," and "like a low-grade electric shock." He jerked away and stumbled back toward his car. During his walk to the car, George fell repeatedly. He noted that his legs had become numb and were rubbery from the electrical shocks he had received.

George drew closer to his car and staggered against a tree, attempting to regain his balance and catch his breath. As he tried to pull himself together to continue onward, a blood-curdling scream pierced the air. It was Edith. George, in fear for his wife and child, instinctively overcame his physical distress and dashed back to the car. He shouted to her, "Edith - for God's sake -

256

what's the matter?" Edith was paralyzed with fear. George stated, "Her lips moved and her eyes were wide open and staring at something behind me." George turned to look, seeking the source of her terror, and the image he saw buckled his knees. George Snitowsky gave this statement regarding what he saw that night, "The figure was standing immobile, on the fringe of the road, about 30 feet off to my right." It was silhouetted in the light emanating from the large spheroid. George described the giant figure as, "a good eight or nine foot tall and in the general shape of a man." He further described it as having "a head and shoulders and a bloated body."

Paralyzed with fear, George "fumbled" with the car door handle, then climbed in and "slammed the door." Their baby was crying hysterically from all of the commotion. He stated, "'Try to quiet him! Muffle his mouth - !' I said to my wife. She was whimpering in sheer terror." He grabbed for the glove box where he kept a knife, and pulled his wife and baby down to the relative safety of the car floor. He huddled over them, shielding them from what was standing only a short distance from their car.

According to George, while they were "on the floor for several minutes," they were unaware that the huge alien figure had moved closer to their car. George raised his head to assess the situation and was shocked to see the "monster" standing directly in front of the car.

He stated, "My chest was hammering like a sledge. I poked my head up and got a close-up of whatever it was—out there." The hysterical couple, anticipating their next move, stayed on the floor of the car. George, still peering over the dashboard saw the giant creature near the car. He stated, "Reaching across the windshield from above, a long, spindly arm was forked into two soft ends. It seemed to be examining the surface of the car." George added, "If I ever prayed in my life, I was praying then."

He then explained, "Seconds later, without making any hostile moves toward us, the creature started back to the woods." He said, "It wasn't walking and I couldn't make out anything that might be called legs." Furthermore, "the lower torso was a single solid mass that seemed to glide across the uneven road surface" as it made its way back into the woods. The sickening stench was still in the air as George watched the creature hover away. He stated, "The figure vanished among the trees." Shortly thereafter, with the mysterious giant gone, George assisted his wife and child up from the car floor.

George stated, "My wife became hysterical and I put the baby in the car crib and tried to calm her." He suddenly "caught sight of the ascending iridescent globe over the trees" as it moved up into the sky. The object he had seen hovering over the forest floor only moments before was now airborne.

George gave the following description of the object he saw departing: "It rose slowly and made intermittent stops, hanging in mid-air for a split second before continuing upward. And then, at about 3,000 feet I guess, it swung back and forth like a pendulum gathering momentum. Suddenly it swooped up in an elliptical arc and with a dazzling trail of light, shot completely out of sight."

George, still badly shaken, instinctively attempted to start the car again. This time the engine started without any problem. He then drove until reaching a 24-hour truck stop/diner, which I believe was in the Sutton area. The Snitowskys went into the diner to unwind after their ordeal. They decided not to tell anyone about what they had just experienced, not then, anyway.

After a short stay at the diner, they left, stopping at a hotel for the night. The following morning, as they were preparing to leave, George noticed something odd on the hood of his car. The hood showed a discoloration, which was dark in appearance where the creature had touched their car the night before. It looked as though the metal on the hood of the car "had been singed. The outline was fork shaped. The following are comparisons between the "Flatwoods Monster" and George Snitowsky's account of the Frametown creature:

- Both George Snitowsky and Eugene Lemon vomited from a nauseating odor that was present in the area where a so-called "monster" had been seen.
- Both Snitowsky and the Flatwoods witnesses described an alien figure that was huge, very tall and had no legs.
- In both cases, witnesses described a cloudy, foggy mist in the area of their encounter.
- In both cases, a burning smell and sulfur odor were noticed in their vicinity.
- Both cases took place in Braxton County, about seventeen miles apart.
- Both cases took place one day apart.
- In both cases, the figure was described as gliding, hovering, or floating above the ground as it moved.

The "Flatwoods Monster" was described as about "twelve feet tall" by all of the witnesses. The "Frametown Monster" was described as being "a good eight or nine feet tall, in the general shape of a man, with a head and shoulders and a bloated body." In comparison, by adding a three-foot high helmet onto the shoulder area of a nine-foot tall figure contained in a space suit would make the overall spacesuit apparatus, twelve feet tall. Based on the sizes and the heights of the figures seen in both incidents, it is feasible that an eight-or-nine-foot figure in the general shape of a man could easily have fit inside a twelve-foot metallic-like space suit.

By comparing the descriptions of both figures from the eyewitness testimonies in both incidents, I have concluded that the "Frametown Monster" was actually the same creature seen in Flatwoods the night before. I will explain. After the alien landed in Flatwoods on September 12, it was seen wearing a full space-suit apparatus when it was outside its ship. The space suit, which also functioned as a vehicle, was capable of hovering and traveling over and above the ground. It carried the alien via a propulsion system, which was contained in the lower half of the suit. When the alien was seen the following night in Frametown, it had removed the upper half of its spacesuit apparatus. In reference to the lower portion of the figure Snitowsky said, "The lower torso was a single solid mass that seemed to glide across the uneven road surface." The lower torso was actually the lower half of the metallic-like space suit, which contained the propulsion system.

Snitowsky could not see any legs on the figure because the alien was standing inside the lower torso section. The lower half of the space-suit apparatus carried the alien above and across the area of the road. What George Snitowsky saw when he described the upper torso of the huge figure was the exposed body of the alien. The odor that these witnesses smelled was actually the exhaust emitted from the propulsion system. As the alien hovered and passed near the areas where it had been observed, it polluted the air around it.

On September 12, the alien was wearing its entire space suit when it landed in Flatwoods after having been shot down. After the "monster" was seen, it departed Flatwoods and made another emergency landing in Frametown, on James Knob, and was stranded overnight. Subsequently, it abandoned its damaged ship. The "monster" left the area where its ship went down in the event the military located the crash site and attempted to capture it or take further hostile actions.

While roaming the area of Frametown, and hovering in its vehicular suit, the Snitowsky family who were simply in the wrong place at the wrong time inadvertently saw it. The Snitowskys actually witnessed the rescue of the stranded "Flatwoods Monster." An associate who worked with Major Donald Keyhoe on the book, *Flying Saucers from Outer Space*, spoke about the "Flatwoods Monster." He wished to remain anonymous in his interview with Keyhoe for the book. This man whom Keyhoe called James Riordan was a captain in the U.S. Air Force. He also had connections with the Air Technical Intelligence Center, the headquarters for Project Blue Book. This officer was an F-86 Sabre jet pilot who fought in the Korean War.

The following conversation took place between Keyhoe and this captain concerning the "Flatwoods Monster:"

Keyhoe: "I started to ask him about the Sutton Monster story. What was the ATIC's conclusion?"
Captain: "They swear they didn't analyze it, but I'm positive they did check into it."
Keyhoe: "I told him what I knew about the case."
Captain: "(shaking head dubiously) It sounds as if there was something to it. Not a —I still can't see that—but it might have been a robot of some kind, the way they [witnesses] described it."

Ivan T. Sanderson spoke with the boys who saw the "monster" and had them draw it. He concluded that the "Flatwoods Monster" was a large suit that contained a being. Sanderson stated, "They all did sketches and we put together a composite of it. It looks exactly like one of the most modern Navy diving suits, which is solid [outer shell], the person is inside." Sanderson also likened the being inside to a "pilot" or "occupant." This spacesuit or the equivalent of our deep-sea-diving bells was regulated to counteract gravity by adjustment to the density of air at ground level. Sanderson believed the "pilot" of the UFO that landed in Flatwoods was "obviously contained in some kind of suit."

It is obvious from the testimony of the witnesses that what was called a "monster" was instead a living being inside a space suit. This space suit was metallic in nature and served as a protective outer covering. It also served as a small vehicular craft, by which the creature could move around.

The living entity inside of the space suit had emerged from a large ovoid craft, which it had controlled and landed. This metallic-like space suit was actually a mechanical probe. Its function was life-supportive, maintaining a controlled environment and protecting the entity within from hostile atmospheric conditions or beings. This creature's space suit also seemed to be damaged; it was hot, leaking an oily substance and making odd noises. The damage most likely occurred during the aerial confrontation with military jets over the Atlantic Ocean. The following eyewitness testimonies concern points involving the damaged space suit:

*Colonel Dale Leavitt: "Well, there was something here that could fly backwards or wherever they wanted to go, just anywhere, I think, as long as they don't tear up their equipment."
*Mrs. May: "It was making a hissing noise and sounded like it was frying bacon." (Possibly very hot and burning up.)
*Mrs. May: "I was as close to it as the length of a car, a small car. I was close enough that it squirted oil all over my uniform...You could feel it was like a warm mist. It must have come from the creature."
*Lee Stewart Jr.: "I walked up and down the skid marks area and that's when I realized I was getting oil on my clothes. The oil was darker than tar grass and adhered to your clothes. There were rocks turned over in the skid mark area, and that's when I found the piece of metal...it was a dripping, like a piece of dripped solder, it was rugged on the edges . . . it was shiny like silver."

It is evident that this metallic-like space suit or vehicle was severely damaged. Once the alien left Flatwoods and landed in Frametown, it removed the upper portion of its suit, which also acted as armor. The suit had built up heat within its shell and had become intolerable to wear because it was extremely hot. Subsequently, the upper portion was discarded because the alien was able to tolerate the Earth's environment. Furthermore, the upper torso of the suit and helmet was probably nonfunctional and not needed. During a rescue mission in Frametown, a large spherical object had landed to retrieve the stranded alien. Subsequently, the alien encountered the Snitowsky family, disappeared into the woods, boarded the sphere craft and took off later.

An interesting point to rise involving the Frametown and Flatwoods incidents is the comparison of lights noted at each of the sights. Purple and violet covered lights were described in each of these cases where the objects were located. Mrs. May stated the following information concerning a flaring light she saw on the Fisher Farm, "As soon as I stepped down into the road and was startin' up the hill, I noticed this great, big red flare, a purplish-looking flare." This was the vicinity where the "Flatwoods Monster" craft landed.

George Snitowsky also gave a similar description of light where he saw the object hovering above the ground in Frametown. He described the color of light as "A soft violet hue, blinding to the eyes." Snitowsky also stated it was "a dazzling flash of light with a wavering unsteady beam." Both witnesses had "seen the light," and it was intense.

Prior to the 8:00 p.m. EST rescue of the stranded alien being in Frametown, another series of UFO events had occurred. Project Blue Book received several reports of UFOs sighted on September 13, 1952, between 6:40 p.m. and 7:07 p.m. EST over Pennsylvania, Virginia, and Maryland. I read all of the reports, dissected them, and plotted their locations including the times they were seen, and their directional headings. After analyzing the information, I established that there were four objects sighted over those areas, which was contrary to the conclusions that Blue

Book officials had reached. Moreover, I concluded that those four objects had a motive that night; they were on a search and rescue mission to retrieve the stranded alien in Frametown.

On the previous night, September 12, there had been no communications to or from the downed "Flatwoods Monster" craft. The specific location of the downed craft in Braxton County was unknown. A last minute ditch-effort to locate the craft by circling over the intended rendezvous point of the Fisher Farm for fifteen minutes had proved futile. The transmitter device of the overheated craft was nonfunctional when it landed in Frametown on Friday night, September 12. On the night of September 13, the circumstances were much different. I have reached the following scenario from my UFO research findings, which involved a military-style search and rescue mission that began Saturday night, at about 6:30 p.m. EST.

The series of events unfolded when the transmitter of the downed craft was repaired and charged by its occupant. Now functioning, it began to transmit a signal from the Frametown area. Subsequently, the Mothership located above Washington, D.C. had received a transmission, a faint signal. A rescue ship was quickly dispatched to obtain a fix on it and head to the area of the downed craft. The ship descended into the atmosphere over Allentown, Pennsylvania and followed the beacon signal. Project Blue Book lists this UFO case as case #2085, an "Unidentified." The location was Allentown, PA. The witness was W. A. Hobler of New York. Mr. Hobler was an inactive Air Force Reserve captain at the time. He submitted a letter to the Commanding General at Mitchel AFB in New York regarding his UFO encounter, which was sent to Blue Book officials at ATIC. The following information is the verbatim letter from Mr. Hobler:

Dear Sir:

If I had not seen the enclosed clipping, I probably would not make the following report. However, since other people in the vicinity where I saw an unusual phenomenon, saw the same thing, I thought perhaps I should describe my experience. On 13 September 1952 at about 1940 [about 6:40 p.m. EST], I was flying alone at ten thousand feet from Allentown, PA. to the Caldwell-Wright Omni Station in a Beech craft Bonanza. Visibility at that altitude was about twelve miles. There were no clouds of any kind although there was some haze . . . from the ground to more than 12,000 feet.

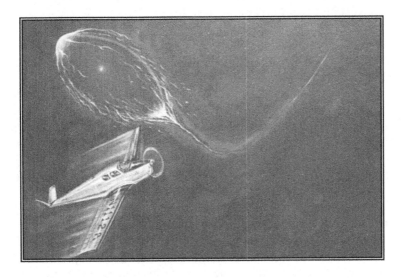

I was approximately 15 to 20 miles NE of Allentown when suddenly a bright object, which appeared to be shaped like a fat football and three feet in diameter, flaming orange-red in color, appeared at a distance of 150 to 200 yards ahead of me at eleven o'clock high.

It was descending at about a 30-degree angle. My first impression was that it was a "falling star" and that I was on a collision course with it. I immediately pulled up into a steep climb to avoid hitting it; but the object, instead of continuing on its downward course, very suddenly pulled up into about a 65-degree climb and went directly over my windshield. I quickly made a 180 to the right but could no longer see the ball of fire. If the object was at the distance and was of the size that it appeared to me to be, I would estimate it was traveling at better than 700 miles an hour. If what I saw was actually a physical object, the rapidity with which it altered its course was astonishing.

Since I was able to see it for not more than two seconds, I hesitated to report what I saw. After the object went by, I resumed my course and for the next 20 minutes tried to be sure that what I had seen was not a light reflection on the windshield. I regret now that I did not make this report immediately.

Even though the description of this oval-shaped object is similar to several other objects seen the previous night on September 12, the Air Force identified this object as an "Unknown," not a meteor. After this UFO had been sighted during a near-collision, it quickly descended below the five-thousand-foot radar range. With the rescue mission now in jeopardy, the craft looked for an isolated landing area. The craft flew southwest and landed in York County after traveling more than 100 miles.

York County borders Dauphin County, separated by the Susquehanna River. Olmsted AFB, located in Middletown, is located in Dauphin County, near the Susquehanna. The oval-shaped UFO came down in a wooded area near Conewago Lake and awaited orders from the main craft. The object sat on the ground until it received orders to abort the mission. It then departed the Conewago Lake area, traveled north at a very low altitude and was sighted by witnesses from several counties. The UFO then passed over Middletown, Pennsylvania. Shortly after, base employees sighted it over Olmsted AFB. This was actually the third sighting of an object over the vicinity of Olmsted AFB in two days. They are as follows:

1). The first sighting occurred September 12 at 2:35 a.m. EST/3:35 a.m. EDT. An Olmsted AFB base guard stated that while on patrol he became aware of the object after hearing what "sounded like heavy projectile artillery and saw a blue light in the sky."
2). The second sighting occurred later that night at 8:07 p.m. EST/9:07 p.m. EDT. This object was the #13 Rescue Ship that was the sentry of the "Descending Guardians." A base employee "sighted a strange object while at work." The witness "described the object as a bright white light...The light was visible for 3 or 4 minutes...Its speed was described as slower than an airplane."
3). The third sighting occurred on September 13 at 7:04 p.m. EDT/8:04 p.m. EDT. Project Blue Book explained and recorded this sighting as being a meteor, which flew near the ground.

I was able to establish that this sighting was a UFO based on several Project Blue Book documents. The first document was the original Teletype report from Olmstead AFB, designated "RE AFL 200-5" [reference Air Force Letter 200-5]. This report was typed at 10:09 p.m. EST to four different Air Force facilities. Along the top of this document were two hand-stamped messages. In large letters were the words "OPERATIONAL IMMEDIATE" and underneath was the word "ACTION." The following is the "FLYOBRPT" [Flying Object Report]:

On 13 Sept 1952 at 0004Z observers from Dauphin and adjacent counties sighted object in sky. Number of base employees sighted same object and reported it to be a meteor traveling from Southeast to Northwest. Apparent size was approximately 25 inches in diameter [size of object at distance] out near ground. Last sighted at 40-10N, 76-40W appearing to go below hills to west of field across Susquehanna River. Light was bluish-white turning to yellow. Fast rate of speed. No sound. Slight tail said by observers to be merely due to great rate of speed. Weather at time of sighting clear with 7 miles visibility. Surface winds calm 2000 feet 280 degrees at 7 knot. (95 4000 ft 320 degrees at 6 knots). No air traffic at time. All observers making reports were on ground, observers appear to be reliable at least two are base guards.

Upon examining this Olmsted AFB teletype, I had questions about this alleged meteor:

1). Several observers in various counties sighted this "object," yet it was reported to be a meteor by the Olmstead base employees who "sighted it." There, the low-flying fast moving object, which was seen "near ground," made no sonic boom, nor did it land. Was it really a meteor?
2). If the object was indeed a meteor, why did Olmstead AFB officials send a teletype describing the incident to the Director of Intelligence at the Pentagon, ATIC at Wright Patterson AFB, the Commanding General of Air Materiel Command at Wright Patterson AFB, and the Commanding General of Ent AFB?
3). Why did this alleged meteor sighting receive a hand stamp by ATIC officials designating the report "OPERATIONAL IMMEDIATE" warranting "ACTION"?

Following procedure by sending this report was actually appropriate for a bogey or an Unidentified Flying Object. It does not seem like a valid response if Air Force personnel had spotted a passing meteor. I conclude that Olmsted AFB officials relayed the original report about the flying object because it was in reality, a UFO, which passed very low and near the vicinity of their Air Materiel Area that housed air defense equipment and supplies. Furthermore, this was the third object that had flown over the base in two days!

Three days later, Olmsted Intelligence Officers followed up their initial teletype report with an additional report. This report was an "AIR INTELLIGENCE INFORMATION REPORT." Two copies of this report were sent to Wright Patterson AFB in Dayton, Ohio. One of the reports was filed at ATIC. Project Blue Book officials then forwarded the other copy to Strategic Intelligence located in Washington, D.C. In part, this September 16, 1952 "AIR INTELLIGENCE INFORMATION REPORT" stated the following information on a standard form: (Note: The typed-in answers on this report are italicized).

COUNTRY – *United States*
SUBJECT – *(UNCLASSIFIED) Unidentified Flying Objects. Reporting (Short Title: FLYOBRPT).*
FROM – *Intelligence Office-Olmsted Air Force Base, Middletown, Pa.*
DATE OF REPORT – *16 September 1952*
DATE OF INFORMATION – *13 September 1952*
SOURCE – *Civilian Observer*

PREPARED BY – *John L. Spiegel, 2d Lt. USAF*
EVALUATION- _____

It is interesting to note that the "EVALUATION" segment of this report was left blank. The reason this follow-up report was filed is stated in the following summary statement:

SUMMARY-*Reference teletype 13/0259Z [September 13/10:59 p.m. EDT], this headquarters, according to base observers this object was unquestionably a meteor. This report is submitted only to nullify teletyped referenced above.*

The above September 16, 1952 "AIR INTELLIGENCE INFORMATION REPORT," was submitted to cancel or "nullify" the initial September 13, 1952, teletype that "this object was unquestionably a meteor." Olmsted AFB intelligence officials suddenly had a change of mind during their investigation. They filed yet another "AIR INTELLIGENCE INFORMATION REPORT" on the following day. This report is dated, "DATE OF REPORT – *17 September 1952*," and the "DATE OF INFORMATION – *16 September 1952*. [Handwritten-14]." The summary section of the report is as follows:

SUMMARY. In reference to FLYOBRPT teletype reporting the observation of an unidentified flying object by Mr. [entire line blacked out] Pa., investigation has established that both objects can be explained. From the information furnished by the observer, it appears that the object seen on 12 September was in reality, a blimp and the object seen on the succeeding night [Sept. 13] was either a bright star or a planet. These explanations are, of course, not 100 % conclusive; however, at this time they seem to suffice.

The summary section now explains what Olmsted officials believed the September 13 object to be, "either a bright star or planet." It also gives a "blimp" explanation for an object sighted over the base on September 12, 1952. On September 12, there were actually two reported sightings, yet the report does not state if it was the early morning sighting at 3:35 a.m. EDT, or the 9:07 p.m. EDT night sighting!

By re-reviewing the 8:07 p.m. EST/9:07 p.m. EDT night sighting, we find that the "Air Information Intelligence Report" for this case was a "Civilian Observer." The Summary reported, "[Name blacked out] an employee of this base reported seeing an unidentified flying object while at work at 0107z [8:07 p.m. EST/9:07 p.m. EDT] on 12 Sept 1952. Mr. [blacked out] described the object as a bright white light that looked like an automobile headlight at a considerable distance. The light moved in a straight line from the southwest to the northwest and disappeared behind a tree. Its speed was described as 'slower than an airplane.'

The light was visible for 'three or four' minutes, but Mr. [blacked out] reported that during this time it dimmed 'considerably' for a period of approximately five seconds after which it regained its former brilliance. No exhaust or sound was noted. There were no local aircraft in the air at the time." Here, the Intelligence report states, "there were no local aircraft in the air at that time." Yet, in the Project 10073 Record Card, the U.S. Air Force stated its conclusion as "possibly aircraft." By reviewing the first sighting that occurred at 3:35 a.m. EDT, we find the "TENTATIVE OBSERVERS QUESTIONNAIRE," was made by an Olmsted AFB base guard.

He stated that while on "patrol" he became aware of the object after hearing what "sounded like heavy projectile artillery and saw a blue light in the sky." The guard described the flying object as a "solid." He remarked that it emitted a "bright blue" light. Moreover, the object was said to be only "1,000 feet" above the earth and disappeared, "suddenly." The guard wrote, "When object disappeared-noise ceased." Which September 12 incident involved the alleged "blimp?"

Finally, I reveal the explanation for the September 13 UFO over Olmsted AFB, which was documented by officials at Project Blue Book. A "Project 100073 Report Card" told the following information about the object. (Note: the answers in the first two sections were typed-in and are italicized. The "CONCLUSIONS" answer was marked-off in a box and has a hand-written note next to it). It states:

LOCATION – *Middletown, Pa.*
BRIEF SUMMARY OF SIGHTING – *Bluish white to yellow. Very fast.*
COMMENTS - *Possible meteor.*
CONCLUSIONS – [X] Possibly astronomical. "Meteor" (is handwritten)."

The September 12, "blimp" explanation and the September 13, "bright star or planet" explanation, which Olmsted AFB officials reported are absurd. Olmsted AFB officials first explained the September 13 object as a "meteor." Then it was said to be a "bright star or planet," even though their teletype reported it had a "Fast rate of speed." Regardless, intelligence officials at both Olmsted AFB and Wright Patterson AFB were inconclusive about the UFO sighted on September 13, 1952. Furthermore, all of the intelligence answers reflect confusion and a massive cover-up.

This UFO, a reconnaissance ship, had passed near Olmsted AFB at 7:04 p.m., made its atmospheric ascent out of Pennsylvania toward the Mothership and then boarded it shortly after. Meanwhile, at approximately 7:00 p.m. EST, another reconnaissance and rescue plan had been implemented, which involved three other objects. The first ship departed the Mothership and made its atmospheric descent over Richmond, VA. It was sighted at 7:02 p.m. EST. One minute later the second ship made its atmospheric descent over Colonial Heights, VA. Two minutes later the third ship descended over Patuxent, MD at 7:05 p.m. EST. The three ships immediately began to search for the transmission signal from the downed craft waiting in West Virginia.

Project Blue Book recorded these sightings in three different documents by the 771st AC&W installations, located in Fort John Eustis, VA. The Virginia sightings were all reported to this installation, but the Maryland sighting was reported to the 26th Air Division Defense (Roslyn, NY) and then relayed to the 771st AC&W. The AC&W is defined in the United States Air dictionary as follows, "Aircraft control and warning. A service or activity in which aircraft (including guided missiles) are detected and tracked in flight and reported, followed by evaluation and plotting of the information obtained, which information is then used in a warning network and in the control of fighter aircraft, anti-aircraft artillery, and other combative forces."

The 771st AC&W initially recorded these incidents, documented them, and relayed the information via Teletype to five different Air Force installations across the United States. When received by Project Blue Book, it was hand-stamped "ACTION." The most interesting point I found when analyzing these three documents was that even though the 771st informed all these Air Force installations about the sightings, the ATIC later evaluated the incident as a single meteor. The following information was contained in the original Teletype document sent to ATIC before a final evaluation was made by officials at Project Blue Book. A summary reported:

One blue ball of fire with a long tail was sighted heading west over Lovingston, VA at 0007z [7:07 p.m. EST]. The observer stated that a four-engine aircraft was in the area at the same time and the pilot could possibly have seen the object. Two airmen of the Richmond Filter Center of the GOC (Ground Observers Corps) reported seeing an object of the same description approximately five minutes earlier [7:02 p.m. EST]. The object danced for a few seconds then took off toward the West. At 0115z [8:15 p.m. EST] the Richmond Filter Station called this station again with the report that the same object had been sighted over Colonial Heights, VA., at 0003z [7:03 p.m. EST].

After analyzing and dissecting the information in these four reports, I realized that there were actually four different sightings of three separate objects. My research concludes that the three Virginia UFO sightings actually involved two objects, which were sighted over three different areas. The other object was sighted near Patuxent, MD, Charles County, near Washington, D.C. The four locations and the times that these three objects were seen follow:

1). First Sighting: 7:02 p.m. EST. The sighting of the first object occurred over Richmond, VA. This object "danced" and was observed for a few seconds.
2). Second Sighting: 7:03 p.m. EST. The sighting of the second object occurred over Colonial Heights, VA.
3). Third Sighting: 7:05 p.m. EST. The sighting of the third object occurred over the Patuxent, MD area. (A Cavalier aircraft pilot sighted a *meteor* at 7:05 p.m. EST near Patuxent, MD).
4). Fourth Sighting: 7:07 p.m. EST. The second sighting of the first object had occurred over Lovingston, VA.

The USAF said the Colonial Heights object was the same object that was later seen over Richmond VA, which would be impossible, and they knew that. The Richmond object left on a westerly course at 7:02 p.m. EST. Colonial Heights lies almost twenty-five miles south of Richmond! The third Virginia sighting was made four minutes later over Lovingston, VA at 7:07 p.m. Lovingston is to the northwest of Richmond and Colonial Heights. Lovingston is also near the West Virginia border, southeast of Braxton County. The document gave a more detailed accounting of the Lovingston, VA sighting. It stated, "One blue ball of fire with a long tail was sighted heading west over Lovingston, Virginia at 0007z [7:07 p.m. EST]. The observer stated that a four-engine aircraft was in the area at the same time and [the pilot] possibly could have seen the 'object.'"

The 7:02 p.m. Richmond sighting and the 7:07 p.m. Lovingston sighting had the same description. The Richmond sighting was seen five minutes earlier because it was the same object, traveling on a westward trajectory. This object, the first Virginia object had been seen over two different locations and reported twice. It was seen five minutes apart and traveling from east to west. This object was the first reconnaissance ship to descend into the area. Here, the two Virginia objects and the lone Maryland object were actually part of the second search and rescue mission.

My conclusions regarding these rescue ships were reinforced after reviewing the ATIC's Project Blue Book "Project 100073 Worksheet" and the "Project 100073 Report Card." The documents related to the Virginia and Maryland sightings contained many errors. The Project 10073 Worksheet was the follow-up report made by Project Blue Book to the original report made by the 771st A C & W. Section 2 of the worksheet shows an error. One of the questions in the section was standard, but the response was inaccurate. It states the following information:

Q. **What astronomical activity was noted?** A. *Yes.* The answer to this question was handwritten and stated, "Yes," which is not an answer to the question!

The section that was highly questionable was the evaluation portion. There were three evaluation questions asked in this section. Taken from multiple choices given on the form, the answers for each section were checked off:

Evaluation of Source [x] "poor"
Details of Report [x] "fair."
Final Evaluation [x] "was astronomical."

The Lovingston, VA object that was seen near Patuxent, MD was explained as a meteor. This evaluation was based on the information from the "26th Air Division Defense" in Roslyn, NY. The following inconsistencies and oddities are contained in the Project 10073 Worksheet. They declared all of the Virginia sightings and the Maryland sighting were the same single meteor.

I raise the following points:

1). The comment section of the document said several people in the Washington, D.C. area had seen this same alleged meteor. However, the original document stated that a "pilot of cavalier aircraft sighted meteor," which was the only witness on record!
2). ATIC intelligence officials at Wright-Patterson AFB received the original Richmond 7:02 p.m. report from the 771st AC&W and were aware that "two airmen of the Richmond Filter Center of the GOC" had sighted an object that fit the same description of the Lovingston object sighted five minutes later. At that point, they knew the 5-minute time span discounted this object as a meteor!
3). This alleged single meteor seen over Richmond, VA at 7:02 p.m., could not have flown south over Colonial Heights at 7:03 p.m., then flown northeast to Patuxent, MD at 7:03 p.m., turned and redirected back to the southwest and then flown over Lovingston at 7:07 p.m. The flight of this very active object would definitely discount it as a single meteor as ATIC officials had stated.
4). Another inconsistency in the Air Force's meteor explanation was the flight description given of this alleged meteor; "the object danced for a few seconds then took off." It seems highly unlikely that two men in the U.S. Air Force would have mistaken a UFO that "danced," for a meteor!
5). Yet, another weak point in the Air Force's stance was their evaluation of the eyewitness source, which was stated as "multiple" source and evaluated as "poor." This seems odd since the first Virginia sighting was made by trained aviators.

The Air Force's low estimation of a sighting by trained personnel seems like an effort to facilitate the cover-up. The final document pertaining to this case is the evaluation report, Project Blue Book's "Project 10073 Record Card." The ATIC recorded inconsistencies follow, "**Type of observation** - Ground visual, air visual."

The ground visual sightings were made in Virginia. The air visual sighting was made in Maryland. ATIC labeled all the sightings over Virginia and Maryland as one single meteor, "**Source** – multiple." Once again, the Air Force tried to label these reports as one lone meteor, seen by multiple witnesses from two states, "**Length of observation** - a few seconds." This is a very general answer. Multiple witnesses sighted the object over three Virginia locations and one witness saw it over Maryland.

How did the ATIC arrive at its conclusion, "a few seconds" when the alleged meteor was seen over a five-minute time span? It also records and states, "**Number of objects** – One," and "**Course** – West." The ATIC's flight path analysis was equally illogical. One meteor could not have passed over all the specified locations if it had been heading in a westerly direction.

The section, "**Brief Summary of Sighting**" states the Lovingston, VA object was, "a ball of fire" that "appeared to dance for a few seconds." Real meteors do not dance. It is a physical impossibility for a meteor to "dance" during its trajectory for a few seconds and then take off. Another inconsistency in the 10073 Record Card was the attribution of the prior description to the Lovingston object. The description of an object that appeared to "dance for a few seconds" was made over Richmond, not Lovingston, as the record card stated.

The Lovingston sighting occurred at 7:07 p.m. EST, five minutes later. It gave the directional heading as west, and there was no mention of the object dancing over Lovingston. It reads:

Comments - Several sources saw an object with a tail streak across the sky, seen for a few seconds only. Aircraft in the area reported a meteor at approximately the same time.

The several sources who saw an object with a tail streaking across the sky were the Virginia witnesses. The aircraft in the area that reported a meteor at approximately the same time was actually in Maryland. This report concludes, "**Conclusion** [x] Was astronomical." [Answer checked off in block; next to this standard response, the word "**meteor**" was typed in.]

My conclusions differ drastically from those of Project Blue Book. Based on my research and the plotted points of each individual sighting, I have concluded the four objects seen over Virginia, Maryland and Pennsylvania were rescue ships. After the Mothership obtained a fix on the signal from the downed "Flatwoods Monster" ship, the four rescue ships descended and followed it.

When the first object had a near collision over Pennsylvania, the rescue mission was temporarily aborted. Soon thereafter, three more ships descended south of Washington, D.C. to find their comrade. The first Virginia object was seen over the Richmond area at 7:02 p.m. EST, the second Virginia craft was seen over Colonial Heights at 7:03 p.m. and the third UFO was seen over Patuxent, MD. at 7:05 pm. The 7:02 Richmond UFO "danced for a few seconds then took off toward the West." This blue ball of fire with a long tail was next seen over Lovingston, VA five minutes later at 7:07 p.m. After this ship flew over Lovingston, it continued to follow the signal west to West Virginia. The other two descended rescue ships followed as part of the mission.

The lead ship continued into Braxton County and passed high over Frametown, following the signal. Moments later, the downed ship was spotted on James Knoll, but something was wrong. The homing signal was not being directly transmitted from the downed craft and there was no sign of life nearby. The signal of the transmitter was actually coming from an area further away in the region of some densely populated woods. At that point, it was realized that the stranded alien was on the move and in hiding. The being had removed the transmitter from the downed ship and adapted it to a portable device. It had left the vicinity of its ship for fear of being captured by the military, kept moving and sought cover in the forest of Frametown. There, it roamed and waited.

The West Virginia National Guard was already in the Flatwoods area and traveling throughout Braxton County. It was unknown if troops were reconnoitering the dense woods of Frametown and looking for the downed craft and its occupant. Since it was not dark enough to descend unnoticed into the area, which would have drawn attention to the stranded alien and a possible capture or a likely confrontation with troops, the rescue attempt was delayed. At that point, the rescue operation was too risky to attempt in daylight.

The rescue object then ascended out of the area, into the upper atmosphere and toward the other two high hovering objects that were awaiting it. The three ships then rendezvoused, flew east and ascended back to the Mothership. The ship chosen to go back to West Virginia after dark and attempt to retrieve the stranded being was the original Pennsylvania craft. This was the large football-shaped object involved in the near collision near Allentown. Shortly after, it descended from the Mothership on its mission. The craft followed the homing signal and headed toward West Virginia while flying high above the atmosphere. It descended toward Braxton County and into the densely wooded Frametown area looking for the stranded alien.

The Mountainous and Wooded Terrain of Frametown

The rescue ship continued to descend, followed the transmission signal from the woods, then circled at a low altitude making a visual inspection of the wooded terrain. Shortly thereafter, the alien sighted the low-flying rescue ship and moved out of the woods into a clearing, where it could easily be spotted. This clearing was a paved road. Moments later, the alien was sighted by the rescue ship. The ship landed a short distance away in the cover of some woods and waited for the stranded alien to reach it. This is when George Snitowsky drove his car into the area. The alien quickly left the road and went back to the edge of the woods. Minutes later, the alien emerged back on the road. As it headed toward the waiting rescue ship, it encountered Snitowsky. After the alien reached the ship, Snitowsky saw the object shoot "completely out of sight." The rescue had finally been completed. The aliens had rescued their stranded comrade.

I have established that the "Flatwoods Monster" was actually a mechanical probe of metallic-like construction which contained an alien being that used it as a mode of transportation. On Sept. 13, the Snitowskys saw the upper portion of the alien being during their encounter. The upper half of the metallic-like suit including the torso shell, inner helmet and outer protective ace of spades helmet were removed. This revealed the head, bloated body, arms and hands of the being that was standing inside of the lower half of the probe. The lower half of this probe was a flared shell that consisted of a mechanical propulsion system. This enabled the probe to hover, enabling the occupant standing inside of it to traverse above and across the ground.

When the being landed in Flatwoods and left its craft, it was wearing, the full armored metallic-like space suit. On the following evening, only the lower half of the space suit was utilized to transport the being. The lower shell of the suit apparatus was very large. Witness Fred May told me, "The lower part of it flared out and was over four foot wide at the bottom." He also stated that, "there were pipes that went around it, and they were as thick and round as a fireman's hose." These pipes were part of the propulsion system and emitted a gaseous odor similar to sulfur, when it propelled the apparatus. When the being removed the upper protective armor section of the suit in Frametown, why did it still use the lower half?

This portion of the suit apparatus was very large and cumbersome. Even though it was being used as a transportation device, it would not be easy to maneuver a machine over throughout the densely wooded area of Frametown, especially a four-foot wide machine between trees, shrubs and rough terrain of the West Virginia Forest. The alien's mobility would be severely limited.

Why had the alien not discarded the lower transport section and simply walked. This would have allowed it to move easier and faster throughout this wooded area than a hovering probe would have. Furthermore, that segment of the suit emitted an obnoxious sulfur-like odor that drew its attention to the occupant, thereby making it conspicuous. Did the alien need the transport device because it was slow and not agile? Was the alien even capable of walking, and better still, did it have legs? Who were these aliens and what race of beings were they. Did these aliens leave any physical evidence behind, which gave some information about them?

There were several landings made throughout West Virginia and Tennessee that night. Numerous landings occurred in Braxton County, including Flatwoods, Sugar Creek and Frametown. In Sugar Creek, biological evidence was found in the area where a landing occurred. It was found by investigator Ivan T. Sanderson and a group of his men.

Sanderson gave details about the specimens he found at Sugar Creek on two occasions. This information was contained in his "Uninvited Visitors" book and his 1968 interview with Long John Nebell. The following information given by Ivan T. Sanderson is from those two sources, "We made the best attempt possible to investigate the hill at Sugar Creek, but the terrain was difficult. There were five of us, Eddie Shoenberger, Gray Barker, Raymond Walter and one other gentleman from Monsanto and myself. The first cliff rose about 800 feet almost perpendicularly. There was a mile-long saddle above and two 500-foot hills beyond.

We searched this mountainside on our hands and knees clawing our way up, because it was so steep. We found nothing until we got to the top. There was a little swamp up there with small trees behind the big forest, of tall trees. In there I found a huge –like a skid mark, which had knocked these bushes down."

Sanderson also stated an observation made by Shoenberger, who looked up at the trees from the direction that the object had come in, before it landed. He states, "Before it had apparently crashed in the swamp, he said 'look at that,' and there was a whole treetop knocked off and several other branches, all recently shattered. As though there was a hole in the top of the trees."

Ivan T. Sanderson explains what he found in the vicinity of where the object crash-landed, "There was a depression in that [area] and also two of these tremendous hoof-life things pushed into the ground and beyond it, a whole mass of little pieces, little coils of white plastic-like material, scattered all over the ground."

Sanderson states, "The depression itself was about 15 foot across, we measured it – 15 or 16 foot but you couldn't, of course, tell where it ran out. It was a disc-shaped [round] depression." At this point, I will analyze Mr. Sanderson's findings at Sugar Creek. The UFO that landed at Sugar Creek was the damaged #1 North Carolina Rescue Ship. When the object landed, it did not hover and descend vertically to make a soft landing when it touched down. It descended on a downward trajectory, knocked off an entire treetop and shattered other nearby branches. The damaged object continued on this trajectory until hitting the ground. It made a belly-landing and crashed, leaving a skid mark path and knocking down bushes as it plowed through the earth.

When the elliptical-shaped object came to a halt, it left a depression in the terrain about 15 foot across that was disc-shaped in nature. The other depressions found near the landing site were the two "tremendous hoof-like things pushed into the ground." These large hoof-shaped impressions seem to indicate the shape of the lower torso section of the heavy space suit made by the occupant upon touching down after hovering out of the downed ship.

It seems the alien occupant departed the object in its spacesuit probe and when it settled to the ground, its tremendous weight caused the lower torso to be "pushed into the ground." Thus leaving a partial impression described as, "hoof-like things." Were there actually two aliens? Sanderson expounded on the evidence he found concerning the "white plastic-like material", he found. He states, "On the comparatively open saddle above the cliff, we found three shallow holes. Beyond each of these, there were wedge-shaped spatters of a strange white substance in small, curled cylinders. This at first looked to us like dried up snake or turtle egg shell, but we collected some and had it subjected to x-ray and general chemical analysis.

Ivan T. Sanderson explained what occurred, "We did have this funny white stuff analyzed. My friends took it down to Monsanto and they couldn't be much better there." Sanderson, actually references the "Monsanto Chemical Company." Plastics and synthetic fabrics had become a primary segment of Monsanto's business by the 40s and during that era. An ideal place for Sanderson to have his "white plastic-like material" specimens analyzed.

He also states what the lab discovered, "They had numerous spectrograph analysis machines and they were unable to find out what it was. It seemed to be of a plastic nature, but – to be of an organic structure. The only thing that they could think it was, that it looked more like the dried up skin of a snake more than anything else." Mr. Sanderson explained the structural characteristics of this material as well as an analysis of it, "It proved to have three layers, the outer smooth, the inner rough, the central, columnar in structure, as far as it could be ascertained. It contained aragonite, and the whole was porous, which would seem to agree with the description of a reptile shell."

Mr. Sanderson went into further detail about material and said, "However, one of the lab assistants down there managed to soften it up. They had been trying to soften it up in everything. He said, 'Why don't you try water' and they did. One of these little rolls of stuff, which were only about the size of my little finger, when outstretched, measured nine and one half inches." Sanderson then asked, "I would like to know, what snake's egg found in the United States, or anywhere else [pauses] from which you could get a strip nine and one half inches long?" Ivan T. Sanderson made the following statement and ended his 1968 interview with Long John Nebell by saying, "The parting shot, was a humorous one made by John DuBarry when I told him all about this.

He said, 'UT-oh, perhaps they were space people, but perhaps they're reptiles and were looking for somewhere to lay an egg." In 1968, this "reptiles" statement may have seemed to be witty and humorous. However, did Sanderson and his associates have the evidence right in their hands, which would have identified the race of aliens that landed on September 12, 1952? It seems they probably did but didn't fully realize it! Were these gigantic beings actually the "Reptilians" that had snake-like bodies and without legs or feet? Were the lower segments of these armor suits flared-out to accommodate their coiled bodies? Is that why these aliens needed mechanical probes to transport their bloated, slow moving and bulky bodies?

The Reptilians with Upper Spacesuit Removed

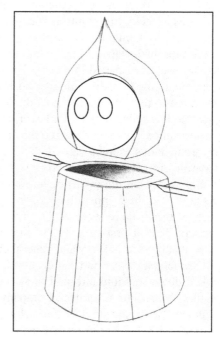

"Bashful Billy"

The drawing of "Bashful Billy" was portrayed as a scaled reptilian with a tail that looks similar to a dragon. The figure was also depicted with arms. The smoke was actually the vehicle's exhaust!

CHAPTER TWENTY-FOUR

THE LETTER

A complex and controversial aspect of the "Flatwoods Monster" case involved a government letter received by Kathleen May. She said the letter explained that the objects seen throughout Braxton County that night were experimental military aircraft. The controversy surrounding this letter involved Kathleen May and A. Lee Stewart, Jr. Since 1952, they have vehemently disagreed with each other about the content of the letter. Mrs. May maintained that the letter was governmental in origin, while A. Lee Stewart, Jr. maintained that it was merely a press release for an upcoming issue of *Colliers* magazine.

This controversy was first reported and documented by Gray Barker in September 1953. He reported in *The Saucerian*, Vol. 1, No. 1, that Mrs. May's "father told me (Barker) that Mrs. May had received a letter from the government, which explained what the whole thing actually had meant, and advised that a report was to be *released* to the public that week, after which she could talk freely about it. Her father said that since the release date had passed he could tell me that the 'monster' was a government rocket ship, propelled by an ammonia-like [sic] fuel, and which could travel at terrific speeds."

Barker also said, "I could hardly wait to look up Editor Stewart who, I was told, could give me details on the government report. Stewart laughed as he pulled out an 8" x 10" photo, attached to a publicity release from *Collier's* magazine. The issue of October 18 was to contain the story about a moon rocket, and the photo was the cover art. It was to be released that week, he explained. He had shown the picture to the May family, because there was some resemblance between the rocket ship and their descriptions of the 'monster.'"

Since that time, there have been many opinions expressed about the contents of this letter and the integrity of the involved parties. Some researchers believed A. Lee Stewart, Jr. actually showed Mrs. May a magazine press release and that Mrs. May simply misinterpreted the source of the material as being governmental. Some researchers have tried to explain the dispute by alluding to increased age and a failing memory on the part of Mrs. May. Those opinions are unfair and inaccurate. Since 1952, Mrs. May has never wavered in her assertion that the letter was from the government. Some researchers have even suggested that Stewart intentionally misled Mrs. May into believing this letter was from the government. Mrs. May always maintained the same story. Not once did she ever waver on a single point.

The following story was related to me during an interview with Mrs. May. She informed me, "It was a week or ten days after we got back from New York. Stewart called and wanted to know if I could get the boys gathered up and have them at my house at seven o'clock that evening. He said he had received a letter from the government and he couldn't open it until seven o'clock. That is when *Collier's* magazine went to the newsstand, seven o'clock that night. He opened the letter and they had a 5" x 7" picture in there of the machine that they were building to send to the moon. And they said that the Navy Department had put the machine up, you know, the one that had come over that evening and that I had given the best description of it even to those that had built it, helped to build it." The conversation continued:

Frank: "Now the letter was actually from the Navy, or from Washington?"

Kathleen: "From Washington, the government, uh-huh. They said the Navy Department was putting it up, building the machine."

Frank: "Now this photograph, that came with the letter, it was an actual picture of the craft?"

Kathleen: "Yes, uh-huh."

Frank: "And it looked similar to it?"

Kathleen: "Yes, uh-huh, the one that I-the one that we saw. They said there'd be two men in it or more." Frank: "Inside the actual craft?"

Kathleen: "And they told us how they would be strapped down, you know, and all this, that and the other and how they would get around and operate in the machine."

Frank: "And this was the Navy who supposedly built this?"

Kathleen: "Yeah, the Navy, and they also said, in the letter, that there were four ships around in the vicinity that night."

Frank: "They said there were four of them that night?"

Kathleen: "Uh-huh, and one of them landed in Flatwoods." Mrs. May added, "It also said the one that landed in Flatwoods was having oil trouble."

Mrs. May's mother also attended when the letter was presented to the gathered witnesses. She made the following statement to Terry Marchal of *The Sunday Gazette-Mail State Magazine*, in 1966, "The letter said it was a test plane with two men in it and then took off again." This next portion of Mrs. May's testimony clarifies her assertions that the information she received was from the government.

Kathleen: "The National Guard and A. Lee Stewart wrote the government and told them they wanted a report. They wanted to know just exactly, what it was. And they were concerned over the children with the gas, you know, and they said they wanted to know if it was one of our own."

This would explain Mrs. May's claims regarding the letter she had received informing her about the experimental ships. It is a fact that Colonel Leavitt did ship off samples from the landing site to Washington, D.C. upon their request. When I asked Colonel Leavitt if any reports or explanations ever came from Washington, he replied, "No! They never gave me anything back."

Stewart informed me that when the Treasury Department acquired his metal sample they informed him "in no way were they connected to the federal government as far as this trip was concerned." Stewart claimed they also took the balance of his metal fragment without his knowledge or permission. It was clear that the Treasury Department people who visited Stewart and obtained his metal samples were actually government investigators.

Mrs. May said that the government letter reported the results of the site samples. "They [government] said it was our own native oil and metal." A press release would not have contained information on the results of the oil and metal samples found at the landing site. Mrs. May did possess knowledge of four experimental ships seen throughout Braxton County that night. She also stated that these experimental craft had a two-man crew, and one craft had landed in Flatwoods.

The October 18, 1952 issue of *Collier's* magazine was only a one-part segment in a series of space articles. Collier's editor, Gordon Manning, created a symposium from a team of space experts; they created the series. The articles dealt with all aspects of theoretical space exploration, and were published by Collier's in 1952, 1953, and 1954. In 1952 there were only two titles released from the series.

The first article, "Man Will Conquer Space Soon," was published on March 22, 1952. The following article, "Man on the Moon," appeared in two consecutive issues published on October 18 and 25, 1952.

Stewart claimed *Collier's* magazine sent him a press release for the October 18, 1952 issue that had a photo attached to it of a moon ship. He in turn showed it to Mrs. May and the witnesses. What puzzled me about Mrs. May's letter was why the United States government would send a letter to Stewart rather than to Colonel Leavitt. The following transpired:

> Frank: "Why do you think that Colonel Leavitt didn't receive any letters, and they sent it to a news reporter? What baffles me is that the newspapers are usually the last people the government wants to deal with, given their propensity for blowing a story out of proportion. Colonel Leavitt, who ran the investigation, told me he didn't get any information at all."
> Kathleen: "No, I don't know either."
> Frank: "Doesn't that sound. . . ."
> [Interrupted]
> Kathleen: "A. Lee had that letter that he brought down and didn't open it until he came out to our home."
> Frank: "But the government sent it to him, right?"
> Kathleen: "Uh-huh."
> Frank: "What do you think about the whole story yourself?"
> Kathleen: "Well, I didn't know and I still don't know. The government just tells you what they want you to believe."

In closing, I asked Mrs. May about the whereabouts of the letter. I asked her if she had it or if Stewart had it. She said, "He never would release the letter, and I don't know what he's done with it." During my interview with Stewart, he explained his version of the controversial letter. Before I started taping, I asked him if he still had the letter. He told me it might be in storage in his attic. I explained that it would be great evidence for my story. It would clarify that Mrs. May might have actually been wrong in interpreting that the letter had come from the government.

Stewart told me he had kept several boxes of documents from *The Braxton Democrat* over the years. He said that some of this was the original correspondence concerning the "Flatwoods Monster." He said his late wife had taken care of the old Braxton Democrat records, packing them away, and that he did not know where she had put them. He told me we didn't need the letter anyway, that he was going to tell me what had happened. When I stressed the importance of the letter as the only hard evidence to prove who was right, he grew upset with me. I decided not to push the issue and started taping his testimony.

To aid in his recollection of events, I gave Stewart my copy of the October 18 *Collier's*. I also gave him a copy of the infamous photograph of Mrs. May holding the "monster" drawing, the one drawn by the *We the People* artist. This is A. Lee Stewart's version of the events:

Collier's contacted me after seeing the television show, remarking about the similarity to what they were getting ready to use in their magazine, to the subject they saw on television.

So here are the two side-by-side, which there is some similarity, maybe you need a broad view of mind to see it, but there is some similarity, much more similarity in 1952 than in 1996.

The only reason that I received this piece of material was the fact that they had seen this on television. It had nothing to do with the federal government, or anything to do with this, except the fact of the similarity, which they saw. We didn't. We hadn't seen this yet.

Stewart Explains his Version of the Letter and the *Collier's* Issue

After hearing his statement, I was no closer to understanding the controversy than when I had started. Both Mrs. May and Stewart were still telling me the same stories they told Gray Barker in 1952. As Stewart and I discussed the story off camera, I again brought up the point about the gaseous odor at the landing site on Fisher Farm. Earlier he had told me, "We got close down to the ground, and we could still pick up an odor." I then told Stewart that I knew he entered the Air Force after high school and his training prompted him to check close to the ground for the gas odor knowing that gases settled.

Innocently, I asked him to expound upon his military experience on camera during the next segment of his interview. Much to my shock, Stewart adamantly told me, "There's no need for anybody to know about my Air Force background." I pushed the issue but he refused to discuss any of his Air Force experience with me so I backed off.

Actual Issue of the *Collier's* October 18, 1952 Magazine

The following day was my last with A. Lee Stewart, Jr. I asked Stewart what he really thought had taken place that night. He told me that something unusual did land on the Fisher Farm. He then asked what I thought had really happened. I told him I believed that the "monster" was actually an alien in a space suit who had landed in a damaged space ship. He answered, "You're probably right." Stewart said that after the incident he had returned to the landing site on numerous occasions. Over the years, he had attempted to piece together the strange encounter on the farm. He would sit out at the farm, sketchpad in hand, attempting to retrace the steps of the event and the flight paths of the objects.

I went out to my car to retrieve one of my paintings, the full color illustration that depicted the farm at the moment of the encounter. I showed it to Stewart and he said, "You know, it didn't land there. It landed on the mountaintop and moved into the valley."

I was stunned that he knew this. Stewart then took my sketchpad and started to draw the Fisher Farm. We drew a compilation sketch together and compared notes while we reviewed the incident. Amazingly, our facts about the encounter on the farm coincided. I had underestimated Stewart's knowledge of the story.

I said to Lee, "So you believe it was an alien in a space ship, too." He replied, "Yes, it was." Lee then looked back at my painting and said, "There were more trees in the valley, to the left of where the ship landed the second time. They were pear trees." He told me I should correct the picture if I wanted it to be accurate.

Shortly thereafter, I began to pack up my equipment for the long trip home. As I thanked Lee for helping me in my research and having me in his home for four days, he made one more comment. I was walking out the door when Lee said, "My dad said, 'I think the aliens knew to land in West Virginia because no one would ever believe us here.'" After spending four days with A. Lee Stewart, Jr., I came away with a much clearer understanding of the "Flatwoods Monster" case, and a much deeper understanding of A. Lee Stewart, Jr. Because of my opportunity to speak with Stewart at length, over a period of four days, the letter incident that had confused me had taken on a new dimension.

I began to see this story from a different angle—an angle I dreaded even thinking about. I tried unsuccessfully to contact Stewart numerous times to see if he had found any documents, supposedly packed away in storage in his home. I continued to call sporadically for over a year, but was unable to reach him. During that time, Freddie May made an arrangement for me to interview his mother once more. I wanted to review some final details for the book before finishing it. During our meeting in November 1998, Mrs. May informed me that A. Lee Stewart, Jr. had recently passed away. It was a sad moment for us.

As our conversation progressed, I showed Mrs. May some of my research that she knew nothing about. I showed her the U.S. Air Force's Project 10073 Record Card, which had explained the "West Virginia Monster"

11. COMMENTS

The West Virginia monster so called.
Actually the object was the well known Washington area meteor of 12 Sep landing near Flatwoods, W. Va.
Have confirmation of an Astronomy Club from Akron, Ohio. Letter from E.C. ～～～～President - Akron Ast. Club

as the "Washington area meteor." I then showed Mrs. May other Project Blue Book reports, information she had never known about, and she was shocked. Even though Mrs. May claimed the government letter contained information about experimental ships, she was puzzled as to why they explained the "monster" as a meteor.

We discussed the illustration of the moon ship seen on the cover of *Collier's*. The illustration attached to the controversial letter. The dimensions in scale of this theoretical moon ship would in fact have been far too large for the "Flatwoods Monster." The height of this proposed "moon ship" was to be, "160 feet long and about 110 feet wide." In reference, the height of this ship at 160 feet would have been 9 feet taller than The Statue of Liberty. The base was to have "a battery of thirty rocket motors" and "topped by the sphere which houses the crew members, scientists and technicians on five floors." According to *Collier's* magazine, the moon ship vehicle would have contained a crew of twenty men.

What Kathleen May did not know about the craft that was pictured on the cover of *Collier's* was the scale of the illustration. Consequently, Mrs. May was unable to interpret the discrepancy in size and height between the illustration and the "Flatwoods Monster". Had the supposed moon ship been scaled down to the size of The "Flatwoods Monster," mice would have been the appropriate-sized occupants. It is obvious that Mrs. May was intentionally misled into believing the far-fetched experimental ship explanation.

We spoke again of the controversial letter. Mrs. May ran through the story once more and said, "It was from the government and he could not open it until seven o'clock that night." The letter said, "It was a rocket that they were building to send to the moon and there were two—[pauses] supposed to be two men in it, and they said four [ships] had come down in Braxton County that night." She was informed that three of the ships were looking for the one that landed on the Fisher Farm. Mrs. May stated, "The rest of them were looking for that one." At this point, I ran run through a synopsis of the story, and then asked her some verifying questions. The following conversation transpired:

Frank: "So this letter came to Stewart, and it came from Washington?"
Kathleen: "Uh-huh."
Frank: "And it explained everything in it?"
Kathleen: "Yeah."
Frank: "And Stewart took the letter back?"
Kathleen: "Yeah. He even took the picture."
Frank: "The picture?"
Kathleen: "He didn't give me anything."

Until Kathleen May received the letter from the government, she did not know what the "monster" was. While in New York for *We the People*, Mrs. May was asked if she knew what the "monster" was. "They asked me if I knew what it was, you know, [pauses] and Lord I didn't know, I had no idea. I know it wasn't an airplane. That's the only thing I'd seen in the sky besides a kite." In 1952 after reading the letter, Mrs. May was convinced, it was an experimental rocket ship.

It struck me as very peculiar that Stewart had taken away both the letter and the photograph. Four years after the incident, on October 7, 1956, *The Charleston Gazette* printed the following headline: "What Happened to the Monster?" The sub-headline read, "Braxton County Woman Feels Glowing Object Was Jet Ship Discovery in 1952 Stirred Up Nation-Wide Martian Debate." The article stated, "Flatwoods, Oct. 6 - The woman who set off a four-year debate when she saw a mysterious object near her home here said today she was convinced she didn't stumble on a craft from Mars. Mrs. Kathleen May said the 'Braxton County Monster' was nothing more than some new type governmental-owned jet or rocket plane."

I showed Kathleen May a microfilm copy of this article from my compilation of research and asked her the following question, "Have you had any change of mind over the years, or do you still think it was something from the government, or you just don't know?"

She answered, "I just don't know. Never will know, don't guess. The way things are happening now, it's hard to tell what it was." Concerning the letter, Kathleen then told me, "I never could understand why A. Lee took that, and why they sent it out to him anyway." Then it hit me why the U.S. had sent the letter to Stewart. I believe there were actually two different letters. The letter shown to Mrs. May and the witnesses by Stewart was an informative letter from the United States. It stated that what had been seen was not a "monster", but one of four Navy ships, and that one was having oil trouble. It also revealed that three of the four experimental craft were searching for the fourth ship.

This letter also contained a small amount of information about rocket fuel, information derived from the *Collier's* article. The government further stated that the metal and oil samples taken from the landing site were from one of their own experimental ships. I believe this letter was to alleviate Mrs. May's concern about the side effects of the oil and gas that the witnesses encountered. Attached to this letter was a photograph of the moon ship that *Collier's* was planning to use on the cover of its October 18, 1952 issue. This photo reinforced the cover-up of the experimental ship explanation. There was, it would seem, a second letter, which was nothing more than an ordinary press release concerning *Collier's* upcoming article, "Man on the Moon." This letter included the attached photo as well.

It appears to me that a switch was made with the letters, which were similar in appearance. I believe that when A. Lee Stewart, Jr. appeared on national television with Mrs. May and Eugene Lemon, government officials saw him. The officials wasted no time in contacting *Collier's* to engineer a cover-up using the national media. This was a commonly accepted practice in the Cold War era, and one in which the media felt obliged to help, as a matter of national security.

In 1953, Major Donald Keyhoe stated, "Mrs. May and the Lemon boy appeared on *We the People* and retold their frightening experience. It was obvious the boys believed the monster was real, and a dozen papers and magazines sent staff writers to Sutton for new angles on the story. 'This could get out of hand,' I told Chop. 'Why doesn't the Air Force squelch it?' 'We've already said the object was a meteor,' he retorted. 'A lot of people don't believe it, and the way this has built up, its bad." Because the government feared mass hysteria because of the statements Mrs. May had made on national television, the story had to be squelched.

When Mrs. May appeared on television and told the American public that she didn't know what the "monster" truly was, her story was very real, sincere, and convincing. Shortly thereafter, the media began to report this from a UFO angle. The Washington UFO flap had only occurred a few weeks prior to the "Flatwoods Monster" incident. As tensions ran high across the United States, the American public was starting to believe that the "Flatwoods Monster" might have actually been an alien.

I have concluded that the U.S. government contacted Stewart, because of his recent ties to the Air Force. He was given instructions to deliver false information to Mrs. May and the other witnesses. Under the circumstances, he probably would have followed the instructions to prevent the story from escalating any further. I think Stewart could have rationalized any reservations he had about delivering a letter as part of a disinformation campaign. My stance is both letters were mailed to him with instructions for delivery. It would not surprise me if the government had coerced or threatened Stewart had he not agreed. Moreover, Mrs. May read a fabricated letter, switched by Stewart when he produced an ordinary press release to Gray Barker. By misleading a few witnesses and spreading misinformation to them, the government may have prevented a nationwide panic. In 1938, the Halloween radio broadcast of "War of the Worlds" caused a nationwide panic. That radio show was broadcast only fourteen years before the "Flatwoods Monster" incident.

I am sure the decision makers in the U.S. government felt they had a valid reason for covering the truth regarding the "Flatwoods Monster" incident. Presenting the letter through Stewart left a natural door open for him to remove the letter after Mrs. May had read it. Stewart could also be on hand to gauge the reactions of the witnesses as the letter was read to them. Had the "experimental craft" letter been sent directly to Mrs. May, she would have had proof and been able to question and disprove the government's official meteor explanation.

The government chose to discredit the primary adult witness, making it appear that she had misinterpreted the letter, and was perhaps unreliable. The misinformation plan was successful; some of the best UFO investigators have been stymied by it. This is an example of a well-executed exercise in deception. However, another point had struck me as odd. Three days after the incident, an article appeared in *Time Magazine*, and read in part, "The International Astronautical Federation, in Stuttgart, Germany, discussed ways and means of launching man-carrying rockets into outer space... The federation heard that long-range rockets like Hitler's V-2s can and probably will be fired to the moon or to Mars within the next ten or 20 years."

During the course of my investigation, I met Professor Harvey Wolf, a physicist who worked in the aerospace industry. His career spanned the late 1950s through the early 1970s. One project that Mr. Wolf worked on was for Lockheed Aircraft, testing re-entry vehicles. After several discussions with Mr. Wolf, he agreed to be interviewed in front of a camera. During that interview, I asked Professor Wolf about the possibilities of manned space exploration in the 1950s. Wolf told me the following, "I don't know anything about the early 50s, but in the mid-50s we were beginning to talk about men in space and actually tried to figure out how to run some experiments on weightlessness."

He also stated, "At that point, none of the people I was working with were talking about putting a man on the moon or interplanetary travel beyond the science fiction aspect of it. We were interested in how one would do repairs in space. I ran an experiment with the Navy off Point Mugu in which we used underwater divers in an attempt to figure out what weightlessness does to the ability to work. We didn't have any vehicle ready for sending people up at that point, in the late 50s."

While speaking about the "Flatwoods Monster," I asked, "Harvey, these drawings are made by witnesses to this particular incident in 1952. In the aerospace program that you were involved with, or at any time, have you ever seen a craft that looked like this?" He replied, "I've never seen a craft that looked like that." Mr. Wolfe concluded, "I've never seen a missile that looked like that."

The moon ship explanation told to Mrs. May in the mysterious letter was not even remotely possible in 1952. The Air Force knew that the fireball in the sky was not a meteor, nor was the "monster" an owl seen by Mrs. May perched on a tree limb in Flatwoods. Therefore, they convinced her that it was something explicable, like an experimental ship. However, there were no manned-experimental ships in 1952! In 1952, their story seemed more believable than it does more than 50 years later. This misinformation strategy apparently worked, because Mrs. May throughout the years has believed that the "monster" was an experimental ship—until now.

In this book, I have outlined a logical, cohesive scenario explaining the numerous UFO-related events of September 12, 1952 from the best sources I was able to obtain. I relied on eyewitness testimonies and factual reports by sources such as our own government agencies and print media from the world over. I provided information and misinformation about the events that occurred during the summer of 1952. Yet, despite all my years of research there are still many people who do not believe in flying saucers and extraterrestrials. Well, if my accounts seem less than plausible, I offer another explanation to the events that occurred during that time and appeared in *The Wheeling News Register* on September 16, 1952.

In an article titled "Bethany Professor Blames Imagination - Citizens 'Hypnotized Into Seeing Saucers,'" a West Virginia College Professor, Dr. J .S. V. Allen of Bethany University, when questioned about the summer of 1952 incidents, brilliantly concludes that the citizens of this nation were "hypnotized into seeing flying saucers from other planets." Physicist Dr. Allen explained, "We are a very gullible people and our imagination can add greatly to our observations." The article attempts to add substantial proof to Allen's theory by backing him up that all the witnesses of this and other incidents suffer from cases of flying 'sorcery.'" Dr. Allen also talked about the impossibilities of space travel between the Earth and the nearest star and other cosmic conundrums. The article states, "The physics instructor points out that should our country have been viewed by persons in flying saucers, would it not be reasonable to expect that scientists would have contacted the saucers native land by radio." The good doctor goes on to state what we all should really accept as the absolute truth; that all the witnesses of the "Flatwoods Monster" incident were simply under "flying saucer 'hypnosis.'"

Apparently, the entire United States was 'hypnotized" into seeing the entire UFO flap during the summer of 1952. Furthermore, since 1952, it seems these bouts of hypnosis have not ceased. In fact, to this day, the *Associated Press* reports monthly accounts of more "hypnotized" US citizens. It seems that someone forgot to snap their fingers!

The following is a top 20 list of the most UFO reports received by Project Blue Book per month between the years 1951 and 1956.

1. 536 - July 1952	11. 68 – August 1955
2. 326 - August 1952	12. 67 – January 1953
3. 148 - June 1952	13. 63 – July 1955
4. *124 - September 1952*	14. 61 – October 1952
5. 123 - August 1956	15. 60 – July 1954
6. 91 – February 1953	16. 57 – September 1955
7. 82 – April 1952	17. 56 – November 1956
8. 79 – May 1952	18. 55 – October 1955
9. 72 – July 1956	19. 54 – May 1955
10. 71 – September 1956	20. 53 – October 1956

The four months that rank highest on this Blue Book top 20 list are the summer months of 1952. That year also charted six of the eight highest months on the list. There are seven months out of the top twenty months with the most received UFO sightings per month - the year 1952. The years 1955 and 1956 each had five months on the top 20 list for that six-year period but 1956 had three months in the top ten of highest months. Did Mrs. May and a group of boys sight an owl in an Oak tree on September 12, 1952 or did they actually see an extraterrestrial space suit?

The December 1952 issue of *Sky and Telescope* magazine had an article titled "Astronomical Highlights of 1952." The article gave a list of the top ten astronomical highlights for 1952, as of October when their meeting was held. Amazingly, the overwhelming amount of alleged meteors that the military insisted occurred on September 12 and 13 did not make the list. **On those two nights in question, there were no meteors.**

Comparison between the Moonship and "Flatwoods Monster"

CHAPTER TWENTY-FIVE

FLATWOODS AND WEST PALM BEACH

On August 21, 1952, Project Blue Book chief Captain Ruppelt and his assistant Lt. Olsson were flown to West Palm Beach, Florida in a B-25 plane, to investigate a terrifying close encounter incident that had occurred on August 19, 1952. This UFO incident occurred only twenty-five days prior to the "Flatwoods Monster" incident and had quickly made worldwide headlines. The incident involved Mr. Sonny DesVergers, a 30-year old WW II Marine veteran and scoutmaster, who was accompanied by three boy scouts when the encounter unfolded. After a scout meeting, at about 10:30 p.m., the scoutmaster was driving the three boys' home in his car on Military Trail about 12-miles south of West Palm Beach. DesVergers was driving along the road when he saw a series of lights descending into the woods. The lights lit up to the side of the road to his left.

He immediately thought a plane had crashed in the woods so pulled over, left the boys and went to look for survivors. DesVergers wearing a denim cap brought two flashlights and a machete and told the boys to wait. He walked through brush toward the area in question where he had just seen the descending lights. The scoutmaster moved on, waving his flashlight in front of him but something seemed peculiar. He didn't see any flames; he didn't hear any sounds of crackling metal or wood and didn't see any aircraft wreckage.

DesVergers continued and used the North Star to guide him through the woods but still did not see the lights ahead of him. The scoutmaster then noticed an open spot ahead of him and suddenly stopped, when he thought it might be a lake. Pointing his light on the ground ahead of him, DesVergers saw the area was actually a clearing and proceeded on. He walked a few steps into the clearing and the noticed a very pungent odor and an intense heat that seemed to come from above. DesVergers then looked up and noticed the sky was blacked out above him and he couldn't see any stars.

He aimed his flashlight upwards and suddenly discovered why. To his dismay, DesVergers saw a 30-foot wide flying saucer over his head. The craft was silently whirling and hovering about 10-feet above the ground and only inches over the pine trees near the outskirts of the clearing. The scoutmaster, paralyzed with fear, froze in his tracks. Shortly after, he gained control of himself, backed away from under the saucer's edge and noticed the heat wasn't intense.

Simultaneously, the craft was moving away from him. DesVergers noticed the edge of the craft glowing like phosphorous against the black sky. As he continued to back away from it, the scoutmaster saw a dome shape on top of the craft and claimed to have seen beings.

Moments later, DesVergers heard a metal against metal noise as if something had opened like

a hatch. Shortly after, a misty flare blossomed from the whirling saucer. This ball of fire quickly floated down at DesVergers head as he covered his face to protect his eyes.

Upon impact, the ball of fire hit his arms, which shielded his face, and DesVergers had received minor burns to his arms, which resembled a flash radiation exposure. Later it was also noticed that his hat was burned and had small holes in it.

Donald Keyhoe explains what happened after the DesVergers incident, "About three months later, when the scoutmaster's story appeared in the *American Weekly Magazine*, DesVergers said he had seen a terrifying creature in the saucer's turret - so dreadful he would not even describe it. But in September, when the Sutton case broke, this was not widely known." This article, written by Marta Robinet was titled, "Burned by a Flying Saucer."

The DesVergers incident also has some interesting points to talk about. The incident also involved the sighting of alien beings was and investigated by government officials. There was one difference though; Project Blue Book officials had openly investigated the Florida incident, which was publicly known.

During that investigation, they had also obtained samples from the site. Writer George Sand covered the story and wrote about it in the April 1953 magazine issue of *STAG-True Men's Adventures*. In the article, He Was Burned by a Flying Saucer, Mr. Sand explained the repercussions of the DesVergers story. He stated, "No sooner had the story hit the news wires when telegrams, phone calls and letters began to descend upon the area from all parts of the nation.

People who ordinarily might have paid attention to the hapless scoutmaster now clamored at his door night and day. The public seemed to want to believe that the strange ship had come from another world. And there was no evidence to prove that it had not." He also told what Deputy Sheriff Partin went through because of the publicity. Mr. Sand stated, "He continued to receive long distance calls, letters from as far away as Australia. One determined voice on the phone insisted that the harassed sheriff make a statement for the British news services."

Mr. DesVergers statements also appeared in Mr. Sand's article. DesVergers stated, "I saw the saucer in every detail as it hissed and hovered horizontally about 10 feet from the ground. It was about three feet thick and rimmed with a phosphorous effect." Sand then explained what DesVergers told West Palm Beach police officers, "The hissing saucer had contained beings, he told them grimly." The writer then reported the involvement of Project Blue Book in the incident.

In part, Mr. Sand stated:

The Air Technical Intelligence Center at Dayton, Ohio, quickly flew an officer to the scene. This center has the responsibility of analyzing reports of unusual aerial objects. Officials from Washington, too, conducted inquiries and combed the wooded area too. "We cannot tell yet just what it was there," an Air Force spokesman said. "We are going to continue to check and get all the facts together, however." What ever those "facts" may have been, they were not being made known. Instead, it was reported that the government investigators had spoken to him "like a Dutch uncle."

DesVergers, following his final interview with the "high brass" had clammed up. He admitted that the Government had no legal hold on him, yet he indicated that a "gentleman's agreement," obligated him to hold back part of the story. "It's not foolish to say that it will determine the future of all of us some day," was the scoutmaster's final statement, "I know what it is and it's of vital importance. But it is better for me not to go any farther because it may cause another Orson Wells panic."

The case was initially handled by Captain Carney of the "Wing Intelligence Office," located at the "1007th Air Wing Base," which was located at the West Palm Municipal Airport. On August 22, 1952, the Project Blue Book investigators openly began their on site investigation of the DesVergers incident. Quickly, the story had started to receive a lot of publicity and attention. Newspapers and magazines from around the world featured the saucer incident and reported it in a straightforward manner. Yes, the DesVergers scoutmaster incident was indeed being taken very seriously by everyone.

A Project Blue Book Official on Site in West Palm Beach during August of 1952

During the Air Force's investigation, grass samples from the area of the encounter were obtained as well as DesVergers baseball hat and subsequently analyzed. Ruppelt had obtained grass samples from a flattened circular area where the incident took place. Later, other samples of grass were obtained from an area approximately "fifty-yards from the location of the sighting" according to an ATIC memorandum. Subsequently, all of the samples were sent to the Batelle Memorial Institute in Columbus, Ohio to be analyzed by their "Agronomy Laboratory."

Under the code name, "Project Stork" this institute was in contract with the ATIC to provide scientific and technical support to Project Blue Book's UFO cases. Then, as details of the scoutmaster case continued to surface and become more complicated, Captain Ruppelt and Lt. Olsson made a second trip to Florida. In the early part of September, they continued their investigation into the incident.

Desvergers

American Weekly Magazine

In his 1956 book, Captain Edward Ruppelt wrote the following, "Everyone who was familiar with the incident, except a few people in the Pentagon, were convinced that this was a hoax until the lab called me with the grass samples we'd sent in. 'Wow did the roots get charred?' Roots charred? I didn't even know what my caller was talking about. He explained that when they'd examined the grass they had knocked the dirt and sand off the roots of the grass clumps and found them charred."

Ruppelt then stated, "The only way it could have been faked would have been to heat the earth from underneath to 300 degrees F., and how do you do this without using big and cumbersome equipment and disturbing the ground. You can't." Project Stork's "Sixth Status Report" recorded as "Contract AF-19741 – PPS-100" and dated, "10 October 1952," was sent to the ATIC. It reported soil and analysis information about two different cases that involved individuals that claimed to have encountered an unidentified craft at close range. The cases were the Bill Squyres August 25 incident in Kansas and the Sonny DesVergers August 19 incident in Florida. The status report document states the following information: The cases were the Bill Squyres August 25 incident in Kansas and the Sonny DesVergers August 19 incident in Florida.

The William Squyres close encounter incident occurred in Frontenac, Kansas near Pittsburg, one week after the DesVergers incident of August 25, 1952. At the time of his encounter, Mr. Squyres, a 42-year old musician, was also a staff member at the local KOAM radio station. When the story first broke in the press, the incident was thought to be a hoax. Since it occurred only a week after the well-publicized Scoutmaster incident in Florida, many thought it was copycats story that Squyres made-up to gain publicity.

When the details of the incident were revealed, Squyres had described the craft involved in his close range sighting and said it had "propellers" mounted to it. This propeller account was uncommon to the many UFOs described in other cases and this account was deemed preposterous. Many asked; why would a technologically advanced craft have propellers? Additionally, the witness claimed to have seen figures through the windows of the craft, which included a seated "human being" in another part of the craft.

These details described by the witness only raised more question about the validity of the incident, however there was trace evidence at the area of the sighting. On August 26, 1952, newspaper reporter Bob McKnight of the *Nehoso Daily Democrat* interviewed Squyres and the witness received a lot of good press concerning the incident. Quickly, the Kansas UFO story spread throughout the media. A couple days after the incident, Project Blue Book officials became involved in the matter, went to Kansas and investigated the site of the encounter. It was then, that the case was looked at and taken more seriously than it had appeared at first glimpse.

The Squyres incident was recorded in the Blue Book files as case 1972 and later evaluated as an "Unknown." A document contained in Project Blue Book that records the Squyres incident reads, "OSI Records" or Special Office of Investigations Records. It is dated, "7 October 1952," which is just three days before the Project Stork "Sixth Status Report" dated, "10 October 1952." This OSI Record states the following, "Special Inquiry by S/A Blair T. Lian, DO #13, Offut AFB, Nebr." The Squyres incident was also studied in *Flying Saucers: An Analysis of the Air Force Project Blue Book Special Report No. 14*, which was conducted by the Batelle Memorial Institute for Blue Book. The Kansas incident is recorded as "Casc XII (Serial 3601.00) in that study.

In part, the October 7, 1952 Blue Book report gives the following information, "At approximately 0550 hours [5:50 a.m.], CST, on 25 August 1952, Squyres left his home driving a 1952 Jeep Station Wagon and started driving south on a rough gravel Road, Known as Yale road. When he reached a point approximately one-fourth mile from US. Highway 160, which runs east and west, he noted the unknown object off to his right side of the road at a horizontal angle of about 40 degrees and at a distance of about two hundred fifty yards."

It further reported, "Squyres said the sun was just rising as he was going to work that morning and it was light enough to see all objects in the area." Here, the witness was talking about the visibility of other objects in the area; such as objects of the terrain like trees, a nearby ditch, a fence etc. The report states there was only one UFO sighted, "There was only one object seen." He continued to drive and shortly after, Squyres pulled his Jeep over, got out of the vehicle and continued to watch the hovering object. The report states, "After stopping his car, Squyres turned off the ignition and when stepping out of his car, he heard a deep throbbing sound coming from the object."

At this point, Squyres said that, "he was about one hundred yards from it." He stated that, "The object was hovering about ten feet from the ground." The Blue Book Special Report No. 14 stated, "The object was not absolutely still, but seemed to rock slightly as it hovered." The witness also observed, "The grass was moving under the object when it was hovering." The "7 October 1952," document also stated the length of the observation, "Squyres estimated he viewed the object for about one-half minute."

Blue Book and the media also reported that the witness commented, "My hair rose straight up on the back of my neck." The "7 October 1952," report also gives the following account of the UFO's description, "Squyres described the object as platter-shaped; by this he said it looked like two platters or bowls had been put together by reversing one platter and placing it over the first one. He estimated it was about seventy-five feet long and forty feet wide and about fifteen feet through the mid-section, measuring vertically in center of the object." Squyres said, "It was dull aluminum in color," and had a "smooth surface.

The witness gave a further description of the object's structure that he described as the propellers, "Along the outer edge of object, there were a series of propellers about six to even inches in diameter." He added, "Spaced closely together, these propellers were mounted on a bracket so they revolved in a horizontal plane along the edge of the object." Squyres reported that the propellers "Were revolving at a high rate. The witness also described the two types of windows of the craft. He said there was, "one window in front section" that was described as,

288

"clear glass." Squyres said it had a "medium blue continuous light" emitting from within that section of the craft. He also saw the silhouette of a figure behind the glass. The report stated "with head and shoulders visible of one man sitting motionless facing forward." This area could be described as the cockpit of the craft. The witness also told Air Force investigators, "I definitely saw a human being through the window."

The upper portion along the mid-section of the craft had several rectangular windows. They were located behind the front portion of the cockpit area where the seated figure was located and were situated in rows but did not reach the rear end of the craft. The Blue Book report stated, "In the mid-section of the object were several windows extending from top to near edge of object; mid-section of ship had a blue light which gradually changed to different shades."

Squyres also saw figures moving around behind the rectangular windows but they were obscured. He explained to the Blue Book investigators, "Like a window shade pulled down. I could see figures moving around." The Blue Book Special Report No. 14 stated, "There was a large amount of activity in the mid-section that could not be identified as either human or mechanical, although it did have a regular pattern of movement."

After watching the UFO hover over the area, Squyres said it "began a rapid vertical descent." The "7 October 1952," report states, "When the object started it's ascent it emitted a sound like a large covey of quails starting to fly at one time." The witness stated, "A covey of a hundred quail taking off." The "7 October 1952," document also states, "There was no visible exhaust or color detected by viewer." The incident ended when the UFO continued to ascend and disappeared from Squyres sight. The "7 October 1952," report stated, "When object reached a height 'about as high as an airplane files' object then increased acceleration at a tremendous speed disappeared from view, straight up through broken clouds."

The report also said, "Squyres stated he wanted to go to the area over which the object had hovered; however, he did not as the terrain was rough (ditch, fence, tall woods, etc.) and he has an artificial leg which prevents normal movement." After the incident, Mr. Squyres drove to work and told two men of his encounter with the UFO. One of those men was an inactive Air Force lieutenant reservist and the other was a businessman that worked next to the radio station. The witness and the two men spoke about the encounter and then went to the site of the UFO sighting at about 10:20 a.m.

The two men were later interviewed by Air Force officials. Each man gave their testimony about what they had observed at the site. The "7 October 1952," document deleted their names but reported their findings. The report stated that one of the men had, "walked directly to the area which Mr. Squyres described as being below the object was sighted and noted that the weeds and grass in the area seemed to be 'pushed down' and twisted." The Blue Book Special Report No. 14 stated, "Investigation of the area soon afterward showed some evidence of vegetation being blown around."

The other man interviewed, "stated that he noted many small dead weeds that seemed to have been blown around in the area, and the broken weeds were found lying on top of some of the other growing weeds." The man added, "The weeds seemed to have a newly broken appearance which was substantiated by the fact that the inside of the broken weeds were still soft and had not dried out like a weed that had been broken for some time."

One of the men stated, "Mr. Squyres was a very reliable man whom he had known for a period of over four years." The Blue Book Special Report No. 14 stated, "Reliability of observer was considered good."

Subsequently, Blue Book officials obtained soil and vegetation samples from the ground areas of the Squyres UFO sighting. The Project Stork "Sixth Status Report" dated, "10 October 1952," reported the soil and analysis information about the DesVergers and Squyres incidents in August. The document states the following information:

SOIL AND VEGETATION SAMPLE: During the month, two sets of soil and vegetation samples were studied by an agricultural specialist and by physicists. Regarding the "Florida" samples, no difference was observed between the two samples of soil, but it was found that the root structure of the plants from the area in question [DesVergers' site of encounter] was degenerated, apparently by heat, while the root structure of a control sample [50-yards away] was undisturbed. In addition, the lower leaves, those nearest the ground under normal conditions, were slightly deteriorated, apparently by heat. No logical explanation is possible for this alteration in the first sample, beyond the suggestion that a high soil temperature around the plants could have been the cause. No radioactivity was found in any of these samples.

Regarding the "Kansas" samples, no difference was found between either the soil and vegetation from the two areas from which the specimens were obtained. These samples are now being examined for radioactivity.

Blue Book Photo of the "Charred" Roots from the Site of the Encounter

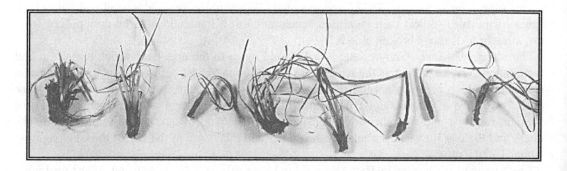

In reference to the burned hat, Ruppelt wrote, "The pattern of the scorch showed that the hat was flat when it was scorched, but the burned holes-the lab found some minute holes that we missed-had very probably been made by an electrical spark."

Ruppelt also stated, "The scoutmaster's burns weren't proof of anything; the flight surgeon had duplicated these by burning his own arms with a cigarette lighter. But we didn't make step one in proving the incident a hoax. We thought up dozens of ways that the man could have set up the hoax but couldn't prove one."

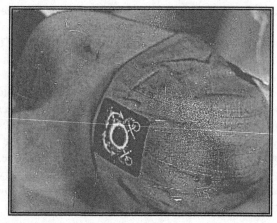

Ruppelt added, "In the scout masters favor were the two pieces of physical evidence we couldn't explain, the holes in the cap and the charred grass roots." Even though Edward Ruppelt stated intelligence's findings in the case he said, "We wrote off the incident as a hoax. The best hoax in UFO history."

Ruppelt then talked to a "scientist" about the DesVergers case and stated something that the scientist said to him, "What do you want...Does a UFO have to come in and land on your desk at ATIC?" Even though Intelligence officials had thought up dozens of ways that DesVergers could have "set up a hoax", they "couldn't prove one."

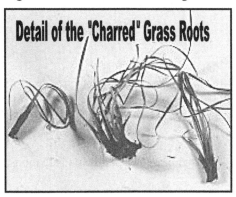

Detail of the "Charred" Grass Roots

According to Ruppelt, they "didn't make step one in proving the incident a hoax." Even though Edward Ruppelt admits that Intelligence had "physical evidence" that they "couldn't explain," they still "wrote off the incident as a hoax." Yes, the DesVergers case was covered-up by the Project Blue Book officials, just as the "Flatwoods Monster" incident would be only 25-days later.

Now, I will talk about another piece of information that involves yet another sample that was obtained from another UFO encounter incident during the summer of 1952. It involves a sample comparison between the DesVergers scoutmaster case and another UFO case that occurred shortly after. This UFO case is actually the "Flatwoods Monster" incident, which occurred on the Fisher Farm in Flatwoods, West Virginia.

Sites in Flatwoods, West Virginia and West Palm Beach, Florida

This documentation was contained in an "**Air Force Office of Special Investigation**" File that was in Project Blue Book. The OSI, is, "An activity under the Inspector General, USAF, providing a centrally directed criminal, counter intelligence, and special investigative service for all AF activities." This document, a "ROUTING AND RECORD SHEET" is dated "Oct 3 1952," which is only one week before Project Stork's "Sixth Status Report" of "10 October 1952."

It states the following information and has the name "DESVERGERS" handwritten across it with the numbers, "24-185-7-5X."

HQ 33 (20 May 44)
        (Stamped CONFIDENTIAL)
      HEADQUARTERS UNITED STATES AIR FIRCE   TALLY
                                                   NO.

ROUTING AND RECORD SHEET   FILE
                                                          NO.

SUBJECT: **(Restricted) Lab Analysis of Soil Samples Having Possible Relation to Unidentified Flying Objects**

TO: Counter Intelligence Division   DATE: OCT 3 1952
    Directorate of Special Investigations, The IG   COMMENT NO. 1
                                            Major Fournet/dbv/75990

FROM: Topical Division
    Deputy Division for Estimates, D/I. DCS/O

1. Reference our R&R dated 5 September 1952. Same subject as above recent developments have prompted the attachment of increased importance to these samples. Specifically, a deposit seeming to have the general same characteristics and also related to a flying object has been reported from Flatwoods, West Virginia.

2. In view of this possible relationship and the necessity for a prompt analysis of these two incidents, it is requested that utmost priority be given to the lab analysis of subject samples.

                           SIGNATURE of William A. Adams

                           WILLIAM A. ADAMS
                           Colonel, USAF
                           Chief, Topical Division
                           Deputy Director for Estimates
                           Directorate of Intelligence, DCS/O

Here, the "SUBJECT" of this document states, **"(Restricted) Lab Analysis of Soil Samples Having Possible Relation to Unidentified Flying Objects."** It refers to a deposit sample that was obtained in the DesVergers case, which was compared to another case, "Specifically, a deposit seeming to have the general same characteristics and also related to a flying object has been reported from Flatwoods, West Virginia."

    The information then adds, "In view of this possible relationship and the necessity for a prompt analysis of these two incidents, it is requested that utmost priority be given to the lab analysis of subject samples." Yes, there were "deposit" samples obtained in West Palm, Florida and Flatwoods, West Virginia that were similar.

In other words, once it was realized that there was a "possible relationship" between the samples in these two incidents there was an urgency to compare them. Here, the samples in question were "soil samples" that contained a "deposit." In particular, one such deposit found on the farm in Flatwoods was an "oil" deposit, which was also described as a "gray grease-like" fluid.

In the Flatwoods case, the oil was emitted from the "Flatwoods Monster," which was actually a machine. Furthermore, a machine that was leaking fluid all over the Fisher Farm! Moreover, the document asserts, that the "deposit" was "related to a flying object" that was "reported from Flatwoods, West Virginia." Was the deposit in question, actually the leaking gray fluid, which was spread across the Fisher Farm?

Moreover, was the "flying object" referred to in the document actually the "Flatwoods Monster" machine? If not, I ask, which "deposit" sample had shared "the general same characteristics" in both the Desvergers and Flatwoods incidents? Was it actually, the gray grease-like substance, the black, plastic-like material, or the scraps of metal material?

Regardless, intelligence officials were serious about the matter and had "requested that utmost priority be given to the lab analysis of subject samples. Now, I will reiterate a segment of the Flatwoods case that concerns my interview with Colonel Leavitt. The Colonel told me that he had received a phone call from Washington, DC. on the night of the incident. Leavitt explained that the USAF wanted him to gather various samples from the Fisher Farm site.

He told me the following information on site of the Fisher Farm, "They called me on the phone and asked me to get them what they wanted, and I told them I would send it back to them. I did. And I came up here and got it. I dug some dirt, and all that sort of thing, leaves off the trees, and sent them in. That's all I did." I asked him, "Where did you have to send all this? Did you have to send it to Washington?" Colonel Leavitt sternly answered, "The Air Force, that's what they wanted me to do." The following conversation transpired:

Frank: "And they never told you any of the results?"
Colonel Leavitt: "No results. Never. They never do."

Frank: "Why do you think that? Do you think? . . ."
Colonel Leavitt: [interrupting] "You think something's wrong"!

Frank: "Do you think they were trying to cover something up?"
Colonel Leavitt: [Caught off guard by the question, he answered] "Maybe."

Frank: "Now, when these samples were sent out, they were sent to Washington directly. How did that process work?"
Colonel Leavitt: "Air Force people, that's who wanted… [Frank interrupts]"
Frank: "Now, they contacted you?"
Colonel Leavitt: "Yeah."

Frank: "Through Washington?"
Colonel Leavitt: "Yeah and they wanted to know what it was. So I got some leaves and some dirt from underneath and all that sort of stuff. "

Frank: "Were there any other reports from Washington?
Colonel Leavitt: "No! They never, they never gave me anything back."

Frank: "It was just this one time that they called you and you sent the samples?"
Colonel Leavitt: "Yeah."
Frank: "Yeah and that was the end of it?"
Colonel Leavitt: "That was the end of it for them.

Frank: "What about the tree limbs or leaves? What did they look like? Were they wilted, burnt or singed at all?"
Colonel Leavitt: "No! It wasn't burned at all, the ones I got. I got them off the tree. But I got some of this oil, the little bits of this and that to see what it was, and I never did know what it was."

Frank: "Now this oily substance that was on the ground, did you have to take samples of that also?"
Colonel Leavitt: "I did, I did, and I took dirt, and leaves and some of the wood."

In closing, I asked Colonel Leavitt, "How did you have to package up this stuff – just put it in bags or cans? Leavitt replied, "I put it all in a great big box, [gestures pushing down] I put it all in the bottom and shipped it all off [gestures a waving motion]." Yes, Colonel Leavitt and the West Virginia National Guard were an instrumental organization that had obtained the first Flatwoods samples and sent them out to the Air Force.

Mrs. May and Frank during One of their Many Interviews

Two undercover intelligence officers who visited Flatwoods and posed as reporters/writers obtained the other samples. Let us now recap that segment of the story, which I discovered from Major Keyhoe and an interview with Mrs. Kathleen May.

During the course of Donald Keyhoe's investigation into the Flatwoods case between 1952 and 1953, he said, "Later from a source outside the Pentagon, I heard that intelligence had followed this up by sending two men in civilian clothes who posed as magazine writers while interviewing witnesses. Even if this was not true, and the Air Force denied it, their check through the state police showed more interest than they had admitted."

Mrs. Kathleen May told me that intelligence did send men to Flatwoods the day after the incident. She said, "Two men came and knocked on my door and they told me they were editors from Clarksburg. Well, they said they were reporters from Clarksburg at first and they would like to go up and see the place where it landed. Freddie went up with me, Eddie was too sick to go, and we went up there."

Then, Mrs. May, Freddie, and the two supposed reporters went to the Fisher Farm. This was Freddie and Mrs. May's first visit to the farm since the incident had occurred. Upon reaching the farm, they went to the field in the valley. Mrs. May said, "And one said he was going to cross over the fence and go down toward Shaversville. That's the way the thing came in that night and landed." While Kathleen, Freddie and the two supposed reporters were standing in the valley near the track marks and second landing area, they conversed about the events that had taken place.

Mrs. May explained, "We were just talking about the thing and they saw the skid marks. These skid marks went right down a little slant."

She added, "One stayed there with Freddie and me, and one went across [the fence] and went down. Well, he was gone about thirty minutes and came back." Mrs. May explained what happened when the supposed reporter came back from the tree area and covered in oil.

Photo Taken from the Woods that Shows the Backside of the Oak Tree:

This Area is where the Alleged Reporter Investigated and became Covered in Oil

Project Blue Book Chief Captain Edward J. Ruppelt

She said, "He came back and said to the other guy, *'Now what do you think Ed's gonna think of this when we send these in for analysis?'* That's just the way he said it** [Gesturing with her arms down at her sides and held out away from her body]. And he was covered. They had beautiful, nice suits on with hats to match, and he was striped. He looked like a zebra, with oil. Everything he touched left oil marks on his suit and hat."

Questioning her further, I asked, "So when this guy came back he held his arms out and he was covered with oil?" She replied, "Yeah, he was just covered, on his arms, his legs, his hat and everything. He had oil all over him." Shortly after these events, the two supposed reporters left the scene and the Fisher Farm.

295

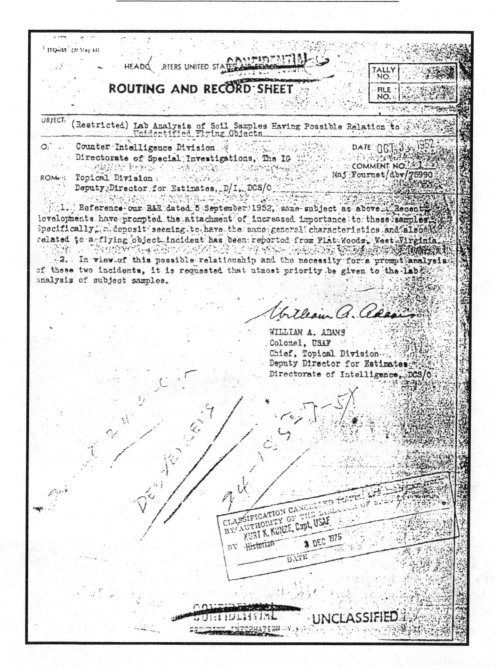

HEADQUARTERS UNITED STATES AIR FORCE

ROUTING AND RECORD SHEET

TALLY NO.

FILE NO.

SUBJECT: (Restricted) Lab Analysis of Soil Samples Having Possible Relation to Unidentified Flying Objects

TO: Counter Intelligence Division
Directorate of Special Investigations, The IG

DATE OCT 3 1952

COMMENT NO. 1

FROM: Topical Division
Deputy Director for Estimates, D/I, DCS/O

Maj Fournet/dbv/75990

1. Reference our R&R dated 5 September 1952, same subject as above. Recent developments have prompted the attachment of increased importance to these samples. Specifically, a deposit seeming to have the same general characteristics and also related to a flying object incident has been reported from Flat Woods, West Virginia.

2. In view of this possible relationship and the necessity for a prompt analysis of these two incidents, it is requested that utmost priority be given to the lab analysis of subject samples.

WILLIAM A. ADAMS
Colonel, USAF
Chief, Topical Division
Deputy Director for Estimates
Directorate of Intelligence, DCS/O

CLASSIFICATION CANCELLED
BY AUTHORITY OF THE DIRECTOR OF ...
KURT K. KUNZE, Capt, USAF
BY Historian   3 DEC 1975
DATE

CONFIDENTIAL
SECURITY INFORMATION   UNCLASSIFIED

On Sunday, September 14, the same two men who spoke with Mrs. May returned and took her back up to the Fisher Farm. She said, "And then the next day they came back and they begged apologies. They said they were from Washington, D.C. They said they were from Washington and they had flown in and rented a car and came up here."

I asked, "Why do you think they didn't tell you the truth the first time?" She replied, "They were afraid that if they wanted information and we knew they were investigators we wouldn't tell them anything." Mrs. May and the two men conversed about the incident.

Pressed further, Mrs. May again mentioned that during her encounter she was squirted with oil. One investigator was adamant about getting a sample. She explained, "They did go down to the house and scrape some oil out of my uniform." Mrs. May added, "So I guess he just wanted it for analysis or something, to see what kind of oil it was." I asked, "Do you remember the oil in particular? Did you get it all over yourself when the "monster" sprayed it on you?" She replied, "No. It just hit the front of my uniform." I asked, "What did you do with your uniform? Did you keep it or did you throw it out?" She answered, "I kept it for a while and then I think I threw it away. I'd never have gotten that (oil) out of it anyway."

These statements by Kathleen May demonstrated the government's involvement and interest in the case. It also corroborated Keyhoe's source who had heard that intelligence had sent two men in civilian clothes posing as magazine reporters while interviewing witnesses.

Moreover, behind closed doors, the Air Force was actually taking both of the Flatwoods and DesVergers incidents very seriously, more serious than they had led the public to believe! On September 12, 1952, the witnesses did not see a meteor, an owl or opossum. They saw the result of a military assault on a UFO, which landed in their back yard in Flatwoods, West Virginia...a downed UFO and its occupant. Subsequent military involvement occurred with the West Virginia National Guard, Captain Ruppelt and two Project Blue Book officials to obtain samples, which indicate the United States Government, did take the incident seriously!

I will reiterate a quote by Keyhoe who stated what happened after the August 1952 DesVergers incident. "About three months later, when the scoutmaster's story appeared in the *American Weekly Magazine*, DesVergers said he had seen a terrifying creature in the saucers turret - so dreadful he would not even describe it. But in September, when the Sutton case broke, this was not widely known." I ask were these two cases, which involved the same deposits, spacecraft and frightening aliens related? Was there a connection between these two cases, which occurred less than a month apart? It certainly seems so, but only time will tell!

In closing, I will give the following quote made by the great author, Sir Arthur Conan Doyle, "When you have eliminated the impossible, whatever remains, *however improbable*, must be the truth." My research and investigation into the, "Braxton County Monster" incident continues...

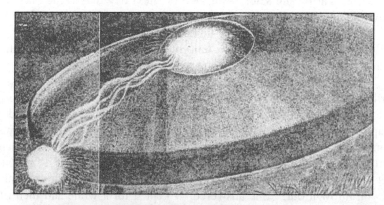

Eddie May

Eddie May

Ron Shaver

Fred May

Mrs. May

Fred May

REFERENCE LISTS FOR THE SEPTEMBER 12, 1952 UFOS

During my investigation, I researched, gathered and used several sources of information about the September 12, 1952 UFO flap. I reviewed Project Blue Book documents including; Intelligence Reports, Tentative Observers Questionnaires, Project 10073 Record Cards and radio broadcast transcripts. I also read several newspaper and magazine articles from around the country, read books about past investigations and interviewed several first hand eyewitness.

Next, I extracted the information about the numerous UFO sightings and events that occurred that day. I then categorized all of this information and compiled the following lists for reference.

THE TEN EAST COAST STATES WHERE UFO SIGHTINGS OCCURRED

1. Delaware
2. Maryland
3. North Carolina
4. Ohio
5. Pennsylvania
6. South Carolina
7. Tennessee
8. Virginia
9. Washington, DC.
10. West Virginia

THE SIX TYPES OF OBJECTS SIGHTED

1. OVAL OBJECTS. Elliptical-shape. Tear drop shape. Oval and tapered.
2. ROUND OBJECTS. Ball-shape. Sphere shape.
3. ROUND OBJECTS with a flat side.
4. TOP-SHAPED OBJECT.
5. CIGAR OR JET-SHAPED with no appendages. Emitted flames and balls of fire.
6. FLYING SAUCER.

THE 25 OBJECTS SIGHTED ON SEPTEMBER 12, 1952

During the September 12, 1952 flap, civilians and military personnel reported UFO sightings to the Pentagon, Air Force bases, Air Defense Command headquarters, Government offices, and Civil Aeronautics Administration officials. Civilians also contacted the FBI, state and local police stations as well as newspaper offices in 10 east coast states.

Throughout the course of the day, there were 116 east coast locations where witnesses reported UFO sightings. I plotted the locations of these sightings and then created a time line of events. I was able to differentiate and establish that there were actually 25 different objects and four of them were damaged.

The 25 objects are listed below:

1. Bladensburg, OH Object. Windows on one side.
2. Middletown, PA #1 Object. Oval with blue light. (Olmsted AFB).
3. Tennessee #1 Object. Round. Bluish-green in Flames. (*Damaged*).
4. Baltimore #2 Object. Oval. Greenish-white in Flames. (*Damaged*).
5. Washington, DC. #3 Object. Oval. Reddish-orange in flames. (*Damaged*).
6. North Carolina #1 Object. Round with a flat side. Large ball of fire. (*Damaged*).
7. North Carolina #2 Object. Round. White.
8. North Carolina #3 Object. Shooting star.
9. North Carolina #4 Object. Flying saucer.
10. North Carolina #5 Object. Huge ball with a tail. Greenish-blue.
11. Rescue Object #1. WDC. Ball. Yellow-white
12. Rescue Object #2. WDC. Oblong. Green.
13. Rescue Object #3. WDC. Balloon/Onion-shaped. Greenish-blue w/red trailer.
14. Rescue Object #4. WDC. #1 Jet-shaped. White to red w/ green tail.
15. Rescue Object #5. VA. Ball-shaped/ a little flattened. Luminous green w/a short orange tail.
16. Rescue Object #6. WDC. Ball. Bluish-yellow w/yellow tail.
17. Rescue Object #7. WDC. (Georgetown). #2 Jet-shaped. Light green-flame color.
18. Rescue Object #8. WDC. Ball. Silvery-white w/ red-orange tail.
19. Rescue Object #9. VA. Oblong. Greenish-white w/ a white rim.
20. Rescue Object #10. MD. Oval. Bright blue and green white in center w/blue-green tail. Size of an automobile. (This thing was being flown).
21. Rescue Object #11. MD. Round and large. Light blue w/light blue- green tail.
22. Rescue Object #12. VA. Round front that tapered to a point. Yellowish-white.
23. Middletown, PA #2 Object. # 13 Rescue Object. Round. Bright white light that dimmed. 3-4 minute sighting. (Olmsted AFB).
24. Allen, MD Object. Round object. With streamers, flashing green, white light with red rim. (35-minute sighting).
25. Claymont, DL. Top-shaped. Slightly smaller than a dirigible.

LOCATIONS WHERE THE OBJECTS WERE SIGHTED DURING A 21-HOUR FLAP

The following Master List indicates the 116 locations where the 25 UFOs passed over, crash-landed or landed in ten east coast states over a 21-hour period. The locations are listed in a chronological order from the first to last sighting of that day.

Four of the twenty-five objects seen that night were damaged and sighted repeatedly as they flew over various locations and made crash- landings. I was able to track each of their flight paths and courses as they flew across the United States. Those damaged objects have been given designated names and title headings. They are as follows:

1. The Tennessee #1 Object.
2. The Baltimore #2 Object.
3. The Washington, DC. #3 Object.
4. The North Carolina #1 Object.

The locations where these 4-damaged objects were sighted as they traveled along their flight paths are listed in sequential order. I have also listed and given title headings to the three strategic "Rescue" missions that also occurred that night, The Extraction Rescue Mission, #1 Search and Rescue Mission and #2 Search and Rescue Mission.

THE MASTER LIST

1. Bladensburg, OH. Object. (1:30 A.M. EST).
2. Middletown, PA. #1 Object. (Olmsted AFB). (2:35 A.M. EST)

THE TENNESSEE #1 OBJECT-*DAMAGED*
Target: Oak Ridge National Laboratory. Oak Ridge, Tennessee

The Wilmington Journal. Wilmington, DL. September 13, 1952. "Fiery Object in Sky Stirs 'Saucer' Reports in 4 States. Baltimore, Sept. 13 (AP)…The streak of fire was reported over Baltimore shortly after dusk about 8 p.m. EDT…A ball of fire seen in the sky over Kingsport, Tenn., about the same time, set off a search for a wrecked plane."

The Kingsport Times-News. Kingsport, TN. September 14, 1952. "A brilliant ball of fire which flashed across the sky in the vicinity of Kingsport at about 7 p.m. Friday put the top on all previous 'strange object reports.

The Kingsport Times-News. Kingsport, TN. September 13, 1952. "Sky Object Seen Here-Search Ends For Wrecked Aircraft… "Reportedly fell to the ground somewhere in the Bloomingdale area about 7 p.m. Friday [7:00 P.M. EST/8:00 P.M. EDT]."

The Kingsport Times-News. Kingsport, TN. September 13, 1952. "Sky Object Seen Here-Search Ends For Wrecked Aircraft…Mrs. Lucille Kenny, also of the Moccasin Gap section, said she saw something which she thought was a 'plane on fire' near her home at 7:15 p.m. [EST]."

3. Roanoke, VA. (Approximately 6:50 P.M. EST/7:50 P.M. EDT).
4. Pulaski, VA.
5. Johnson City, VA. (Tri-Cities Airport sighting).
6. Arcadia, TN. Bloomingdale area. *(Crash-landed about 7:00 P.M. EST)*.
7. Kingsport, TN.
8. Rogersville, TN.
9. Moccasin Gap, TN. *(Crash-landed/went down at 7:15)*.
10. Wadlow Gap, TN.
11. Elizabethton, TN.
12. Greensboro, NC. (Later sighting which occurred at 7:45 P.M. that involved the damaged North Carolina #1 Object).

THE BALTIMORE # 2 OBJECT-*DAMAGED*
Target: Wright Patterson AFB. Dayton, Ohio

The Mercury. Pottstown, Pennsylvania. September 13, 1952. "Reported Plane Crash is Just Another Meteor. Sept. 13. Dr. I.M. Levitt, director of Fels Planetarium in Philadelphia said a meteor passed over the area at the time, lasting three seconds...Mrs. Eva Hilbert, Monocacy, reported to *The Mercury* soon after she had seen the 'flaming object' in the sky...Edward Rea, 783 Haycreek Road, Birdsboro, saw the meteor."

The Baltimore Sun. Baltimore, Md. September 13, 1952. "Scores of Baltimoreans See Meteor-Like Object in Skies...The 'mass of flaming, incandescent material' which flashed across the sky about 8 p.m. [8:00 P.M. EDT/7:00 P.M. EST]."

The New Haven Register. New Haven, Ct. September 13, 1952. "Fiery Object Streaks Across Skies Of 4 States – A Meteor? Could Be. Baltimore, Sept. 13 (AP)...The streak of fire was reported over Baltimore shortly after dusk about 8 p.m. E.D.T. [7:00 P.M. EST]."

13. Philadelphia, PA (Fels Planetarium Sighting)
14. Monocacy, PA.
15. Birdsboro, PA
16. Baltimore, MD. (Approximately 6:50 P.M. EST/ 7:50 P.M. EDT).
17. Catonsville, MD.
18. Frederick, MD.
19. Hagerstown, MD.
20. Cumberland, MD.
21. Garret County, MD.
22. Preston County, WV.
23. Morgantown, MD.
24. Fairmont, WV.
25. Columbus, OH.
26. Zanesville, OH.
27. St. Clairsville, OH.
28. Wheeling-Ohio County Airport. (Near mid-air collision).
29. Oglebay Park Resort, WV. *(Crash-landed).*

The Charleston Daily Mail. Charleston, WV. September 13, 1952. "Fiery Objects Flash Across Sky In W. Va. – Many From Wheeling To Bluefield Puzzled Over Weird Spectacle...Residents from Wheeling, McMechen, Fairmont, Parkersburg, Elkins, Morgantown and Bluefield all reported fiery objects in the sky about 7 p.m. [7:00 P.M. EST/8:00 P.M. EDT]."

30. Wheeling, WV.
31. McMechen
32. Parkersburg, WV. (Wood County Airport sighting).
33. Nitro, WV.

34. St. Albans, WV. *(Crash-landed).*
35. Charleston, WV. Spring Hill Cemetery
36. West of Charleston, WV.
37. Charleston, WV. South Hills. *(Crash-landed).*
38. Charleston, WV. Watt Powell Park area. *(Crash-landed).*
39. Ward, WV.
40. Cabin Creek, WV. *(Crash-landed).*
41. Bluefield, WV.
42. Greensboro, NC area. (Later sighting by crew of a USAF B-25 plane that occurred at 8:03 P.M. EST).

THE WASHINGTON, DC. # 3 OBJECT-*DAMAGED*
Target: Washington, DC. and Flatwoods, West Virginia.

Project Blue Book 10073 Record Card. "Actually the object was the well known Washington area meteor of 12 Sep. landing near Flatwoods, W. Va. Have confirmation of an Astronomy Club from Akron, Ohio. Letter from E.C. [blacked-out] President – Akron Ast. Club."

Akron Astronomy Club Report. "FIREBALL – SEPTEMBER 12, 1952…Time: Approximately 7:00 P.M. E.S.T."

43. Washington, DC. (Shortly after 7:00 P.M. EST/8:00 P.M. EDT).
44. Front Royal, VA. (Pilot sighting from small plane).
45. Elkins, WV.
46. Burnsville, WV.
46. Heaters, WV.
48. Flatwoods, WV. *(Crash-landed at 7:25 P.M. EST. "Flatwoods Monster").*
49. Little Birch, WV.
50. Frametown, WV. *(Crash-landed on James Knoll).*

EXTRACTION RESCUE MISSION

THE TWELVE RESCUE UFOS
7:00 P.M. EST – 7:10 P.M. EST/8:00 P.M. EDT - 8:10 P.M. EDT.
These Twelve Rescue Objects Descended upon Washington, DC, Virginia and Maryland when the damaged Washington, DC. #3 Object Passed West Over Washington, DC.

The Baltimore Sun. Baltimore, Md. September 13, 1952. "Scores of Baltimoreans See Meteor-Like Object in Skies…As it turns out, the object was not a source of wonderment to Maryland alone. Associated Press reports early this morning told of 'similar objects seen all over Virginia.' And the United States Army Intelligence in Washington received reports about the sky visitor from that city, as well as nearby points in Maryland."

51. #1 Rescue Object. Washington, DC. (7:00 P.M. EST/8:00 P.M. EDT).
52. #2 Rescue Object. Washington, DC. (7:00 P.M. EST/8:00 P.M. EDT).

53. #2b. 2nd sighting. Mclean, VA. (7:00 P.M. EST/8:00 P.M. EDT).
54. #3 Rescue Object. Washington, DC. (7:00 P.M. EST/8:00 P.M. EDT).
55. #4 Rescue Object. #1 Jet-shaped Object. Washington., DC. (7:00 P.M. EST/8:00 P.M. EDT).
56. #5 Rescue Object. Arlington, VA. (7:00 P.M. EST/8:00 P.M. EDT).
57. #6 Rescue Object. Washington, DC. (7:00 P.M. EST/8:00 P.M. EDT).
58. #7 Rescue Object. #2 Jet–shaped Object. Washington, DC. Georgetown. (7:01 P.M. EST/8:01 P.M. EDT).
* #7b. 2nd sighting. Georgetown. (7:02 P.M. EST/8:00 P.M. EDT).
59. #8 Rescue Object. Washington, DC. (7:03 P.M. EST/8:03 P.M. EDT).
60. #9 Rescue Object. Fairfax, VA. (7:03 P.M. EST/8:03 P.M. EDT).
61. #10 Rescue Object. District Heights, MD. (7:04 P.M. EST/8:04 P.M. EDT).
62. #11 Rescue Object. Beltsville, MD. (7:05 P.M. EST/8:05 P.M. EDT).
63. #12 Rescue Object. Alexandria, VA. (7:10 P.M. EST/8:10 P.M. EDT).

THE #2 JET-SHAPED OBJECT - # 7 RESCUE OBJECT

The New Haven Register. New Haven, Ct. September 13, 1952. "Fiery Object Streaks Across Skies Of 4 States – A Meteor? Could Be. Baltimore, Sept. 13 (AP)… LIKE A FLAMING JET. Persons throughout Virginia saw what they described as 'a big star,' 'a flying saucer' and something 'like a flaming jet plane.' They said it ranged in color from pale yellow to greenish and reddish and was noiseless. It moved from east to west."

The Columbus Citizen. Columbus, Oh. September 13, 1952. "Fireballs Shower City Area…Residents in Harrisonburg, Va., reported a 'cigar-shaped object trailing blue-green flame' streaked across the sky."

64. Harrisonburg, VA.
65. Har, WV.
66. Flatwoods, WV. (Dropped homing beacon on Fisher Farm between 6:50 P.M. and 6:55 P.M. EST).
* Washington, DC. # 7 Rescue Object. (Georgetown, 7:01 P.M. EST and 7:02 P.M. EST. #53).
67. Freeport, OH. Piedmont Lake. Later sighting. *(Landed)*.

#1 SEARCH AND RESCUE MISSION

THE FIVE NORTH CAROLINA OBJECTS.

The Damaged Southern Object Descended over South Carolina and crash-landed on a Farm in Florence. It then ascended and flew northeast towards Lumberton, then rendezvoused with two other Objects and descended over North Carolina at approximately 6:50 P.M.EST/7:50 P.M. EDT.

Those three Objects Flew Northwest towards West Virginia to Rendezvous with the Westbound Washington, DC. #3 Damaged Object at Flatwoods. The Fourth NC Object Descended over Flat Rock and then Flew to Eastern Ohio to Partake in a Second Search

306

and Rescue Mission. The Fifth NC Object Patrolled the North Carolina Escape Corridor and descended about one hour later.

THE NORTH CAROLINA #1 OBJECT-*DAMAGED*

68 Florence, SC. (Crash-landed on Barnes Farm)
69. Mars Bluff, SC.
70. Lumberton, NC. (At about 7:00 O'clock [7:00 P.M. EST]).
71. Greensboro, NC. (CIRVIS report made by USAF C-46 crew).
72. Reidsville, NC. (6:50 P.M. EST)
73. Draper, NC.
74. Gauley Mills, WV. ** (Flew in formation with two other objects).
75. Flatwoods, WV. (Failed rendezvous with the damaged # 3 Washington, DC. Object on the Fisher Farm).
76. Holly, WV. *(Crash-landed)*.
77. Sugar Creek, WV. *(Crash-landed along the Elk River)*.
78. Frametown, WV. *(Crash-landed along the Elk River)*.
79. Duck Creek, WV. (Encounter with automobile).
80. Greensboro, NC. (Later sighting which occurred at 7:45 P.M. EST that involved the damaged Tennessee # 1 Object).

THE NORTH CAROLINA #2 OBJECT

81. Lumberton, NC. (On Friday afternoon, Sept. 12, 1952 at dusk).
82. Reidsville, NC. (6:50 P.M. EST)
** Gauley Mills, WV. (The location of this sighting is previously listed. This object flew in formation with the two other North Carolina objects).
83. Heaters, WV.

THE NORTH CAROLINA #3 OBJECT

84. Winston Salem, NC. (At about 7 o'clock [At about 7:00 P.M. EST]).
85. Mt. Airy, NC.
** Gauley Mills, WV. (The location of the sighting is previously listed. This object flew in formation with the other two other North Carolina objects).
86. Braxton County Airport

THE NORTH CAROLINA #4 OBJECT

87. Flat Rock, NC.
88. Lafferty, OH.

THE NORTH CAROLINA #5 OBJECT

89. Lake Waccamaw, NC. (2359z [6:59 P.M.EST]).

90. Elizabethtown, NC.
91. Fayetteville, NC. (After 1900 Eastern Time [After 7:00 P.M. EST]).
92. Raleigh, NC.
93. Rocky Mount, NC.
94. Arcola, NC.

#2 SEARCH AND RESCUE MISSION.

For Approximately Two Hours, between 7:05 P.M. and 9:00 P.M. EST/8:05 P.M. and 10:00 P.M. EDT, Several Objects Descended Over PA, WV and OH. They were in Search of a Stranded Occupant from the Damaged Baltimore #2 Object that Went Down in Oglebay Park, WV.

The Wheeling Intelligencer. Wheeling, WV. September 13, 1952. "Mystery Lights Zip Through Skies Here Causing Mild Furor…The Intelligencer editorial room was swamped with calls between 8 and 10:00 o'clock from residents on both sides of the river."

The Times-Leader. Martins Ferry-Bellaire, Ohio. September 13, 1952. "Authorities Probe Flashes In Area Skies… Civil Aeronautics authorities officers were still trying to find an explanation today for a flurry of bright flashes seen by hundreds of people in the skies of eastern Ohio and three other states last night shortly after 8 p.m…All witnesses agreed that the blazing objects, planes, meteors, rockets, or whatever, zoomed horizontally and awful low."

The Wheeling Intelligencer. Wheeling, WV. September 13, 1952. "Mystery Lights Zip Through Skies Here Causing Mild Furor…A series of brilliant flames flashed across the sky over the Ohio River last night and jittery valleyites feared they were in for another siege of 'flying saucers.'"

The Columbus Citizen. Columbus, Ohio. September 13, 1952. "Fireballs Shower City Area…Reports of 'balls of fire' and 'flaming planes' deluged newspaper offices and police stations in four states Friday night…Police in the 'bombarded' states reported they were searching the countryside for some clue to the strange phenomenon."

The Boston Globe. Boston, Massachusetts. September 13, 1952. "Four States 'Bombarded' by Meteor-Like Objects. Pittsburgh. (UP) Authorities sought an explanation today for the flurry of meteor-like objects sighted over four states that caused jittery citizens to report airplanes plunging from the skies in flames…Descriptions of the weird spectacle varied widely but all witnesses agreed the blazing objects moved horizontally and 'awfully low.'"

Two UFOs involved in this episode over Ohio are previously listed on #67 and #88:

*** *Freeport, OH. #2 Jet-shaped Object. (Landing 7:05 P.M. EST/8:05 P.M. EDT).*
 *** *Lafferty, OH. The NC #4 Object. (7:05 P.M. EST/8:05 P.M. EDT).*

95. West Liberty, WV. Rescue Mission #5 Object. (7:06 P.M. EST/8:06 P.M. EDT).
96. Glenwood Heights, WV.
97. Triadelphia, WV. *(Landing)*.
98. Wheeling, WV.
99. Akron, OH.
100. Chillicothe, OH. *(Landing about 8:30 P.M. EST/9:30 P.M. EDT)*.
101. Frankfort, OH. *(Landing)*.
102. Martins Ferry, OH. *(Landing on hill between radio tower transmitter)*.
103. Millwood, OH. *(Landing)*.
104 Mount Vernon, OH. *(Landing)*.
105. Pittsburgh, PA.
106. Uniontown, PA
107. Bitner, PA.
108. Markleysburg, PA. *(Landing in woods near residence)*
109. Smock, PA.
110. Franklin Township
111. Smithfield, PA.
112. Greensboro, PA.
113. Middletown, PA #2 Object. (8:07 P.M. EST Olmsted AFB).

THE LAST SEPTEMBER 12, 1952 UFO SIGHTINGS

114. Allen, MD. (Sighting lasted from 9:30 P.M. until 10:05 P.M. EST).
115. Claymont, DL.
116. Flatwoods, West Virginia. Rescue Mission #5 Object- VA.
    (Object was sighted as it circled over the Fisher Farm for 15-minutes between 10:30 P.M. - 11:00 P.M. EST. It was previously sighted over *Arlington, VA,* and *West Liberty, WV*).

Fireballs Shower City Area

Meteor Fall Blamed As Cause of Scare

Reports of "balls of fire" and "flaming planes" deluged newspaper offices and police stations in four states Friday night.

SHOCKING

Four Frederick farmers saw "a ball shooting across the horizon."

Near Washington, three United Press correspondents said it was like this:

• "A rocket with a fiery tail . . . It shocked us, it looked so close." (Frank Eleazer.)

• "A big magnesium flare . . . It gave off sparks." (Robert Loftus.)

• It plunged out of the sky "very fast," like a plane shot down in the war. It was trailing a tail of flame."—(John A. Goldsmith.)

George Lincoln, of 756 S. Greenbrier-st, Arlington, saw something "about as big as a washtub. I was sure it was going to crash, some place," he said.

THE FOUR-DAMAGED OBJECTS

The 13 Crash-Landing Sites of the 4 Damaged Objects

1. Tennessee #1 Object. Arcadia, Tennessee.
2. Tennessee #1 Object. Moccasin Gap, Tennessee.

3. Baltimore #2 Object. Oglebay Park, West Virginia.
4. Baltimore #2 Object. St. Albans, West Virginia.
5. Baltimore #2 Object. Charleston, West Virginia. South Hills.
6. Baltimore #2 Object. Charleston, West Virginia. Watt Powell Park area.
7. Baltimore #2 Object. Cabin Creek, West Virginia.

8. Washington, DC. #3 Object. Flatwoods, West Virginia. Fisher Farm.
9. Washington, DC. #3 Object. Frametown, West Virginia. James Knoll

10. North Carolina #1 Object. Florence, South Carolina. Barnes Farm.
11. North Carolina #1 Object. Holly, West Virginia.
12. North Carolina #1 Object. Sugar Creek, West Virginia. Elk River area.
13. North Carolina #1 Object. Frametown, West Virginia. Elk River area.

KEY QUOTES DESCRIBING THE 4-DAMAGED OBJECTS

Locations of the Sightings Are Listed in Sequential Order

THE TENNESSEE # 1 OBJECT

Kingsport, Tennessee. "A brilliant ball of fire which flashed across the sky in the vicinity of Kingsport at about 7 p.m. Friday put the top on all previous 'strange object reports.

Arcadia, Tennessee. "A flying object... 'big as a car with a flaming exhaust' reportedly fell to the ground somewhere in the Bloomingdale area about 7 p.m."

Arcadia, Tennessee. "Mrs. Taylor and her husband G.W. Taylor saw the object from their front porch. She described it as a 'flaming streak of silver.'"

Arcadia, Tennessee. "It was shining bright and big as a car and when it went down over the hill back of Joe Newland's tobacco patch it sprouted a tail."

Arcadia, Tennessee. "Since most of the early reports came from Arcadia about five miles out the Bloomingdale Road, Tennessee Highway Patrolman and county officers, led by people who saw the object, formed search parties to comb the area. An ambulance and the Kingsport Life Saving and First Aid Crew stood by after patrolmen reported sighting what they believed to be distress flares from the ground where the object was said to have fallen."

Rogersville, Tennessee. "A ball of fire *resembling* a meteor passed over there about 7 p.m. Miller said it looked 'like a full moon with a tail on it.'"

Moccasin Gap, Tennessee. "Saw something which she thought was a 'plane on fire' near her home at 7:15 p.m."

Moccasin Gap, Tennessee. "Six were talking together on the front porch when they saw an object 'almost big as a full moon and with a fluorescent glow' streak past. Bowlin said the 'thing seemed to burst as it went down over some trees on top of a mountain and left only a short glowing trail."

Moccasin Gap, Tennessee. "Reports throughout the evening placed the fallen object 'just over the ridge' in Wadlow Gap, Moccasin Gap."

Greensboro, North Carolina. Later sighting which occurred at 7:45 P.M. EST that involved the damaged North Carolina # 1 Object: "Saw a huge light proceeding in front of a fiery ball object [damaged #1 North Carolina Object]."

THE BALTIMORE #2 OBJECT

Monocacy, Pennsylvania. "Mrs. Eva Hilbert, Monocacy, reported to *The Mercury* soon after she had seen the 'flaming object' in the sky.'"

Baltimore, Maryland. "A fiery object that streaked through the night sky with a 'greenish-white light.'"

Baltimore, Maryland. "Suddenly this thing came swooping down from the eastern skies. It looked like it was right above the housetops. It was a ball of bright greenish fire with a long tail."

Baltimore, Maryland. "I thought it was a flying saucer. I thought it was a flare at first-that is, I thought it was a flare until the darned thing swooped down-and then up again. It seemed to follow the contours of the road. (Army veteran)."

Baltimore, Maryland. "To Herman Rosenthal when he first saw it swinging 'treetop height' near his home in the 2700 block of Springhill Avenue, it looked at first, like a 'plane on fire.' He soon realized that it was no plane, however. 'But it was that big.' He said."

Catonsville, Maryland. "Numerous Catonsville residents saw it too. Most of them thought it would hit the ground in that area. It didn't though."

Morgantown, West Virginia. "A large ball of fire."

Fairmont, West Virginia. "About 40 persons in the Fairmont area said the object looked like a spotlight with a greenish tail and was traveling from 300 t0 500 miles per hour."

Zanesville, Ohio. "In Zanesville, CAA officials at the Municipal Airport said an Army pilot at 10,000 feet reported what looked like a flaming plane."

St. Clairsville, Ohio. "Flashed over the west horizon, sped away toward the east, broke into several small pieces and vanished in a sparkling shower."

Oglebay Park, West Virginia. "A luminous ball that was moving diagonally...there was no noise she [witness] stated and was confident it was not a plane. Apparently it should have come down in the vicinity of Oglebay Park."

Wheeling, West Virginia. "A 'Brilliant flaming object' blazing across the sky at a low altitude."

McMechon, West Virginia. "Appeared without any noise and was spitting blue and white flame from one end. It disappeared over the Riley hill at McMechon."

Parkersburg, West Virginia. Wood County Airport: "A bright ball of fire flashing through the sky around dusk and disappearing to the south or southeast. According to the spotters, the thing seemed to disintegrate in their general area."

St. Albans, West Virginia. "[Witnesses] declared they saw a lighted object float lazily to the ground and disappear.

Nitro, West Virginia. "I told the passengers in the car to look. My sister-in-law said she saw something dropping from the thing. It was a greenish color; shaped like a top...It seemed to disappear about the edge of the entrance to the rubber plant."

Charleston, West Virginia. Spring Hill Cemetery: "Suddenly this enormous light appeared and veered in the general direction of Shadowlawn or Meadowbrook. It looked like a big star and was brighter than anything I had seen before. It made sort of a 'putt-putt' noise. One corner seemed to fall off. And I saw sparks for a moment. Then it seemed to just disappear." Another report stated, "The object gave off a 'putt-putt' noise and [the witness] said a piece fell off near the airport."

Charleston, West Virginia. West of Charleston: "Mrs. Alice Williams-informed us [Ivan T. Sanderson and associate] that she had witnessed the disintegration of still another fiery object in the air at a height of not more than a few hundred feet, to the west of Charleston...when the object disintegrated 'a lot of ashes fell to the ground.'"

Charleston, West Virginia. "In Charleston, a number of persons said they saw what looked to be a bright ball of fire apparently fall to earth. Varying reports described the object from a weird green to a yellowish orange."

Charleston, West Virginia. South Hills: "It was very close and at first I thought it was an airplane in trouble. Then it appeared to be a very bright light and it looked as though some little pieces fell from it. It seemed to fall right in South Hills."

Charleston, West Virginia. Watt Powell Park area: "It appeared to be falling in a very slight arc to the south-in the hills back of Watt Powell Park. It looked like a giant skyrocket and there was a very bright light. The light seemed to go out just before the thing hit and it looked like a very, very faint puff of smoke rose where it landed."

Charleston, West Virginia. "The object was variously reported to have made hissing sounds and to have 'backed up and started over.'"

Charleston, West Virginia. "It...had sparkles all around it. It was white. I was standing out in our front yard and it went to the right behind a neighbor's house."

Cabin Creek, West Virginia. "It was round and yellowish-orange in color and it looked like it dropped in Mill hollow or the hollow to the right. It seemed to be about 20 or 30 feet across. I don't think it was a meteor because it looked like it stopped right in mid-air just before it came down."

Greensboro, North Carolina area. 8:03 p.m. EST: "Flying Object Report: One oblong fiery object, whitish glow trailing red sparks was observed from a B-25 Aircraft... Object was observed for approximately 15 seconds."

THE WASHINGTON, DC. #3 OBJECT

Washington, DC. United Press correspondent, John A. Goldsmith: "It plunged out of the sky very fast, like a plane shot down in the war. It was trailing a tail of flame."

Washington, DC. "Residents of Montgomery County-said it descended at a 45-degree angle about 1000 feet above the ground."

Washington, DC. "I was sure it was going to crash, some place."

Washington, DC. United Press correspondent, Robert Loftus: "A big magnesium flare...it gave off sparks."
Washington, DC. "Green Fireball...Round to tear drop."

Washington, DC. "A brilliant flame."

Washington, DC. "The blazing object moved horizontally across the heavens and came 'awfully low.'"

Washington, DC. Radio broadcast: "Most witnesses agreed that the blazing object moved horizontally and came 'awfully low.'"

Washington, DC. "Flaming Object Seen at Capital."

Washington, DC. Radio broadcast: "A flaming object whizzed through the sky over Washington tonight."

Front Royal, Virginia. "A pilot enroute to Wheeling from the east reported sighting the object from the vicinity of Front Royal, Va. over this general area. He noted it was, 'tremendously large' and 'seemed to disappear in a bunch of sparks.'"

Elkins, West Virginia. "Fiery object."

Burnsville, West Virginia. "It looked like a ball. It wasn't on fire, but it was reddish-orange and went very fast but I knew as low as it was, just clearing the tree tops, that it was going to land someplace close, someplace very close in our county."

Heaters, West Virginia. Mrs. May: "Jerry Marples from Heaters called the Sheriff's office and said there was a flying saucer coming down behind the hill in Flatwoods."

Flatwoods, West Virginia. "We all looked up and saw a ball of fire coming from over the mountain here. It was a round ball of fire...oval-shaped. Flames were trailing behind it... It was slowing down as it was coming in, decelerating. It came down and lit on the other side of the mountain right up there."

Flatwoods, West Virginia. "A pear shaped glowing red object, which was pulsing from cherry red to bright orange...It stopped and sank slowly down the hill and they [boys] could see this light pulsing behind the crest of the hill."

Flatwoods, West Virginia. "It was an oblong-shaped object lit up...It had a clearer, brighter illuminated light from the top and kind of orange-red. Then as it came down a little farther, the object was a little duller orange. The top of it had the reflection of a light that I would describe as a mercury vapor light...It was just clearing the tree tops, just a little above the height of the trees there. I had the general feeling that whatever it was had landed...I knew it was up there. And I knew with the reflection, the light stopped there, and I could see the reflection of it through the trees. It was very obvious to see."

Flatwoods, West Virginia. "Well, it landed gently and undoubtedly because it didn't go down in the dirt or anything like that."

Frametown, West Virginia. "Landed on an overgrown and isolated field at the top of a hill known as James' Knoll or Knob but that, although seen by the two young James boys, it had not been investigated because it had been regarded as a fireball."

Florence, South Carolina. "A search by ground and air will begin this morning for remnants of a meteor believed to have fallen north of Florence last night. The meteor thought to be "four to five feet in diameter" and weighing possibly 50 tons was reported to have fallen on farmland near the residence of Smith Barnes on the Douglas Street Extension...Barnes said the object, first glowing red and then flaring brilliant white as it approached the ground, moved earthward at a 45-degree angle. It made no noise but lighted up sides of trees indicating it might have fallen in woods about 1,000 feet from the Barnes home. The highway patrol conducted an initial investigation but found nothing."

Lumberton, North Carolina. "I saw a seeming ball of fire. It seemed to be a bright glowing mass with a contrasting tail at least three times the diameter of the ball...traveling on a downward plane. When it got below tree level, it seemed to level off...The mass or object appeared round and flat with the flat side down...I have seen falling stars and meteors but this was larger and different from any that I have seen. The object appeared to be a mile and a half away and 12 to 15 feet in diameter. "

Greensboro, North Carolina. CIRVIS report made by USAF C-46 crew: "Unidentified flying object flying over Greensboro, North Carolina." [Pilot] Observed one unidentified flying object...After object had passed observing aircraft it appeared as a round ball of fire which then erupted into sparks and disappeared...Also observing phenomena were persons in control tower at Greensboro Highpoint Airport."

Reidsville, North Carolina. "It was a round object, reddish in color and leaving a trail of fire."

Reidsville, North Carolina. "Object passed over them [witnesses] trailing fire."

Draper, North Carolina. "A large light bulb...it flew low straight across the sky and was traveling at a fast rate of speed. The red streak it left looked like fire."

Gauley Mills, West Virginia. Flying in formation with two other objects: "They were large and very bright. They were flying in a triangular formation...They were not airplanes or jets-there were no contrails."

Flatwoods, West Virginia. Failed rendezvous with the Mid-Atlantic #3 Damaged Object on the Fisher Farm: "A fiery object coming over the horizon though in a different direction than the others reported. It had not landed but had gone across the sky. It went over the Bailey Fisher cistern...a piece of fire broke off. As it neared the horizon toward the Sutton Airport, it exploded and went out.

Holly, West Virginia. Crash-landed: "One went down over in Holly."

Sugar Creek, West Virginia. Along the Elk River: "Woodrow Eakle [sic Eagle] of Duck along the Braxton-Clay line was traveling toward Flatwoods as the aerial phenomenon made its appearance. He reported to Braxton County Sheriff Robert Carr a small airplane had crashed against a mountainside. A later search failed to disclose any remnants of wreckage." Another report stated, "He saw a flaming object, which he thought from his army experience to be a small piper plane, shoot over a saddle to his left, cross the main road, and the rail beyond, and crash into the wooded side of a steep hill immediately to the south."

Sugar Creek, West Virginia. Along the Elk River: "A flaming bucket with a tail...smoke that hung about the face of the hill. There had been a 'strong smell of woods burning.'"

Frametown, WV. Along the Elk River: "A piper cub plane, an excited hitchhiker was reporting, had crashed into a hillside near Frametown and was burning. He had seen it from a car which he had received a 'lift' then driven to the first available phone to report this incident. Sheriff Carr and a deputy [Burnell Long] rushed seventeen miles to the scene but could find no trace of the burning plane."

Duck Creek, WV. Encounter with an automobile: "I heard a man and wife were driving through Duck [Creek] when they saw the thing. She was scared to death and in the hospital for about two days." Another report stated, "They said it [UFO] shut the engine off and they said they couldn't get it started again. Then when it left, they went up the road."

Greensboro, North Carolina. Later sighting which occurred at 7:45 P.M. EST that involved the damaged Tennessee #1 Object: "Ball of fire in rotation...it traveled close to the ground. Saw a huge light [damaged Tennessee #1 Object] proceeding in front of a fiery ball object."

UFO DESCRIPTIONS

Descriptions of the UFOs sighted over nine east coast states on September 12, 1952:

1. Aerial object.
2. Airplane in trouble.
3. Aircraft plunging from the skies in flames.
4. Ball shooting across the horizon.
5. Ball. White and spherical-shaped.
6. Ball. Flaming ball.
7. Ball. Yellow and white.
8. Ball-shaped object.
9. Ball. Green and a little flattened.
10. Ball of greenish fire with a long tail. It looked like it was right above the treetops.
11. Balloon-shaped, onion. (Size of a dirigible).
12. Ball of fire. It was barely clearing the treetops.

13. Ball of fire and brilliant.
14. Ball of fire and bright.
15. Balls of fire.
16. Balls Of Fire Over Pittsburgh.
17. Big magnesium flare. It gave off sparks.
18. Blazing objects.
19. Blazing matter.
20. Big star.
21. Big star that made a putt-putt noise and pieces fell off.
22. Bright blue. Bluish green tail. (Size of automobile).
23. Bright lights.
24. Cigar-shaped object trailing a blue green flame.
25. Exploding plane.
26. Fiery object.
27. Fiery objects.
28. Fireballs Shower City Area.
29. Flame Over Washington.
30. Flames, a series of brilliant.
31. Flaming object.
32. Flashes in Area Skies.
33. Flashing light.
34. Flashing meteor.
35. Flying objects.
36. Flying saucer.
37. Flying saucer. The darned thing swooped down-and then up again. It seemed to follow the contours of the road. (Army veteran).
38. Frying pan shape. Very white and bright. Sparks shooting from the tail.
39. Great big flare. Low on the horizon.
40. Green ball of fire.
41. Green object.
42. Green light.
43. Greenish-colored object.
44. Greenish-white object.
45. Jet-shaped object. No wings or appendages and shooting balls of fire from back.
46. Jet- shaped. Flaming jet plane.
47. Light. Bright and similar to an automobile headlight.
48. Light, enormous.
49. Lights.
50. Meteor, about ten times as large as the normal sized meteor which you would see in the sky during this time of year… Mass of incandescent flaming material.
51. Meteor. Especially bright and big.
52. Meteor.
53. Meteor. Tremendously large and seemed to disappear in a bunch of sparks. (Pilot sighting from aircraft).
54. Meteor-like object.
55. Meteor-Like Objects, Four States Bombarded by.

56. Meteor shower.
57. Mystery light.
58. Object, nearly clipped the wing of his craft. (Commercial airline pilot).
59. Object. It was lit up brightly…and seemed to have windows on only one side. It circled near the ground for nearly half an hour making very little noise.
60. Object. Made hissing sounds. Backed up and started over.
61. Object. Spotlight with a greenish tail.
62. Object, spitting blue and white fire from one end.
63. Object. The size of a two-car garage.
64. Objects.
65. Objects, flashed by two or three commercial planes while aloft.
66. Oblong-shaped.
67. Oval-shaped. With a blue light. Unconventional maneuvers.
68. Oval-shaped. Greenish-blue and in flames.
69. Oval-shaped. Reddish-orange and in flames.
70. Plane-like. It plunged out of the sky very fast like a plane shot down in the war. It was trailing a tail of flame. (John A. Goldsmith).
71. Plane about to crash.
72. Plane, crashing.
73. Plane fuselage-shaped object, light green in color with flames.
74. Plane afire, crashed to the ground.
75. Plane on fire.
76. Plane on fire, it was big. It was sun colored with a tail.
77. Plane dashing to the ground.
78. Plane on fire going down.
79. Plane in flames.
80. Propane tank-shaped object.
81. Rocket with a fiery tail.
82. Roman candles, objects looked like.
83. Round and yellowish in color. It stopped in mid-air just before it came down.
84. Round and fiery object.
85. Round object with flat side that emitted flames from either side.
86. Round object. White in color.
87. Round object. Blue in color.
88. Round object. Tapered to a point and yellowish-white.
89. Round object. With streamers, flashing green, white light with red rim. (35-minutes).
90. Round thing. Light blue in color.
91. Rocket. Soundless.
92. Something. Witness George Lincoln…I was sure it was going to crash, someplace.
93. Sphere.
94. Sphere-shaped object.
95. Shooting star, larger-than-usual.
96. Skyrocket, that seemed to go out as it fell to earth east of the city.
97. Skyrocket, giant.

98. Skyrocket, enormous.
99. Spinning tops in the sky.
100. Strange lights.
101. Strange objects.
102. Streak of fire.
103. Streak of light.
104. Streak of silver.
105. Tear drop shape.
106. Thing. (Several different references).
107. Thing went down.
108. Top-shaped Object.
109. Two-in-one meteor.
110. Unidentified aerial object.
111. Unidentified flying object.

Four States "Bombarded" by Meteor-Like Objects

PITTSBURGH. Sept. 13 (UP)— Authorities sought an explanation today for the flurry of meteor-like objects sighted over four states that caused jittery citizens to report airplanes plunging from the skies in flames.

Residents of Washington. Pittsburgh, Virginia, West Virginia and Ohio swamped telephone switchboards in police stations. newspaper and government offices last night with reports of "balls of fire" streaking through the heavens.

In Washington. residents of the nation's capital. feared they were in for another siege of "flying saucers."

Civil Aeronautics Administration officials at Wheeling, W. Va., Pittsburgh and Zanesville. O., were deluged with telephone calls reporting great numbers of aircraft plunging from the skies in flames.

Residents in Harrisonburg, Va., reported a "cigar-shaped object trailing blue-green flame", streaked across the sky.

Three commercial pilots told the CAA that meteor-like objects flashed past their planes. One pilot said one nearly hit his ship.

Police in the "bombarded" states reported they were searching the countryside for some clue to the strange phenomenon. However, police officials said they believed the objects sighted were meteors.

A spokesman at the United States Naval Observatory said the reports "sound like a typical meteor display."

Descriptions of the weird spectacle varied widely, but all witnesses agreed the blazing objects moved horizontally and zoomed "awfully low."

W. A. Garrison of West Liberty, W. Va., told the Wheeling Intelligencer newspaper that he sighted objects which resembled "roman candles" at 8:06 p. m.

Mrs. Mary Curitti of McMechen, W. Va., reported an object which "appeared without noise and was spitting blue and white fire from one end."

The Ohio highway patrol reported calls from all over the eastern section of the state.

THE WHITE HOUSE

WASHINGTON

TELEPHONE MEMORANDUM

The President

Sep 12   , 19 52

TIME	NAME	ANSWER
	KC	
10 09	**J. Vivian Truman**	***Out"***
3 47	*Leslie Billes* *out*	"
4 17	*Sister Strats*	"
425	*Norma Archibald Mcleod* *Roosevelt LJ*	*Ca*
450	*Eugene Field*	*Thad Hutchison*
500	*Troy Birnes* *Houston, Texas*	*Collect*
6.12 P	**Kenny Rose** **Padukah Ky**	**unavail**
7.05 P	**Walter Greer** **Baltimore Md.**	"Agent Campion
8.02 P	**Paul Williams** **Norfolk VA**	**unavail**
9.22 P	**Bud (Not Legible)** **Salem Wis**	**unavail**
10.12 P	**Usher** out	"Agent Danta
10.30 P	**John Reances Fort** **Worth Tex**	**unavail**

This graph is a transcribed copy of the "Telephone Memorandum" for President Harry Truman, dated September 12, 1952. The information contained within the graph is entirely handwritten. The information just above the graph, *The President,*" and the date "*Sep. 12, 1952,*" are also handwritten. Three different persons logged in the twelve calls for that day. The times listed are EDT or Eastern Daylight Time.

The person who wrote, "*The President*" and "*Sep. 12, 1952,*" also logged in the first call at 10:09 A.M. This person also wrote their initials "KC" in the NAME section at the top of the graph. The next five telephone phone calls were logged in by a second person. The next six telephone calls were logged in by a third person.

It is interesting to note that during the last six entries between 6:12 P.M. and 10:30 PM., President Truman was unavailable. On two separate occasions, 7:05 P.M. and 10:12 P.M., agents answered the telephone in President Truman's office, first Agent Campion and then Agent Danta. Furthermore, the 10:12 P.M. log "NAME" entry actually states, "usher out."

According to my research and reconstructed events that day, the Gulf of Mexico air battle I first describe off the Florida coast was in progress when Truman was first unavailable at 6:12 p.m. EDT. Later, the "Flame Over Washington," passed over Washington D.C. at about 8:00 P.M. EDT. Between 8:00 P.M. and 8:10 P.M. EDT, twelve other the UFOs descended over the Washington, D.C., Maryland and Virginia areas. During that time at 8:02 P.M., President Truman was unavailable when a phone call was received from Norfolk, Virginia. Furthermore, President Truman was unavailable for the rest of the night on September 12, 1952!

FLAME OVER WASHINGTON

Brilliant Streak Across the Sky Probably a Meteor

WASHINGTON, Sept. 12 (UP)— A brilliant flame, apparently a meteor, flashed across the sky near the nation's capital tonight, prompting jittery Washingtonians to believe they were in for another "flying saucer" scare.

Newspaper offices were flooded by calls from witnesses of the phenomenon who sought an explanation.

Descriptions of the flame varied widely, but they agreed the blazing object moved horizontally across the heavens and came "awfully low."

The National Airport's observation tower said the object was not a "flying saucer." There was no trace of any unidentified object on radar screens.

At the United States Naval Observatory a spokesman said the reports "sound like a typical meteor."

The Air Force said it knew absolutely nothing about the object.

Flaming Object Seen at Capital

Washington, Sept. 12 (INS)—A flaming object believed to have been a falling meteor tonight flashed across the skies startling hundreds of Washington area residents.

The object was seen over the capital and nearby Maryland and Virginia.

The Weather Bureau, Naval Observatory and newspaper offices were jammed with a flood of calls from persons wanting to know what the mysterious looking object was.

National Airport observation tower crewmen said there was no trace of an unidentified object on their radar screens. A U. S. Naval Observatory spokesman said "it sounds like a typical meteor" which probably burned itself up before it hit the ground.

The "Flatwoods Monster" Cutaway Drawings

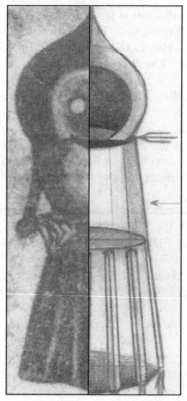

Scale Drawing of Occupants and Craft
Craft Height: 16 Feet Length: 32 Feet

FRIEDMAN VISITS FLATWOODS

In 1996, I met nuclear physicist Stanton T. Friedman at a UFO Conference in Gulf Breeze, Florida and told him about my "Flatwoods Monster" investigation. We spoke for about an hour and he told me he knew about the case and seemed interested in it. We sporadically kept in touch over the years and I met with him one more time in Florida.

In 2002, Flatwoods Mayor Margaret Clise and I invited Mr. Friedman to speak at the "Flatwoods Monster" 50th Anniversary Celebration in Flatwoods. I made the phone call and Mr. Friedman accepted. He went to Flatwoods for the 3-day gathering and lectured twice on two days.

Mrs. Kathleen May and Stanton T. Friedman in Flatwoods

During that time, Mr. Friedman met the late Mrs. May, Eddie May, Fred May and spoke to them at length. On the actual 50th anniversary of the "Flatwoods Monster" incident, September 12, 2002, I led a group of more than fifty people onto the Bailey Fisher Farm with the late Mrs. Clise. I gave a step-by-step guided tour of the farm and retraced the footsteps of the witnesses as they did on the night of their encounter. We went to all of the exact locations involved in the incident and I explained what occurred on the night of September 12, 1952 as it was explained to me by the eyewitnesses that I worked with.

Stanton T. Friedman walked with me as I led the group across the Fisher Farm property. I led the group up onto the mountaintop of the farm where the "Flatwoods Monster" craft had initially landed. On site, Stanton Friedman then spoke to the group about several other 1952 UFO incidents that occurred during the summer of 1952 near the date of the Flatwoods incident.

Mrs. Feschino, Mr. Friedman and Frank C. Feschino, Jr. on the Fisher Farm

At 8:00 p.m., Mr. Friedman stated the time and announced the "Flatwoods Monster" encounter anniversary, "It's 50 years ago – right now!" Stanton and I spoke then to the group and we departed the farm and went back into town.

After we finished the tour, Mr. Friedman had a much better understanding of the events that occurred on the actual night of the encounter. During those three days, I also drove around the area with Mr. Friedman. I showed him some of the other landmark sites that were also involved in the incident on September 12, 1952.

In closing, Mr. Friedman later stated, "I was astonished in talking with Frank and he was sending me material, to see the enormous amount of information that he had collected. Flatwoods is a good solid case. Frank Feschino has collected more data on that case than any other case that I am aware of." Now, ten years later, my ongoing investigation the "Braxton County Monster" has brought you this "Revised" book to commemorate the 60th anniversary of the incident. Did a 32-year-old woman and six country boys all misinterpret an animal or a bird perched in a tree and all describe the same vision of what was called a "monster"? The evidence I have set forth in this case clearly demonstrates beyond a reasonable doubt, no.

The "Braxton County Monster" Photo Gallery

Back row: Jeff Burie, Rick Fisher, Alfred Lehmberg, Kenneth Bailey, Gilbert Bailey, Scott Bailey and Robert Breeze.
Front row: Frank Feschino, Jr., Don Hobar, Scott Ramsey, Suzanne Ramsey, Anthony Sica, Stanton T. Friedman, Larry Bailey and Trent.

In 2007, Frank Feschino, Jr. and West Virginia promoter Larry Bailey of "Brothers Bailey Promotions," held the "Flatwoods Monster 55th Anniversary and Flying Saucer Extravaganza" event in Charleston, West Virginia. The two-day event was held at the Capitol Center Theatre on September 7 - 8, 2007, to commemorate the 55th Anniversary of the "Flatwoods Monster" incident. The show featured several well-known researchers and guests from the UFO and paranormal fields and was a success.

The 2008 "Flatwoods Monster Anniversary and Flying Saucer Extravaganza" event was held in the city of St. Albans, West Virginia. The two-day event was held at the beautiful and newly renovated Alban Art and Conference Center on September 12-13. The show featured West Virginia's two most popular paranormal entities, the "Flatwoods Monster" and "Mothman." UFO investigators Frank Feschino, Jr., Stanton T. Friedman and "Mothman" researcher Jeff Wamsley were the featured guests. With the support of Mayor Dick Callaway, Larry Bailey, Gilbert Bailey, Scott Bailey, Kristen Bailey, Robert Breeze and others, the event was once again a success.

The "Flatwoods Monster" 2007 *UFO Magazine* Cover

326

Feschino Taping the *Monsterquest* TV Show in Flatwoods

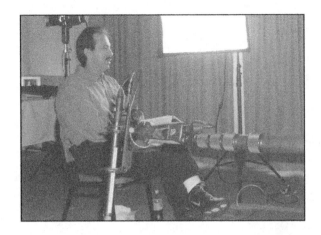

Frank Feschino, Jr. and Travis Walton in Philadelphia during 2012

Frank Standing next to a 1952 Chevy in West Virginia

2012 Daytona Beach *News-Journal* Article

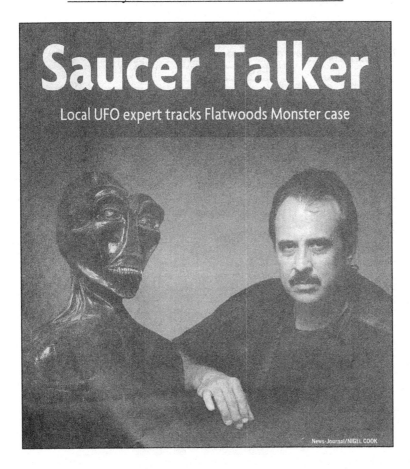

2012 Photo of Frank and Johnny Barker – Investigator of the "Monster" Story for WCHS Radio in 1952

Feschino Displays an Actual 2.75 inch "Mighty Mouse" Rocket that Armed the F-94C "Starfire" Jet

HOLD FOR RELEASE UNTIL 7:00 P.M., EDT, 2 JULY 1952.

#44562 AC - AIR FORCE ANNOUNCES PRODUCTION OF NEW
                AIRCRAFT.
    The Air Force has announced that the new Lockheed
F-94C, "Starfire," an all-weather interceptor, is
in production. The two-place jet, armed with
twenty-four 2.75 inch rockets, was developed from
the earlier F-94A, but has a new type engine,
wing, and electronic system which makes it
virtually a new aircraft.

            WASHINGTON, D.C., 2 JULY 1952

    OFFICIAL AIR FORCE PHOTO, RELEASED BY DEPT. OF DEFENSE

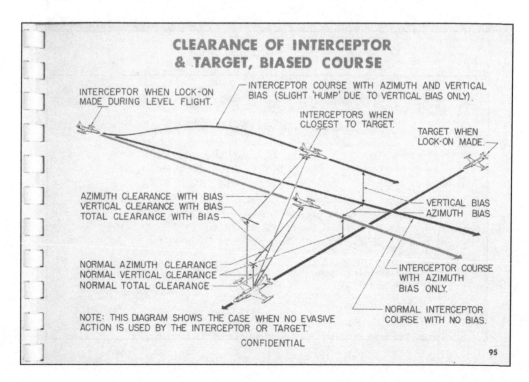

CLEARANCE OF INTERCEPTOR
& TARGET, BIASED COURSE

INTERCEPTOR WHEN LOCK-ON MADE DURING LEVEL FLIGHT.

INTERCEPTOR COURSE WITH AZIMUTH AND VERTICAL BIAS (SLIGHT 'HUMP' DUE TO VERTICAL BIAS ONLY).

INTERCEPTORS WHEN CLOSEST TO TARGET.

TARGET WHEN LOCK-ON MADE.

AZIMUTH CLEARANCE WITH BIAS
VERTICAL CLEARANCE WITH BIAS
TOTAL CLEARANCE WITH BIAS

VERTICAL BIAS
AZIMUTH BIAS

NORMAL AZIMUTH CLEARANCE
NORMAL VERTICAL CLEARANCE
NORMAL TOTAL CLEARANCE

INTERCEPTOR COURSE WITH AZIMUTH BIAS ONLY.

NORMAL INTERCEPTOR COURSE WITH NO BIAS.

NOTE: THIS DIAGRAM SHOWS THE CASE WHEN NO EVASIVE ACTION IS USED BY THE INTERCEPTOR OR TARGET.

CONFIDENTIAL

95

332

WESTERN UNION

CLASS OF SERVICE		SYMBOLS
This is a full-rate Telegram or Cablegram unless its deferred character is indicated by a suitable symbol above or preceding the address.	(40)	DL = Day Letter
		NL = Night Letter
		LC = Deferred Cable
		NLT = Cable Night Letter
		Ship Radiogram

JOSEPH L. EGAN
PRESIDENT

The filing time shown in the date line on telegrams and day letters is STANDARD TIME at point of origin. Time of receipt is STANDARD TIME at point of destination

1952 SEP 15 PM 3 48

AB65

A TP A 62 LONG GOVT PD=MACDILL AFB FLO 15 327P=

ASHBY GLEN JONES=

PALMETTO AVE SANFORD FLO=

DAAD-4 53042. IT IS WITH DEEP REGRET THAT I OFFICIALLY
INFORM YOU THAT YOUR BROTHER, JOHN A. JONES, JR. HAS BEEN
REPORTED AS MISSING. HE WAS ON A LOCAL ROUTINE TRAINING
FLIGHT FROM TYNDALL AFB ON 12 SEPT. 1952 WHEN THE WEATHER
DETERIORATED. ALL AIRCRAFT WERE RECALLED AND INSTRUCED TO
PROCEED TO MOODY AFB. GEORGIA WHICH WAS THE ALTERNATE LANDING
FIELD. YOUR BROTHER WAS UNABLE TO CONTACT MOODY BY RADIO
AND NOTIFIED TYNDALL AFB THAT HE WAS NOT POSITIVE OF HIS
POSITION. THE TYNDALL CONTROL TOWER WAS DIRECTING HIM TO
MACDILL AFB FLO. WHICH WAS THE NEAREST BASE. WHEN HE INFORMED
THEM THAT HIS ENGINE HAD FAILED. IMMEDIATELY THEREAFTER
TYNDALL AFB LOST RADIO CONTACT WITH YOUR BROTHER. NO FURTHER
INFORMATION IS AVAILABLE AT THIS TIME. HOWEVER. PLEASE BE
ASSURED THAT EVERYTHING IS BEING DONE TO LOCATE THE AIRCRAFT.
ADDITIONAL INFORMATION AS IT BECOMES AVAILABLE WILL
IMMEDIATELY BE FORWARDED TO YOU=

GENERAL BENJAMIN W SHIDLAW COMMANDING GENERAL
AIR DEFENSE COMMAND ENT AFB COLORADOSPRINGS COLORADO=

AD AD-4 53042 AFB 12 1952 ENT AFB=

THE COMPANY WILL APPRECIATE SUGGESTIONS FROM ITS PATRONS CONCERNING ITS SERVICE

9-17-52 Letter from Colonel Kleine to the Brother of
Pilot 2nd Lt. John Anderson Jones, Jr.

HEADQUARTERS
3625TH FLYING TRAINING WING
(ADVANCED INTERCEPTOR)
Tyndall Air Force Base, Florida

17 September 1952

Mr. A. G. Jones
2544 Palmetto Avenue
Sanford, Florida

Dear Sir:

    In addition to our telephone conversations, perhaps this letter
will bring a little more light as to just what happened last Friday
afternoon. John and his Radar Observer, Lt Del Curto, were on a
routine weather training mission. When the weather started to become
near our minimums, all of the aircraft were called to come back to the
field. Supervisory personnel in the Control Tower advised John and
three other aircraft to go to Moody Air Force Base about 15 minutes
north of Tyndall; however he was unable to contact the Moody tower
or the Moody Approach Control. He indicated that he was not sure of
his position at 4:20; however, the Tyndall radio directional finding
gave him a steer to Tyndall Air Force Base. MacDill Air Force Base
directional finding was able to pick up John's voice and gave him a
steer also. Shortly afterward, he said he had a flame-out at 15,000
feet.

    Immediately, Air Sea Rescue was alerted for a search. Since last
Friday, almost 125 sorties, which at one time included 52 airplanes,
have been searching. Over 46,000 square miles have been searched with
aircraft and surface vessels. All available leads are being thoroughly
investigated. I wish that I could give you some positive hope and information; however, at this time all I can say is that the Air Force is
doing everything possible to find John and his Radar Observer. Search
is continuing. I am sure that you have received some information from
the newspapers that is not, in all cases, factual information; however,
any leads that we get are thoroughly investigated. For example, today
an area is being searched thoroughly by helicopter in an attempt to run
down a lead that some fishermen possibly heard shouting. Please be
assured that the Air Force will continue to search in hopes of finding
John and his Radar Observer. My deepest sympathies are with you at this
time. In the event we develop any additional leads, I will call you
direct.

                                        Very sincerely yours,

                                        B. T. KLEINE
                                        Colonel, USAF
                                        Commanding

The 3 Mysterious Articles that Appeared on the Same Page of
The Daytona Beach Morning Journal – 9-16-52

RNING JOURNAL Tues., Sept. 16, 1952

UR BOYS

drew J. Goodwin, is serving with the 7th Infantry Division on the central front in Korea.

Pfc. Rufus C. Harper, 332 Harris St., recently qualified as an expert in 81 mm. mortar gunnery at the Berlin Military Post in Germany. Pfc. Harper is a member of the 6th Infantry Regiment, which provides security for American installations in the former German Capital.

EMERGENCIES

Lost Pilot Was From Sanford, AF Reports

PANAMA CITY (AP) — The Air Force yesterday identified a jet pilot and radar operator missing since Friday in a flight from Tyndall Air Force Base here to MacDill Field, Tampa.

The pilot was 2nd Lt. John A. Jones, Jr., 544 Palmetto Ave., Sanford, attached to the Air Defense Command. The radar operator was 2nd Lt. John S. Del Curton, of Pine, Ore., a trainee at Tyndall.

A large scale airsea search has been under way for the two since their F-94 all weather night fighter and interceptor radioed it was having trouble at 5:52 p. m. Friday.

The search continued yesterday after shifting 200 miles west of Tampa in the Gulf of Mexico.

FLORIDA

Repeat Arrest Not Legal, Court Says

TAMPA (AP) — A court ruling yesterday put a crimp in Sheriff Hugh Culbreath's policy of repeatedly arresting on sight every person in Hillsborough County who has a Federal gambling stamp.

Circuit Judge Harry N. Sandler ruled at a habeas corpus hearing that Rolando Rodriguez could not be arrested twice on a vagrancy charge after he purchased a gambling stamp.

Rodriguez was arrested twice Friday, two hours apart, on charges of vagrancy. He put up bonds on both counts. Judge Sandler said he could not be arrested legally the second time.

The first charge, unaffected by the ruling, is to be heard in Peace Justice Court Sept. 23.

Other than persons compelled after Federal Court convictions here to buy gambling stamps, Rodriguez is the first Hillsborough County man to purchase a Federal stamp.

Culbreath had announced a policy that he considered possession of a gambling stamp prima facie evidence of gambling activities.

He emphasized the policy after a verbal tiff with Sheriff Jack Henderson of Dade County.

After scores of Dade County persons obtained gambling stamps on July 31, Henderson was asked why so many in the Miami area were buying stamps and what he did about them.

Henderson said in reply "there are just as many gamblers in Hillsborough County selling bolita, for instance, as there are in Dade County."

Culbreath retorted that if all counties "would adopt the same policy we have in Tampa and Hillsborough County it would go a long way toward stamping out gambling entirely throughout Florida."

That policy, said Culbreath, is to arrest a stamp holder every time he showed up. Rodreguez was the first person he had a chance to try it out on.

16 Year Old Gets Pilot's License

TALLAHASSEE (AP) — Ronnie

Mystery Object Frightened His Cattle

BELLE GLADE (AP) — Floyd Brown, a milker at the Everglades Experiment Station, said yesterday "a large red lighted object" scared some cattle he was trying to milk early Sunday.

Brown told civil defense authorities he went out to milk the cows about 4:30 a.m. and saw "a large red lighted object over the barn in the trees, about 100 feet above the ground."

The lighted object settled down to within about 40 feet of the ground with a whistling sound and the cattle bolted, he declared. Then the object moved off.

Brown said he rounded up the cattle and was just driving them into the barn when the object appeared again and again the cattle bolted.

The milker was alone at the time. He said the object did not return again.

Belle Glade is on the south side of Lake Okeechobee.

Odd Balloon Is Found In Tree

TALLAHASSEE (AP)—Members of the Tallahassee Civil Air Patrol yesterday reported recovering a strange paper balloon about 20 feet in diameter from the top of a tall pine tree where they saw it land Saturday.

CAP men engaged in a search for a missing plane spotted the object drifting along about 25 miles an hour near the Tallahassee airport.

CAP Col. Wally Schanz, State Aviation Director, reported the location of the tree in which it landed. The next morning, a CAP cadet shinnied up the tree and pulled it down.

It was a hot air balloon apparently made of rice paper over a wire frame. The paper was in panels of white, green and blue. Attached to it were streamers of green, white and red paper. It contained no writing or markings.

In the inside there was a wire bracket for a heating element. The interior was badly smoked but there was no indication of what type of fuel was used to provide hot air to raise the balloon.

It is being turned over to military authorities.

Child Found

Frank in Florida at the Memorial Headstone of Missing Pilot 2nd Lt. John Anderson Jones, Jr.

Crash-Landing Site

FISHER FARM SIGHTINGS:

1). 6:50 PM EST. Jet-shaped Object. low balls of fire from rear. A.M. Jordan

2). 7:15 P.M. EST. Round Object - fiery #1 NC. Object. Mr. Hoard. (12-15. ft.)

3). 7:25 P.M. EST. Oval Object in flames. #3 Wash., DC.Object. Boys & Jack Davis

4). 10:30 - 11. P.M. EST. Round Object w/ flat side. flames- either side. circled Fisher Farm for 15-minutes. Baily Frame.

Feschina Jr-

Feschino's USPS Signed "Return Receipt"
for the Package he Mailed to George Snitowsky in 1993

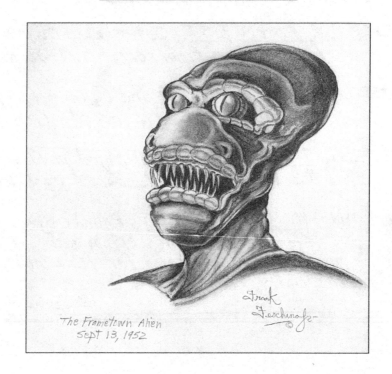

SENDER: Complete items 1 and 2 when additional services are desired, and complete items 3 and 4.
Put your address in the "RETURN TO" Space on the reverse side. Failure to do this will prevent this card from being returned to you. The return receipt fee will provide you the name of the person delivered to and the date of delivery. For additional fees the following services are available. Consult postmaster for fees and check box(es) for additional service(s) requested.
1. ☐ Show to whom delivered, date, and addressee's address. 2. ☐ Restricted Delivery
(Extra charge) *(Extra charge)*

3. Article Addressed to:
MR. George Snitowsky
69-53 218th St.
Flushing. N.Y.
11364

4. Article Number
P 089490 051
Type of Service:
☐ Registered ☐ Insured
☒ Certified ☐ COD
☐ Express Mail ☒ Return Receipt for Merchandise
Always obtain signature of addressee or agent and DATE DELIVERED.

5. Signature – Addressee
X
6. Signature – Agent
X
7. Date of Delivery

8. Addressee's Address *(ONLY if requested and fee paid)*

PS Form 3811, Apr. 1989 ✦U.S.G.P.O. 1989-238-815 DOMESTIC RETURN RECEIPT

Drawing of the "Frametown Monster" Sighted
in Frametown, WV on 9-13-52

The Frametown Alien
Sept 13, 1952

Frank
Feschino Jr.

The "Reptilian" Sighted by Snitowsky was Seen Inside of the Lower Portion of its Hovercraft

Sept. 13, 1952
Frametown
Alien

Frank ©
Feschino Jr.

339

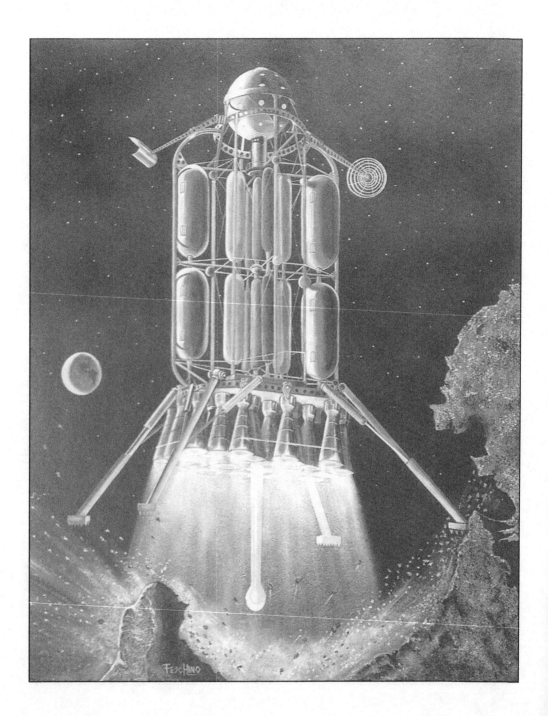

Collier's October 18, 1952 Moonship Cover

President Harry Truman in Arlington, VA.

EPILOGUE BY STANTON T. FRIEDMAN

It is clear from the previous chapters that Frank C. Feschino, Jr. has continued to do an incredible job of collecting, arranging and chronicling data about the Flatwoods incident and the overwhelming amount of UFO events that occurred on that day. His "Flatwoods Monster" work informs us about Project Blue Book, the press, the key players involved during that time and much more. On September 12, 1952, there were a host of UFO sightings, close encounters, and in most of the sightings, a simple explanation was provided...meteors. The facts did not support that explanation though. Meteors don't land, they don't make sharp turns, they don't reverse course; they don't fly from city to city, following rivers and airport flight lines. When they do impact into the ground, there are often sonic booms, craters and shock waves that are very noticeable.

The fact of the matter is that there are meteor showers in September that even *Sky and Telescope* Magazine, which often listed significant meteor flights, recorded none for September 12, 1952. Furthermore, the Harvard Meteor Project that was operated between 1952 and 1954 and recorded 2401 meteor passages recorded none on September 12, 1952. The project was under the direction of Harvard Astronomer, Dr. Donald Howard Menzel, who was a well-known UFO debunker.

A more detailed investigation, as reported in my book, *TOP SECRET/MAJIC*, indicated Menzel was up to his ears in highly classified activities for such government agencies as the National Security Agency, the Central Intelligence Agency, the Office of Naval Intelligence, and was a member of Operation Majestic 12. One suspects that if he could have found a meteor (or several) to explain the events of Sept. 12, he would have. One is reminded of how often Venus has been identified as the source of a UFO report even in cases when it was not visible at the time and location of the sighting.

On September 12, the press noted many reports of high-speed objects in their local area, often ignoring events in other locations and blindly accepting "meteor" even when it was clear from witness testimonies that what was observed *could* not have been a meteor. Obviously, there were no UFO reporters looking at the big picture for the news wire services, or apparently for Project Blue Book either. Painstakingly, Frank Feschino, Jr. did manage to piece together the Blue Book file and it was woefully inadequate.

There are aspects of the events that at first glance seem quite puzzling including the glowing varying color regions around what was observed. Now that we know how important plasma phenomena can be with regard to potential propulsion systems such as those involving magneto aerodynamics, they make more sense. We have the intriguing comments by one of the boys that even where there had been glowing regions of air, there was not high heat.

The tree from behind which the "monster" emerged was not burned nor the leaves charred. Plasma is often called the fourth state of matter along with liquid, solid and gas. Most of the universe is made of plasma including the stars, the ionosphere, much of deep space. In simplest terms, everyday matter is electrically neutral. But if some electrons are separated from the atoms around which they revolve, one can create electrically conducting fluid, plasma. Fluorescent bulbs have plasmas inside them when turned on. Some plasma is relatively cool and some, such as those produced by nuclear explosions, are very hot indeed.

When the Apollo astronauts were returning from the moon, some of the command modules' energy when striking the atmosphere went in to ionizing the air around the blunt end of the system. Because it is an electrically conducting fluid, that plasma prevented radio signals from the command module from reaching the earth causing the temporary but well-known communications blackout. When we observe high-speed "shooting stars," we are actually observing the plasma created by the much smaller meteor.

The point here is that we now know that having plasma around a high-speed object moving in the atmosphere can allow one to avoid many of the problems of high-speed flight. With appropriate electric and magnetic fields, one can control lift, drag, heating, sonic boom production, and radar profile. Plasmas are produced when nose cones on Intercontinental Ballistic Missiles re-enter the atmosphere. There has been a great deal of research dealing with this atmospheric plasma problem, most of it classified. If one wants the nose cone to hit a target, one must understand the effect of the ionized atmosphere on the drag (frictional slowing down) on the nose cone. One can try to change the plasma characteristics by incorporating easily ionized (broken up into ions and electrons) substances in the outer layer to fool the defense radar into mistaking a decoy for a real nose cone.

Way back in 1969 while working for McDonnell Douglas Astronautics on possible UFO propulsion schemes, I had a search done of the technical report literature produced under government contracts for the DOD and NASA. The keyword that was used was magneto aerodynamics. There were 900 references located of which 90% were classified. Powerful radar beams, microwave beams, infrared beams, charged particles from radioactive substances, can all affect the object and the plasmas around it.

The new systems being used by the Lockheed F-94C in 1952 to get a radar lock-on and fire the plane's air-to-air missiles at an intruding Soviet aircraft or flying saucer would certainly have been a concern to the inhabitants of the saucers. Once they learned what the radar lock-on meant, they may have taken immediate action to destroy the aircraft on the verge of firing a missile at them. The many descriptions of glowing colored regions of gas around the objects, sound very much like manifestations of plasma phenomena and interactions with electromagnetic systems described as well as possible by people who knew nothing about such phenomena.

Dr. Stewart Way, an outstanding scientist with the Westinghouse Research Laboratory in Pittsburgh, Pennsylvania, actually supervised the building of an analogous 9' long electromagnetic submarine in 1966 at the University of California, Santa Barbara. Seawater, an electrically conducting fluid akin to ionized air, was influenced by electric and magnetic fields. There were no moving parts, but the submarine moved through the seawater. A number of years later a large Japanese company built a much larger electromagnetic ship actually using superconducting magnets to provide very strong magnetic fields while using little electrical power. Larger superconducting magnets are used in medical MRIs and in big accelerators.

I had a quiet conversation with a military radar operator who, while based in Kalispell, Montana, in the early 1950s, had the experience of being told by Canadian Air Defense people that a saucer was headed his way. A USAF interceptor in the neighborhood was vectored toward the intruder. The scenario was being watched on radar and then the interceptor disappeared. Even though they knew its direction and speed of flight and altitude, no wreckage was ever found.

The radar operator told me that after that, the message went out "Do not shoot at intruding UFOs, take gun camera pictures." Many years ago, I had a quiet conversation with an individual who had worked for the National Security Agency listening post nearest to Cuba. The Soviets in the Cuban base were told in March 1967, of an approaching UFO at 30,000 feet and moving at

344

Mach one. Two MIG 21's were scrambled to meet the saucer heading SW toward Cuba. It did not respond to their demands to go away. The lead pilot, after describing it over the airwaves as spherical with no appendages, was told to shoot it down. His missile was armed, the radar locked on, and then suddenly the wingman shouted that the first plane had disintegrated. The UFO ascended to 90,000 feet and headed Southeast at Mach several. Certainly, the saucer could tell when the lock-on was achieved. The NSA asked for a copy of the original tape, though this was very rare, and the base was told to list the loss of the MIG as due to equipment malfunction. Attempts to obtain more information through the freedom of information act were met with strong intimidation by the FBI and the office of the Air Force's Inspector General.

Unfortunately, records of all such encounters between intruding aircraft, including flying saucers, and our air defense systems are born classified and remain that way as are records of many other observations of "Uncorrelated targets" inspected by the Air Defense Command. One wonders how many of the almost completely whited-out TOP SECRET National Security Agency UFO documents (obtained through a long legal battle) dealt with observed intercepts by alien spacecraft of Earthling aircraft. I am reminded of a comment by USAF General Carroll Bolender in a memo dated October 20, 1969, and dealing with his recommendation that Project Blue Book be closed (Which it was that December).

Bolender, with whom I later spoke, noted that closing Project Blue Book would get rid of a place for the public to report UFO sightings. He stated, "Moreover, reports of unidentified flying objects which could affect national security are made in accordance with JANAP (Joint Army Navy Air Force Publication) 146 or Air Force Manual 55-11 and are not part of the Blue Book System." Two paragraphs later, "However, as already stated, reports of UFOs which could affect national security would continue to be handled through the standard Air Force procedures designed for this purpose." I checked and found that Project Blue Book was not on the distribution list provided in the noted regulations.

This iceberg of data is still clearly under the water of secrecy. One wonders what it would take, starting with the extensive data compiled by Frank, to obtain the full-uncensored accident reports of events taking place more than 50 years ago. One excuse given by authorities to families seeking details of a pilot's demise is, "We want all interviewed people connected with the airplane to speak freely without fear of being sued if it turns out that a certain aircraft component had malfunctioned." Thus, the secrets of these too-close encounters are doomed to secrecy if no major press group makes the effort to cut through the secrecy.

Much less understandable is the failure of CSICOP "Investigator" Dr. Joseph Nickell to do an adequate investigation of the event. He visited the Fisher Farm, but didn't get past the first pasture and didn't see the important oak tree on the other side of the gate. Nickell didn't view the flat clearing on the mountaintop where the alleged "meteor" landed after making a slow turn over the town...without a sonic boom, without a crater, and no meteoric residue being found.

In addition, Nickell didn't view the gulley where the damaged craft relocated. Moreover, he didn't talk with Mrs. May or her sons. Does anybody really believe his story of the 6-foot owl? Journalist A. Lee Stewart, Jr. went to the May home shortly after the event, talked to the witnesses and went onto the farm. Were the boys so frightened by this alleged owl that they became sick and Lemon threw up all night from fright, though Stewart had noted a gaseous odor near the ground at the site? Furthermore, the Air Force document, which compares the 1952 Flatwoods and Desvergers cases, actually proves that samples were indeed retrieved from Flatwoods and both cases were actually taken seriously. Nickell obviously missed this very important document during his research investigation!

Moreover, he thought that, while the boys had certainly been frightened, they had genuinely been ill from some substance emitted by the "monster." In short, Nickell's investigation typified debunking at its worst, applying four major rules:

1). What the public doesn't know, I won't tell them.
2). Don't bother me with the facts my mind is made up.
3). If you can't attack the data, attack the people.
4). Do your research by proclamation; investigation is too much trouble. For shame!

Any persons with first or second hand knowledge about the "Flatwoods Monster" incident or those who may know of any close encounters between military aircraft and UFOs please contact me toll free, at 1-877-457-0232. Witness names won't be used without permission. Of course, information will be shared with Frank Feschino, Jr. Clippings can be sent to me at PO. Box 958, Houlton, ME 04730-0958.

My email is **fsphys@rogers.com**
Web Site: http://www.stantonfriedman.com
Stanton T. Friedman

<u>Frank C. Feschino, Jr. and Stanton T. Friedman in Kansas at the 2011 OZUFO Reykawvik Summit held by Daniel Lauing</u>

SOURCES

BOOKS

Ageton, Arthur A. *The Naval Officers Guide.* 4th Ed. New York: McGraw-Hill, 1951.

Air Force ROTC-Air Science II. *Applied Air Power.* ConAC Manual 50-2 Part 3. Mitchell AFB, NY: Continental Air Command, n.d.

Air Navigation for Pilots. AFM No. 51-43. Washington, D.C.: Dept. of the Air Force. 1952.

The Air Officer's Guide. 2nd ed. rev. Harrisburg, PA: The Military Publ. Co., 1951.

Aircraft Industries Assoc. The Aircraft Yearbook 1952. 34th ed. Washington, D.C.: Lincoln Press, n.d.

The Airman's Handbook. 1st ed. rev. Harrisburg, PA: The Military Publ. Co., 1950.

The Airman's Handbook. 2nd ed. rev. Harrisburg, PA: The Military Publ. Co., 1951.

The Blue Jackets Manual. 14th ed. Annapolis, MD: U.S. Naval Inst., 1950.

Casamassa, Jack V., Editor. *Jet Aircraft Power Systems.* McGraw-Hill Book Company, Inc., 1950

Filter Station Operation. AFM No. 50-13. Washington, D.C.: Dept. of the Air Force, 1952.

Green, William and Cross, Ray. *The Jet Aircraft of the World.* Hanover House Edition, 1955.

Ground Observer's Guide. AFM 50-12. Washington, D.C.: Dept. of the Air Force, 1951.

Hillman, William. *Mr. President.* New York: Farrar, Strauss, & Young, 1952.

Keyhoe, Donald. *Aliens From Space.* Doubleday & Company, Inc. 1973.

Keyhoe, Donald. *The Flying Saucer Conspiracy.* Henry Holt & Co., 1955.

Keyhoe, Donald. *Flying Saucers from Outer Space.* Henry Holt & Co., 1953.

Mason, Jr., Herbert Molloy. *The United States Air Force-A Turbulent History.* Mason-Carter.1976.

NASA. *The Dictionary of Technical Terms for Aerospace Use.* Washington, D.C.: U.S. Govt. Printing Office, 1965.

Povenmire, Harold. *Fireballs, Meteors and Meteorites.* Indian Harbour Beach, FL: JSB Enterprises, 1980.

Rolfe, Douglas and Dawydoff, Alexis. *Airplanes of the World.* Simon & Shuster, 1962.

Ruppelt, Edward J. *The Report on Unidentified Flying Objects.* New York: Doubleday & Co., 1956.

Sanderson, Ivan T. *Uninvited Visitors: A Biologist Looks at UFOs.* New York: Cowles Educ. Corp., 1967.

STARFIRE F-94C weapon data. California Division, Lockheed Airport Corporation - Burbank, California. 27 April 1953.

Theory of instrument flying. AFM No. 51-38. Washington, D.C.: Dept. of the Air Force. April 1954.

The Unicorn Book of 1952: Outstanding Events of the Year. New York: Unicorn Books, Inc., 1953.

The U.S. Air Force Dictionary. Washington, D.C.: U.S. Govt. Printing Office, Air University Press, 1956.

Wolfe, Tom. *The Right Stuff.* Rev. Ed. New York: Farrar, Strauss, Giroux, 1983.

MAGAZINES AND PERIODICALS

"Agricultural Almanac for the year 1952." Lancaster, PA: John Baers Sons, 1951.

"Almanac for the year. 1952," Winston-Salem, NC: Blum's Almanac Syndicate 1951. Winston-Salem, NC.

"Astronomical Highlights of 1952," *Sky and Telescope.* (Dec. 1952): 45.

Barker, Gray. "Flatwoods W.Va. Monster, A Full Report of Investigation," *The Saucerian*, no. 1. (Sept. 1953).

Barker, Gray. "The Monster and the Saucer," *FATE.* Vol. 6. (Jan. 1953): 12-17.

"Conferences—The International Astronautical Federation," *Time.* no. 11 (Sept. 15, 1952): 32.

"Here and There with Amateurs," Sky and Telescope. (Sept. 1952): 289.

Hamilton, C. L. "Defense of the Homeland - Taking Saucers Seriously," *Flying.* (August 1952):48 Ley, Willy. ("Man on the Moon" comp.) "Inside the Moonship," *Collier's - The National Weekly.* 130, no. 16.(Oct. 18, 1952): 56.

Hansen, L. Taylor. The Night I Saw a Spaceship Orbit the Earth. *Flying Saucers-The Magazine of Space Conquest.* FS-19 (May 1961): 59-61.

Keyhoe, Donald. "What Radar Tells Us About Flying Saucers." *TRUE Magazine.* December 1952.

Lieb, Paul (interview with George Snitowsky). "The West Virginia Monster," *Male.* 5, no. 7. (July 1955): 39, 78-79.

Luyten, Prof. William. J. "If a Giant Meteor Hit a Modern City," *Science and Invention.* Vol. 17, no. 4. (1929): 296-297, 365.

Montgomery, Jack. "Report from the Readers - Circling Object," *FATE.* Vol. 6 (Feb. 1953): 108 Parrish, Wayne W., ed.

"Worldwide Airline Schedules, Fares and Information," *Official Airline Guide* – An American Aviation Publication. 8. no. 12. (Sept. 1952).

Perreault, William D. "Extra Section," *American Aviation* (September 1, 1952): 42.

"Production Highlights...Lockheed F-94C Starfire," *American Aviation.* (July 7, 1952).

Sand, George X. "He Was Burned by a Flying Saucer." *Stag."* VOL. 4, NO.4. (April 1953): 22, 58, 60.

Sanderson, Ivan T. "Sutton Monster Real?" *Infinity.* Contained in Project Blue Book. 1 Page article.

TIME. SCIENCE. (August 11, 1952):58.

UFO Investigator, NICAP 1958. VOL. I, NO. 5.

Von Braun, Wernher Dr. ("Man on the Moon" comp.) "The Journey," *Collier's, The National Weekly.* 130. no. 16 (Oct. 18, 1952): 52-58.

Wilson, W. L., ed. *The Aircraft Flash – Official G.O.C. Magazine* 1, no. 1 (Oct. 1952).

NEWSPAPERS

"Aerial Whazzit Seen Here Friday," *The Greensboro Record*. 16 September 1952.

"Air Force Alerts Jets to Chase 'Flying Saucers' Anywhere In U.S," *United Press-(UP)*. July 29, 1952.

"Air Force Explains 2 - Hour Delay in Chasing 'objects' Over Capital" *The New York Times*. 29 July 1952.

"AIR FORCE ORDERS 11 NEW JET TYPES," *The New York Times*. 14 September 1952.

"Air Force Orders Jet Pilots To Shoot Down Flying Saucers If They Refuse To Land," *The Seattle Post Intelligencer*. 29 July 1952.

"AIR FORCE PROBES FLYING SAUCERS-Four State 'Disc' Reports Unexplained," *The Greensboro Daily News*. 13 September 1952.

"Air Force's New Supersonic Jet Plane –F-94C Starfire, All-Rocket Jet Interceptor," *The New York Times*. 3 July 1952.

"Air Force Seeks Solution; Gives 'Shoot Down Order, '" WASHINGTON-INS. International News Service. 28 July 1952.

"ALERT JETS TO HUNT SAUCERS," *New York Daily News*. 29 SEPTEMBER 1952.

"An Artists Conception" *Weston (W.V.) Democrat*. 26 September 1952.

"Apparso UN Mostro nel West della Virginia," *Il Giornale D'Italia*. 17 September 1952.

"Authorities Probe Flashes In Area Skies—Strange Lights Observed Over Four States," *The (Martins Ferry-Bellaire, Ohio) Times-Leader*. 13 September 1952.

"Balls of Fire In Pittsburgh: Jittery Citizens Report Planes In Flames Over Wide Area," *Wilmington (Del.) Sunday Star*. 14 September 1952.

"'Bashful Billy' Plagues Patrol," *The Wheeling Intelligencer*. 17 September 1952.

"Bethany Professor Blames Imagination – Citizens 'Hypnotized' into Seeing 'Saucers.'" *The Wheeling News Register*. 16 September 1952.

"Boogie Man Has B.O.-Monster From Space Roaming W.Va. Hills?" *The Wheeling Intelligencer*. 15 September 1952.

"Braxton County Monster," *The Braxton (W.V.) Democrat*. 18 September 1952.

"Braxton Co. Residents Faint, Become Ill after Run-In With Weird 10-Foot Monster," *The Charleston Daily Mail*. 14 September 1952.

"Braxton Folks Divided Over Visitor-'Monster May Have Been Due To Dead Tree, Meteor, Beacon," *The Charleston Daily Mail*. 15 September 1952.

"Braxton Monster Left Skid Marks Where He Landed," *The Charleston Gazette*. 15 September 1952.

"BULLETIN; TAMPA-AP," *Panama City News Herald*. 14 September 1952.

"CAP To Continue Plane Search," *The Tampa Tribune*. 17 September 1952.

"Centerville, Virginia," International News Story. (INS). 22 September 1952.

"City Dust Haze Replaces Interest in Sky Objects," *Kingsport (Tenn.) Times-News*. 14 September 1952.

"'Crashing' Plane Believed Meteor," *Ohio State Journal*. 13 September 1952.

"Did It Ride Meteor?—Boys Spot Appalling Creature near Flatwoods, Link It to Fiery Objects In Skies," *The Charleston Gazette*. 14 September 1952.

"Don't Shoot Them Down, Rocket Man Says," *The Louisville Courier-Journal*. 30 July 1952.

"EMERGENCIES-Lost Pilot Was From Sanford, AF Reports," *The Daytona Beach Morning Journal*. 16 September 1952.

"Falling Meteor Startles Ohioans," *Ohio News-Register Star* (Sandusky, OH). 14 September 1952.

"Fiery Object Seen by Man at Clearwater," *The Wichita Evening Eagle*. 16 September 1952.

"Fiery Object Streaks across Skies of 4 States—A Meteor? Could Be," *The New Haven Register*. 13 September 1952.

"Fiery Objects Flash Across Sky in W.Va.—Many From Wheeling To Bluefield Puzzled Over Weird Spectacle," *The Charleston Daily Mail*. 13 September 1952.

"15 'Flying Saucer' Reports from N. E. Unexplained-Objects Spotted Form Holyoke, Long Meadow, Westover on List; Most of Sightings Identified," *The Springfield News*. 13 September 1952.

"Fireballs Shower City Area—Meteor Blamed As Cause Of Scare," *The Columbus (Ohio) Citizen*. 13 September 1952.

"FLAME OVER WASHINGTON," *The New York Times*. 13 September 1952.

"Flaming Object Seen at Capitol," *The Springfield (Mass.) News*. 13 September 1952.

"Flashes of Life. Green Monster with Blood-Red Face Scares Wits Out of Seven Hill Folk," *The Binghamton (N.Y.) Press*. 15 September 1952.

"Flat Rock Man Calls News To Report Flying Saucer," *The Mount Airy News*. 19 September 1952.

"Flatwoods Revisited," *The Sunday Gazette-Mail*. 6 March 1966.

"Flatwoods Visit Convinced Skeptic Saucers Are Real," *The Charleston Gazette*. 30 April 1968.

"Fliers Hunt Tyndall Pair," *Panama City News Herald*. 14 September 1952.

"Flying Objects 'Invade' State; 6 Seen From Highland Park," *The Topeka Capital*. 15 September 1952.

"'Flying Saucer' Reported seen By Mrs. Blackwell," *Leaksville (N.C.) News*. 18 September 1952.

"Flying Saucers In District Once More – Reports of Sighting The Discs In From All Sections; Some Citizens Jittery," *Evening Standard* (Uniontown). 13 September 1952.

"Four States 'Bombarded by Meteor-Like Objects,'" *The Boston Globe*. 13 September 1952.

"Green Bodied, Red-Faced and Smelly. Huge 'Monster' on West Va. Hill Frightens Woman and Six Boys," *The Manchester Union Leader*. 15 September 1952.

"Jet Plane, Running Low On Gas, Brought In At MacDill," *The Tampa Tribune*. 17 September 1952.

"Jets Couldn't Find Them-Air Force After D.C. 'Saucers'" *The Washington Daily News*. 29 July 1952.

"Jets On 24 Hour Alert to Shoot Down Saucers," *The San Francisco Examiner*. 29 July 1952.

"Jets Ready to Chase Lights, 24-Hour Alert Ordered After Second Appearance Here," *The Washington Daily News*. 28 July 1952.

"Jets Ready to Chase Lights," *The Washington Daily News*. 28 July 1952.

"Jets Told to Shoot Down Flying Discs," *The Fall River (Mass.) Herald-News*. 29 July 1952.

"Large Meteorite Sighted In This Section," Morgantown (W.V.) *The Dominion News*. 13 September 1952.

"Last Heard From Yesterday-MacDill Searches For Pilot Down In Flight Over Gulf," *The Tampa Daily Times*. 13 September 1952.

"Lt. John A. Jones Is Reported Missing," *The Sanford Herald*. 15 September 1952.

"Many Report Thing In Sky At Reidsville," *The Greensboro Daily News*. 16 September 1952.

"Metallic Odor Indicates Meteor — Officers Shake Heads Over W.Va. Ogre Tail,"
The Wheeling News-Register. 15 September 1952.

"Meteor Hunt Today-Fifty-Ton Flaming Object Seen Falling Near City," *Morning News,*
(Florence, SC). 13 September 1952.

"Meteor Seen Whizzing Across Maryland Skies," *The Charleston Gazette.* 13 Sept. 1952.

"Meteorite Spotted In Kanawha Area," *The Charleston Gazette.* 13 September 1952.

"Meteorite Viewed By Many Residents In Early Evening," *The Greensboro Daily News.*
13 September 1952.

"Military Accident Toll" *The New York Times.* 11 October 1956

"Missing Airmen's Names Announced," *The Tampa Daily Times.* 16 September 1952.

"The Monster of Braxton County: Around A Bend They Saw A Pair Of Bulging Eyes,"
The Washington Daily News. 15 September 1952.

"Monster Still Top Subject," *The Braxton Democrat.* 25 September 1952.

"Monster Story To Be Broadcast," (Ohio) *The Times-Leader.* 17 September 1952.

"Mystery Lights Zip Through Skies Here Stirring Mild Furor," *The Wheeling Intelligencer.*
13 September 1952.

"Mystery Object Frightened His Cattle," *The Daytona Beach Morning Journal.*
16 September 1952.

"Odd Balloon Is Found In Tree," *The Daytona Beach Morning Journal.* 16 September 1952.

"Ohio, Columbus," *Associated Press.* 24 July 1952. (AP).

"Pilot Bails Out, Lands Safely After MacDill Hears Distress Call," *The Tampa Tribune.*
13 September 1952.

"Pine Airmen Lost In Flight," *The Baker Democrat Herald.* 15 September 1952.

"Planes Hunt For Missing Jet Fighter," *The Tampa Sunday Tribune.* 14 September 1952.

"Planes Press Search for Jet Fighter," *Panama City News Herald.* 16 September 1952.

"Police Say Braxton Monster Product of Mass Hysteria," *The Fairmont Times.*
15 September 1952.

"Powered By Suggestion? – 'Monster' From Outer Space Arrives Here Via 'Saucer,'"
The Wheeling Intelligencer. 16 September 1952."

"Reported Plane Crash Is Just Another Meteor," *Mercury,* (Pottstown, PA). 13 September
1952.

"Residents of Ohio Valley Excited as Heavenly Meteor Hurls off Bright Fragments,"
The Wheeling News Register. 13 September 1952.

"Saucer or Meteor? Residents of 4 States Saw Green Light," *Courier News,* (Arkansas).
13 September 1952.

"Scores of Baltimoreans See Meteor-Like Object in Skies," *The Baltimore Sun.*
13 September 1952

"Scores See 'Green Light Over Area,'" *The Washington Post.* 13 September 1952.

"Seven Chased By Saucer Monster Scared To Death," *The Statesville Record and Landmark.*
15 September 1952.

"60 'Saucer' Reports Fly At Air Force in 2 Weeks," *The New York Times.* 18 July 1952.

"Sky Object Seen Here—Search Ends For Wrecked Aircraft," *The Kingsport Times-News.*
14 September 1952.

"Space 'Thing' 17 Feet High Has Red Face, Very Bad BO: Seven in W. Virginia Swear
'Glowing Monster' Had Green Body, Odor Made Them Ill," *The Springfield News.*
15 September 1952.

"Strange Sky Object Viewed By Many In This Area," *Evening Telegram*, (Rock Mount, NC). 14 September 1952.

"Strange Objects in Worcester Sky," *The Lawrence Tribune*. 23 July 1952.

"Suggests No Shooting at 'Saucers,'" *The Manchester Union-Leader*. 30 July 1952.

"The Thing, 10 Feet Tall, Terrifies Party of 7," *The New York Daily News*. 15 September 1952.

"Truman To Stump Through 24 States," *The New York Times*. 13 September 1952.

"Truman Vows To Be 100 As He Gets Lifetime Pass," *The New York Times*. 13 September 1952.

"2 In One Meteor Seen Over Ward" *The Charleston Daily Mail*. 14 September 1952.

"Unidentified Jets 'Buzz' R.I. Town," *The Boston Globe*. 13 September 1952.

"Urges USAF Not To Shoot Saucers," *The Lawrence Tribune*. 31 July 1952.

"Was Monster A Hoax? Are UFOs For Real? Hmmm A Possibility," *The Charleston Daily Mail*. 7 December 1977.

"Weather," *Panama City News-Herald*. 12 September 1952.

"The Weather," *The Tampa Morning Tribune*. 12 September 1952.

"The Weather in the Nation," *The New York Times*. 12 September 1952.

"Weather Map," *The Tampa Daily Times*. 12 September 1952.

"Well, It Was Some Ball of Fire," *The Washington Daily. News*. 13 September 1952.

"West Virginia Town Divided Over Report of Monster," *The (Martins Ferry-Bellaire, Ohio) Times- Leader*. 15 September 1952.

"What Happened To the Monster – Braxton County Woman Feels Glowing Ship Was Jet Ship – Discovery in 1952, Stirred Up Nation-Wide 'Martian' Debate," *The Charleston Gazette*. 7 October 1956.

"You Can't Get One Out at Night By Hisself," *Washington Daily News*. Sept. 19, 1952.

MISCELLANEOUS

ARTC untitled document. "Log of 26 July 1952."

ATIC-Wright Patterson AFB. *Project Blue Book*. Washington, D.C.: National Archives Microfilms, June, July, August, and September 1952.

Barker, Gray. *Letter to Major Donald Keyhoe* [USMC Retired]. 9 November 1953. Henry Holt & Co., New York.

Berliner, Donald. *"The Unexplained UFO Reports from the Files of the U.S. Air Force's Project Blue -Book UFO Investigations."* Fund for UFO Research (1974).

Canadian UFO Report. Summer 1976. Vol. 3, # 8.

Civilian Saucer Investigation, *"More On The Green Monster."* Quarterly Bulletin – Los Angeles, CA. Vol. 1, No. 2. Winter 1953.

Norton AFB, *Microfilm* case numbers; 52-7-27-3, 52-7-28-5, 52-9-12-4, 52-8-5-5.

Maxwell Air Force Base Historical Research Agency. *USAF Pamphlet 1993-0-738-833.*

ABOUT THE AUTHOR

Frank C. Feschino, Jr. grew up in Connecticut. He is a graduate of the prestigious Paier School of Art in Hamden, Ct. where he studied illustration, commercial art, and photography. He was trained by several world-renowned artists including Kenneth Davies and Rudolph Zallinger, became an exceptional illustrator and earned his diploma in 1981. Feschino also studied film and video production at Phillips Jr. College in Florida where he earned an Associates Degree in 1994. As a result, Feschino honed additional communication abilities enhancing his stunning literary skills. In 1990, he became interested in UFOs when he visited a relative's farm in Braxton County West Virginia, where crop circles appeared overnight and UFO sightings were frequent. He documented these anomalies and shared his research with world-renowned crop circle enthusiast Colin Andrews.

Frank then discovered the story of the "Flatwoods Monster" incident. He investigated this case for several years, becoming an authority on the event and wrote, *The Braxton County Monster-The Cover-Up of The Flatwoods Monster*. He also applied a ceaselessly assiduous investigation into the UFO events that occurred throughout the summer of 1952, and wrote, *Shoot Them Down!-The Flying Saucer Air Wars of 1952*. Frank C. Feschino, Jr. has been investigating the UFO phenomena for more than twenty years and continues to do so, often working with Stanton T. Friedman. The author/Illustrator resides in central Florida.

<u>Stanton and Frank display Frank's Custom-embroidered</u>
<u>"Shoot Them Down" Satin Jacket at a UFO Conference in Las Vegas</u>

For more information, visit: www.FlatwoodsMonster.com

354

Made in United States
Orlando, FL
15 November 2023

39023387R00207